WORK AND PERSONALITY:

An Inquiry Into the Impact of Social Stratification

MODERN SOCIOLOGY
A Series of Monographs, Treatises, and Texts

Edited by
Gerald M. Platt

Bellman and Jules-Rosette • A Paradigm for Looking

Borman • The Social Life of Children in a Changing Society

Cottle • Like Fathers, Like Sons: Portraits of Intimacy and Strain

Gresson • The Dialectics of Betrayal: Sacrifice, Violation, and the Oppressed

Hammond • The Politics of Benevolence: Revival Religion and American Voting Behavior

Jules-Rosette (Ed.) • The New Religions of Africa

Jules-Rosette • Symbols of Change: Urban Transition In A Zambian Community

Louis and Sieber • Bureaucracy and the Dispersed Organization: The Educational Extension Agent Experiment

McCann • Chemistry Transformed: The Paradigmatic Shift from Phlogiston to Oxygen

Blum and McHugh (Eds.) • Friends, Enemies and Strangers: Theorizing in Art, Science, and Everyday Life

Merton and Riley (Eds.) • Sociological Traditions from Generation to Generation: Glimpses of the American Experience

Rosenfeld • The Legacy of Aging: Inheritance and Disinheritance in Social Perspective

SanGiovanni • Ex-Nuns: A Study of Emergent Role Passage

Wilken • Entrepreneurship: A Comparative and Historical Study

In Preparation:

Borman, Quarm, and Gideonese • Women in the Workplace: Effects on Families

Duster and Garrett • Biological Rhythms

Harris • Rationality and Collective Belief: Advances in Social Psychology

WORK AND PERSONALITY:
An Inquiry Into the Impact of Social Stratification

by
Melvin L. Kohn and Carmi Schooler
with the collaboration of

Joanne Miller, Karen A. Miller, Carrie Schoenbach, and Ronald Schoenberg,
all, the National Institute of Mental Health

Ⓐ ABLEX PUBLISHING CORPORATION
NORWOOD, NEW JERSEY 07648

Cover photograph:
David Smith
SITTING PRINTER, 1954, bronze.
87¼ ″ x 15¾ ″ x 16″
Collection of the Storm King Art Center, Mountainville,
New York.
Reproduced by permission of Candida and Rebbecca Smith.
Photograph courtesy of the Archives of American Art,
Smithsonian Institution.

Published 1983 by Ablex Publishing Corporation.

Printed in the United States of America.

Library of Congress Cataloging in Publication Data

Kohn, Melvin L., 1928—
   Work and personality.

   (Modern sociology)
   Includes bibliographical references and index.
   1. Job analysis. 2. Social classes. 3. Quality
of work life. 4. Personality and occupation.
I. Schooler, Carmi, II. Title. III. Series.
HF5549.5.J6K64   1983   155.9′2   82-24485
ISBN 0-89391-121-6
ISBN 0-89391-199-2 (pbk.)

Ablex Publishing Corporation
355 Chestnut Street
Norwood, New Jersey 07648

Contents

v

APPENDICES

Preface

This book is the product of a collaboration that began more than two decades ago. Kohn had asked Schooler to critique an interpretive essay (later published as Kohn, 1963) about the relationship between social stratification and parent-child relationships. That essay proposed, inter alia, that the key to understanding why middle-class and working-class parents differ in their values lies primarily in their different educational and occupational experiences, particularly the differential opportunity to exercise self-direction in work. Schooler responded that the interpretation was certainly subject to empirical test and that we should get to work immediately on that test. Thus began our planning for the cross-sectional survey of employed men that was carried out in 1964.

As planning proceeded, the scope of the intended research was considerably broadened. An initial focus on middle-class and working-class parents developed into a more general inquiry into the psychological concomitants of social stratification. The conceptualization of job conditions was sharpened and extended. The range of psychological phenomena to be studied was enlarged considerably beyond parental values, to include also values for oneself, orientations to self and society, and even cognitive functioning. By the end, we would develop a partial but useful conceptualization of personality and attempt to model the causal interrelationships of job conditions and personality so conceived.

In 1962 we were only dimly aware that the research we were then planning could establish only a prima facie case that job conditions play an important part in shaping personality. To demonstrate the actual causal impact of job conditions on personality would eventually require a follow-up study and the use of complex methods of analysis that were not to be developed for nearly a decade. By the same token, we were then only dimly aware of just how powerful the concept, occupational self-direction, would turn out to be and of how far our interpretive model could be applied.

Fundamental to our approach was the decision to study *dimensions* of work—job conditions such as heaviness, time-pressure, job complexity, and closeness of supervision—rather than particular occupations, such as lawyer, bank clerk, and carpenter. We see job conditions, particularly those that are determinative of self-direction in one's work, as basic to understanding the relationship between social structure and adult personality. Admittedly, job conditions are not the only experiential links between position in the larger social structure and individual personality. Job conditions do, however, provide a particularly strategic way of examining the processes by which social position affects those immediate conditions of life that are central to an individual's perceptions of and stance toward social reality.

This book presents the development of our analytic strategy for assessing the impact of social structure on personality, beginning with our initial analysis of the relationship of social stratification with values and orientations, continuing with the progressive refinement of our models of job conditions and personality, and then generalizing the interpretive model in ways little anticipated when the research was begun. As the scope of the research has expanded, so too has the collaboration, which has grown to include Joanne Miller, Karen A. Miller, Carrie Schoenbach, and Ronald Schoenberg.

We faced a dilemma in deciding how to present the work of two decades, much of which had been published along the way as journal articles. One strategy would have been to reanalyze all the data, using the most advanced methods now at our command, to redefine concepts, using our most recent thinking—and generally to present everything as we now think of it. An alternative would have been simply to reprint the previously-published papers in chronological order, adding new chapters at the end, thereby showing most clearly the process of conceptual and methodological development. There are advantages and disadvantages to both approaches. The former would be more coherent and easier to follow, but it would lose much in the telling and would be unfair to our collaborators, whose work would become grist for the mill of Kohn and Schooler's reanalysis and retelling. The latter would have the distinct advantage of telling an exciting story of the development of ideas and methods—a story that may have considerable heuristic value. It would have the disadvantages, though, of being somewhat repetitious; of perhaps being confusing in those places where we have changed terminology; and of letting chronology dominate logical development in those places where the two do not march in step.

We have chosen a compromise, intended to maximize the advantages of both strategies. We have deliberately not changed terminology or methods wherever we thought it instructive to show their development. We have presented previously-published analyses as they were originally done, not as we would now do them. We have not greatly altered the structure of previously-published papers; but we have revised the earlier versions, some of them substantially, wherever we thought that doing so would tell a more coherent story without distortion. Errors have been corrected. Terminology that we no longer consider accurate has been revised. (A prime example is that we did not differentiate between social class and social stratification in the original articles; in this book, we do so.) Duplication has been removed, ambiguities have been explained. Methodological discussions have been moved to the earliest chapter in which they apply. Some materials that journal editors thought nonessential, but which are useful for the continuity of the book, have been reincorporated. Five new chapters have been written. In a host of ways, large and small, what had been a collection of separate, if closely related, papers has been transformed into a book.

In the main, the sequence of chapters follows the chronological sequence in which the papers were prepared, simply because the chronological and logical sequences are essentially the same, but new chapters have been interpolated and all analyses that we see as extensions of the principal model have been placed in the Section of the book that deals with the generalizability of the interpretive model.

Section I presents our initial interpretations of the relationships of social stratification and of bureaucratization with values and orientations. In these analyses, we look to the job conditions attendant on social-structural position for much of the explanation of how position in some larger social structure affects individual psychological functioning.

In Section II, the focus shifts to occupational structure itself, the intent being to search out just which job conditions are related to psychological functioning and in just which ways. We assess the more than 50 job conditions indexed in our survey, isolating those that are related to psychological functioning independent of each other and of education. Then we appraise the relative importance for alienation of two sets of job conditions, one emphasizing control over the product of one's labor, the other emphasizing control over the work process. In this Section of the book, too, we come face-to-face with a focal problem of the research—whether the relationships between job conditions and personality solely reflect processes of occupational selection and job molding or whether, in addition, the job actually does affect personality. Still using the cross-sectional data of the 1964 survey, we demonstrate that job probably does affect personality—thus justifying the investment in time and money required for undertaking a follow-up study.

Section III, which utilizes the longitudinal data provided by the follow-up study, is the heart of the book. We begin by presenting a prototypic analysis of the reciprocal effects of one key dimension of work—its substantive complexity—and one principal facet of personality—cognitive functioning. Next, we expand the model considerably, to include not just one dimension of occupational structure and one facet of psychological functioning, but the structure of the job as a whole and several facets of personality. We then bring the methods and concepts developed in this inquiry back to the theoretical problem with which the work began, the role of occupational self-direction in explaining the impact of social stratification on psychological functioning. These analyses are the direct outgrowth of our decision to present the previously-published analyses as they were originally done. This decision left a void: How would we now assess the interrelationship of social stratification, occupational self-direction, and psychological functioning? Moreover, since we now differentiate between social stratification and social class, does our interpretive model apply as well to social class? These analyses are meant to fill that void.

The penultimate Section of the book (Section IV) presents several generalizations of the interpretive model. The model having been based on data about men, we first consider whether job conditions affect women similarly—and demonstrate that they do. The model having dealt almost entirely with the intrapsychic concomitants of work, we next consider whether work bears a similar relationship to one important aspect of (reported) behavior—the intellectuality of people's leisure-time activities. It does, for both men and women. The model having dealt with the conditions of work experienced in paid employment, we then consider whether the experiences of work encountered in housework may have similar psychological consequences; for women, they do. Finally, we deal with the most far-reaching extension of the interpretive model, the intergenerational transmission of the values and orientations developed by one's forebears from their conditions of work in an earlier historical epoch.

The concluding Section of the book (Section V) utilizes the work of many investigators, particularly in other countries, to assess the universality of the interpretative model. In this Section, we summarize the results of two major replications of our work, in Poland and Japan. Finally, we discuss a number of unresolved interpretive issues. In this context, we summarize our ongoing research on the relationship of children's "educational self-direction" to their personality development—an exciting and potentially important extension of our interpretive model.

We have tried to provide sufficiently detailed information about method-ology that other investigators will be able to judge our research and to repli-cate it, should they wish to do so. But this book is not addressed principally to specialists. To make our research more broadly accessible, we have tried to present a heuristic, entirely nonmathematical introduction to linear structural-equation measurement and causal modelling. Our way of trying to achieve the apparently conflicting goals of providing both detailed tech-nical information for specialists and more general nontechnical explana-tions for other readers is to present different types of information in different places. In the text, we describe the general logic of the analysis and interpretation. More detailed technical information is provided in footnotes and Appendices.

There are Introductions to all but the last Section of the book, each giving an overview of the chapters that constitute that Section. These Intro-ductions provide a general picture of the main themes of the research. They also provide a brief description of the data that are employed in the analyses presented in that Section.

Acknowledgements

This book is based on the work and ideas of many people. Our indebtedness is considerable.

We are deeply indebted to our four collaborators. Joanne Miller played the lead role in the analysis and interpretation of the relationship between women's job conditions and psychological functioning, collaborated in other analyses, and has taken responsibility for overseeing the comparative analyses of social stratification and psychological functioning in Poland and the United States that are discussed in the penultimate chapter. Karen A. Miller played the lead role in the analysis of job conditions and the intellectuality of leisure-time activities, collaborated in other analyses, and has taken responsibility for the analysis of educational self-direction and the personality development of children, discussed in the final chapter. Both Joanne Miller and Karen Miller have also made major contributions to the research as consultants and critics. Carrie Schoenbach has played a host of roles of ever-increasing importance. She began as research assistant, became our principal computer programmer, then data-coordinator, finally collaborator in the longitudinal analysis of social stratification, job conditions, and psychological functioning. She has also made extensive and invaluable editorial contributions to the entire book. Ronald Schoenberg is the methodologist to whom we have repeatedly turned for expert advice on causal modelling, particularly with respect to identifying complex models.

Starting with the original version of LISREL, Schoenberg has also created MILS, a computer program for estimating structural-equation models. By repeatedly improving MILS, he has met our ever-increasing needs and made MILS an ever more flexible and powerful program.

At various stages of the inquiry, we have also benefitted greatly from advice on methods of statistical analysis provided by Samuel Greenhouse, Elliot Cramer, Jacob Cohen, Hubert M. Blalock, Robert M. Hauser, Otis Dudley Duncan, George W. Bohrnstedt, David R. Heise, Karl G. Joreskog, William M. Mason, and John W. Meyer. Duane F. Alwin introduced us to linear structural-equation analysis and taught us how to do measurement models.

As will be apparent to all who read Chapter 12, our interpretation has been greatly enriched by the studies conducted by our Polish and Japanese collaborators. Kazimierz M. Slomczynski and Atsushi Naoi not only carried out major replications of our studies in Poland and Japan, respectively, but also, while working as Visiting Scientists at the National Institute of Mental Health, joined with us in the comparative analysis of the U.S., Polish, and Japanese data. Wlodzimierz Wesolowski and Ken'ichi Tominaga not only sponsored the replications in Poland and Japan, but also, as Visiting Scientists, played valuable roles as consultants and critics.

So many colleagues critiqued earlier drafts of one or more chapters of this book that we refrain from thanking anew those whose help was acknowledged in previously published papers. We do want to thank here those who critiqued one or another of the five newly published chapters: Wlodzimierz Wesolowski, Erik Olin Wright, and Richard Suzman. Kazimierz M. Slomczynski was not only a constructive critic of Chapters 12 and 13, but also originated many of the ideas on which the analyses of Chapter 7 are based.

Many fine research assistants have worked on one or another facet of the research; their contributions are acknowledged in the chapters that report the analyses they did. We would like to acknowledge here the research assistants whose work has contributed to the analyses newly reported in this book: Bruce Roberts, Carol Richtand, Margaret Renfors, Cheryl Keller, and Gloria Anderson. Cynthia Ann Gal, a student volunteer, verified the accuracy of the References and helped develop the Index. Diane Mueller prepared the Figures and played a major role in preparing the Index.

Without Virginia Marbley, who typed the innumerable drafts of the manuscript, while simultaneously handling all the administrative functions of our research unit, the book would not have been possible. Without her equanimity, writing the book would have been a much less pleasurable experience than it actually was.

We have enjoyed the consistent administrative support of John C. Eberhart and Robert A. Cohen, former Director and Deputy Director, respectively, of the Intramural Research Program of the National Institute of Mental Health, Frederick K. Goodwin, present Director of the Program, Hazel W. Rea, the Associate Director for Program Management, and Patrick G. Talmon, the Administrative Officer.

WORK AND PERSONALITY:

An Inquiry Into the Impact of Social Stratification

SECTION I | *Posing the Issues*

The two chapters in this Section present our general strategy for interpreting the relationship between position in the structure of society and individual psychological functioning. These chapters serve also to pose the critical issue that will confront us again and again throughout the book: how to go beyond correlations to deal with causality.

The underlying premise of our interpretation of the relationship of social structure to values and orientations is that social structure is significant for psychological functioning because it embodies systematically differentiated conditions of life that profoundly affect people's views of social reality. These two chapters differ considerably in which aspects of social structure they examine, Chapter 1 being concerned with the social-stratification system, Chapter 2 with bureaucratization. Still, the two chapters use the same theoretical approach. Whether attempting to explain the psychological impact of social stratification or of bureaucratization, the strategy is to look to the experiences that are attendant on people's social-structural positions. In particular, we focus on job conditions—in the first instance, job conditions that are concomitants of higher or lower stratification position; in the second instance, job conditions that are concomitants of the bureaucratization of a firm or an organization.

In Chapter 1, we interpret the relationships of social stratification to values and orientations as resulting from the cumulative effects of education and occupational experience. Education may affect values and orientations directly, by fostering intellectual flexibility and breadth of perspective. Education may also affect values and orientations indirectly, because of its role in job placement—the more education people have, the more likely they are to be recruited into responsible jobs that provide opportunity to be self-directed in their work.

This brings us to the heart of the thesis: that the relationships of social stratification to values and orientations result mainly from the greater opportunity to be self-directed in one's work that is afforded by higher educational level and occupational position.

Occupational self-direction—by which we mean the use of initiative, thought, and independent judgment in work—is greatly facilitated by some job conditions and constrained by others. Insofar as people do substantively complex work, are free of close supervision, and engage in non-routinized tasks, their work is necessarily self-directed. Insofar as people do work of little substantive complexity, are subject to close supervision, and engage in highly routinized tasks, their work cannot be self-directed. Our interpretation proposes that doing occupationally self-directed work results in valuing self-direction, both for oneself and for one's children, and in having self-directed orientations to self and society. We do not at this stage of the research actually demonstrate such causal effects.

In Chapter 2, the same interpretive strategy is applied to bureaucratization. Just as in our interpretation of the psychological effects of social stratification, we look to immediately impinging job conditions for the explanation of bureaucracy's psychological effects on its employees. Those effects are not at all what past sociological theory and popular belief would have led one to expect. Bureaucratic employment is associated with greater, not less, intellectual flexibility, openness to new experience, and self-direction in one's values than is non-bureaucratic employment. These relationships are attributable primarily to three job conditions: the substantive complexity of the work, job protections, and job income. Here, again, the focal problem is sharply posed: Do these job conditions actually affect psychological functioning, or do the relationships solely reflect selective recruitment and retention processes?

In these chapters we only pose that issue, reserving for later the task of actually assessing the causal effects of social-structural position on personality and of personality on social position.

Sample and Methods of Data Collection

The research discussed in this Section of the book is based on interviews conducted for us by the National Opinion Research Center of the University of Chicago in the spring and summer of 1964. Thirty-one hundred men, representative of all men throughout the United States then employed in civilian occupations, were interviewed. For most of the analyses discussed in these chapters, the entire sample is used. The analysis of parental values, however, is limited to about half the men—those who had one or more children aged three through fifteen living at home. Each father was asked about his values for a child of the same age and sex as a randomly-selected child of his own.

Of the 4105 men chosen to be in the study, 3101 (i.e., 76 percent) gave reasonably complete interviews, the median interview taking two and one-half hours. As far as can be learned from city directories in those cities where they exist, rates of nonresponse do not vary with occupational status.

About half the interview questions were directed to job, occupation, and career, the remainder to background information and to values and orientations. We shall discuss the content of the questions, the concepts that guided the inquiry, and the indices developed to measure them, as they become relevant to the substantive analysis.

Appendix A provides a more detailed description of sampling and interview procedures and an analysis of the characteristics of the nonrespondents.

Stratification, Occupation, and Orientation*

Melvin L. Kohn
and Carmi Schooler

This chapter describes and interprets the relationship of social stratification to values and orientations. Its impetus comes from earlier research on social stratification and parental values conducted in Washington, D. C. (Kohn, 1959) and in Turin, Italy (Pearlin and Kohn, 1966). Both studies found a distinct difference in emphasis between middle-and working-class parents' values for children—a higher valuation of self-direction by middle-class parents and of conformity to externally-imposed rules by working-class parents. The first objective of this chapter is to confirm that finding, insofar as it applies to fathers, in a sample broadly representative of men at all levels of social stratification throughout the United States.

A second objective is to determine whether the distinction between self-direction and conformity to external authority is basic, not only to the relationship of social stratification with fathers' values for children, but also to the relationship of social stratification with men's values for themselves and their

* This chapter is a substantially revised version of a paper entitled "Class, Occupation, and Orientation," originally published in the *American Sociological Review* (Kohn and Schooler, 1969). It summarizes the principal analyses reported in Kohn's (1969) book, *Class and Conformity*. Those analyses pose the substantive and methodological problems pursued in this book. In that sense, this book begins where *Class and Conformity* left off.

We are indebted for critical advice and essential help to our associates in this research—Lindsley Williams, Elizabeth Howell, Margaret Renfors, Carrie Schoenbach, and Mimi Silberman; and, for statistical advice, to Samuel Greenhouse, Elliot Cramer, and Jacob Cohen.

conceptions of social reality. Implicit in fathers' values for their children are values for themselves. We should expect men of higher stratification position to value self-direction for themselves, just as they do for their children. Moreover, values imply a great deal about conceptions of reality. Thus, if men value self-direction, they should tend to see the world and their own capacities in ways that make self-direction seem possible and efficacious. If they value conformity, they should tend to see the world and their own capacities in ways that make conformity seem necessary and appropriate. We therefore expect social stratification to be related, not only to men's values, but also to their conceptions of the external world and of self. We call these conceptions "orientations," thereby emphasizing that they serve to define men's stance toward reality. We examine men's orientations to three major aspects of reality—work, society, and self.

Our final and most important objective is to interpret the relationships of social stratification with values and orientations—to discover which of the many conditions of life associated with social-stratification position are most pertinent for explaining why social stratification is related to values and orientations. The focus of this analysis is *occupational* conditions, particularly those that are conducive to, or restrictive of, the exercise of self-direction in work. Our principal hypothesis is that stratification-related differences in men's opportunities to exercise occupational self-direction—that is, to use initiative, thought, and independent judgment in work—are basic to the relationship of social stratification with values and orientations. Few other conditions of life are so closely bound up with education and occupational position as are those that determine how much opportunity, even necessity, men have for exercising self-direction in their work. Moreover, there is an appealing simplicity to the supposition that the experience of self-direction in so central a realm of life as work is conducive to valuing self-direction, off the job as well as on the job, and to seeing the possibilities for self-direction not only in work but also in other realms of life.

INDEX OF SOCIAL STRATIFICATION

We conceive of social stratification as the hierarchical distribution of power, privilege, and prestige.[1] Our index of stratification is based on the two variables that seem most important for defining social-stratification position in industrial societies—education and occupational status. The index of stratification that we employ is Hollingshead's "Index of Social Position," a weighted combina-

---

[1] In the original publications on which this chapter is based (Kohn and Schooler, 1969; Kohn, 1969), we used the term, social classes, to refer to "aggregates of individuals who occupy broadly similar positions in a hierarchy of power, privilege, and prestige." We have since come to think it useful to reserve the term social class for its specifically Marxian usage, meaning a group defined in terms of its relationship to ownership and control of the means of production (see Wesolowski, 1969, 1979; Ossowski, 1963; Wright and Perrone, 1977).

tion of education and occupational status (see Hollingshead and Redlich, 1958:387-397), arbitrarily divided into five socio-economic levels.[2] We treat the five levels (or "classes") as merely a convenient division into a small number of categories of what is actually a continuum.

Hollingshead's classification of education is straightforward, but one might question his classification of occupational status. Essentially, he has modified the U.S. Census occupational classification (Edwards, 1938), making appropriate refinements, but validating the resulting classification only against expert opinion. Duncan (1961) proposed an alternative system, also derived from the Census classification, that weights the occupational categories to conform to the judgments of occupational prestige held by society at large. Given the evidence of consensus and stability in people's judgments of the relative prestige of occupations (Reiss, et al., 1961; Gusfield and Schwartz, 1963; Hodge, et. al., 1964), Duncan's approach seems well justified. But the classification is dependent on the sometimes imprecise distinctions employed in the Census. Fortunately, the correlation between Duncan's and Hollingshead's occupational classifications, based on a random sample of 90 men in our study, is sufficiently high (.89) to indicate that they measure much the same thing. Where the two indices differ, it is usually because Duncan has had to use one of the grosser Census categories; the Hollingshead index generally seems more appropriate. We therefore retained Hollingshead's classification of occupational status, in effect having validated it against Duncan's conceptually well-buttressed but less precise alternative.

VALUES AND ORIENTATIONS

Parental Values

By values, we mean standards of desirability—criteria of preference (see Williams, 1960:402-403). By parental values, we mean those standards that

---

[2] Hollingshead classifies occupational status into seven categories, education into another set of seven categories, then weights the occupational scores by seven and the educational scores by four, adds the two, and finally divides the resulting composite scores into five socioeconomic levels.

The major occupational categories are: (1) Higher executives, proprietors of large concerns, and major professionals. (2) Business managers, proprietors of medium-sized businesses, and lesser professionals. (3) Administrative personnel, proprietors of small independent businesses, and minor professionals. (4) Clerical and sales workers, technicians, and owners of little businesses. (5) Skilled manual employees. (6) Machine operators and semiskilled employees. (7) Unskilled employees.

The educational categories are: (1) Professionally trained. (2) College graduate. (3) Some college. (4) High school graduate. (5) 10-11 years of school, some high school. (6) 7-9 years of school, approximately grade school graduate. (7) Less than 7 years of school, approximately some grade school.

The detailed occupational classification has been included in a compilation of sociological indices by Bonjean, et al., 1967: 441-448.

parents would most like to see embodied in their children's behavior. Since values are hierarchically organized, a central criterion of value is choice. For this reason, our index requires men to choose, from among 13 desirable characteristics (listed in Table 1.1), the three most desirable, the one most desirable of all, the three least important (even if desirable), and the one least important of all. This procedure makes it possible to place men's valuations of each characteristic along a five-point scale:

5 = The most valued of all.
4 = One of the three most valued, but not the most valued.
3 = Neither one of the three most nor one of the three least valued.
2 = One of the three least valued, but not the least valued.
1 = The least valued of all.

We must recognize that fathers are likely to accord high priority to those values that are not only important, in that failing to achieve them would affect the children's futures adversely, but also problematic, in that they are difficult of achievement. Our index of values measures conceptions of the important, but problematic.

We find that the higher fathers' social-stratification positions, the more they value characteristics indicative of self-direction and the less they value characteristics indicative of conformity to external authority.[3] That is, the higher men's positions, the greater is their valuation of consideration, an interest in how and why things happen, responsibility, and self-control, and the less their valuation of manners, neatness and cleanliness, being a good student, honesty, and obedience (Table 1.1).

It is instructive to note two pairs of apparently similar characteristics whose members are oppositely related to social-stratification position. Manners, with its emphasis on the proper forms of behavior, is more highly valued at lower levels; consideration, with its emphasis on an empathic concern for the other person, at higher levels. Being a good student, with its emphasis on how one's performance is judged by others, is more highly valued at lower levels; an interest in how and why things happen, with its emphasis on intellectual curios-

---

[3] The analyses reported in this chapter are based on the computer program for multivariate analysis of variance initially developed by Dean J. Clyde, Elliot M. Cramer, and Richard J. Sherin (see Clyde, et al., 1966) and further developed by Cramer. The test of statistical significance is the F-ratio.

We are treating all dependent variables in the analyses reported in this chapter as if they were interval scales (see Blalock, 1964:94; Labovitz, 1967; Cohen, 1965, for justification).

In our analyses, we use control variables as factors in an analysis of variance, first testing the interaction terms, then attributing all possible variation in the dependent variables to the control variables. Finally, we test the relationship of the independent variable to the residual variation in the dependent variables. (In doing this, we control both the linear and non-linear components of the control variables.)

For more general discussions of the logical bases of our statistical procedures, see Blalock, 1960, Chapters 15–21; Cohen, 1968.

Table 1.1.   PARENTAL VALUES, BY SOCIAL STRATIFICATION

	Individual Values													Canonical Correlation	Factor Scores Self-direction/ Conformity	Sample Size
Mean Scores For:	Considerate of Others	Interested in How and Why Things Happen	Responsible	Self-control	Good Manners	Neat and Clean	Good Student	Honest	Obeys Parents	Good Sense and Sound Judgment	Acts as a Boy (Girl) Should	Tries to Succeed	Gets Along with Other Children			
Class 1	3.40ᵃ	3.12	3.07	2.95	2.84	2.23	2.53	3.58	3.43	3.16	2.81	2.92	3.07		+.74	(74)
Class 2	3.36	3.00	3.05	2.90	2.94	2.40	2.47	3.54	3.61	3.09	2.77	2.71	3.32		+.56	(192)
Class 3	3.24	2.69	2.85	2.87	3.13	2.70	2.54	3.81	3.64	3.12	2.74	2.65	3.21		+.12	(431)
Class 4	3.06	2.56	2.72	2.84	3.26	2.84	2.70	3.87	3.68	3.03	2.82	2.75	3.16		−.21	(580)
Class 5	2.95	2.39	2.72	2.77	3.40	2.90	2.85	3.76	3.70	3.01	2.74	2.92	3.20		−.43	(222)
Degree of Association (eta)																
Linear component of social strat.	.20**	.18**	.14**	.06*	.20**	.20**	.12**	.09**	.06*	.05	.00	.04	.02	.38**	.34**	
All components of social strat.	.21**	.19**	.16**	.06	.20**	.21**	.13**	.13**	.07	.05	.04	.11**	.07	.38**	.34**	

* $p < .05$.
** $p < .01$.
ᵃHigh valuation is indicated by a score of 5, low by a score of 1. For the factor scores, high valuation of self-direction is indicated by a positive score.

ity, at higher levels. These two pairs of manifestly similar but connotatively opposite characteristics nicely illustrate the differential emphases on internal process and external form that lie at the heart of the distinction we make between valuing self-direction and valuing conformity to external authority.

The essential difference between the terms, as we use them, is that self-direction focuses on *internal* standards for behavior; conformity focuses on *externally* imposed rules. (One important corollary is that the former is concerned with intent, the latter only with consequences.) Self-direction does not imply rigidity, isolation, or insensitivity to others; on the contrary, it implies only that one bases one's actions on internal standards—that one thinks for oneself. Conformity does not imply sensitivity to one's peers, but rather obedience to the dictates of authority.[4]

To secure a single index of parental valuation of self-direction *versus* conformity to externally-imposed rules, we did a factor analysis of the set of value-choices; the first factor produced by this analysis clearly reflects this dimension.[5] Henceforth, we use scores based on this factor as the index of parental valuation of self-direction *versus* conformity to external authority.[6] This index is correlated with social-stratification position, reaffirming that the higher men's social positions, the more highly they value self-direction for their children; the lower their social positions, the more highly they value conformity.

These findings confirm and extend the conclusions of the Washington (Kohn, 1959) and Turin (Pearlin and Kohn, 1966) studies. Not only do middle-class parents have different values from those of working-class parents, but the relationships between social-stratification position and values are consistently linear, from the highest to the lowest (but for the unemployed) socioeconomic

---

[4] People who value self-direction are not necessarily more (or less) altruistic than are those who value conformity to authority. (On this, see Schooler, 1972.) Certainly, people who value self-direction are just as much products of their life-conditions as are those who value conformity. But whatever the process that brought them to hold the values they do, and however noble or selfish their goals, people who value self-direction think it desirable to try to act on the basis, not of authority, but of one's own judgment and standards.

[5] This was an orthogonal principal component factor analysis, rotated to simple structure through the varimax procedure, based on the computer program developed by Clyde, et al. (1966:15). The first factor is the relevant one for present purposes; it contrasts neatness ($r = -.62$), manners ($r = -.56$), being a good student ($r = -.35$), and obedience ($r = -.34$), against an interest in how and why things happen ($r = .51$), consideration ($r = .43$), good sense ($r = .30$), self-control ($r = .29$), and responsibility ($r = .28$). (A second factor reflects the age of the child, contrasting characteristics more valued for older children with those more valued for younger. A third factor reflects one principal characteristic—tries hard to succeed.)

[6] Our procedure for calculating factor scores preserves the orthogonality of the factors and yields correlations of the original variables to the factor scores that are identical to the "loadings" of those variables on the factors (see Ryder, 1965). In constructing the scores, we repeated the factor analysis, limiting the number of rotated factors to two. We left out one of the thirteen values, so that no error in the computation of the inverse of the correlation matrix could result from linear dependency among the values.

strata of American society. (This can be seen in the mean scores presented in Table 1.1, and is attested to by the *etas* for the linear component of social stratification being nearly as large as those for all components of social stratification.[7]) More detailed analyses (see Kohn, 1969: Chapter 4) show that the relationship of social stratification to parental values is essentially the same, whatever the age and sex of the child, in families of varying size, composition, and functional pattern.

It should be noted that the correlations of social-stratification position with the individual values are no larger than .21; the correlation of social-stratification position with the entire set of values, as measured by the canonical correlation, is .38; and the correlation of social-stratification position with valuation of self-direction or conformity, as indexed by the factor scores, is .34.[8] The magnitude of these correlations is only moderate; what makes them impressive is their consistency.

Values for Self

To test our expectation that values for self are consonant with values for children, we use a similar mode of inquiry—modifying the characteristics to be more appropriate for adults (see Table 1.2 for the complete list). As anticipated, characteristics indicative of self-direction—an interest in how and why things happen, good sense and sound judgment, responsibility, self-reliance, the ability to face facts squarely, and the ability to do well under pressure—are more valued at higher social-stratification levels. There is evidence, too, that conformity is more valued at lower stratification levels. But this evidence is limited, because in modifying the list we substituted only one "adult" characteristic—respectability—for four "child" characteristics—manners, obedience, neatness, and being a good student. Moreover, we narrowed, perhaps distorted, the connotations of honesty by changing it to truthfulness. Thus, the only way men could endorse conformity was to choose respectability.[9] At lower

---

[7] The measure of association that we use, *eta,* is the correlation coefficient most easily obtained from an analysis of variance. It is the square root of the ratio of the "between groups" sum of squared deviations from the mean to the total sum of squared deviations from the mean. *Eta* is directly analogous to the product-moment correlation coefficient, in that it represents the square root of the proportion of variation in the dependent variable attributable to the independent variable. When one deals with the linear component of the independent variable, *eta* is identical to the product-moment correlation coefficient, except that its sign is always positive. (See Blalock, 1960:266–269; Cohen, 1965; Peters and Van Voorhis, 1940:312–324 and 353–357).

[8] The canonical correlation is a multiple correlation of one or a set of independent variables with a set of dependent variables. More precisely, it is the maximum correlation between linear functions of the two sets of variables (see Cooley and Lohnes, 1962:35).

[9] For this same reason—we think—the magnitude of the relationship of social stratification to values-for-self is weaker than that to values for children (the canonical correlations being .27 and .38 respectively).

Table 1.2. VALUES FOR SELF, BY SOCIAL STRATIFICATION

Mean Scores For:	Individual Values												Canonical Correlation	Factor Scores		Sample Size
	Interested in How and Why Things Happen	Good Sense and Sound Judgment	Responsible	Self-reliant	Able to Face Facts Squarely	Able to Do Well Under Pressure	Respectable	Able to Do Many Things Well	Truthful	Successful	Able to Get Along Well with People	Helpful to Others		Self-direction/ Conformity	Self-direction/ Competence	
Class 1	2.83[a]	3.73	3.50	3.08	3.33	2.69	2.63	1.94	3.35	2.38	3.40	3.17		+.65	+.31	(138)
Class 2	2.56	3.74	3.42	3.01	3.14	2.61	2.89	2.00	3.45	2.48	3.61	3.18		+.29	+.15	(332)
Class 3	2.33	3.62	3.38	2.93	3.08	2.64	3.11	2.12	3.59	2.54	3.68	3.10		−.01	+.07	(887)
Class 4	2.32	3.52	3.36	2.91	3.09	2.56	3.19	2.33	3.59	2.53	3.56	3.16		−.09	+.02	(1160)
Class 5	2.28	3.47	3.21	2.83	3.01	2.47	3.12	2.50	3.57	2.65	3.78	3.24		−.15	−.30	(544)
Degree of Association (eta)																
Linear component of social strat.	.10**	.10**	.09**	.07**	.06**	.06**	.13**	.16**	.05**	.06**	.05**	.04	.27**	.17**	.14**	
All components of social strat.	.12**	.10**	.10**	.08**	.08**	.07**	.17**	.17**	.07**	.07**	.10**	.07**	.27**	.19**	.15**	

* p<.05.

** p<.01.

[a] High valuation is indicated by a score of 5, low by a score of 1. For the factor scores, high valuation of self-direction is indicated by a positive score.

12

stratification levels, more men did so—thereby providing the only possible evidence that conformity is more highly valued by men of lower social-stratification position.

There is a second cluster of values-for-self associated with lower stratification position, centering around a high valuation of competence, as reflected in valuing the ability to do many things well, success, and the ability to get along well with people. We think this represents an important theme, distinct from conformity, but also in contradistinction to self-direction.

This supposition is borne out by a factor analysis of the entire set of value-choices. Two factors embodying self-direction appear, one contrasting it to conformity, the other to competence. (The first factor is focused on judgment, contrasting reliance on one's own judgment with reliance on other people's judgments. The second is focused on performance, the contrast being between acting on the basis of one's own standards and acting competently.)[10] Both are significantly correlated with social-stratification position, albeit neither very strongly. It adds an essential modicum of information that the higher the men's positions, the more self-directed are their values, with reference both to thought and to action.

Judgments about Work

It seems reasonable to assume that men judge jobs in terms both of the occupational conditions they might ideally want and of the alternatives that are realistically open to them. Again, as with values, judgments about jobs are constrained by what is thought important and what is thought problematic. Consonant with their greater valuation of self-direction, men of higher stratification position should be better able to take for granted such extrinsic aspects of the job as pay and security, to focus instead on the possibilities the job affords for self-expression and individual accomplishment. This expectation is given support in Inkeles's (1960:9) analysis, which shows that among both Americans and refugees from the Soviet Union, men in higher status jobs are "more likely to be concerned about having a job which is 'interesting,' stimulating, challenging, permits self-expression, and so on."

To learn about orientations to work, we asked men to evaluate the importance of various occupational conditions. Our data (Table 1.3) confirm Inkeles's conclusion and extend it. Essentially, men of higher social-stratification position judge jobs more by intrinsic qualities; men of lower social-stratification position, more by extrinsic characteristics. That is, the

---

[10] The first factor contrasts an interest in how and why things happen (r = .57), good sense and sound judgment (r = .45), and the ability to face facts squarely (r = .45) with respectability (r = −.62), truthfulness (r = −.43), and success (r = −.33). The second factor contrasts responsibility (r = .52) and self-reliance (r = .40) with the ability to get along well with people (r = − .68) and the ability to do many things well (r = − .44).

Table 1.3. JUDGMENTS ABOUT WORK, BY SOCIAL STRATIFICATION

Mean Scores For:	How Interesting the Work Is	Amount of Freedom	Chance to Help People	Chance to Use Abilities	Pay	Fringe Benefits	Supervisor	Co-workers	Hours of Work	How Tiring the Work Is	Job Security	Not Being Under Too Much Pressure	Chance to Get Ahead	How Clean the Work Is	How Highly People Regard the Job	Intrinsic Qualities	Extrinsic Benefits	Sample Size
	(Individual Characteristics)															*(Factor Scores)*		
Class 1	2.91[a]	2.59	2.43	2.88	2.25	1.95	2.36	2.25	1.76	1.70	2.30	1.74	2.55	1.65	2.01	+.34	−.75	(133)
Class 2	2.90	2.47	2.47	2.91	2.30	2.04	2.36	2.27	1.79	1.74	2.32	1.88	2.68	1.74	1.99	+.38	−.64	(326)
Class 3	2.75	2.32	2.39	2.81	2.41	2.17	2.34	2.24	1.96	1.88	2.59	2.08	2.68	1.80	2.07	+.13	−.20	(858)
Class 4	2.55	2.25	2.32	2.69	2.59	2.39	2.40	2.28	2.05	1.94	2.76	2.25	2.62	1.75	1.98	−.16	+.21	(1148)
Class 5	2.48	2.31	2.39	2.58	2.66	2.42	2.50	2.35	2.20	2.08	2.71	2.36	2.59	1.83	2.03	−.20	+.43	(522)

Degree of Association (eta)

	How Interesting the Work Is	Amount of Freedom	Chance to Help People	Chance to Use Abilities	Pay	Fringe Benefits	Supervisor	Co-workers	Hours of Work	How Tiring the Work Is	Job Security	Not Being Under Too Much Pressure	Chance to Get Ahead	How Clean the Work Is	How Highly People Regard the Job	Intrinsic Qualities	Extrinsic Benefits	Canonical Correlation
Linear component of social strat.	.25**	.10**	.04*	.20**	.21**	.20**	.06**	.04*	.16**	.13**	.23**	.22**	.03	.03	.01	.20**	.36**	.46**
All components of social strat.	.25**	.13**	.07**	.20**	.21**	.21**	.08**	.05	.16**	.14**	.26**	.22**	.07**	.06	.05	.21**	.36**	.47**

* p<.05.
** p<.01.
[a] High importance is indicated by a score of 3, low by a score of 1. For the factor scores, high importance is indicated by a positive score.

higher men's positions, the more importance they attach to how interesting their work is, the amount of freedom it provides, the chance to help people, and the chance to use their abilities. The lower their positions, the more importance they attach to pay, fringe benefits, the supervisor, co-workers, the hours of work, how tiring the work is, job security, and not being under too much pressure.

That the extrinsic-intrinsic distinction is a central line of cleavage is substantiated by a factor analysis that differentiates an intrinsic from an extrinsic dimension in these judgments.[11] Social stratification is correlated positively with the intrinsic, negatively with the extrinsic. The correlation of stratification with men's interest in the extrinsic is nearly twice as great as with their interest in the intrinsic. Social stratification apparently matters more in determining whether men are forced to focus on the extrinsic than in determining whether they are free to focus on the intrinsic.

Social Orientation

We expect men of higher social-stratification position to see society as so constituted that responsible individual action is practicable; men of lower social-stratification position will be more likely to think that following the dictates of authority is the course of wisdom. This distinction should be manifested in many ways, four of which seem especially pertinent: in how rigidly men define what is socially acceptable, in their definitions of appropriate moral standards, in how trustful they are of their fellow man, and in their stance toward change.

If orientations are consistent with values, men of higher social-stratification position will be more open-minded in their views of the socially acceptable and in their tolerance of nonconformity, while men at lower stratification levels will hold more authoritarian views of what is acceptable and will more rigidly reject behavior that does not conform to the acceptable. This expectation is buttressed by past investigations that have found social stratification to be related to authoritarianism (see Christie, 1954; Hyman and Sheatsley, 1954; Srole, 1956; Lipset, 1959; Kirscht and Dillehay, 1967:37–40) and by Stouffer's (1955) demonstration that intolerance of nonconformity is an essential ingredient of conformity.

The other aspects of social orientation that we investigated are standards of morality, trust, and stance toward change. Self-direction implies personally responsible moral standards; conformity requires only that one follow

---

[11] The first factor focuses on intrinsic qualities of jobs—how much opportunity the job provides for using one's abilities ($r = .68$), how interesting the work is ($r = .64$), and how much opportunity it offers to help people ($r = .67$). The second factor focuses on the extrinsic benefits of the job, emphasizing hours of work ($r = .64$), fringe benefits ($r = .58$), how tiring the work is ($r = .58$), job security ($r = .57$), and not being under too much pressure ($r = .51$).

the letter—not necessarily the spirit—of the law. Self-direction also implies a certain degree of trust in one's fellow man and the belief that change can be for the good; a conformist orientation is more pessimistic.

The indices that we use to investigate the relationship of stratification to social orientation are derived from a factor analysis of a set of 57 questions, mainly of the "agree-disagree" and "how often?" types.[12] Table 1.4 gives the exact wording of each component question that correlates .33 or more with any of these factors. In essence, the four indices of social orientation are as follows:

Authoritarian conservatism. Men's definitions of what is socially acceptable—at one extreme, rigid conformance to the dictates of authority and intolerance of nonconformity; at the other extreme, open-mindedness.

Standards of morality. A continuum of moral positions, from believing that morality consists of strict adherence to the letter of the law and keeping out of trouble, to defining and maintaining one's own moral standards.

Trustfulness. The degree to which men believe that their fellow man can be trusted.

Stance toward change. Men's receptiveness or resistance to innovation and change.

Social-stratification position is linearly related to all four aspects of social orientation (Table 1.5). The strongest correlation, by a very wide margin, is with authoritarian conservatism: The lower men's social-stratification position, the more rigidly conservative their view of man and his social institutions and the less their tolerance of nonconformity. The other aspects of orientation are less strongly correlated with social stratification, but the correlations are altogether consistent with our expectations. The lower men's positions, the more likely they are to feel that morality is synonymous with obeying the letter of the law; the less trustful of their fellow man they are; and the more resistant they are to innovation and change.

---

[12] Fourteen analytically separable, but not necessarily empirically independent, aspects of orientation to society and to self were initially indexed. We borrowed from existing indices where possible (see Adorno, et al., 1950; Srole, 1956; Rosenberg, 1957, 1962; McKinley, et al., 1948 and the references therein), but modified or added questions to provide the necessary connotations. All fourteen indices met the usual criteria for unidimensional scales (Guttman, 1944, 1950; Ford, 1950; Menzel, 1953).

Useful as the Guttman scaling technique is for eliminating questions that do not fall along a single dimension, it provides no definitive evidence that the retained questions all do fall along that dimension (see Schooler, 1968). Nor does it insure that the scales are independent of one another. To overcome these limitations, we subjected the entire battery of 57 questions, of which the 14 original scales were constituted, to a factor analysis. This analysis yielded twelve independent factors, nine of which are directly pertinent to our purposes and are used as indices. The complete factor analysis is given in Kohn, 1969: Appendix D.

Table 1.4. PRINCIPAL ITEMS OF THE SOCIAL ORIENTATION AND SELF-CONCEPTION FACTORS

	Loading[a]		Loading[a]

A. Social orientation

Factor 1. Authoritarian conservatism
(Authoritarian-open-minded)[b]

1. The most important thing to teach children is absolute obedience to their parents. +.61
2. Young people should not be allowed to read books that are likely to confuse them. +.58
3. There are two kinds of people in the world: the weak and the strong. +.58
4. People who question the old and accepted ways of doing things usually just end up causing trouble. +.55
5. In this complicated world, the only way to know what to do is to rely on leaders and experts. +.52
6. No decent man can respect a woman who has had sex relations before marriage. +.51
7. Prison is too good for sex criminals. They should be publicly whipped or worse. +.51
8. Any good leader should be strict with people under him in order to gain their respect. +.45
9. It's wrong to do things differently from the way our forefathers did. +.43
10. Once I've made up my mind, I seldom change it. +.37
11. It generally works out best to keep on doing things the way they have been done before. +.33

Factor 2. Standards of Morality
(Personally responsible-literalistic)

1. It's all right to do anything you want as long as you stay out of trouble. −.66
2. If something works, it doesn't matter whether it's right or wrong. −.57
3. It's all right to get around the law as long as you don't actually break it. −.54
4. Do you believe that it's all right to do whatever the law allows, or are there some things that are wrong even if they are legal? −.51
5. It's wrong to do things differently from the way our forefathers did. −.36

Factor 3. Trustfulness
(Trustful—distrustful)

1. Do you think that most people can be trusted? +.62
2. If you don't watch out, people will take advantage of you. −.48
3. Human nature is really cooperative. +.42
4. It's all right to get around the law as long as you don't break it. −.34

Factor 4. Stance toward Change
(Receptive—resistant)

1. Are you generally one of the first people to try out something new or do you wait until you see how it's worked out for other people? +.61
2. Are you the sort of person who takes life as it comes or are you working toward some definite goal? −.43
3. It generally works out best to keep on doing things the way they have been done before. −.33

B. Self-conception

Factor 1. Self-confidence
(Confident—not confident)

1. I take a positive attitude toward myself. +.62
2. I feel that I'm a person of worth, at least on an equal plane with others. +.61
3. I am able to do most things as well as other people can. +.60
4. I generally have confidence that when I make plans I will be able to carry them out. +.60
5. Once I've made up my mind, I seldom change it. +.38
6. Human nature is really cooperative. +.36

17

Table 1.4. *(continued)*

	Loading[a]		Loading[a]
7. On the whole, I think I am quite a happy person.	+.33	3. How frequently do you find yourself anxious and worrying about something?	+.62
Factor 2. Self-deprecation *(Deprecating—not deprecating)*		4. How often do you feel uneasy about something without knowing why?	+.59
1. I wish I could have more respect for myself.	+.62	5. How often do you feel so restless that you cannot sit still?	+.58
2. At times I think I am no good at all.	+.55	6. How often do you find that you can't get rid of some thought or idea that keeps running through your mind?	+.56
3. I feel useless at times.	+.54		
4. I wish I could be as happy as others seem to be.	+.53	7. How often do you feel bored with everything?	+.55
5. There are very few things about which I'm absolutely certain.	+.43	8. How often do you feel powerless to get what you want out of life?	+.50
Factor 3. Attribution of Responsibility *(Fatalistic—nonfatalistic)*		9. How often do you feel guilty for having done something wrong?	+.48
1. When things go wrong for you, how often would you say it is your own fault?	−.72	10. How often do you feel that the world just isn't very understandable?	+.45
2. To what extent would you say you are to blame for the problems you have—would you say that you are mostly to blame, partly to blame, or hardly at all to blame?	−.68	11. How often do you feel that there isn't much purpose to being alive?	+.40
		Factor 5. Idea-conformity *(Conforming—independent)*	
3. Do you feel that most of the things that happen to you are the result of your own decisions or of things over which you have no control?	−.60	1. How often do your ideas and opinions differ from those of your friends?	−.74
Factor 4. Anxiety *(Anxious—not anxious)*		2. How about from those of other people with your religious background?	−.70
1. How often do you feel that you are about to go to pieces?	+.65	3. According to your general impression, how often do your ideas and opinions about important matters differ from those of your relatives?	−.68
2. How often do you feel downcast and dejected?	+.65	4. Those of most people in the country?	−.67

[a]Plus sign stands for "strongly agree" or "very frequently."
[σ]The first-named pole of the factor, e.g., "Authoritarian," is the positive pole.

Self-conception

We expect men of higher stratification position to see themselves as more competent, more effective, more in control of the forces that affect their lives than do men of lower stratification position. We investigate five aspects of self-conception: self-confidence, self-deprecation, attribution of responsibility, anxiety, and idea-conformity.

The indices are derived from the same factor analysis as are those for social orientation (Table 1.4). They measure:

Table 1.5. SOCIAL ORIENTATION AND SELF-CONCEPTION, BY SOCIAL STRATIFICATION

	Social Orientation					Self-conception						Sample Size
	Authoritarian Conservatism (+=Authoritarian)	Standards of Morality (+=Personally Responsible)	Trustfulness (+=Trustful)	Stance Toward Change (+=Receptive)	Canonical Correlation	Self-confidence (+=Confident)	Self-deprecation (+=Self-deprecating)	Attribution of Responsibility (+=Fatalistic)	Anxiety (+=Anxious)	Idea-conformity (+=Conforming)	Canonical Correlation	
Mean Scores For:												
Class 1	−.91	.22	.33	.03	...	.21	−.08	−.17	−.02	−.26	...	(137)
Class 2	−.67	.30	.31	.17	...	.22	−.11	−.13	−.08	−.16	...	(335)
Class 3	−.13	.12	.08	.16	...	.05	−.09	−.14	−.05	−.09	...	(890)
Class 4	.18	−.04	−.07	.04	...	−.08	.01	.05	.05	.05	...	(1145)
Class 5	.48	−.30	−.26	−.43	...	−.06	.22	.25	.08	.21	...	(528)
Degree of Association (eta)												
Linear component of social strat.	.38**	.17**	.17**	.15**	.47**	.09**	.10**	.13**	.05**	.13**	.23**	
All components of social strat.	.38**	.18**	.17**	.21**	.48**	.10**	.11**	.14**	.06*	.13**	.24**	

*p<.05.
**p<.01.

19

Self-confidence.   The positive component of self-esteem: the degree to which men are confident of their own capacities.

Self-deprecation.   The self-critical half of self-esteem: the degree to which men disparage themselves. (This empirical division of self-esteem accords well with the possibility that one can be simultaneously confident of one's capacities and critical of oneself.)

Attribution of responsibility.   Men's sense of being controlled by outside forces or, alternatively, of having some control over their fate.

Anxiety.   The intensity of consciously-felt psychic discomfort.

Idea-conformity.   The degree to which men believe that their ideas mirror those of the social entities to which they belong.

The relationship of social stratification to self-conception is not nearly as strong as is that of stratification to social orientation; apparently social-stratification position is less relevant for how men view themselves than for how they view the external world (Table 1.5). But the findings are consistent with our expectations. The higher men's social-stratification positions, the more self-confidence and the less self-deprecation they express; the greater their sense of being in control of the forces that affect their lives; the less beset by anxiety they are; and the more independent they consider their ideas to be.

Men's views of how effectively they function are significantly, but not strongly, associated with their social-stratification positions, men at the top being more confident of their own capacities than are men lower in the social hierarchy.[13]

DIMENSIONS OF SOCIAL STRATIFICATION

In interpreting the relationships of social stratification to values and orientation, the logical first step is to examine stratification itself, its components, and its correlates. This analysis yields four principal findings. The first is apparent in the tables already presented—the relationships of social

---

[13] More detailed analyses of the relationships of social stratification with values and orientations show that these relationships are essentially invariant for all major segments of American society—regardless of race, religious background, national background, region of the country, and size of community. Moreover, the magnitudes of the relationships are little affected by statistically controlling these other social variables. In fact, social stratification—controlled on all these other major lines of social demarcation—is more strongly related to values and orientations than are all the other major lines of social demarcation combined, when controlled on social stratification.

Detailed analyses also show that the relationships of social stratification with values and orientations remain statistically significant when respondent's age and such artifacts of the interview procedure as the respondent's tendency to agree with statements put to him, his tendency to give extreme answers, the length of the interview, and his apparent attitude toward the interview, are statistically controlled.

stratification with values and orientations are preponderantly linear, with virtually no significant curvilinear or higher-order relationships, no sharp breaks, no departures from pattern. Therefore, in interpreting these relationships, it is profitable to think of a continuous hierarchy of positions, rather than of discrete categories.

Second, the two components of our index of social stratification—education and occupational status—are each related, independently of the other, to almost all aspects of values and orientation, and these relationships are essentially additive.[14] Thus, any explanation of the relationships must take into account that both education and occupational status are involved.

Third, such other aspects of stratification as income and subjective class identification bear only a small relationship to values and orientations when social-stratification position (as we have indexed it) is statistically controlled. On the other hand, social-stratification position is nearly as strongly related to values and orientations when income and subjective class identification are statistically controlled as when they are not. Income and subjective class identification may, of course, be more important for explaining the relationship of social stratification to other psychological phenomena.

Finally, present social-stratification position matters for values and orientations more than do social origins. Although we cannot overlook the obvious and critical fact that parents' socio-economic status plays a major part in determining one's own present stratification position, our data show that when men move into positions different from those of their parents (and their grandparents), their values and orientations come to agree with those of their achieved positions.

OCCUPATIONAL CONDITIONS

Interpreting the relationships of social stratification to values and orientations requires that we determine which of the many conditions of life associated with social-stratification position actually contribute to explaining these relationships. We have narrowed the range of possibilities by finding that only those conditions of life that vary continuously with education and occupational status can be of any great relevance for explaining the relationships of social stratification to values and orientations. Primary among the conditions of life that vary continuously with education and occupational status are the *occupational* conditions conducive to or restrictive of the exercise of self-direction in work. Our further analysis is focused on these occupational conditions.

---

[14] A note of caution is in order here. In dealing with variables as substantially correlated as are education and occupational status ($r = .63$), it may not be possible to precisely assess their independent effects on values and orientations (see Blalock, 1963; Farrar and Glauber, 1967; Gordon, 1968).

Occupational Self-direction

Although many conditions of work either facilitate or deter the exercise of occupational self-direction, three in particular are critical.

First, a limiting condition: Men cannot exercise occupational self-direction if they are closely supervised. Not being closely supervised, however, does not necessarily mean that men are required—or even free—to use initiative, thought, and independent judgment; it depends on how complex and demanding is their work.

A second and far more important condition for occupational self-direction is that the work, in its very substance, require initiative, thought, and independent judgment. Work with "data" or with "people" is more likely to require initiative, thought, and judgment than is work with "things". Granted, there are exceptions. For example, even though most work with things does not require a great deal of self-direction, some work with things is highly self-directed—consider the sculptor. Conversely, work with data may not always be self-directed—consider routine office jobs. Still, complex work with data or with people—synthesizing or coordinating data, teaching or negotiating with people—is especially likely to require initiative, thought, and judgment. Thus, occupational self-direction is most probable when men spend some substantial amount of their working time doing complex work with data or with people.

The third condition for occupational self-direction is that the work allow a variety of approaches; otherwise the possibilities for exercising initiative, thought, and judgment are seriously limited. The organization of the work must be complex, involving a variety of tasks that are in themselves complexly structured.

No one of these conditions is definitional of occupational self-direction. Together, though, the three job conditions largely determine how much self-direction men can exercise in their work. Insofar as men are free of close supervision, do complex work with data or with people, and work at complexly organized tasks, their work is necessarily self-directed. Insofar as they are closely supervised, work with things, and work at simply organized tasks, their work does not permit self-direction.

The Relationship of Occupational Self-direction to Values and Orientation

We begin this phase of the analysis by ascertaining whether specific stratification-related occupational conditions are significantly related to values and orientations, independent of their relationship to social stratification. We statistically control social-stratification position, to avoid spuriously explaining the relationship of social stratification to values and orientations in terms of phenomena that can themselves be explained as functions of social stratification. It is unimportant that the partial correlations—of occupational conditions with values and orientations, controlled on social stratification—will necessarily be small; all that matters is that there be some statistically significant, independent association between a given occupational condition and one or, preferably, several aspects of values and orientation.

Closeness of supervision. The index here is a scale based on five questions about how much latitude men's supervisors allow and how supervisory control is exercised:[15]

1. How closely does (the man who has the most control over what you do on the job) supervise you—does he decide what you do and how you do it; does he decide what you do but let you decide how you do it; do you have some freedom in deciding both what you do and how you do it; or are you your own boss so long as you stay within the general policies of the firm (organization, department)?
2. When he wants you to do something, does he usually just tell you to do it, does he usually discuss it with you, or is it about half and half?
3. How free do you feel to disagree with him—completely free, largely but not completely, moderately, not particularly, or not at all free?
4. Is the speed at which you work controlled mostly by you, your boss, your work group, the speed of machinery with which you work, or what? (The relevant aspect here is whether or not the supervisor controls the speed at which the man works.)
5. [How important is it for doing your job well that you] do what you're told?

Closeness of supervision, thus indexed, is associated with a constricted orientation (Table 1.6, column 1). Closely supervised men tend to value conformity for their children, to emphasize extrinsic benefits that jobs provide rather than opportunities for intrinsic accomplishment, to have standards of morality keyed to the letter rather than the spirit of the law, to be distrustful, to be resistant to innovation and change, to lack self-confidence, and to be anxious.

The substance of work with data, things, and people. The indices here are based on detailed inquiry about precisely what men do and how much time they spend working with things, with data or ideas, and with people. Early in the interview—immediately after learning the title of

---

[15] Reproducibility = .93; the pattern of errors seems essentially random, using Ford's (1950) criteria.

the man's principal occupation and its institutional locus—the interviewer asked these questions:

One thing we'd like to be able to pin down particularly accurately is how much of your working time is spent reading and writing, how much working with your hands, and how much dealing with people. We realize, of course, that you can be doing two or even all three of these at the same time.

1. First—reading or writing. Here we should like to include any type of written materials—letters, files, memos, books, or blueprints. About how many hours a week do you spend reading, writing,

Table 1.6. VALUES AND ORIENTATION, BY THE CONDITIONS DETERMINATIVE OF OCCUPATIONAL SELF-DIRECTION[a]

	Closeness of Supervision	Substance of the Work: Data, Things, and People	Organization of the Work: Repetitiveness and Structural Complexity	Total of All Three Components of Occupational Self-direction
A. Parental Values				
Self-direction/conformity	.06*	.12**	.10*	.15**
B. Values for Self				
Self-direction/conformity	.02	.08*	.04	.08
Self-direction/competence	.01	.05	.05	.07
C. Judgments about Work				
Importance of intrinsic qualities	.11**	.14**	.10**	.18**
Importance of extrinsic benefits	.07**	.15**	.15**	.18**
D. Social Orientation				
Authoritarian conservatism	.03	.10**	.11**	.14**
Standards of morality	.12**	.13**	.11**	.18**
Trustfulness	.04*	.09**	.05	.10**
Stance toward change	.06**	.13**	.07*	.15**
CANONICAL CORRELATION	.14**	.21**	.18**	.26**
E. Self-conception				
Self-confidence	.08**	.09**	.04	.12**
Self-deprecation	.02	.07*	.07*	.10**
Attribution of responsibility	.02	.06	.05	.08
Anxiety	.07**	.04	.04	.09*
Idea-conformity	.03	.07*	.06	.09*
CANONICAL CORRELATION	.11**	.13**	.08	.16**

[a] Entries are partial correlations, either *eta* or the canonical correlation, always controlled on social stratification. Closeness of supervision and the seven component indices of the substance of the work have been tested linearly, the organization of the work has been tested *in toto*.
*$p < 0.05$.
**$p < 0.01$.
N>2900, except for parental values, where N=1450.

dictating, or dealing with any kind of written materials on your job?

>(If any time at all)
>a. What do you do?
>b. What are they about?

2. Second—working with your hands, using tools, using or repairing machines. We should like to include everything that involves working with your hands—operating a lathe or a dentist's drill, moving furniture, playing the piano. About how many hours a week do you spend working with your hands on your job?

>(If any time at all)
>a. What do you do? (Probe: What operations do you perform?)
>b. What materials do you work on?
>c. What tools or equipment do you use?
>d. (If relevant) What do you do to set up and maintain your equipment?

3. Third—dealing with people. Here we do not mean to include passing the time of day, but only conversations necessary for the job; for example, talking to your boss, teaching, supervising, selling, advising clients. About how many hours a week does your job require you to spend dealing with people?

>(If any time at all)
>What kinds of things do you do—do you teach students, supervise subordinates, receive instructions from the boss, sell to customers, advise clients, discuss the work with co-workers, or what?

From this information, we rated the overall complexity of men's work, the degree of complexity of their work with things, with data, and with people, and the amount of time they spend at each of the three types of activity.[16] Examining the combined effect of these seven indices of time and complexity of work with data, with things, and with people, we find (Table

---

[16] See Appendix B for our classifications of complexity. Our ratings of the complexity of work with things, with data, and with people are modelled on those used in the third edition of the *Dictionary of Occupational Titles* (United States Department of Labor, 1965). The *Dictionary's* ratings, based on *in situ* observations by trained occupational analysts, provide objective appraisals of typical job requirements for all major occupations. Our ratings for particular jobs prove to be highly consistent with the *Dictionary's* ratings for entire occupations.

Although the third edition of the *Dictionary* appeared long after our survey was undertaken, our plans were keyed to it—thanks to the foreknowledge and advice provided by Sidney Fine, the originator of this valuable classificatory system.

1.6, column 2) the substance of work to be significantly related to virtually all aspects of values and orientation. Doing complex work with data or with people is consistently associated with valuing self-direction and holding a consonant orientation; working with things is consistently associated with having conformist values and orientations.

The specifics of men's work with data, with things, and with people—the types of data with which they work, the tools they use, the nature of their relations with the people with whom they interact—are relatively unimportant. What does matter for values and orientations is the complexity of work with data and with people, the time spent working with data, things, and people, and the overall complexity of the job. Each of these is independently relevant, and their multiple correlations with values and orientations are a bit greater than are the correlations for any one of them.

The complexity of organization of work. Some jobs are endlessly repetitive, others offer a variety of different tasks or at least variety in the ways that essentially similar tasks can be performed. In some jobs, the "units" of which the stream of work is composed are nearly identical; in others, the units are complex entities—each with a structural integrity of its own—or the work is so highly diversified that it cannot be split into meaningful units. Again the essence of the matter is complexity, but, in this case, from the perspective of the organization of the work. Simply organized jobs cannot allow much self-direction; complexly organized jobs require it.

Our indices here are based on men's appraisals of what constitutes "a complete job" in their occupation and of how repetitive their work is.[17] These two aspects of the complexity of organization of work are independently related to values and orientations, their effects being additive. Men who work at complexly organized jobs tend to value self-direction for children, to emphasize intrinsic aspects of the job, to be open-minded and tolerant of nonconformity, to have moral standards that demand more than conformity to the letter of the law, to be receptive to change, and not to be self-deprecatory (Table 1.6, column 3).

---

[17] Concretely, we asked:
  (1) What it takes to do a complete job varies a great deal from occupation to occupation. To a worker on an assembly line a complete job may be to tighten two or three bolts; to an auto mechanic a complete job is to repair a car; to a coal miner, a complete job may be to load eighteen tons.
    a. What do you ordinarily think of as a complete job in your occupation? (Probe: What do you have to do in order to feel that you've finished a piece of work? Second Probe: Do you ever feel that you've finished? At what point?)
    b. How long does it take you to do a complete job? (If it varies: What is the range of variation?)
  (2) Does your work involve doing the same thing in the same way repeatedly, the same kind of thing in a number of different ways, or a number of different kinds of things?

In sum, each of the three conditions that are determinative of occupational self-direction—closeness of supervision; the substance of work with data, with things, and with people; and the complexity of organization of work—is consistently related to values and orientations. Thus, each of these conditions of work might help explain the relationships of social stratification with values and orientations. Moreover, each is significantly related to values and orientations independent of the other two. Of the three components of occupational self-direction, the substance of work with data, with things, and with people bears the strongest relationship to values and orientations; but closeness of supervision and the complexity of organization of work add to the total impact. As a result (Table 1.6, column 4), occupational self-direction, independent of its close association with social stratification, is significantly related to almost all aspects of values and orientation with which we have dealt.

Other Facets of Occupation

Previous theoretical and empirical studies suggest many other stratification-related occupational conditions that might be related to values and orientations and therefore might help explain the relationships of social stratification with values and orientations.[18] We find, in fact, that several of these occupational conditions are significantly related to values and orientations, independent of their relationship to social stratification—the principal ones being ownership, amount of competition, job security, size and supervisory structure of the firm or organization, position in the supervisory hierarchy, time-pressure and the consequences of time-pressure, and the average amount of overtime.

For our immediate purposes, the primary importance of these findings lies not in their intrinsic interest but in the opportunity they afford for contrasting the conditions determinative of occupational self-direction with an alternative set of occupational conditions that we expect will not prove to be as relevant for explaining the stratification relationships. This gives us a basis for a clear-cut test of our principal hypothesis: that the conditions

---

[18] Our inquiry focused particularly on (a) ownership (a dichotomy, contrasting men who have full or partial ownership of the firm where they are employed to those who do not), job rights, and job security; (b) bureaucratization—as measured by the size and supervisory complexity of the employing firm or organization—and place in the supervisory structure; (c) the use and organization of time—including both the several facets of how work time is internally structured and how work time is separated from nonwork time; (d) patterns of interpersonal relations in work; and (e) job satisfaction, occupational commitment, and subjective reactions to the job. Of the many occupational conditions studied, only those enumerated in the text proved to be independently related to values and orientations in a way that could be pertinent for explaining the relationships of social stratification with values and orientations. For the details of this analysis, see Kohn, 1969, Chapter 10.

determinative of occupational self-direction are highly relevant for explaining the relationships of social stratification to values and orientations, and that other occupational conditions (even though related to values and orientations) are of less relevance for explaining these relationships.

THE RELEVANCE OF OCCUPATIONAL SELF-DIRECTION FOR EXPLAINING THE STRATIFICATION RELATIONSHIPS

To test our hypothesis, we statistically control (singly and in sets) all those occupational conditions that have proved to be independently related to values and orientations, to see how much this reduces the correlations of social stratification with values and orientations. It must be emphasized that in dealing with these occupational conditions we are concerned, not with distinctions that cut across social stratification, but with experiences constitutive of stratification. The objective is to learn whether these constituent experiences are pertinent for explaining the relationships. Our procedure is altogether hypothetical, for it imagines an unreal social situation—stratification levels that do not differ from one another in the occupational conditions experienced by their members. It is nevertheless analytically appropriate to use such hypothetical procedures, for it helps us to differentiate occupational conditions that are relevant for explaining the relationship of social stratification to values and orientations from those that are not.

We need not discuss the effects of controlling each occupational condition, for the major lessons of this analysis are sufficiently well documented by a summary presentation (Table 1.7). The relationships of social stratification to most of the values and orientations are substantially attributable to those occupational conditions that are conducive to or restrictive of occupational self-direction. That is, statistically controlling the conditions determinative of occupational self-direction greatly reduces the correlations of social stratification with values and orientations—in almost all instances by half and in several by two-thirds or more. Controlling the other occupational conditions has much weaker effects—in general, reducing the correlations by less than one-third. Controlling both sets of conditions reduces the correlations of social stratification to values and orientations by no more than does controlling the conditions determinative of occupational self-direction alone. Thus, the relationships of social stratification to values and orientations are in large measure attributable to those conditions that are determinative of occupational self-direction.

This analysis can be pursued further by considering the relevance of occupational self-direction to each of the components of our index of social stratification: education and occupational status. Since education and occupational status are substantially correlated ($r = .63$), the variance in values and orientations "explained" by social stratification has three components: a portion that is due solely to education, a portion that is due solely to occupational status, and a sizeable portion that cannot be exclusively attributed to either. Dealing with the third portion requires more complex modelling of the interrelationship of education, occupational status, and job conditions than can be attempted in this chapter. We can, however, test whether occupational self-direction is pertinent primarily for explaining the uniquely educational component of the relationships of social stratification with values and orientations, primarily for explaining the uniquely occupa-

Table 1.7. EFFECTS ON THE STRATIFICATION CORRELATIONS OF CONTROLLING SETS OF OCCUPATIONAL VARIABLES

	Initial Correlation with Social Stratification[a]	Proportional Reduction in the Magnitude of the Correlation When Controlling:		
		Occupational Self-direction[b]	Other Occupational Conditions[c]	All Significant Occupational Conditions
A. Parental Values				
Self-direction/conformity	.33**	.65	.33	.67
B. Values for Self				
Self-direction/conformity	.16**	.56	.23	.54
Self-direction/competence	.15**	.49	.25	.50
C. Judgments about Work				
Importance of intrinsic qualities	.19**	.94	.36	.94
Importance of extrinsic benefits	.35**	.57	.21	.58
D. Social Orientation				
Authoritarian conservatism	.38**	.50	.21	.50
Standards of morality	.18**	.87	.32	.87
Trustfulness	.17**	.61	.22	.61
Stance toward change	.15**	.95	.58	.99
CANONICAL CORRELATION	.48**	.56	.22	.56
E. Self-conception				
Self-confidence	.09**	.99	.64	.96
Self-deprecation	.09**	.87	.23	.86
Attribution of responsibility	.12**	.45	.30	.49
Anxiety	.06**	.35	.10	.38
Idea-conformity	.13**	.57	.30	.60
CANONICAL CORRELATION	.22**	.57	.31	.60

[a] *Eta* or the canonical correlation. These figures differ slightly from those of preceding Tables because respondents for whom data were not complete are dropped. $N > 2600$, except for parental values, where $N > 1285$.

[b] Substance of the work with data, things, and people + closeness of supervision + complexity of organization of the work.

[c] Size and supervisory structure of the organization + time-pressure and its consequences + position in supervisory hierarchy + amount of competition + likelihood of loss of job or business + ownership status + amount of overtime.

*$p < 0.05$.

**$p < 0.01$.

tional status component of the relationships, or equally for explaining both. We find that it is relevant to both, but more to the occupational status than to the educational component (Table 1.8). That is, the correlations of the uniquely educational component of social stratification with values and orientations are in small to moderate part attributable to occupational self-direction; but the correlations of the uniquely occupational status component with most aspects of values and orientations (with the notable exception of self-conception) are largely attributable to occupational self-direction.[19]

One implication is that occupational status would cease to be relevant for most aspects of values and orientation if higher occupational status did not mean greater occupational self-direction. A second implication is that, although the magnitude of the correlations would be reduced, education would still be revelant for almost all aspects of values and orientation even if educated men were not disproportionately situated in self-directed jobs. Why, then, is education pertinent? In part, of course, it is because education is important to job placement—an importance reflected in the variance that education and occupational status share with occupational self-direction. But there is more to education than its role in job placement. Our hypothesis is that educational level is pertinent to values and orientations, in part, because education provides the intellectual flexibility and breadth of perspective that are essential for self-directed values and orientations; lack of education must seriously interfere with men's ability to be self-directed.

We do not have the data to test this hypothesis directly. We can, however, show that intellectual flexibility is involved in the relationship of education to values and orientation. As an approximate measure of intellectual flexibility, we use scores based on a single factor comprising several indices of how well men dealt with problems they encountered in the interview.[20] This measure of intellectual flexibility is correlated with education, hence

---

[19] Since the object of this analysis is to see how controlling occupational self-direction affects the specifically educational component of the relationships, occupational status is also controlled. Similarly, when we examine how controlling occupational self-direction affects the relationships of occupational status to values and orientation, education is controlled.

[20] The components of this factor (together with the factor loadings) are: (1) A rating of the adequacy of men's answers to the question, "Suppose you wanted to open a hamburger stand and there were two locations available. What questions would you consider in deciding which of the two locations offers a better business opportunity?" $(r = .37)$. (2) A rating of their answers to: "What are all the arguments you can think of for and against allowing cigarette commercials on TV? First, can you think of arguments for allowing cigarette commercials on TV? And can you think of arguments against allowing cigarette commercials on TV?" $(r = .41)$. (3) A measure of the frequency with which men agreed when asked agree-disagree questions $(r = -.52)$. (4) Their summary scores on a portion of the Embedded Figures Test (see Witkin, et al., 1962), which was given at the end of the interview $(r = .67)$. (5) The interviewers' appraisals of their intelligence $(r = .60)$. (6) Witkin, et al.'s (1962) summary score for the Draw-A-Person test (administered at the end of the interview) $(r = .75)$. (7) The Goodenough estimate of intelligence (see Witkin, et al., 1962), also based on the Draw-A-Person test $(r = .78)$.

with social stratification, and is independently associated with most aspects of values and orientation. Controlling intellectual flexibility reduces many of the correlations of social stratification with values and orientations, notably the correlations with social orientations. Most correlations of social-stratification position with values and orientations are reduced by 25 percent to 50 percent when intellectual flexibility is controlled. All correlations except that with self-deprecation remain statistically significant.

Most importantly, the reductions in the correlations are specific to the educational component of social stratification; for example, statistically controlling intellectual flexibility reduces the canonical correlation of education with social orientations by 40 percent, but it reduces the correlation

Table 1.8. EFFECTS ON THE EDUCATION AND ON THE OCCUPATIONAL STATUS CORRELATIONS OF CONTROLLING OCCUPATIONAL SELF-DIRECTION

	Education (Linear) Controlled on Occupational Status		Occupational Status (Linear) Controlled on Education	
	Initial Correlation[a]	Proportional Reduction When Controlling Occ. Self-direction	Initial Correlation[a]	Proportional Reduction When Controlling Occ. Self-direction
A. Parental Values				
Self-direction/conformity	.23**	.18	.09**	.83
B. Values for Self				
Self-direction/conformity	.12**	.12	.05*	1.00
Self-direction/competence	.13**	.11	.02	. . .
C. Judgments about Work				
Importance of intrinsic qualities	.04*	. . .[b]	.14**	.86
Importance of extrinsic benefits	.20**	.18	.15**	.70
D. Social Orientation				
Authoritarian conservatism	.32**	.13	.05**	.98
Standards of morality	.08**	.44	.08**	.87
Trustfulness	.09**	.27	.08**	.70
Stance toward change	.06**	.58	.05*	.00
CANONICAL CORRELATION	.36**	.15	.14**	.62
E. Self-conception				
Self-confidence	.05*	.31	.05*	.37
Self-deprecation	.03	. . .	.03	. . .
Attribution of responsibility	.03	. . .	.05**	.43
Anxiety	.04*	. . .	.09**	.19
Idea-conformity	.08**	.19	.02	. . .
CANONICAL CORRELATION	.11**	.24	.12**	.24

[a] Respondents for whom occupational data are incomplete have been excluded.
[b] Proportional reduction not computed where the initial correlation is less than 0.05.
*p<0.05.
**p<0.01.
 N>2625, except for parental values, where N=1366.

of occupational status with social orientations by less than 10 percent. Although this finding is hardly definitive, it does strengthen the supposition that one important reason why education is related to values and orientations lies in education's contribution to the intellectual flexibility that may be essential for self-directed values and orientations.

CONCLUSION

Much of the variation in men's values and orientations results from idiosyncratic personal experience, unrelated to the positions men occupy in the general social structure. Still, social structure does have pronounced and consistent effects, and, of all aspects of social structure, social stratification is by far the most important.

The higher their social-stratification positions, the more value men place on self-direction and the more confident they are that self-direction is both possible and efficacious. The lower their social-stratification positions, the more value men place on conformity to external authority and the more certain they are that conformity is all that their own capacities and the exigencies of the world allow. Thus, it would appear that men's values, their appraisals of their own abilities, and their understanding of the world are consistent. Self-direction is a central value for men of higher social position who see themselves as competent members of an essentially benign society. Conformity is a central value for men of lower social position who see themselves as less competent members of an essentially indifferent or threatening society. Self-direction, in short, is consonant with an orientational system premised on the possibilities of accomplishing what one sets out to do; conformity, with an orientation system premised on the dangers of stepping out of line.

These relationships of social stratification to values and orientations are substantially attributable to variations in the degree to which jobs allow and require self-direction. More specifically, the job conditions determinative of occupational self-direction are of great importance for explaining the uniquely occupational-status component of the stratification relationships, but are decidedly less important for explaining the uniquely educational component of these relationships. Occupational status seems to matter for values and orientations because it helps determine the opportunity and need for exercising self-direction that jobs provide or preclude. Education, on the other hand, seems to matter for values and orientations not only because of its role in job placement but also because it can be very important for intellectual flexibility and breadth of perspective. Thus, the relationships of social stratification with values and orientations are built on the cumulative effects of educational training and occupational experience.

We must acknowledge that nothing has been said about such issues as the relationship of occupational selection and of job-molding to values and orientations. The reinforcing processes by which jobs affect values and orientations, and values and orientations reflect back on jobs, are undoubtedly more complex than we have represented. The thrust of our thesis is not that all influence is in one direction, but rather that the occupational conditions attendant on social-stratification position are important in shaping men's values and orientations. We recognize the great difference between demonstrating that the relationships of social stratification with values and orientations are statistically attributable to occupational conditions and demonstrating that these occupational conditions do, in fact, enter into the processes by which social-stratification position affects values and orientations. This issue is a major focus of subsequent chapters.

We believe that, in industrial society, where occupation is central to men's lives, occupational experiences that facilitate or deter the exercise of self-direction come to permeate men's views, not only of work and of their role in work, but also of the world and of self. The conditions of occupational life at higher social-stratification levels facilitate interest in the intrinsic qualities of the job, foster a view of self and society that is conducive to believing in the possibilities of rational action toward purposive goals, and promote the valuation of self-direction. The conditions of occupational life at lower social-stratification levels limit men's view of the job primarily to the extrinsic benefits it provides, foster a narrowly circumscribed conception of self and society, and promote the valuation of conformity to authority. Conditions of work that foster thought and initiative tend to enlarge men's conceptions of reality; conditions of constraint tend to narrow them.

Bureaucratic Man:
A Portrait and
an Interpretation*

Melvin L. Kohn

It is often asserted that bureaucracy makes for unthinking, literalistic conformism. So self-evidently correct does this view seem that Webster's Third New International Dictionary defines bureaucracy as, among other things, "a system of administration marked by...lack of initiative and flexibility, by indifference to human needs or public opinion, and by a tendency to defer decisions to superiors or to impede action with red tape." Moreover, there is plausible theoretical reason why bureaucracy should have such effects. As Merton (1952) pointed out, the social psychological corollary of the efficiency, rationality, and predictability that Weber prized in bureaucratic organizational practice must be a certain "overconformity" in the behavior of bureaucrats.

But does working in a bureaucracy merely make automatons of men, or are there compensating features that encourage individualistic qualities? Surprisingly, there has been little empirical study of how bureaucracy af-

* This chapter is a slightly revised version of a paper of the same title (Kohn, 1971), originally published in the *American Sociological Review*. I am indebted for critical advice and essential help to my associates: Carmi Schooler, Lindsley Williams, Elizabeth Howell, Margaret Renfors, Carrie Schoenbach, and John Westine.

fects those who spend their working hours in its employ.[1] One objective of this chapter is to ascertain whether "bureaucrats" really are conformist in their values and in their appraisal of social reality, resistant to innovation and change, literalistic in their moral judgments, and inflexible in their thinking.

A further and more important objective is to discover how bureaucratization exerts its social-psychological impact, whatever that impact may be. The overall structure of the organization matters, for those who work there, through its impact on occupational conditions that bear directly on men's lives—"proximate" occupational conditions, such as closeness of supervision, time pressure, and the substantive complexity of the work. Bureaucratization affects many of these conditions, but most discussions seem to have arbitrarily focused on only one, supervision. In this inquiry, we attempt a systematic examination of the many occupational concomitants of bureaucratization to see which ones contribute to its impact.

We are not here concerned with the efficiency of bureaucratic organization for getting things done, with the effect of the system on outsiders who must deal with it, or even with the adequacy of bureaucrats' performance in their occupational roles. We deliberately limit our attention to how (and why) the experience of working in a bureaucracy affects men's values, social orientations, and intellectual functioning.

PRINCIPAL INDICES

Bureaucracy: Definition and Index

Our conception of bureaucracy is derived from Weber's classic analysis (see Gerth and Mills, 1946:196–244; Weber, 1947:329–341). As summarized by Merton (1952:362), the main characteristics of bureaucratic structure are that: "[B]ureaucracy involves a clear-cut division of integrated activities which are regarded as duties inherent in the office. A system of differentiated controls and sanctions is stated in the regulations. The assignment of roles occurs on the basis of technical qualifications which are ascertained through formalized, impersonal procedures (e.g., examinations). Within

---

[1] The few relevant studies give apparently contradictory results. Whyte (1956) argued that large corporations co-opt junior executives, to the detriment of their individuality; and Miller and Swanson (1958) found that bureaucratization leads parents to de-emphasize self-reliance in favor of accommodation as values for children; but Blau (1955:183-200) found that the job securities provided to the employees of a government bureaucracy generate favorable attitudes toward change; and Bonjean and Grimes (1970) failed to find any consistent evidence to support the hypothesized positive relationship between bureaucracy and alienation.

the structure of hierarchically arranged authority, the activities of 'trained and salaried experts' are governed by general, abstract, clearly defined rules which preclude the necessity for the issuance of specific instructions for each specific case.''

In this study, we are able to index only one of these several dimensions of bureaucracy, the hierarchical organization of authority. This limitation is the price we pay for a sample sufficiently large and diverse to permit a systematic assessment of the occupational conditions attendant on bureaucratization. In studying men who work in a multitude of organizations, we cannot assess organizational structure at firsthand, but must rely on reports by the men who work there, some of whom know little about their employing organization except insofar as it directly impinges on them. The one facet of organizational structure that we can measure; because it necessarily impinges on all men, is authority.

How much is lost by our inability to index other dimensions is uncertain, because there is contradictory evidence as to whether or not bureaucracy's several dimensions are highly intercorrelated (see Hall, 1963; Hall and Tittle, 1966; Miller, 1970). But even the research that finds low intercorrelations concludes that the hierarchical organization of authority "may be the central dimension...of the overall degree of bureaucratization" (Hall, 1963:37). Moreover, hierarchy of authority is conceptually central: bureaucracies can operate with greater or lesser specialization, with more or less impersonality, with or without a multiplicity of codified rules and procedures, but it is basic to the very idea of bureaucracy that authority be hierarchically organized (see Gerth and Mills, 1946:197; Rheinstein, 1954: 336–337; Blau, 1970:203).

We treat the hierarchical organization of authority as operationally equivalent to the number of formal levels of supervision. Although many men do not have a comprehensive view of the authority structure of the firm or organization in which they work, even the man at the bottom of the hierarchy knows whether his boss has a boss and whether that man is the ultimate boss. So we asked the respondents: "Is this [an organization] where everyone is supervised directly by the same man, where there is one level of supervision between the people at the bottom and the top, or where there are two or more levels of supervision between the people at the bottom and the top?"[2]

To distinguish further, we assume that when an organization reaches at

---

[2] The question was asked only of men working in a firm or organization that employs 10–499 workers. Men who told us that they work in a firm or organization employing fewer than ten people were not asked about supervisory structure, because pretest interviews had shown these men to take it so completely for granted that there can be only one boss that they find such questions baffling. We simply assume that such firms have only one level of supervision. Correspondingly, we assume that firms or organizations employing as many as five hundred people must have at least three levels of formal authority.

least three levels of formal authority, greater differentiation of structure is roughly proportional to size, at least in organizations of about 100 to 1,000 employees—an assumption given some empirical support by Blau's (1970:205) work. (We cannot make the same assumption about organizations of more than 1,000 employees; nor would we even trust respondents' estimates of size when the number surpasses 1,000.) Thus, the index of bureaucratization is as follows: (1) One level of supervision; (2) two levels of supervision; (3) three or more levels of supervision, fewer than 100 employees; (4) three or more levels of supervision, 100–999 employees; and (5) three or more levels of supervision, 1,000 or more employees.

This index makes explicit what is in any case implicit: that it is impossible to index hierarchical structure without also indexing size—their correlation (.71) is too great. For now, we simply accept as empirical fact that bureaucratization implies large size; later we shall attempt to separate the consequences of bureaucratic structure, as such, from those of size.

Indices of Values, Social Orientation, and Intellectual Functioning

Valuation of conformity. By values, we mean standards of desirability—criteria of preference (see Williams, 1960:402–403). Specifically pertinent here, because of the assertion that bureaucracy breeds conformism, is men's relative valuation of self-direction or of conformity to external authority. The index is based on a factor analysis of men's rankings of the relative desirability of a number of generally valued characteristics (see Chapter 1). Self-direction, as thus indexed, means regarding as most desirable such characteristics as curiosity, good sense and sound judgment, and the ability to face facts squarely; valuing conformity means giving priority to respectability.

Social orientation. At issue here is whether bureaucratization is conducive to intolerance of nonconformity, literalism in moral positions, and resistance to innovation and change. We attempt to measure all three, by means of the indices developed in Chapter 1.

1. *Authoritarian conservatism,* that is, men's definitions of what is socially acceptable—at one extreme, rigid conformance to the dictates of authority and intolerance of nonconformity; at the other extreme, open-mindedness.
2. *Standards of morality,* by which we mean a continuum of moral positions, from believing that morality consists of strict adherence to the letter of the law, to holding personally responsible moral standards.

3. *Stance toward change,* that is, men's receptiveness or resistance to innovation and change.

Intellectual Functioning. The most serious charge against bureaucracy is that it inhibits men's readiness to think for themselves. For one test of this assertion, we have measured men's intellectual flexibility, evidenced in several appraisals of actual performance deliberately built into the interview. These include cognitive problems that require weighing both sides of an economic or a social issue; a test involving the differentiation of figure from ground in complex color designs; and a test of men's ability to draw a recognizably human figure whose parts fit together in a meaningful whole. We also asked the interviewers to evaluate each respondent's "intelligence"; and we did a simple count of the respondent's propensity to agree with agree-disagree questions. All these we take to reflect, in some substantial part, intellectual flexibility.

As a single index of intellectual flexibility, we use scores based on a factor analysis of these diverse measures (see Chapter 1). We also extracted from these same data two rotated factors, which provide measures of two distinct aspects of intellectual functioning.[3] One is "perceptual," based primarily on inferences from the figure-drawing and form-perception tests. The other is "ideational," manifested primarily in problem-solving and in impressing the interviewer as being an intelligent person.

One final index examines the demands men put on their intellectual resources, no matter how great or limited those resources may be. This index, based on a factor analysis of questions about a wide range of leisure-time activities, focuses on how intellectually demanding are those activities. The relevant factor contrasts spending a large amount of one's leisure time watching TV with engaging in such intellectually active pursuits as going to museums and plays, reading books, reading magazines, and working on hobbies.[4] Some of the latter activities are facilitated by education and income; that fact will be taken into account in our analyses.

THE SOCIAL-PSYCHOLOGICAL CONCOMITANTS OF BUREAUCRATIZATION

The most difficult problem in assessing the social-psychological impact of bureaucratization is deciding who to compare with whom. Who are bureau-

---

[3] In the two-factor solution, the first factor is based primarily on the Draw-A-Person Test (summary score, .91; Goodenough estimate of intelligence, .91) and the Embedded Figures Test (.43). The second factor is based on the interviewer's appraisal of the respondent's intelligence (.69), the cigarette-commercials problem (.61), the respondent's "agree" score (−.56), the hamburger-stand problem (.54), and the Embedded Figures Test (.52).

[4] The factor loadings are: frequency of visits to plays, concerts, and museums (.60); number of books read in the past six months (.54); time spent working on hobbies (.35); whether or not reads magazines (.61); and time spent watching television (−.35).

crats? The narrowest definition would be that they are the higher, nonelective officialdom of government. But there is reason and ample precedent to expand that definition to include all employees of all organizations that are bureaucratic in structure—blue-collar as well as white-collar workers, employees of profit-making firms and nonprofit organizations as well as government. To whom should bureaucrats be compared—entrepreneurs, employees of nonbureaucratic organizations, or both? Again, the answer is not self-evident.

Rather than make a priori decisions, we prefer to deal with these questions empirically. We begin at the simplest descriptive level, using analysis of variance to ascertain what relationship there may be between bureaucratization, as we have indexed it, and those aspects of values, orientation, and intellectual functioning on which it has been thought to bear.[5] No man employed in a civilian occupation is excluded from this analysis, whether he be employee or entrepreneur, whether he works in a profit-making firm, a nonprofit organization, or a governmental agency.

The correlations of bureaucratization with values, orientations, and intellectual functioning are small, ranging from only .05 to .17; they are nonetheless impressive, because they consistently contradict preconception (Table 2.1).[6] Men who work in bureaucratic firms or organizations tend to value, not conformity, but self-direction. They are more open-minded, have more personally-responsible standards of morality, and are more receptive to change than are men who work in nonbureaucratic organizations. They show greater flexibility in dealing both with perceptual and with ideational problems. They spend their leisure time in more intellectually demanding activities. In short, the findings belie critics' assertions.

Now we can consider what difference it makes if the definitions of bureaucrat and nonbureaucrat be altered.

Ownership. Many discussions of bureaucracy assume that the antithesis of the bureaucrat is the entrepreneur. We find, to the contrary, that entrepreneurs are remarkably similar to bureaucrats, particularly to bureaucrats of comparable occupational status. (The one notable difference is that bureaucrats are more intellectually flexible—another refutation of stereotype.) The real contrast is not between bureaucrats and entrepreneurs, but

---

[5] This and subsequent analyses of variance are based on the computer program initially developed by Clyde, et al. (1966:20-28) and further developed by Cramer. The test of statistical significance is the F-ratio. We are treating all dependent variables in these analyses as interval scales (for justification, see Blalock, 1964:94; Cohen, 1965; Labovitz, 1967).

For more general discussions of the logical bases of the statistical procedures used in this chapter, see Blalock, 1960, Chapters 15-21; Blalock, 1964; Cohen, 1968.

[6] It is apparent in Table 2.1 (and has been confirmed in more detailed analyses) that the *etas* for the linear component of bureaucratization—in its relationships with the several aspects of values, orientation, and intellectual functioning that we have investigated—are nearly as large as those for all components. It is therefore appropriate to treat our index of bureaucratization as essentially linear.

Table 2.1. VALUES, SOCIAL ORIENTATIONS, AND INTELLECTUAL FUNCTIONING, BY BUREAUCRACY—TOTAL SAMPLE

| | Mean Scores for: | | | | | | | | | |
| | Values and Orientations | | | | Intellectual Functioning | | | | | |
Index of Bureaucracy:	Valuation of Self-Direction/Conformity (+ = Self-direction)	Authoritarian Conservatism (+ = Authoritarian)	Standards of Morality (+ = Personally Responsible)	Stance Toward Change (+ = Receptive)	Perceptual Component of Intellectual Flexibility (+ = Flexible)	Ideational Component of Intellectual Flexibility (+ = Flexible)	Overall Index of Intellectual Flexibility (+ = Flexible)	Intellectual Demandingness of Leisure-time Activities (+ = Demanding)	Canonical Correlation[a]	Number of Cases[b]
One level of supervision	-1.01	.91	-.59	-.57	-1.47	-.74	-2.17	-.49		(840)
Two levels	.12	.16	-.63	.01	-.69	-1.06	-2.34	-1.22		(121)
Three or more levels:										
<100 employees	-.23	.12	.50	.33	.68	-.03	.15	-.32		(307)
100-999 employees	.97	-.36	.08	.13	.26	1.07	.54	-.07		(456)
1000 + employees	.61	-1.29	.66	.68	1.20	1.82	1.78	1.35		(1,023)
Degree of association (Eta):										
Linear component of bureaucracy	.07**	.09**	.05**	.05*	.11**	.11**	.17**	.08**	.17**	
All components of bureaucracy	.08**	.09**	.06	.05	.11**	.12**	.17**	.09**	.17**	

[a]The canonical correlation excludes the overall index of intellectual flexibility, because it is a linear function of the two component indices.
[b]354 respondents for whom data are incomplete are excluded from this and subsequent tables.
* = $p < 0.05$.
** = $p < 0.01$.

between both these groups and the employees of nonbureaucratic organizations.

To properly assess the effects of bureaucratization, we must limit the analysis to employees, comparing the employees of bureaucratized organizations to those of nonbureaucratic organizations. Thus limiting the analysis strengthens the contrast between bureaucrats and nonbureaucrats (Table 2.2). Most of the correlations are increased in magnitude, the overall (canonical) correlation increasing by one-third. The picture of the bureaucrat as self-directed and intellectually flexible becomes a little more sharply etched.

Sector of the economy. Just as the entrepreneur has been thought to be the antithesis of the bureaucrat, the government official is usually thought to be its prototype. In fact, employees of government (and of nonprofit organizations) do exemplify what we have found to be the social-psychological characteristics associated with bureaucratization; they are more tolerant of nonconformity, have more personally responsible moral standards, evidence greater flexibility in dealing with ideational problems, and make more intellectually demanding use of their leisure time than do employees of equally bureaucratized profit-making firms.

To distinguish the impact of bureaucratization from that of employment in the public versus the private sphere, we further limit the analysis to profit-making firms—the one sector of the economy where there is any substantial variation in conditions of bureaucratization. We find (again see Table 2.2) the correlations of bureaucracy with values, orientations, and intellectual functioning to be nearly the same for employees of profit-making firms as for all employees.[7] Thus, our earlier findings do not simply reflect the bureaucratization of the public sector of the economy, for bureaucracy's influence extends to the private sector as well.

Occupational status. Many discussions of bureaucracy have been addressed only to its salaried, its white-collar, or its professional staff. It is therefore necessary to see if bureaucratization bears the same relationship to values, orientations, and intellectual functioning for blue-collar as for white-collar employees. To do this, we examine the two groups separately, recognizing that in so doing we partially control variables correlated with occupational status, such as education, the substantive complexity of the

---

[7] It could hardly be otherwise, since employees of profit-making firms constitute two-thirds of the total sample. For the same reason, all conclusions drawn from analyses of this subsample apply as well to the sample as a whole. We focus on employees of profit-making firms, not to secure different empirical findings, but for conceptual clarity. There is no advantage in further focusing the analysis on particular types of industries, for more detailed analyses show that bureaucracy has essentially the same psychological correlates in all types of industries. Moreover, excluding nonurban occupations from the analysis has no noticeable effect.

Table 2.2. CORRELATIONS OF BUREAUCRACY WITH VALUES, SOCIAL ORIENTATIONS, AND INTELLECTUAL FUNCTIONING—FOR SPECIFIED SAMPLES

Correlations[a] of Bureaucracy and:	All Men Employed in Civilian Occupations (Owners and Employees)	Employees Only	Employees of Profit-Making Firms		
			All	White-Collar	Blue-Collar
Values and Orientations					
Valuation of self-direction/ conformity	.07**	.09**	.08**	.07*	.09**
Authoritarian conservatism	.09**	.09**	.07**	.08*	.00
Standards of morality	.05**	.11**	.11**	.00	.15**
Stance toward change	.05*	.09**	.10**	.07*	.09**
Intellectual Functioning					
Perceptual component of intellectual flexibility	.11**	.09**	.08**	.08*	.06*
Ideational component	.11**	.17**	.18**	.14**	.14**
Overall index of intellectual flexibility	.17**	.19**	.19**	.17**	.13**
Intellectual demandingness of leisure-time activities	.08**	.15**	.15**	.07*	.13**
Canonical correlation[b]	.17**	.23**	.24**	.19**	.23**
Number of cases	(2,747)	(2,268)	(1,855)	(702)	(1,140)

[a] *Eta,* or the canonical correlation, for the linear component of bureaucracy.
[b] The canonical correlation excludes the overall index of intellectual flexibility (see note to Table 2.1).
$* = p < 0.05.$
$** = p < 0.01.$
Note: Mean scores are not presented in this table. The direction of all relationships is the same as indicated by the mean scores in Table 2.1.

work, and the job protections attendant on unionization. Even so (Table 2.2), bureaucracy's social psychological correlates are similar for blue-collar and for white-collar workers.[8] Moreover, the canonical correlation is as strong for blue-collar as for white-collar workers. Thus, any explanation of the social-psychological impact of bureaucratization must apply to the entire work force, not just to the white-collar portion.[9] It is true, of course, that the explanation need not be the same for both groups.

---

[8] To distinguish white-collar from blue-collar workers, we use Hollingshead's classification of occupational status, dichotomizing the population between category 4 (clerical and sales workers, technicians, and owners of little businesses) and category 5 (skilled manual employees).

[9] We also find that the social-psychological correlates of bureaucracy are essentially the same regardless of men's own positions in the supervisory hierarchy (as measured by the number of subordinates they have).

We conclude that bureaucratization bears essentially the same relationship to values, orientations, and intellectual functioning wherever and to whomever it occurs. Why? What is there about working in a bureaucratic organization that makes men more self-directed, open to change, and intellectually flexible?

We must also ask: Why are the correlations so small? The comparable correlations for several other aspects of occupation are much stronger (see Kohn, 1969:165–182). Does the small size of bureaucracy's correlations imply that we have used an inadequate index, or does bureaucratization have a weaker impact than had been supposed?

EXPLAINING BUREAUCRACY'S IMPACT

Bureaucrats and nonbureaucrats are drawn from rather different segments of the population. Bureaucrats necessarily live where large firms are located: disproportionately in big cities along the Great Lakes and in the Northeastern and Pacific states. Not only are they now urban, but they grew up in urban places. Their forebears are more likely to have come from northern or western Europe than from southern or eastern Europe. Few are black; few are Jews. They are disproportionately Catholic. Those who are Protestant are a little more likely to be members of large, established denominations than of smaller sects. Most notable of all, bureaucrats are more highly educated than are nonbureaucrats.

Of all these differences in the composition of bureaucratic and nonbureaucratic work forces, only education seems to matter for explaining why bureaucrats differ from nonbureaucrats in values, orientation, and intellectual functioning (Table 2.3). That is, statistically controlling education markedly reduces bureaucracy's impact: The canonical correlation is reduced by nearly 30 percent and the correlations with authoritarian conservatism and with the perceptual component of intellectual flexibility are reduced to statistical nonsignificance. Further controlling any or all of the other measures of social background reduces the correlations little more than does controlling education alone. Thus, education is clearly implicated in explaining why bureaucrats differ from nonbureaucrats; but aside from bureaucracies' employing more educated men, the composition of the work force appears to have little explanatory relevance.

Important though education may be, it provides only a partial explanation of the differences between bureaucrats and nonbureaucrats. That is, even with education statistically controlled, bureaucrats are found to value self-direction more highly than do nonbureaucrats, to have more personally demanding moral standards, to be more receptive to change, to be intellectually more flexible (especially in dealing with ideational problems), and to

Table 2.3. EFFECTS ON BUREAUCRACY CORRELATIONS OF
CONTROLLING EDUCATION, REGION, SIZE OF
COMMUNITY, RACE, NATIONAL BACKGROUND,
RELIGION, AND RURALITY OF CHILDHOOD (LIMITED
TO EMPLOYEES OF PROFIT-MAKING FIRMS)

		Partial Correlation with Bureaucracy, Controlling:	
	Initial Correlation with Bureaucracy[a]	Education	Education + Region, Size of Community, Race, National Background, Religion, and Rurality of Childhood
Values and Orientations			
Valuation of self-direction/ conformity	.08**	.07**	.06*
Authoritarian conservatism	.07**	.00	.01
Standards of morality	.11**	.09**	.07**
Stance toward change	.10**	.07**	.06*
Intellectual Functioning			
Perceptual component of intellectual flexibility	.08**	.05	.03
Ideational component	.18**	.11**	.10**
Overall index of intellectual flexibility	.19**	.11**	.09**
Intellectual demandingness of leisure-time activities	.15**	.08**	.09**
Canonical correlation[b]	.24**	.17**	.16**
Number of cases = 1,855 in columns 1 and 2 and 1,807 in column 3			

[a] *Eta*, or the canonical correlation, appropriately controlled, for the linear component of bureaucracy.
[b] The canonical correlation excludes the overall index of intellectual flexibility (see note to Table 2.1).
* = $p < 0.05$.
** = $p < 0.01$.
Note: Mean scores are not presented in this table. The direction of all relationships is the same as indicated by the mean scores in Table 2.1.

spend their leisure time in intellectually more demanding activities. The explanation of these differences must lie either in bureaucracies' somehow recruiting more self-directed, intellectually flexible people (a possibility to which we shall return), or in bureaucracies' subjecting their employees to occupational conditions that foster these social-psychological attributes.

Bureaucratization does make for widespread, and in some instances substantial, differences in the conditions of occupational life, few of them attributable to educational disparities and most of them applicable (although not always in equal degree) to both the white-collar and blue-collar work forces (Table 2.4). These differences are, principally, that the employees of bureaucracies tend to work at substantively more complex jobs than do other men of comparable educational level, but under conditions of somewhat closer supervision by a supervisor more remote in the hierarchy; to work under an externally-imposed pressure of time that results in their having to think faster; to work a shorter week; to work in company of, but not necessarily in harness with, co-workers; to face greater competition; to enjoy much greater job protections,[10] and to earn more than other men of similar educational background (even when in jobs of comparable occupational status). White-collar employees of bureaucratic organizations tend to work at less routinized tasks, but blue-collar employees of bureaucratic organizations tend to work at more routinized tasks, than do men of comparable occupational status in nonbureaucratic firms and organizations.

In assessing the possible explanatory relevance of these occupational conditions, we statistically control education throughout and limit the analysis to those social psychological correlates of bureaucracy that remain significant even with education controlled.[11] From one point of view, this procedure gives undue weight to education, which may matter primarily because it is a precondition for certain types of jobs—substantively complex jobs, for example. But since most men come to their jobs only after completing their educations, it is incumbent on us to show that occupational conditions matter above and beyond any effect that might be attributed to education. We continue to focus the analysis on employees of profit-making firms.

Three of the occupational concomitants of bureaucracy—job protections, job income, and the substantive complexity of the work—prove to have substantial pertinence (Table 2.5). The combined effect of controlling all three is to reduce the canonical correlation of bureaucracy with values,

---

[10] In particular, bureaucrats are more likely to enjoy the basic job protections given by tenure or by contractual guarantees based on seniority; by the existence of formal grievance procedures; and by sick pay. These correlations are more pronounced for blue-collar than for white-collar workers, and are linked to the greater unionization of the blue-collar work force. Even for non-union and for white-collar workers, though, job protections are decidedly greater in bureaucratic firms. (And they prove to be as important for younger as for older men.)

It is noteworthy that the critical difference bureaucratization makes is not in the risks to which men are subject but in the protections that their jobs afford. Bureaucrats are no less exposed to occupational risk than are nonbureaucrats, but they are better protected, should those eventualities occur.

[11] Since bureaucrats are more educated than are nonbureaucrats, they are necessarily higher in social-stratification position, too. But we regard education, not stratification, as the appropriate variable to control in these analyses, because education is what men bring to the job. Other components of social stratification, notably occupational status, are conferred by the job. (In fact, if education is controlled, occupational status has little importance.)

Table 2.4. THE OCCUPATIONAL CONCOMITANTS OF EMPLOYMENT IN BUREAUCRATIC ORGANIZATIONS (LIMITED TO EMPLOYEES OF PROFIT-MAKING FIRMS)

	Correlation[a] With Bureaucracy	Partial Correlation, Education Controlled	White-collar Employees Only	Blue-collar Employees Only
1. Substantive Complexity	.40**	.31**	.37**	.33**
2. Supervision				
a. Closeness of supervision	.02	.05*	.04	.04
b. Positional disparity between man and his effective supervisor	.17**	.18**	.13**	.18**
3. Time Pressure				
a. Frequency of time pressure	.10**	.05	.10**	.06*
b. Determinants of time pressure: workflow, not own volition	.10**	.13**	.12*	.19**
c. Consequences of time pressure: think faster, not make faster movements or work longer hours	.19**	.14**	.21**	.16**
4. Average Hours Worked per Week	−.28**	−.29**	−.20**	−.29**
5. Interpersonal Setting				
a. Time spent in the company of five or more co-workers	.22**	.24**	.11**	.27**
b. Time spent alone	−.12**	−.13**	−.03	−.15**
c. Participation in coordinated workteam	.02	.04	.01	.04
6. Amount of Competition	.17**	.13**	.19**	.11**
7. Job Protections				
a. Tenure, or seniority guaranteed by union contract	.37**	.42**	.16**	.56**
b. Formal grievance procedures	.39**	.45**	.20**	.57**
c. Sick pay	.33**	.30**	.25**	.34**
d. Job protections: overall index	.50**	.52**	.30**	.60**
8. Income and Income Fluctuations				
a. Job income	.27**	.21**	.19**	.31**
b. Fluctuations in income	−.04*	−.02	−.07*	.02
9. Routinization of Work	.08**	.09**	−.18**	.15**

[a]*Eta*, or (in the case of 1, 3b, 3c, 7d, and 9) the canonical correlation, for the linear component of bureaucracy. In column 2, a partial correlation, controlled on education, is reported. Columns 3 and 4 report total correlations, computed for the appropriate subgroups. In lieu of presenting a multitude of mean scores, we have arbitrarily used signs to indicate the direction of relationships.
* = $p < 0.05$.
** = $p < 0.01$.
Note: N's vary from 1,826 to 2,059 for the sample of all employees of profit-making firms, from 646 to 749 for the white-collar subsample, and from 1,169 to 1,289 for the blue-collar subsample.

Table 2.5. EFFECTS OF CONTROLLING THE PRINCIPAL OCCUPATIONAL CONCOMITANTS OF BUREAUCRACY (LIMITED TO EMPLOYEES OF PROFIT-MAKING FIRMS)

Values, Orientations, and Intellectual Functioning	Partial Correlation With Bureaucracy, Education Controlled[a]	Percentage Reduction in This Partial Correlation When Controlling:								
		Job Protections	Job Income	Substantive Complexity	Amount of Competition	Time Pressure	Hours of Work	Interpersonal Setting	Closeness of Supervision and Positional Disparity	Job Protections, Income, and Substantive Complexity
Valuation of self-direction/ conformity	.07**	17	20	14	−06	08	20	−03	06	44
Standards of morality	.09**	50	24	25	−02	05	12	00	−08	85
Stance toward change	.07**	39	19	08	21	10	−19	10	12	80
Ideational component of intellectual flexibility	.11**	24	21	29	05	03	01	−06	−03	64
Overall index of intellectual flexibility	.11**	32	12	16	05	−05	−07	−01	−05	66
Intellectual demandingness of leisure-time activities	.08**	11	35	33	00	05	01	−01	05	71
Canonical correlation	.17**	29	21	18	03	02	00	00	−01	66
Number of cases	(1,855)	(1,774)	(1,662)	(1,823)	(1,829)	(1,846)	(1,762)	(1,761)	(1,804)	(1,569)

[a]From Table 2.3. In the computations that follow, these partial correlations (*etas*) have in each instance been recomputed for all respondents for whom the relevant occupational data are known.

* = $p < 0.05$.
** = $p < 0.01$.

orientations, and intellectual functioning by two-thirds and to render this and all the individual correlations statistically nonsignificant.[12]

Job protections contribute particularly to the relationship between bureaucracy and men's orientations to morality and to change and to the relationship between bureaucracy and intellectual flexibility. It thus appears that men who enjoy job protections are less fearful of the new and the different, are better able to accept personal responsibility for their acts, and are even able to make fuller use of their intellectual talents. Substantive complexity is particularly pertinent for explaining bureaucrats' flexibility in dealing with ideational problems and their making intellectually demanding use of leisure time. The experience of working at substantively complex jobs thus appears to have direct carry-over to the use of one's intellectual resources in nonoccupational endeavors. Job income, not surprisingly, is most pertinent for explaining bureaucrats' more intellectually demanding use of their leisure time.

We conclude, then, that job protections, substantive complexity, and income all contribute to, and together may largely explain, the social-psychological impact of bureaucratization. Separate analyses of the white-collar and blue-collar work forces do indicate, though, that job protections contribute more to bureaucracy's psychological impact on blue-collar workers; substantive complexity, to its impact on white-collar workers. It would seem that the job protections afforded by bureaucracy matter most for men in occupations that do not already enjoy a substantial measure of security; substantive complexity comes to the fore only when some degree of security has been attained.

DISCUSSION

Observers of bureaucracy, impressed by its need to coordinate many people's activities, have assumed that a primary effect of bureaucratization must be to suppress employees' individuality. We have found, to the contrary, that bureaucratization is consistently, albeit not strongly, associated with greater intellectual flexibility, higher valuation of self-direction, greater openness to new experience, and more personally responsible moral standards. In part, this seems to result from bureaucracies' drawing on a more educated work force. In larger part, it seems to be a consequence of the occupational conditions attendant on bureaucratization—far greater job protections, somewhat higher levels of income, and substantively more complex work. Job protections matter particularly for bureaucracy's psy-

---

[12] Multiple-regression analyses, not shown here, confirm that job protections, income, and substantive complexity all contribute to bureaucracy's psychological impact, independent of each other and of other job conditions.

chological impact on blue-collar workers; substantive complexity, for its impact on white-collar workers.

There are four issues that our data do not fully resolve. The first is whether the effects we have attributed to the experience of working in a bureaucratic organization might really be an artifact of what types of people bureaucracies recruit. We have found that the educational disparities between bureaucratic and nonbureaucratic work forces cannot provide a sufficient explanation, and that other disparities in the social and demographic compositions of the work forces have little relevance. There remains the possibility that bureaucracies may hold a special attraction for self-directed, intellectually flexible men who are receptive to innovation and change. Perhaps, for example, intellectually active people seek jobs in bureaucratic organizations because that is where challenging work is to be found.

We cannot test this interpretation, because we have no information about the men's values, orientation, and intellectual functioning prior to their employment in bureaucratic (or nonbureaucratic) organizations. There are, however, two reasons to doubt that "self-selection" can explain our findings. The interpretation assumes that men have more complete and accurate knowledge of working conditions in bureaucratic organizations, before starting to work there, than is usually the case—especially in light of widely-held stereotypes about bureaucracy. The interpretation also assumes that men have a fuller range of choice in deciding on jobs than is usually the case—particularly when one remembers that our findings apply to men of all educational and skill levels and that many types of jobs can be found only in bureaucratic or only in nonbureaucratic settings. It would be more consonant both with our broader knowledge of occupational realities and with the specific data of this study to conclude that bureaucrats differ from nonbureaucrats primarily because they have experienced different conditions of occupational life.

The second issue is why the correlations are so small. We may have underestimated their size by limiting this investigation to one dimension of bureaucracy, by employing an inadequate index of this dimension, or by failing to take account of measurement error. Our data, however, suggest an alternative explanation: that bureaucracy really does have a smaller psychological impact than had been assumed. The psychologically most potent occupational conditions are those that maximize men's opportunities for self-direction in their work: freedom from close supervision, substantively complex work, and a varied array of activities (see Kohn, 1969:139–167). Bureaucracies do provide substantively complex work. They conspicuously fail, however, to provide freedom from close supervision, and although they provide a wide variety of complexly interrelated jobs to their white-collar workers, they tend to entrap their blue-collar workers in a routinized flow of simply-organized tasks. It is ironic and probably self-defeating that bureaucracies hire educated men, give them complex jobs to perform, and then fail to give them as much opportunity for occupational self-direction as their educational attainments and the needs of the work allow.

The third issue is whether our findings reflect bureaucratization or only size. Two of the three occupational conditions that have come to the fore in our analyses—income and substantive complexity—may be only ancillary features of bureaucracy. It is not intrinsic to bureaucratic organization that it pay its employees more or that its work be substantively more complex. These are, instead, products of the very conditions that give rise to bureaucracy itself—large size, technology, the need for highly skilled employees, and the problems of coordination, planning, and record-keeping that result from size and technology. Job protections, though, are an essential feature of bureaucracy. As Weber long ago recognized (see Gerth and Mills, 1946:202–203), it is necessary to bureaucratic organization that its authority be circumscribed. A principal finding of this research—that job protections are central to the impact of bureaucratization on its employees—cannot be attributed to size alone; they reflect the structural essentials of bureaucracy. (It is perhaps ironic that these structural essentials may be more important for the blue-collar work force, whom theories of bureaucracy have largely ignored, than for the white-collar work force.)

It is hardly crucial to the argument (but nonetheless reassuring) that the correlations of bureaucracy with all our principal indices of values, orientations, and intellectual functioning remain statistically significant not only when we employ a truncated version of the bureaucracy index that makes no use of information about the size of the organization, but even when we impose the extreme restriction of statistically controlling size of organization.

Last, and most important, is the issue of whether our focus on one dimension of bureaucratic structure—the hierarchical organization of authority—produces so partial a picture as to be misleading. Had we also studied such facets of bureaucracy as impersonality of procedures or specificity of rules, proximate occupational conditions other than (or in addition to) job protections, income, and substantive complexity might have come to the fore. The picture we have presented may be seriously incomplete.

Even if this be true, our findings are so at variance with common presuppositions as to require a rethinking of how bureaucracy impinges on its employees. Many writings about bureaucracy assert that a system based on the hierarchical organization of authority necessarily imposes tight discipline, leaving little leeway for initiative. Our data do indicate a tendency in this direction—employees of bureaucratic firms are supervised a little more closely than are other men of their educational levels, and close supervision does have the constricting effects ascribed to it. Still, the propensity of bureaucracies to supervise employees too closely is more than offset by the protections it affords from the arbitrary actions of superordinates.

Bureaucracies must ensure that superordinate officials are limited in what facets of their subordinates' behavior they are allowed to control and how they may exercise that control; superordinates cannot dismiss subordinates at will, and questionable actions can be appealed to adjudicatory agencies. The power of nonbureaucratic organizations over their employees is more complete and may be more capricious. Thus, the alternative to bureaucracy's circumscribed authority is usually, not less authority, but personal, potentially arbitrary authority. What is notable about bureaucratic practice is not how closely authority is exercised but how effectively it is circumscribed.

SECTION II

Job Conditions and Personality: Cross-Sectional Analyses

The two chapters in this Section focus on job conditions in their own right, not only as mechanisms by which position in the larger social structure affects individual psychological functioning.

Chapter 3 isolates a small set of occupational conditions, twelve in all, which define the "structural imperatives of the job." All twelve are related to psychological functioning independent of other job conditions and of education. At the core of the structural imperatives of the job are the three job conditions that we characterize as determinative of occupational self-direction—the substantive complexity of work, closeness of supervision, and routinization. Other structural imperatives fall into three clusters: job pressures, job uncertainties, and position in the organizational structure. This set of job conditions defines aspects of the work that impinge on the worker directly, insistently, and demandingly; they are imperatives of the work, built into the very structure of the job. Those structural imperatives of the job that elicit effort and flexibility are conducive to favorable evaluations of self, an open and flexible orientation to others, and effective intellectual functioning.

Chapter 4 focuses more specifically on two subsets of these job conditions—one emphasizing control over the product of one's labor, the other emphasizing control over the work process. Marx's analysis implies that both subsets of job conditions may be sources of alienation. Our data show that, in this large-scale, capitalist system, control over the product of

53

one's labor (ownership and hierarchical position) has only an indirect effect on alienation, whereas control over the work process (closeness of supervision, routinization, and the substantive complexity of work) has an appreciable direct effect on three principal facets of alienation—powerlessness, self-estrangement, and normlessness. Again we find the conditions determinative of occupational self-direction to be of focal importance for personality, in this instance, for alienation.

The analyses of both chapters emphasize anew the importance of the issue raised but not answered in the first Section of the book: Do job conditions actually affect psychological functioning, or do they only reflect selective recruitment, selective retention, and the propensity of men to mold their jobs to meet their needs and values? In these chapters, still using the cross-sectional data of the 1964 survey, we attempt to assess causal directionality. In the absence of longitudinal data, such an assessment can only be provisional, but these analyses do establish a strong *prima facie* case that job conditions not only reflect, but also affect, personality.

Sample and Methods of Data Collection

The analyses discussed in these chapters use the data of the 1964 cross-sectional survey of men employed in civilian occupations in the United States (see Appendix A).

3 | Occupational Experience and Psychological Functioning: an Assessment of Reciprocal Effects [*]

Melvin L. Kohn and Carmi Schooler

Our thesis is that adult occupational experience has a real and substantial impact upon men's psychological functioning. This argument, although familiar to social science at least since Marx's early writings, has never to our knowledge been empirically appraised. A widely-believed contrary argument is that all correspondence between men's occupations and personalities results from processes of selective recruitment and modification of the job to meet incumbents' needs and values. This view seems to underlie, for example, the logic of personnel testing, where the object is to select job applicants whose personalities match those of successful job incumbents. This perspective may also underlie the greater attention sociologists have given to occupational choice than to occupational effects.

The question of whether occupation affects or only reflects personality first arose in our analysis of social stratification, occupational self-direction, and values and orientations (Chapter 1). We found that occupational conditions conducive to the exercise of self-direction in one's work—namely, freedom from close supervision, substantively complex work, and a non-routinized flow of work—are empirically tied to valuing

[*] This Chapter is a revised version of a paper of the same title, originally published in the *American Sociological Review* (Kohn and Schooler, 1973). We are indebted for advice and essential help to our associates—Elizabeth Howell, Margaret Renfors, Carrie Schoenbach, and Lindsley Williams.

self-direction and to having orientations to self and to the outside world consonant with this value.

It could be argued that these findings reflect the propensity of men who value self-direction to seek out jobs that offer them opportunity to be self-directed in their work and, once in a job, to maximize whatever opportunities the job allows for exercising self-direction. On the other hand, we know that occupational choice is limited by educational qualifications, which in turn are greatly affected by the accidents of family background, economic circumstances, and available social resources. Moreover, the opportunity to exercise greater or lesser self-direction in one's work is circumscribed by job requirements. Thus, an executive must do complex work with data or with people; he cannot be closely supervised; and his tasks are too diverse to be routinized—to be an executive requires some fairly large degree of self-direction. Correspondingly, to be a semi-skilled factory worker precludes much self-direction. The substance of one's work cannot be especially complex; one cannot escape some measure of supervision; and if one's job is to fit into the flow of other people's work, it must necessarily be routinized. The relationship between being self-directed in one's work and holding self-directed values would thus seem to result not just from self-directed men acting according to their values, but also from men's job experiences affecting these very values.

The issue of the direction of the effects arose again in the analysis of bureaucracy (Chapter 2), which showed that employees of bureaucratic organizations are more intellectually flexible, more open to new experience, and more self-directed in their values than are men who work in nonbureaucratic organizations. It is, of course, possible that bureaucracies hold a special attraction for such men. Still, an explanation based on self-selection assumes that men have more complete and accurate knowledge of working conditions in bureaucratic organizations than is usually the case. An explanation based on self-selection also assumes that men have a wider range of choice in the type of firm or organization for which they will work than is often true. It would thus appear that an important part of the explanation for employees of bureaucratic organizations differing psychologically from those of nonbureaucratic organizations is that they experience different occupational conditions.

In this chapter, we go beyond these essentially a priori arguments to an empirical appraisal of the reciprocal effects of man on job and job on man. Since this analysis is based on cross-sectional data, we lack the measurements of change required for a thoroughgoing analysis of the continuing interplay between job conditions and psychological functioning. Still, our unusually complete occupational data enable us to delineate those facets of occupation that are most closely related to psychological functioning at the present time. These data also enable us to examine systematically the major alternatives to our preferred interpretation—that there is a continuing interplay of man affecting job and job affecting man. Finally, we estimate the magnitudes of the reciprocal effects of one principal facet of occupation, its substantive complexity, and several facets of psychological functioning.

DIMENSIONALIZING OCCUPATIONAL CONDITIONS

The key to our approach is to focus on *dimensions* of occupation. By contrast, the main tradition in the sociology of work has been to focus on a particular occupation, explicitly or more often implicitly comparing it to all other occupations or to those occupations believed to highlight its unique characteristics. Cottrell's (1940) classic study of railroaders, for example, pointed out a multitude of ways that the job conditions of men who operate trains differ from those of men in many other occupations—including the unpredictability of working hours, geographical mobility, precision of timing, outsider status in the home community, and unusual recruitment and promotion practices. Since all these conditions are tied together in one occupational package, it is not possible to disentangle the psychological concomitants of each. More recent comparative studies have faced similar interpretative problems. For example, Blauner's (1964) study of blue-collar workers in four industries, chosen to represent four technological levels, showed that differences in working conditions are systematically associated with the stage of technological development of the industry. These differences, too, come in packages; printing differs from automobile manufacture, for example, not only in technology and in the skill levels of workers, but also in the pace of work, closeness of supervision, freedom of physical movement, and a multitude of other conditions.[1]

We attempt to disentangle the intercorrelated dimensions of occupation by securing a large and representative sample of men from varied occupations, inventorying their job conditions, and differentiating the psychological concomitants of each facet of occupation by statistical analysis. Admittedly, there are serious limitations to securing occupational data by interviewing a representative sample of men. One is that men's descriptions and evaluations of their job conditions may be biased—a problem with which we shall deal later. Another is that men may have only limited information about some aspects of their jobs, such as the overall structure of the

---

[1] Other particularly pertinent studies of occupational experience and psychological functioning are: Chinoy, 1955; Freidson, 1970; Goldthorpe, et al., 1968, 1969; Kornhauser, 1965; Pearlin, 1962; and Turner and Lawrence, 1965. A remarkably prescient analysis of the research literature to its time is Herbert Menzel's (1950) M.A. thesis.

organization in which they work. Moreover, a sample of men scattered across many occupations and many workplaces does not contain enough people in any occupation or any workplace to trace out interpersonal networks and belief systems. Similarly, the method is not well adapted for studying the industrial and technological context in which a job is embedded.[2]

The method is useful, though, for studying the immediate conditions of a man's own job—what he does, who determines how he does it, in what physical and social circumstances he works, to what risks and rewards he is subject. In the interviews, we attempted to secure pertinent information about all these aspects of occupational experience, emphasizing those that we had any reason to believe might influence psychological functioning.[3] In all, we indexed more than 50 separable dimensions of occupation, including such diverse aspects of work experience as the substantive complexity of the work, the routinization or diversity of the flow of work, relationships with co-workers and with supervisors, pace of work and control thereof, physical and environmental conditions, job pressures and uncertainties, union membership and participation, bureaucratization, job protections, and fringe benefits (for complete information, see Kohn, 1969: 244–253). These indices provide the basis for a broadly descriptive picture of the principal facets of occupation, as experienced by men in all types of industry, at all levels of the civilian economy. We shall shortly see which of these many aspects of occupational experience matter most for men's psychological functioning.

INDICES OF PSYCHOLOGICAL FUNCTIONING

Of the myriad aspects of psychological functioning that might be affected by occupational experience, we limit this inquiry to ten, chosen because of their intrinsic importance and because together they cover a wide sweep. These ten deal with subjective reactions to the job itself, valuation of self-direction or of conformity to external authority, orientation to self and to society, and intellectual functioning.

---

[2] For pertinent studies of interpersonal, industrial, and technological context, see Blau, 1960; Blauner, 1964; Chinoy, 1955; Walker, 1957; Walker and Guest, 1952; and Whyte, 1961.

[3] Our search was extensive: We used such diverse sources as past research, our own and our colleagues' occupational experiences, our reading of novels, plays, and even the *Dictionary of Occupational Titles* (U.S. Department of Labor, 1949), and—most valuable of all—semi-structured pretest interviews with a considerable number of men in a wide range of occupations.

In addition to several of the studies previously noted, the following were particularly helpful in our search for relevant dimensions of occupation: Becker and Carper, 1956; Blau, 1955; Edwards, 1959; Foote, 1953; Hughes, 1958; Lipset, et al., 1956; Mills, 1953; Morris and Murphy, 1959; and Rosenberg, 1957.

Subjective Reactions to Occupation

Although our principal interest is in the possible effects of the job on *off-the-job* psychological functioning, we include two indices of men's subjective reactions to their jobs. We see these phenomena as a sort of way-station between the concrete realities of the job and men's orientations to nonoccupational realities.

One index, *occupational commitment,* is meant to measure men's dedication to their occupations, as distinct from their satisfaction or dissatisfaction with the particular jobs they hold. The index is based on a Guttman Scale of four questions about men's willingness to change occupations, their appraisal of what it takes to be good at their occupations, and their sense of the moral worth of their occupations (see Kohn, 1969:180).

Another index, *job satisfaction,* attempts to measure men's satisfaction or dissatisfaction with those aspects of their jobs they deem important. We asked each respondent to rate the importance of many aspects of work—e.g., how interesting it is, how clean it is (see Kohn, 1969:77, 250). We then asked him to tell us how satisfied he is, in his present job, with every aspect of work he considers important. Our index is an average of these judgments, weighting a man's satisfaction with an aspect of work he deems very important twice as much as his satisfaction with an aspect of work he considers only fairly important.[4]

Valuation of Self-direction or of Conformity to External Authority

By values, we mean standards of desirability—criteria of preference (see Williams, 1960:402–403). Our study includes indices of men's values for themselves and for their children, in both cases the focus being on their valuation of self-direction or of conformity to external authority (see Chapter 1). In this analysis, we use only the index of values for children.

Self-conception and Social Orientation

We attempt to measure five facets of self-conception and social orientation, all of them based on a factor analysis of a set of 57 questions, as described in Chapter 1. These are:

Anxiety, by which we mean the intensity of consciously felt psychic discomfort.

---

[4] The correlation between this index of job satisfaction and answers to the single question, "All things considered, how satisfied are you with the job as a whole?," is .67. For a review of studies of job satisfaction, and a discussion of the inadequacies of a single-question index, see Blauner, 1966. For a host of alternative indices, see Robinson, et al., 1969:99–143.

Self-esteem, an index created by combining scores for two factors, self-confidence and self-deprecation.

Stance toward change, that is, men's receptiveness or resistance to innovation and change.

Standards of morality, by which we mean a continuum of moral positions, from believing that morality consists of strict adherence to the letter of the law and keeping out of trouble, to defining and maintaining one's own moral standards.

Authoritarian conservatism, that is, men's definition of what is socially acceptable—at one extreme, rigid conformance to the dictates of authority and intolerance of nonconformity; at the other extreme, open-mindedness.

Intellectual Functioning

We study two aspects of intellectual functioning. The first, *intellectual flexibility,* is evidenced by performance in handling cognitive problems that require weighing both sides of an economic or a social issue, in differentiating figure from ground in complex color designs, and in drawing a recognizably human figure whose parts fit together in a meaningful whole. We also include the interviewers' evaluations of the respondents' "intelligence" and a simple count of their propensity to agree with agree-disagree questions. All these we take to reflect, in some substantial part, intellectual flexibility. A factor analysis of these various manifestations of intellectual flexibility yields two dimensions, one primarily perceptual, the other ideational (see Chapter 2). The latter provides the index used in these analyses.

We measure another aspect of intellectual functioning by examining *the demands men put on their intellectual resources.* This index, based on a factor analysis of questions about a wide range of leisure-time activities, focuses on how intellectually demanding are those activities. The relevant factor (see Chapter 2) contrasts spending a large amount of one's leisure time watching TV with engaging in such intellectually active pursuits as going to museums and plays, reading books, reading magazines, and working on hobbies. Some of the latter activities are facilitated by education and income; we take this fact into account in our analyses.

OCCUPATIONAL CONDITIONS AND PSYCHOLOGICAL FUNCTIONING

Virtually all of the many occupational conditions included in our inquiry are significantly related to one or another of the indices of psychological functioning enumerated above. Many of these relationships, however, may be artifactual—they may merely reflect the interrelatedness of occupational conditions with one another and with education. To distinguish those occupational conditions that have both independent and more-than-limited relevance to psychological functioning, we employ the following criteria:

1. We statistically control education—because education in most cases precedes and is often a prerequisite for a job.[5] (This may be an overly stringent criterion, because it does not allow for the possibility of a causal chain in which education is a determinant of job conditions, which in turn affect psychological functioning.)
2. In assessing each occupational condition, we statistically control all the others.[6] This we do to measure the independent effects of each occupational condition, uninfluenced by its interrelatedness with other aspects of the job.
3. Finally, we require an occupational condition to be significantly related to more than one facet of psychological functioning—so that we may limit the analysis to occupational conditions whose impact on psychological functioning has some degree of generality.

Twelve of the more than 50 occupational conditions we have indexed meet all these criteria (Table 3.1). The magnitudes of the relationships between these twelve occupational conditions and the several facets of psychological functioning are generally not very large; but since our controls are so stringent, the phenomena they depict are exceedingly precise.[7] When we find, for example, that the substantive complexity of the work is related to self-esteem, we can be reasonably sure that substantive complexity is at issue, not education or such correlated occupational conditions as closeness of supervision, routinization, and time-pressure. Moreover, the overall (canonical) correlation between occupational conditions and psychological functioning is fairly substantial: with education controlled, it is .41. Even if subjective reactions to the job are excluded, the canonical correlation is .34. Whatever interpretation one draws, the relationship between job conditions

---

[5] Using multivariate analysis of variance (Clyde, et al., 1966), we tested the interactions between education and each of the occupational conditions. We found them to be generally small and statistically nonsignificant. We also tested the linearity of each occupational condition in its relationships with all facets of psychological functioning. They proved to be preponderantly linear.

[6] For this analysis, we used the multiple-regression program developed by Nie, et al. (1968). We also used multivariate analysis of variance, to test the significance of interactions between pairs of occupational conditions, wherever we had reason to expect them to occur. The interactions were generally small and unpatterned. Even those few that were statistically significant do not affect the essential conclusions drawn from the multiple-regression analyses.

[7] In Table 3.1, the magnitude of relationship between any occupational condition and any facet of psychological functioning is given by the standardized regression-coefficient, which indicates "how much change in the dependent variable is produced by a standardized change in one of the independent variables when the others are controlled" (Blalock, 1960: 345).

Table 3.1. SUBJECTIVE REACTIONS TO JOB, VALUES, ORIENTATIONS, AND INTELLECTUAL FUNCTIONING, BY THE PRINCIPAL DIMENSIONS OF OCCUPATION (CONTROLLING EDUCATION)

	Occupational Commitment (+ = Committed)	Job Satisfaction (+ = Satisfied)	Parental Valuation of Self-direction (+ = High)	Anxiety (+ = Anxious)	Self-esteem (+ = High)	Stance Toward Change (+ = Receptive)	Standards of Morality (+ = Personally Responsible)	Authoritarian Conservatism (+ = Authoritarian)	Ideational Flexibility (+ = Flexible)	Intellectual Demandingness/ Leisure Time (+ = Demanding)
Standardized beta-coefficients[a]										
1. Organizational locus										
a. Ownership	.19	.10	.05	-.12	---	---	---	.05	---	---
b. Bureaucratization	-.07	---	.04	-.06	.05	.06	.09	---	.10	.05
c. (High) position in hierarchy	.05	.10	---	---	---	---	-.04	---	---	---
2. Occupational self-direction										
a. Closeness of supervision	-.10	-.18	-.07	.07	-.09	-.06	-.13	.07	-.07	-.07
b. Routinization of work	-.13	-.06	---	---	---	---	-.06	-.07	-.11	-.07
c. Substantive complexity	.20	.16	.08	---	.09	.09	.07	-.07	.10	.18
3. Job pressures										
a. Time pressure	---[b]	-.10	.10	.11	---	.11	---	-.06	.06	---
b. Heaviness of the work	---	---	---	.07	.07	---	---	-.04	---	.04
c. Dirtiness of the work	---	-.10	---	.07	-.05	---	---	.07	-.05	-.09
4. Uncertainties										
a. Likelihood of "dramatic change"	.05	---	---	.09	---	.07	---	---	---	---
b. Frequency of being held responsible for things outside of one's control	-.07	-.12	---	.09	---	---	---	---	---	---
c. Risk of loss of job or business	-.05	-.14	---	.06	-.06	---	---	---	---	-.04
Multiple-partial correlations[a]										
1. Organizational locus	.18	.13	.07	.13	.05	.07	.10	.07	.12	.07
2. Occupational self-direction	.23	.24	.10	.07	.12	.10	.16	.09	.18	.14
3. Job pressures	---	.14	.10	.12	.07	.11	.04	.09	.08	.09
4. Uncertainties	.09	.18	---	.15	.06	.08	---	---	.04	.07
5. All occupational conditions	.36	.40	.19	.24	.18	.22	.20	.15	.26	.24

N = 3101, except for parental valuation of self-direction, where N = 1499.

[a] Controlling education and all other facets of occupation.

[b] Beta-coefficients and correlations of less than ± 0.04 are omitted from this table; they would not be statistically significant.

Note: The "positive" end of each occupational dimension is implicit in its name; in the case of job pressures and job uncertainties, the "positive" end is assigned to greater pressure or greater uncertainty.

and psychological functioning is large enough to be taken seriously.

Although few in number, the twelve occupational conditions that meet our criteria are sufficient to define the *structural imperatives of the job,* in that they identify a man's position in the organizational structure, his opportunities for occupational self-direction, the principal job pressures to which he is subject, and the principal uncertainties built into his job. Of all these occupational conditions, those that determine occupational self-direction prove to be the most important: They are significantly related to all facets of psychological functioning, in most cases more strongly than are any other occupational conditions. Nevertheless, position in the organizational structure, job pressures, and job uncertainties all make some independent contributions to the overall relationship between the structural imperatives of the job and psychological functioning.

Our more specific findings and the indices on which they are based are as follows:

Position in the Organizational Structure

Ownership/nonownership. All men who have any substantial share in the ownership of the firm in which they are employed are here treated as owners. The advantageous position of owners is reflected in their greater occupational commitment, greater job satisfaction, and lesser anxiety. Owners are more self-directed in their values but are more authoritarian conservative in orientation than are employees.

Bureaucratization is here indexed by the number of formal levels of supervision and the size of the organization (see Chapter 2). Employees of bureaucratic firms and organizations are less committed to their occupations (and more to the organizations that employ them) than are employees of nonbureaucratic firms and organizations. Bureaucratization also has broad ramifications for off-the-job functioning, employees of bureaucratic firms and organizations being more ideationally flexible and making more intellectually demanding use of their leisure time, having more personally responsible moral standards, being more receptive to change, being less anxious, having greater self-esteem, and being more self-directed in their values, than are employees of nonbureaucratic firms. All these findings are consonant with our earlier analyses (Chapter 2), which showed the conditions of work in bureaucratic organizations to be conducive to both intellectual and orientational flexibility.

Position in the supervisory hierarchy is indexed by the number of people over whom a man has direct or indirect supervisory authority. Higher position is associated with job satisfaction and occupational commitment, but position in the supervisory hierarchy has little relationship with off-the-job psychological functioning, independent of other job conditions.

Occupational Self-direction

By occupational self-direction we mean the conditions that facilitate or restrict the use of initiative, thought, and independent judgment in work (see Chapter 1). We conceive three occupational conditions to be critical:

Closeness of supervision   is again indexed by a Guttman Scale based on five questions about how much latitude the supervisor allows and how supervisory control is exercised.

Routinization of the work   (which we earlier called the complexity of organization of the work) is again a composite measure of the repetitiveness of work tasks and the complexity of the "units" of which work is comprised.

The substantive complexity of the work   is based on detailed questioning of each respondent about his work with things, with data or ideas, and with people (see Chapter 1). The index now used comes from a one-dimensional factor analysis of the seven ratings: our appraisals of the complexity of a man's work with data, with things, and with people; our appraisal of the overall complexity of his work; and his estimates of the amount of time he spends working at each type of activity.[8]

All three aspects of occupational self-direction are broadly pertinent for psychological functioning, men whose job conditions facilitate self-direction consistently having more positive reactions to job, self, and society and consistently evidencing more effective intellectual functioning. The substantive complexity of work is clearly the most important of the three components of occupational self-direction, but closeness of supervision and routinization of work add significantly to the total impact.

Job Pressures

Our indices of job pressures are based mainly on respondents' appraisals of their own situations.[9] Three types of job pressure prove to be pertinent:

---

[8] The factor loadings are: complexity of work with data (.85), with people (.82), with things (−.26); overall complexity of the work (.80); time spent working with data (.65), with people (.57), with things (−.68).

[9] The questions used to elicit men's appraisals of job pressures are:
1. Time pressure: How often do you have to work under pressure of time?
    If ever work under pressure:
    When you're working under time pressure, does this involve working longer hours, heavier physical work, faster physical movements, or faster thinking?
2. Heaviness: Our appraisal, based on the respondent's description of his work with things.
3. Dirtiness: How dirty do you get on the job—very dirty, fairly dirty, a little, or not at all?

Frequency of time-pressure. Seeing oneself as working under great pressure of time is associated with job dissatisfaction and anxiety. But working under time-pressure is also associated with valuing self-direction, being receptive to change, being open-minded, and being ideationally flexible. Time-pressure may be unpleasant, but it may nevertheless be conducive to flexibility.

Heaviness of work. Doing heavy work may be a source of pride—it is primarily associated with high self-esteem. It is also associated with open-mindedness and intellectually demanding leisure-time activities.

Dirtiness of work represents how dirty a man gets while doing his job. Doing dirty work has unpleasant concomitants, being associated with greater job dissatisfaction, greater levels of anxiety, and lower self-esteem. Doing dirty work is also associated with authoritarian conservatism, lack of ideational flexibility, and not making intellectually demanding use of one's leisure time.

Job Uncertainties

Finally, there are three aspects of occupational reality (as appraised by the respondents) that are less immediate, more indefinite in scope and time than are job pressures; all deal with the possibility of a potentially threatening change in a man's basic job situation:[10]

The likelihood, in this field, of there occurring a sudden and dramatic change in a man's income, reputation or position. The probability of such a change, whether it is likely to be for the better or the worse, is associated with anxiety. If there is some possibility that the change can

---

[10] The questions used to elicit men's appraisals of job uncertainties are:
1. "Sudden and dramatic change": Is yours a field where there can be a sudden and dramatic change in your income, reputation, or position?
    If yes:
    a. Is the change likely to be for the better or for the worse?
    b. How often does this happen to people in your field?
    c. When it does happen, is it usually because of some achievement, because of a good or bad break, poor performance, or for some other reason?
2. "Held responsible for things outside one's control": How often are you held responsible for things that are really outside of your control?
    If sometimes or frequently:
    For what sorts of things outside of your control are you held responsible?
3. "Risk of loss of job or business":
    a. *(asked of employees)*
    As things look now, how likely is it that you could be laid off from your job in the next year or so because of a cutback in the number of people your (firm, organization, department) employs—is it very likely, fairly likely, not very likely, or not possible?
    b. *(asked of self-employed)*
    How great is the risk of failure in your field—very great, fairly great, some risk but not much, very little risk, or no risk?

be for the better, it is also associated with being generally receptive to change and with occupational commitment.

The frequency of being held responsible for things outside one's control. Perceiving this to be a serious possibility is associated with job dissatisfaction, anxiety, and a weaker commitment to one's occupation.

The risk of loss of one's job or business. This threat has entirely expectable psychological concomitants, primarily job dissatisfaction, anxiety, and lessened self-esteem.

Numerous other facets of work that are only ancillary to the structural imperatives of the job seem to have little independent relevance for psychological functioning. Take, for example, interpersonal relatedness. Those aspects of interpersonal relatedness that are directly involved in occupational self-direction—that is, closeness of supervision and the substantive complexity of men's work with people—prove to have widespread psychological ramifications.[11] But aspects of interpersonal relatedness not involved in occupational self-direction—such as whether a man works primarily alone or in the company of others and, if with others, with how many others; whether he is involved in a team operation; the competitiveness of his relations with fellow employees; and his participation in union or other work-related group activities—prove to have little independent relevance. It may be, of course, that our methods are inadequate for assessing the full impact of interpersonal relatedness. We believe, however, that the explanation lies elsewhere, that on-the-job interpersonal relationships do not greatly affect off-the-job psychological functioning.

We have found, then, a network of statistical relationships between the structural imperatives of men's jobs and their psychological functioning, off as well as on the job. These relationships are meaningful, in the sense that they could be explained straightforwardly as resulting from the direct process of men's generalizing from occupational experience to other realms. Not only is unpleasant occupational experience associated with job dissatisfaction and anxiety, but job conditions—however affectively toned—that elicit effort and flexibility are associated with favorable evaluations of self, an open and flexible orientation to others, and effective intellectual functioning.

---

[11] This statement is based on an analysis of the psychological impact of complexity of work with people, examined separately from the impact of the complexity of work with data and with things.

ALTERNATIVE INTERPRETATIONS

Our preferred interpretation of the links between the structural imperatives of the job and men's psychological functioning is that there is continuing interplay between job and man, in which job conditions both affect and are affected by men's psychological functioning. Our objective is to assess the magnitudes of these reciprocal effects. Before doing so, we must consider a number of alternative interpretations, each of which might explain our findings without according any importance to the effects of job on man. We start with the simplest—that our findings might reflect some inadequacy in our occupational indices—reserving until last the most complex and most important—that our findings might result solely from men seeking out or modifying jobs to fit their personalities.

The Adequacy of Our Occupational Indices

The simplest alternative explanation is that our findings reflect a systematic tendency for respondents to see their conditions of work through the distorting lens of their own needs and values. Our data suggest otherwise.

Consider first the index of substantive complexity. We can compare this index, which is precisely tailored to the specifics of each respondent's description of his own job, with the assessments given in the *Dictionary of Occupational Titles* (U.S. Department of Labor, 1965) for every occupation in the American economy. The *Dictionary's* ratings of the complexity of work with things, with data, and with people are averages for entire occupations, so they lack the specificity of ours; but since they are based on observations by trained occupational analysts, they can serve as a source of external validation. We find the multiple correlation between our index of substantive complexity and the independently coded *Dictionary*-ratings to be .78—sufficiently high to assure us that our appraisals of substantive complexity accurately reflect the reality of men's work.

For no other index do we have so clearcut a standard of comparison. It is, however, possible to ask whether, on the average, men's assessments of their occupational conditions seem realistic. In this analysis, we focus on those occupations for which our sample contains at least 30 men, arbitrarily defining an "occupation" as any occupational grouping to which the *Dictionary of Occupational Titles* assigns a unique identifying number. The technique of analysis is to rank these occupations in order of the median rating their incumbents give to any given occupational condition, to see if this rank-ordering is consonant with our general knowledge of occupational realities. Insofar as it is, we are assured that respondents' appraisals of this occupational condition are essentially unbiased. In fact (Table 3.2), these

Table 3.2. RANK-ORDERS OF MEDIAN RATINGS OF OCCUPATIONAL CHARACTERISTICS GIVEN BY THE MEMBERS OF THE 14 MOST POPULOUS OCCUPATIONS IN THE SAMPLE

Occupations	N=	Closeness of Supervision	Routini-zation	Substantive Complexity	Time Pressure	Heavi-ness	Dirti-ness	Likelihood of Dramatic Change	Freq. of Being "Held Responsible"	Risk of Loss of Job or Business
1. Accountants and auditors	(32)	11	8	2	3	14	14	10	8	12
2. Carpenters (construc-tion industry)	(43)	2	9	12	12	3½	5	8	7	5
3. Farmers (general)	(126)	14	14	9	10	3½	3	1	6	1
4. Farmers (grain)	(31)	12	12	7	9	5½	1½	2	9	2
5. Machinists	(34)	5	11	10	5	10	6	8	14	7
6. Managers and officials, service industries	(41)	13	7	4	2	11	13	4	2	3
7. Managers and officials, wholesale and retail trade	(62)	10	6	3	1	12	11	3	1	6
8. Mechanics	(50)	7	13	8	7½	5½	1½	8	11½	10
9. Packagers and materials handlers	(43)	1	1	13	13	1	8	13	11½	9
10. Porters and cleaners	(39)	4	2	14	14	8½	9	14	13	11
11. Salesmen—drivers	(38)	8	3	5	7½	8½	10	6	3	13
12. School teachers (secondary school)	(36)	9	5	1	11	13	12	12	5	14
13. Service station attendants	(31)	6	10	6	6	7	4	5	4	4
14. Truck-drivers (heavy trucking)	(35)	3	4	11	4	2	7	11	10	8

evaluations conform closely to what we should expect them to be. Thus, it is improbable that systematic biases in respondents' reports about their jobs contribute much to explaining the relationships between occupational conditions and psychological functioning.

Income and Occupational Status

Another possible interpretation of our findings is that actual working conditions are not important in themselves, but only as a reflection of such extrinsic aspects of a job as the income and status it provides. This possibility can be tested by statistically controlling income and occupational status to see whether the relationships between conditions of work and psychological functioning are markedly reduced.

For several facets of psychological functioning (specifically, occupational commitment, job satisfaction, parental valuation of self-direction, and the intellectually demanding use of leisure time), controlling income and occupational status does reduce the multiple correlations noticeably, though not by nearly enough to render them statistically nonsignificant (Table 3.3). The correlations between job conditions and all other facets of psychological functioning are hardly at all reduced. It thus seems clear that the relationships between occupational conditions and psychological functioning do not simply reflect income and status.[12]

Social Selectivity in Recruitment and Retention

Still another possible explanation of our findings is that they reflect social selectivity in occupational recruitment and retention. The pattern of findings might have resulted from occupations recruiting their members from different segments of the society—drawing more heavily from urban or from rural populations, from particular races, religions, and nationalities, from older or from younger segments of the work force. In fact, we find that there are consistent (albeit not very powerful) links between men's social characteristics and their conditions of work. For example, men who do substantively complex work are disproportionately white, older, urban, members of "liberal" religious denominations, and of northern or western European background.

There is, then, a distinct possibility that the relationships between occupational conditions and psychological functioning reflect the social characteristics of workers. For example, substantive complexity may be related to

---

[12] In fact, income and occupational status, controlled on education and occupational conditions, are much less strongly related to psychological functioning than are occupational conditions, controlled on education, income, and occupational status.

Table 3.3.   MULTIPLE-PARTIAL CORRELATIONS BETWEEN
OCCUPATIONAL CONDITIONS AND
PSYCHOLOGICAL FUNCTIONING

Facet of Psychological Functioning	Multiple-partial Correlation between the Set of 12 Occupational Conditions and the Specified Facet of Psychological Functioning; Controlling		
	Education	Education Plus Occupational Status and Income	Education Plus Background Characteristics[a]
Occupational commitment	.36	.25	.33
Job satisfaction	.40	.32	.38
Parental valuation of self-direction	.19	.13	.17
Anxiety	.24	.22	.21
Self-esteem	.18	.16	.19
Stance toward change	.22	.20	.23
Standards of morality	.20	.17	.16
Authoritarian conservatism	.15	.14	.12
Ideational flexibility	.26	.22	.23
Intellectual demandingness of leisure-time activities	.24	.17	.22

Note: N = 3101, except for parental valuation of self-direction, where N = 1499. All correlations shown are statistically significant.
[a] Age, race, urbanness of principal place where the man was raised, religious background, and national background.

self-esteem because men who do substantively complex work come from more advantaged segments of society. To test this and similar possibilities, we statistically control age, race, urbanness, religious background, and national background (just as we earlier controlled occupational status and income) to see whether the relationships between occupational conditions and psychological functioning are appreciably reduced. They are not (Table 3.3). We conclude that social selectivity in occupational recruitment contributes little to our findings.

Occupational Selection and Job-molding

It could also be argued that occupational conditions are related to psychological functioning because of individual selectivity in recruitment and retention—because employers hire men they think are qualified and because men search out jobs that meet their needs and desires. Moreover, men often leave jobs, voluntarily or otherwise, when the jobs do not match their needs, desires, or talents. (To make matters more complicated, men may be promoted out of jobs to which they are especially well suited.) Finally, once in a job, men may mold their conditions of work to meet their preferences.

We readily grant that processes of "occupational selection" and "job-molding'' may contribute to our findings. Intellectually flexible men, for example, may seek and be sought for jobs that allow maximum opportunity to do substantively complex work; once in their jobs, they may make the most of whatever opportunities the jobs provide to exercise occupational self-direction. Similarly, men who hold authoritarian beliefs may gravitate to jobs in which they are closely supervised. It is even possible that men who disparage themselves may welcome dirty jobs that confirm their negative self-evaluations. Not all our findings, however, can be explained by such processes. Few men, for example, choose to be held responsible for things outside their control; and although anxious men may create conditions of time-pressure, it is at least as reasonable to expect them to avoid getting into time-pressured situations.

Moreover, as we have previously argued and can now demonstrate empirically, occupational selection and job-molding take place within rather narrow confines: Occupational conditions are structurally interrelated. Thus, a man who does substantively complex work stands a greater risk of being held responsible for things outside his control than does a man who works at simpler tasks: the correlation of substantive complexity with such a risk is .32. The risk increases if the job is not only substantively complex but also time-pressured (the multiple correlation being .36), and increases still further if the man stands high on the supervisory ladder or is an owner (multiple $r = .40$). From this perspective, an increased risk of being held responsible for things outside one's control is the price one pays for holding an interesting and responsible job. Similarly, jobs that offer freedom from close supervision are likely to be substantively demanding, are somewhat unpredictable, and are also likely to entail some risk of losing one's job or business (multiple $r = .54$). We need not proliferate examples of the structural interrelatedness of occupational conditions. All point to the same lesson: It is not as if one could make a series of independent decisions—to be self-directed, not to be under great time-pressure, to work in a nonbureaucratic organization; their structural interrelatedness means that one has to accept some occupational conditions as the price for securing others.

The data provide a second reason for believing that occupational selection and job-molding cannot sufficiently explain the relationships between occupation and psychological functioning. If these processes fully accounted for the relationships, then statistically controlling an index of men's job preferences should substantially reduce the magnitude of the correlations. We can test this possibility, for we had asked the men to evaluate the importance of many occupational conditions, ranging from pay and job security to the chance to use one's abilities. A factor analysis yields two dimensions to these judgments, one emphasizing the intrinsic, the other emphasizing the extrinsic (see Chapter 1). Using factor scores based on these dimensions, we statistically control both. The relationships between job conditions and psychological functioning are only slightly reduced.

A third reason for believing that occupational selection and job-molding do not provide an adequate explanation of our findings comes from an examination of time-pressure, an occupational condition that varies notably in the degree to which it is subject to workers' control. Having asked the men to tell us who or what controls the pace of their work, we can compare those who say they control the pace of their own work with those who say they work at a pace enforced by a boss, co-workers, the speed of machinery, or some other external agency. We find that, on the whole, the correlations between time-pressure and psychological functioning are as great for men who work at an externally enforced pace as for men who determine their own pace of work (Table 3.4). This being the case, it can hardly be that these findings simply reflect men's ability to select or to mold their occupational conditions to suit their needs and values.

The evidence consistently suggests that, although men undoubtedly do choose and mold their jobs to fit their personal requirements, it is not likely that these processes alone can sufficiently explain the relationships between occupational conditions and psychological functioning. The correlations between occupational conditions and psychological functioning must also reflect the impact of the job on the man.

Table 3.4.   PARTIAL CORRELATIONS BETWEEN TIME-PRESSURE AND PSYCHOLOGICAL FUNCTIONING, SEPARATELY FOR MEN WHO DO AND MEN WHO DO NOT CONTROL THE PACE OF THEIR WORK (EDUCATION CONTROLLED)

Partial Correlation of Time-pressure with	Men Who Control the Pace of Their Own Work	Men Whose Work-pace is Controlled by Boss, Co-workers, Speed of Machinery, or Other External Agent
Occupational commitment	.04	.02
Job satisfaction	−.06*	−.12*
Parental valuation of self-direction	.13*	.11*
Anxiety	.14*	.12*
Self-esteem	.02	.04
Stance toward change	.17*	.11*
Standards of morality	.03	.05
Authoritarian conservatism	−.07*	−.08*
Ideational flexibility	.07*	.17*
Intellectual demandingness of leisure-time activities	.08*	.12*
N^a =	(1730)	(818)

[a] Except for parental valuation of self-direction, where N = 820 and 410.
*$p < .05$.

THE RECIPROCAL EFFECTS OF MAN ON JOB AND JOB ON MAN

We have tried to show that the relationships between occupational conditions and psychological functioning do not simply reflect some inadequacy in our indices; or the effects of education, occupational status, and income; or selectivity in recruitment and retention; or men's efforts to mold their jobs to fit their needs and values. This negative argument has been necessary to establish the plausibility of an interpretative model that assumes reciprocal effects of job on man and man on job. Now we can assess the relative magnitudes of these reciprocal effects.[13]

We want to partition the correlations between occupation and psychological functioning into their components, to assess how large a part of each correlation results from the effects of the job on the man and how large a part from occupational selection, job-molding, and such other processes as can together be thought of as the effects of the man on the job. Statistical procedures that assume causal effects to be unidirectional are of course inappropriate to this task. Fortunately, the simultaneous-equations techniques that econometricians have developed for dealing with reciprocal effects are well suited to our needs (see Goldberger, 1964; Blalock, 1971; Miller, 1971; Duncan, Haller, and Portes, 1968). In this analysis, we employ the technique called two-stage least squares, a relatively simple method for estimating coefficients in simultaneous equations (see Blalock, 1971; Mason and Halter, 1968; Goldberger, 1964:329-38).[14]

The two-stage procedure, in effect, attempts to "purge" each variable of the effects of all those with which it is reciprocally related, by estimating from other pertinent data what an individual's score on each variable would have been if the other variables had not had an opportunity to affect it. These estimated scores are then used for assessing each variable's impact on the others. Clearly, the analysis is hypothetical, albeit no more so than are

---

[13] One might think it possible to assess the impact of job on man by measuring increases in the magnitudes of the correlations between occupational conditions and psychological functioning as men have been in their jobs for longer times. But the expectation that the correlations should be a linear (or even some more complicated) function of time in job assumes that the most important difference between men who have been in their jobs a short time and those who have been in their jobs a longer time is time itself. This assumption disregards the highly selective processes of occupational mobility, both vertical mobility within a single occupation and mobility from one occupation to another. It also fails to take adequate account of social-psychological effects of prior jobs and leaves out of consideration other time-related processes, notably aging.

[14] We are indebted to Hubert M. Blalock for suggesting that we use this technique, and to Ralph Bryant, Roger Craine, and Richard Porter of the Federal Reserve Board for their advice in developing the model used in our analyses.

analyses based on such conventional statistical techniques as partial correlation and test-factor standardization. Equally clearly, the meaningfulness of the analysis depends on the accuracy of the estimated scores.

In doing two-stage least squares analyses, one first computes the multiple regression of each of the endogenous variables (that is, variables that are affected by other variables in the model) on a set of "predetermined" variables (that is, variables that are believed to have some causal effect on one or more of the endogenous variables, but which cannot themselves have been affected by any of the endogenous variables). "Predetermined" variables can be of two types—"exogenous" variables, whose explanation lies outside of the explanatory model, e.g., social background characteristics; and "lagged endogenous" variables, i.e., values of one or more of the endogenous variables at some earlier time or times. The unstandardized regression coefficients from these equations (when multiplied by the respondents' scores on the predetermined variables) provide the basis for creating "purged" estimates of the endogenous variables. These estimated scores are used in the stage-two regression equations, which assess the causal impact of each of the endogenous variables and of relevant predetermined variables. (For a more detailed description of the procedure and the criteria that must be met in using it, see Mason and Halter, 1968; Blalock, 1971.)

In our analysis, the endogenous variables are job conditions and the several facets of psychological functioning. The exogenous variables are those social characteristics that we had a priori reason to think would have an impact on, and in fact proved to be empirically related to, one or another endogenous variable.[15] These alone, without data on past job conditions, do not provide enough information to construct adequate estimators of some of the endogenous variables, notably of current job conditions; nor would an analysis that did not take past job conditions into account be particularly instructive. We also need data about pertinent "lagged endogenous" variables, i.e., past job conditions.

Fortunately, our data include a history of each man's past jobs. This in-

---

[15] The pertinent characteristics are education, race, age, national background, religious background, region of the country in which the man was raised, urbanness of the principal place where he was raised, father's education and occupational status, maternal and paternal grandfathers' occupational statuses, and the number of children in the parental family. The indices of national background, region, and religious background are linear approximations to these nonlinear concepts. In our present use, these linearized indices represent slight underestimates of what would be shown in a more complicated dummy variable analysis. The rationale for these linearizations is given in Schooler, 1972. Essentially, all three indices are ordered in terms of modernity: national background, on the basis of how long it has been since the social organization of the nation's agriculture passed beyond feudalism; region of the United States, on the basis of industrialization and expenditures for education; and religion, on the basis of fundamentalism.

formation is insufficient for inventorying all pertinent facets of each past job, but it does enable us to index the most important facet of the job, its substantive complexity. To create this index, we make use of the finding, reported earlier, that our measure of the substantive complexity of a particular job is highly correlated with the *Dictionary of Occupational Titles'* appraisals of the complexity of work with data, with things, and with people for the occupation as a whole. Because of this correspondence between our ratings and those of the *Dictionary,* we can compute an approximate index of substantive complexity for any past job from a knowledge of the job title alone.[16] Such an index has obvious limitations. It assumes that the levels of complexity of the many occupations in the American economy were similar some years or decades ago to what they are today. Being based on average levels of substantive complexity for entire occupations rather than on precise levels of complexity for particular jobs, the *Dictionary*-based index is also considerably less powerful than is the index of substantive complexity we have thus far employed. Since it extrapolates from the observations and evaluations made by trained occupational analysts, though, it has the advantage that it cannot be influenced by our respondents' styles of reporting.

As a prototypic analysis, we examine the reciprocal effects of substantive complexity and ideational flexibility, the latter deliberately chosen because it appears to offer us the toughest test: Ideational flexibility is obviously pertinent to recruitment into substantively complex jobs, and it might be expected to be the most resistant to change of all the facets of psychological functioning we have studied. As depicted in Figure 3.1, the model assumes that ideational flexibility and job complexity have reciprocal effects; the main purpose of the analysis is to assess the relative magnitudes of these effects. Lacking a measure of ideational flexibility from earlier stages of the men's lives, we cannot estimate the impact of earlier ideational flexibility on the substantive complexity of the present job. It would be inappropriate to measure the impact of past jobs on present ideational flexibility when we cannot measure the corresponding process. We therefore exclude from the model any consideration of the effects of past jobs on present ideational flexibility. Thus, the model attempts only to assess the reciprocal effects

---

[16] The approximate index of substantive complexity is equal to the sum of the *Dictionary of Occupational Titles* score for complexity of work with data, weighted .133, plus the score for complexity of work with people, weighted .119, minus the score for work with things, scored 1 if the man does any significant work with things and 2 if he does not, weighted .711. (These weights represent the unstandardized beta-coefficients from the multiple regression of substantive complexity on the *Dictionary* scores for complexity of work with data, people, and things, with the score for things dichotomized. The weight for "things" is larger than the other two because this score has been dichotomized.)

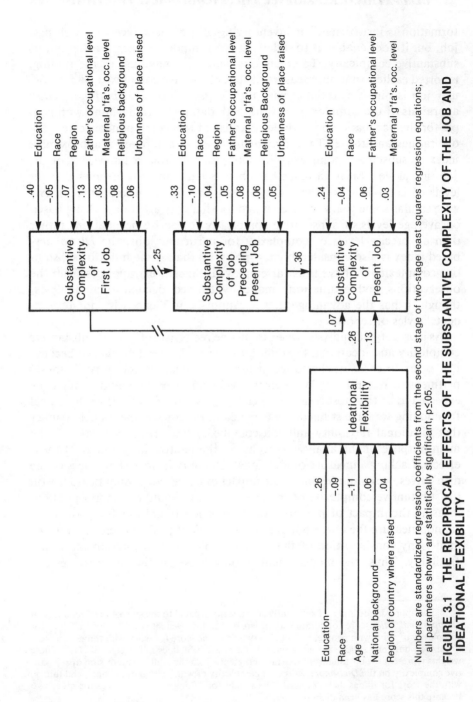

Numbers are standardized regression coefficients from the second stage of two-stage least squares regression equations; all parameters shown are statistically significant, p≤.05.

FIGURE 3.1 THE RECIPROCAL EFFECTS OF THE SUBSTANTIVE COMPLEXITY OF THE JOB AND IDEATIONAL FLEXIBILITY

of the substantive complexity of the *present* job and ideational flexibility at the *present* time.

The model presented in Figure 3.1 shows the reciprocal effects of substantive complexity and ideational flexibility, as well as the effects of those "predetermined" variables that have some statistically significant impact.[17] The numbers shown are standardized regression coefficients from the second-stage equations. These findings bear out our contention that substantive complexity and ideational flexibility do have substantial reciprocal effects.

The most important determinant of the *substantive complexity* of the present job, as would be expected, is the substantive complexity of the immediately preceding job. Education has considerable contemporaneous importance, above and beyond its historical importance as the prime determinant of the substantive complexity of prior jobs. Next in importance is ideational flexibility, which has a greater impact on job complexity than does any exogenous variable other than education. Still significant, even well into men's careers, are race, father's occupational level, and even maternal grandfather's occupational level. Other social characteristics—notably religious background and the region and urbanness of the principal place of residence during childhood—have had some historical importance in shaping earlier career stages, but by the third or later job they no longer have any significant direct bearing.

The most important determinants of *ideational flexibility* are education and the substantive complexity of the work. Their impact greatly surpasses that of age, race, national background, and the region of the country in which the man was raised, all of which have some pertinence for ideational flexibility well into men's careers. No other exogenous variable in our model continues to have a significant impact at this stage of career.

The crucial comparison this model enables us to make is of the relative magnitudes of effect of substantive complexity on ideational flexibility and of ideational flexibility on substantive complexity. The ratio is exactly two

---

[17] As noted, the effects of past jobs on current ideational flexibility are deliberately excluded from the model. So too is the effect of age on the substantive complexity of the present job, for including age in the equation would control the very historical processes whose effects we are trying to measure, thereby overemphasizing the conditions making for mobility among an age cohort. Age is instead used as an instrument for identifying the effect of current ideational flexibility on current substantive complexity, the rationale being that since the model includes past jobs, it takes account of the historical process leading to current levels of substantive complexity of work, but does not do so for ideational flexibility. (For further discussion of the complex topic of identifying reciprocal-effects models, see Chapter 5.)

to one. In terms of their *present* reciprocal relationship, the impact of job on ideational flexibility is greater than the reverse.[18]

It must be emphasized that this conclusion refers only to the present time, not to the historical process. It is but a simple extrapolation from our findings to the conclusion that the reciprocal relationship between ideational flexibility and the substantive complexity of the present job must have been true for past jobs, too. (Moreover, there is every reason to believe that, earlier in the lives of these men, ideational flexibility bore the same type of reciprocal relationship to education that it now bears to the substantive complexity of the job.) Without measurements of the men's ideational flexibility at relevant times in the past, we cannot assess the magnitudes of the reciprocal effects of ideational flexibility and substantive complexity over the course of men's occupational careers. The *present* relationship between the two, though, results more from job complexity affecting ideational flexibility than the reverse.

We can now generalize the model to consider the relationships between substantive complexity and all the other facets of psychological functioning we have measured (Table 3.5). As before, the crucial issue is the effect of substantive complexity on a particular facet of psychological functioning, compared to the effect of that facet of psychological functioning on substantive complexity. In every case, job affects man more than man affects job. In fact, only four of the eight facets of off-the-job psychological functioning have a statistically significant effect on job complexity, and of these four only the two measures of intellectual functioning—ideational flexibility and the intellectual demands men put upon their leisure-time activities—are more than just barely significant. By contrast, substantive complexity

---

[18] Lacking longitudinal data about ideational flexibility, this analysis does not take "earlier" ideational flexibility into account. Robert M. Hauser has suggested an intriguing method for stretching our cross-sectional data to meet some of the requirements of a longitudinal model—synthetic cohort analysis. The essence of the method, as applied here, is to use data provided by the men who have had the median number of jobs (which is 4) to provide estimates of the correlations involving ideational flexibility as of 1964, and data provided by the men who have had one fewer than the median number of jobs to provide estimates of the correlations involving ideational flexibility as of the time of the "immediately prior job." The synthetic-cohort method enables us to answer this important question: What does the model we have constructed from the cross-sectional data imply about the magnitude of the correlation between "earlier" and "later" ideational flexibility? If the model implies an improbably low correlation between earlier and later ideational flexibility, this would cast doubt on its plausibility. If, on the other hand, the model implies an expectedly high correlation between earlier and later ideational flexibility, this would increase the plausibility of the model. Using the basic theorem of path analysis (Duncan, 1966), and following procedures similar to those used in Duncan, Haller, and Portes (1968), we find the implied correlation between "earlier" and "later" ideational flexibility to be .78. Given some degree of unreliability of measurement (an issue we shall address in Chapter 5), this strikes us as being about as high a correlation as should be expected. In fact, the longitudinal data that we shall present in Chapter 5 show this estimate of the "stability" of ideational flexibility to be reasonable, perhaps even too high, for an estimate that does not take measurement error into account.

Table 3.5. THE RECIPROCAL EFFECTS OF THE SUBSTANTIVE COMPLEXITY OF THE JOB AND PSYCHOLOGICAL FUNCTIONING

(Figures Represent Standardized Beta-coefficients from the Second Stage of Two-stage Least Squares Regression Equations)

Facet of Psychological Functioning:	Effect of Specified Facets of Psychological Functioning on Substantive Complexity[a]	Effect of Substantive Complexity on the Specified Facet of Psychological Functioning	Exogenous Variables Included in Equation for Psychological Variable (All Others Non-significant)
Occupational commitment	.02	.16*	Race (−.04), Age (.17), Region of origin (−.09), Urbanness (−.07).
Job satisfaction	.13*	.39*	Education (−.22), Race (−.04), Urbanness (−.05).
Parental valuation of self-direction	−.07	.14*	Education (.21), Race (−.04), Age (−.05), National background (.07), Region of origin (.06), Father's education (.04).
Anxiety	−.04*	−.07*	Age (−.12), Urbanness (.04).
Self-esteem	.04*	.10*	Age (−.05), National background (−.06), Urbanness (.08).
Stance toward change	−.03	.14*	Age (−.16), Region of origin (.09).
Standards of morality	.01	.16*	Education (.09), Race (−.06), Age (.14), National background (.10), Religious background (−.14), Urbanness (−.05).
Authoritarian conservatism	−.01	−.17*	Education (−.21), Age (.19), National background (−.05), Region of origin (−.07), Religious background (−.06), Urbanness (−.04).
Ideational flexibility	.13*	.26*	Education (.26), Race (−.09), Age (−.11), National background (.06), Region of origin (.04).
Intellectual demandingness of leisure-time activities	.14*	.28*	Education (.17), Race (.07), Region of origin (.08), Father's occupational level (.04), Religious background (.07), Father's education (.04), Urbanness (.05).

[a] Substantive complexity of prior jobs, education, father's occupational level, and maternal grandfather's occupational level are always included in the equations. Standardized beta-coefficients for these variables remain essentially the same no matter which facet of psychological functioning is included in the equation.
* Statistically significant, p<.05.

significantly affects all facets of psychological functioning, in several instances to as large a degree as does the most powerful exogenous variable. In short, the substantive complexity of a job is consistently important for psychological functioning and consistently more so than is psychological functioning for substantive complexity.

All this is based on but one dimension of occupation, its substantive complexity. We cannot say whether it is true for other job conditions, as it is for substantive complexity, that the impact of job on man is consistently greater than the reverse. We can conclude that in the continuing interplay between man and job, the effects of job on man are far from trivial.

DISCUSSION

The central issue of this chapter is whether men's adult occupational experiences affect or only reflect their psychological functioning. We believe that the job does play a part in shaping the man, that there is a continuing interplay throughout his career between man affecting job and job affecting man. In support of this belief, we have presented several strands of evidence, none definitive but all consistently indicating that the relationships between the conditions men experience in their work and their psychological functioning do not simply reflect some inadequacy in our data; or the effects of education, status, and income; or men's efforts to mold their jobs to fit their needs and values; or selectivity in recruitment and retention. In fact, for the one occupational condition about which we have sufficient historical data to make an assessment—the substantive complexity of the work—we find that the job has a substantially greater impact on men's psychological functioning than the reverse.

Several limitations of our study need be recognized. First, in the absence of longitudinal data, we can assess only the *current* reciprocal effects of occupational conditions and psychological functioning, not the historical process. Second, our treatment of the data has been broad-brush: We have described the main effects of some principal occupational conditions on the total male civilian work force, ignoring for this analysis the possibility that there may be important variations on the themes we have sketched, and even some exceptions, among various segments of this population. Third, this analysis says nothing about the effects of occupational experience for women. Finally, our methods may be less suited for studying organizational, interpersonal, and technological contexts than for studying the immediate conditions of a man's own work.

These limitations notwithstanding, we believe that our findings have several important implications. Most concretely, they buttress and extend our earlier conclusions about the psychological importance of conditions that facilitate or inhibit the exercise of occupational self-direction. We had earlier found (Chapter 1) that occupational self-direction is of critical importance for understanding the impact of social stratification on men's values and orientation. We can now say that, in addition to its relevance for explaining the psychological impact of social stratification, occupational self-direction has the most potent and most widespread psychological effects of all the occupational conditions we have examined. In terms of these effects, the central fact of occupational life today is not ownership of the means of production; nor is it status, income, or interpersonal relationships on the job. Instead, it is the opportunity to use initiative, thought, and independent judgment in one's work—to direct one's own occupational activities. To state our conclusions more generally, our findings emphasize the psychological importance of the structural imperatives of the job—those aspects of the job that impinge on a man most directly, insistently, and demandingly. Not only the conditions that determine occupational self-direction, but all structural imperatives of the job that elicit effort and flexibility, are conducive to favorable evaluations of self, an open and flexible orientation to others, and effective intellectual functioning. Men thrive in meeting occupational challenges.

These findings also provide some insight into the processes by which occupational experience affects psychological functioning. The findings argue for a learning-generalization model, in contrast to a reaction-formation or compensatory model (see Breer and Locke, 1965). That is, the specific links between particular occupational conditions and particular facets of psychological functioning suggest that men's ways of coping with the realities of their jobs are generalized to nonoccupational realities. Men whose jobs require intellectual flexibility, for example, come not only to exercise their intellectual prowess on the job but also to engage in intellectually demanding leisure-time activities. Nowhere in these data is there evidence that men turn their occupational frustrations loose on the nonoccupational world or try to find compensation in nonoccupational realities for occupational lacks and grievances.

Finally, our findings bear on the issue of whether men similarly located in the structure of society come to share beliefs and values because they experience similar conditions of life or because of some interpersonal process of value-transmission. Marx and the structuralists would have us believe that the former is basic; theorists as diverse as the "human relations in industry" and "culture of poverty" schools stress the latter. Our findings, emphasizing as they do the structural imperatives of the job and questioning the importance of interpersonal relatedness, support the argument of the structuralists. A man's job affects his perceptions, values, and thinking processes primarily because it confronts him with demands he must try to meet. These demands, in turn, are to a great extent determined by the job's location in the larger structures of the economy and the society. It is chiefly by shaping the everyday realities men must face that social structure exerts its psychological impact.

4 Occupational Structure and Alienation*

Melvin L. Kohn

Despite its ambiguity of meaning, alienation is an appealing concept, standing as it does at the intersection of social-structural conditions and psychological orientation. Certainly it has been the subject of a vast literature (see Geyer, 1972). On the structural side, there is the fundamental Marxian analysis, focusing on the meaning for the worker of loss of control over his primary work role. On the psychological side, there is the extensive literature on all the ways in which estrangement from self and others can be expressed. But rarely are the social-structural and psychological aspects of alienation juxtaposed, even more rarely in empirical analysis. This chapter examines the relationship between social structure—in particular, occupational structure—and the subjective experience of alienation, under the conditions that exist in a large-scale, technological economy.

Our starting point is Marx's analysis of occupational structure. Marx emphasized ownership of the means of production and division of labor, both of which were especially salient in the early stages of the industrial revolution (Israel, 1971:30–62; Marx, 1964, 1971). An exact test of the present-day pertinence of these occupational conditions to feelings of alienation would require cross-national comparisons to see whether workers in

* This chapter is a revised version of a paper of the same title originally published in the *American Journal of Sociology* (Kohn, 1976a). I am indebted for advice and essential help to my associates—Margaret Renfors, Carrie Schoenbach, Carmi Schooler, and Erma Jean Surman.

societies having capitalist systems feel more alienated than do workers in societies having noncapitalist systems, and whether workers in economies characterized by a highly specialized division of labor feel more alienated than do workers in less specialized economies. Yet, even within the United States, with its capitalist system and its large-scale, highly specialized economic structure, it is possible to see whether employees feel more alienated than owners, and whether those who work in firms having a specialized division of labor feel more alienated than do those who work in firms where the division of labor is less pronounced. We can also see whether having a position of authority—often thought of as the functional equivalent in large-scale enterprises of ownership in small-scale enterprises—is related to alienation.

As we interpret Marx's discussion, he was concerned with workers' loss of control over the means of production not only for its economic and political import, but also because it signified workers' loss of control over the essential conditions of their own occupational lives. When one sells his labor to an employer instead of working for himself, and when one makes some standardized part instead of an entire entity, he loses control over the "product" of his labor. One can also lose control over the "process" of his labor—by having to do work that does not engage his interests or challenge his abilities. Both a concern with loss of control over product and a concern with loss of control over process are evident in the *Early Writings:*

> What constitutes the alienation of labor? First, that the work is *external* to the worker, that it is not part of his nature; and that, consequently, he does not fulfill himself in his work but denies himself, has a feeling of misery rather than well-being, does not develop freely his mental and physical energies but is physically exhausted and mentally debased . . . . His work is not voluntary but imposed, *forced labor.* It is not the satisfaction of a need, but only a *means* for satisfying other needs . . . . Finally, the external character of work for the worker is shown by the fact that it is not his own work but work for someone else, that in work he does not belong to himself but to another person. [1964:124-25]

Work that is "external" to the worker, in which he cannot "fulfill himself," comes close to being the opposite pole of what we have called "self-directed" work—that is, work involving initiative, thought, and independent judgment (Chapters 1 and 3). Although many occupational conditions are either conducive to or deterrent of the exercise of occupational self-direction, we see three in particular as crucial—closeness of supervision, routinization, and substantive complexity. Insofar as workers are free of close supervision, perform a variety of tasks, and do work that is substantively complex, their work is necessarily self-directed. Insofar as workers are closely supervised, are caught up in a repetitive flow of similar tasks, and do work of little substantive complexity, their work does not permit self-direction. Believing that loss of control over the process of work is conducive to alienation, we hypothesize that being closely supervised, doing routinized work, and doing work of little substantive complexity will result in feelings of alienation. We would further predict that, in a modern capitalist economy, dominated by large-scale enterprise, these occupational conditions will have a greater effect on feelings of alienation than whether one is owner or employee or whether one works in an enterprise having more or less pronounced division of labor.

There is solid empirical reason to make the same predictions. Our analyses of the relationships between some 50 separable dimensions of occupation and each of several facets of psychological functioning (including, for example, intellectual flexibility, anxiety, self-esteem, and authoritarian conservatism), led us to conclude that "...occupational self-direction has the most potent and most widespread psychological effects of all the occupational conditions we have examined. In terms of these effects, the central fact of occupational life today is not ownership of the means of production; nor is it status, income, or interpersonal relationships on the job. Instead, it is the opportunity to use initiative, thought, and independent judgment in one's work—to direct one's own occupational activities" (Chapter 3). This being so, it is probable that the conditions determinative of the degree of occupational self-direction—closeness of supervision, routinization, and the substantive complexity of the work—have an important effect on feelings of alienation as well.

The intent of this analysis, then, is to appraise two related hypotheses suggested by Marx's analysis of the occupational sources of alienation. One hypothesis, emphasizing loss of control over the *products* of one's labor, posits that ownership and hierarchical position are of crucial importance with respect to alienation (and also ascribes an important, if secondary, role to division of labor). The other hypothesis, emphasizing loss of control over the *process* of labor, suggests that (at least within an industrialized, capitalist society) such determinants of occupational self-direction as closeness of supervision, routinization, and substantive complexity overshadow ownership, hierarchical position, and division of labor in their effects on alienation.[1]

---

[1] Little of the empirical literature on the sociology and social psychology of work is directly pertinent to the central issue of this paper. Most occupational studies, of course, do not purport to deal with alienation. Of those that do, some use job dissatisfaction as their index of alienation. But extrapolating from job dissatisfaction or even from a lack of occupational commitment to feelings of alienation is unwarranted. Closer to our purposes are those studies that use as their index of alienation some measure of "alienation from work" (Aiken and Hage, 1966; Miller, 1967; Pearlin, 1962; and Zurcher, Meadow, and Zurcher, 1965). Pertinent as these studies are, though, it is unsafe to extrapolate from their findings about people's job orientations to people's more general orientations toward both occupational and nonoccupational social reality. A few studies *do* examine the relationship between one or more occupational conditions and one or more aspects of off-the-job alienation (notably, Blauner, 1964;

INDICES OF ALIENATION

Before assessing the occupational sources of alienation, we must face the fact that in social-psychological usage, "alienation" is an extraordinarily vague and imprecise term. Alienation refers to people's conceptions of the external world and of self, in other words, to their orientations. Most definitions agree that alienation involves estrangement from (or disillusionment with, or lack of faith in) the larger social world or oneself. There is, however, little agreement on how large a segment of the orientational domain "alienation" should encompass. Lacking an adequate general definition, we follow Seeman's (1959) example, in his classic analysis of the historical uses of the concept, and use the term to refer generally to the five distinguishable facets of orientation that the term has come to imply: powerlessness, self-estrangement, normlessness, isolation (or cultural estrangement), and meaninglessness.

Seeman's analysis demonstrated that alienation has such disparate meanings that the term cannot be used analytically without specifying which meaning is intended. This conclusion remains valid, even though Seeman (1972a, 1972b) and others (Allardt, 1965; Blauner, 1964; Clark, 1959; Dean, 1961; Finifter, 1970, 1972; Horton, 1964; Israel, 1971; Kon, 1967; Nettler, 1957; Olsen, 1969; Zollschan and Gibeau, 1964) have refined the conceptualization of alienation in many ways. In fact, a major controversy revolves around the theoretical utility of retaining as an analytic concept a term with such diverse meanings (see especially Israel, 1971).

We are of course interested in two types of alienation that have been central to theoretical discussion of the alienating effects of occupational structure—powerlessness and self-estrangement. But the other types—normlessness, cultural estrangement, and meaninglessness—also might be affected by occupational conditions. Thus, there is utility in examining them all. To this end, we attempted to develop indices of all five types of alienation, using the same information as was used for our indices of self-conceptions and social orientations. (We deal here, not with new facets of orientation, but with a different conceptualization of the same psychological phenomena.) We actually succeeded in constructing adequate Guttman Scales of four dimensions of alienation, failing only with meaninglessness, for which we were able to develop only a single question.[2] Since the four

---

Bonjean and Grimes, 1970; Goldthorpe et al., 1969; Neal and Seeman, 1964; Nelson, 1968; and Tudor, 1972). But, with the exception of Tudor's study, none of these answers the major question of this chapter, because they do not deal with (or do not directly measure) the dimensions of occupation central to our interests, or because their indices of alienation are inferential.

[2] For enumerations of indices of alienation employed by other investigators, see Bonjean, Hill, and McLemore (1967:27-38); Robinson and Shaver (1969:161-210); and Seeman (1972a).

scales are basic to all our analyses, it is worth examining them carefully (see Table 4.1).

1. Powerlessness.   Seeman says that powerlessness "can be conceived as the expectancy or probability held by the individual that his own behavior cannot determine the occurrence of the outcomes . . . he seeks" (p. 784). The concept implies a continuum, from the individual's seeing himself as being at the mercy of external forces, to his believing that he has some degree of control over his own fate. Seeman speaks of powerlessness as a measure, not of "the objective conditions in society," but of "the individual's expectancy for control of events." It is not the fact of being

Table 4.1.   GUTTMAN SCALES OF ALIENATION

Scale	Attribute
1. Powerlessness	*a)* Do you feel that most of the things that happen to you are the result of your own decisions or of things over which you have no control? *b)* I generally have confidence that when I make plans I will be able to carry them out (agree-disagree). *c)* There are things I can to that might influence national policy (agree-disagree). *d)* How often do you feel powerless to get what you want out of life?
2. Self-estrangement	*a)* How often do you feel that there isn't much purpose to being alive? *b)* How often do you feel bored with everything? *c)* At times I think I am no good at all (agree-disagree) *d)* Are you the sort of person who takes life as it comes or are you working toward some definite goal?
3. Normlessness	*a)* It's all right to do anything you want as long as you stay out of trouble (agree-disagree). *b)* It's all right to get around the law as long as you don't actually break it (agree-disagree). *c)* If something works, it doesn't matter whether it's right or wrong (agree-disagree). *d)* Do you believe that it's all right to do whatever the law allows, or are there some things that are wrong even if they are legal?
4. Cultural estrangement	*a)* According to your general impression, how often do your ideas and opinions about important matters differ from those of your relatives? *b)* How often do your ideas and opinions differ from those of your friends? *c)* How about from those of other people with your religious background? *d)* Those of most people in the country?

Note: All four scales have reproducibilities in the .90s, scalabilities in the .70s, and essentially random patterns of error.

powerless but the sense of being powerless that we attempt to measure; whatever produces a sense of powerlessness, the psychological reality is that to feel powerless is to lack a sense of personal efficacy. This is what the index of powerlessness is meant to, and apparently does, reflect. Other indices in common use have more abstract referents, but even those designed to measure the individual's conception of how power is organized in the larger social order may actually reflect his sense of personal efficacy.

2. Self-estrangement. This is difficult to conceptualize and to index. Seeman says that it "refers essentially to the inability of the individual to find self-rewarding—or in Dewey's phrase, self-consummatory— activities that engage him" (p. 790). The concept overlaps with what we call self-deprecation, the negative component of self-esteem. But self-estrangement implies something more than a negative evaluation of one's own worth; it also implies a sense of being detached from self, of being adrift—purposeless, bored with everything, merely responding to what life has to offer, rather than setting one's own course. Our index attempts to capture this sense of detachment from self.

3. Normlessness. The concept is derived from Durkheim's "anomie" and its psychological counterpart, "anomia."[3] By Seeman's definition, normlessness arises from a situation "in which there is a high expectancy that socially unapproved behaviors are required to achieve given goals" (p. 788). Our index is based on an implicit continuum—from the individual's believing that it is acceptable to do whatever he can get away with, to his holding responsible moral standards. The beliefs that it is morally acceptable to do "anything you want as long as you stay out of trouble," that it is legitimate to "get around the law," that "if something works it doesn't matter whether it's right or wrong," and that it's "all right" to take advantage of "whatever the law allows" provide our index of normlessness. (We must acknowledge, though, that believing that "there are some things that are wrong even if they are legal"—which we treat as the internalization of the moral norms of the larger society—may in some instances represent alienation from the society.)

4. Cultural estrangement (which Seeman originally called isolation). This refers, by his definition, to "assign[ing] low reward value to goals or beliefs that are typically highly valued in the given society" (pp. 788–89). Seeman thinks of cultural estrangement in terms of an individual's rejection of such allegedly dominant cultural themes as success and materialism. We have asked instead whether the respondent believes that his

---

[3] Most empirical studies are based on indices derived from Srole's (1956: 711) definition of anomia as "self-to-other alienation." For informative discussions of the relationship between alienation and anomie/anomia, see Horton (1964) and Lukes (1972).

"ideas and opinions about important matters" differ from those of his friends, his relatives, other people of his religious background, and his compatriots generally. This seems preferable, in that it does not prejudge the dominant cultural themes or what the respondent assumes them to be. Still, we may have missed the essence of what Seeman and others mean by cultural estrangement. Another possible problem with our index (see Antonovsky and Antonovsky, 1974) is that it fails to distinguish between estrangement from primary groups (friends and relatives) and estrangement from secondary groups ("people with your religious background" and "most people in the country"), which are included in the same index. But we do not believe this invalidates the index, for we have found a unidimensionality in such estrangement, regardless of whether primary or secondary groups are involved.

OCCUPATIONAL STRUCTURE

Three aspects of occupational structure are focal to this analysis: ownership and position in the supervisory hierarchy, division of labor, and the conditions that determine how much opportunity a person has to exercise self-direction in his work.

Indices of Occupational Structure

Ownership is indexed straightforwardly: the interviewers asked all men employed in profit-making firms, "Are you an owner?" For these analyses, we simply dichotomize owners and nonowners, disregarding the distinction between full and partial ownership. (An index of "degree of ownership" yields altogether consistent findings.)

Position in the supervisory hierarchy, which some consider the equivalent of ownership, is based on the respondent's estimate of how many people are "under" him—either because he supervises them directly or because they are under people he supervises.

We have no direct index of *division of labor.* The closest equivalent provided in this study is an index of bureaucratization, employed here on the assumption that the division of labor is generally most pronounced where bureaucratization is greatest. Our index of bureaucratization (see Chapter 2 for the complete rationale) is based on one principal dimension of bureaucracy, the hierarchical organization of authority or, operationally, the number of formal levels of supervision and size of the firm or organization.

As mentioned above, we conceive three occupational conditions to be of crucial importance in determining the degree of *occupational self-direction*—closeness of supervision, routinization, and substantive complexity. The indices we employ are the same as those used in Chapter 3.

Occupation and Alienation

We begin the analysis of occupational structure and alienation by examining the correlations between the indices of occupational structure just enumerated and the four types of alienation indexed above (see Table 4.2).

Consider, first, the relationships between occupational structure and a type of alienation particularly germane to Marx's analysis, powerlessness. Ownership per se is related hardly at all to powerlessness, the correlation being − .04. Position in the supervisory hierarchy, though, is more strongly related to powerlessness, this correlation being − .13.

Bureaucratization also is related to powerlessness (the correlation here being − .09), but the direction is opposite to what alienation theorists might predict: Employees of highly bureaucratized firms and organizations— where, presumably, the division of labor is generally greatest—are less likely to feel powerless than are employees of nonbureaucratic firms and organizations. This finding casts doubt on the belief that, under modern conditions, division of labor is itself conducive to powerlessness. (On the other hand, the finding is consistent with our earlier analyses of bureaucratization [Chapter 2], which showed that the occupational conditions attendant on bureaucratization are conducive to intellectual flexibility, openness to new experience, and self-directed values.)

Table 4.2. CORRELATIONS OF ALIENATION SCALES WITH SELECTED OCCUPATIONAL CONDITIONS

Index	Powerlessness	Self-Estrangement	Normlessness	Cultural Estrangement
1. Ownership and hierarchical position:				
Ownership	− .04	− .02	− .03	.00
Position in the supervisory hierarchy	− .13	− .09	− .09	.07
Combined (multiple correlation)	.13	.09	.09	.07
2. Bureaucratization of firm or organization	− .09	− .09	− .11	.06
3. Occupational self-direction:				
Closeness of supervision	.16	.14	.23	− .11
Routinization of work	.08	.04	.13	− .06
Substantive complexity of work	− .19	− .17	− .26	.17
Combined (multiple correlation)	.21	.18	.29	.17

Note: $N = 3,101$. Correlations of approximately ± .04 are statistically significant at the .05 level; correlations of approximately ± .05 are significant at the .01 level. The "positive" end of each variable represents the "higher" or "greater" pole of the dimension (higher position in the supervisory hierarchy, greater degree of bureaucratization, etc.).

All three of the conditions determinative of the degree of occupational self-direction are related to powerlessness, all of them in the expected direction: close supervision, routinized work, and work of little substantive complexity are all related to feelings of powerlessness. The correlations range from .08 for routinization to -.19 for substantive complexity.

This pattern of relationships between occupational conditions and feelings of powerlessness is essentially repeated for self-estrangement and normlessness: Ownership per se is of minor importance at most, position in the supervisory hierarchy is of greater importance, division of labor (as inferred from bureaucratization) is negatively related to alienation, and the three conditions that impede the exercise of occupational self-direction are consistently related to feelings of alienation. In each instance, occupational self-direction is more strongly related to alienation than are ownership and hierarchical position. (Similar analyses, limited to the profit-making sector of the economy, yield identical conclusions.)

The relationships between occupational conditions and cultural estrangement, however, are altogether different from those between occupational conditions and the other types of alienation. The very conditions that are positively related to powerlessness, self-estrangement, and normlessness— namely, holding a low position in the supervisory hierarchy, working in a nonbureaucratic firm or organization, and not being self-directed in one's work—are negatively related to cultural estrangement. So this type of alienation is, at least as judged by its occupational concomitants, quite different from the other three; we shall not consider it further here, its main value for this analysis having been to confirm the view that the various types of alienation must be considered separately.[4] More important for our purposes is that the analysis thus far indicates a pattern of relationships between occupational conditions and the "Durkheimian" type of alienation—normlessness—similar to the pattern for the "Marxian" types of alienation— powerlessness and self-estrangement.

We conclude tentatively that both control over the product of one's labor (i.e., ownership and hierarchical position) and control over the process of one's labor (i.e., closeness of supervision, routinization, and the substantive complexity of work) are related to feelings of powerlessness, self-

---

[4] Analyses of many other dimensions of social structure yield almost entirely consistent confirmation that cultural estrangement bears a different (usually opposite) relationship to social structure from that of the other three types of alienation. (Middleton [1963] reported consonant findings.) A likely explanation of this disparity is that powerlessness, self-estrangement, and normlessness, at least as we have indexed them, all represent a negative judgment of self—in the sense that the individual feels that he lacks personal efficacy, lacks basic worth, or lacks the ability to make his own moral decisions. Cultural estrangement, on the other hand, does not necessarily represent a negative judgment of self, but often means quite the opposite, that the individual is sufficiently secure in his judgments of self to be independent in his values.

estrangement, and normlessness, the latter type of control more strongly so. This, however, is not to say that we have as yet demonstrated that any of these occupational conditions actually results in alienation; there are several other possible interpretations of the findings.

Two logical possibilities are that the relationship between alienation and control over the product of one's labor reflects the greater opportunities of those in high position to be self-directed in their work, or, conversely, that the relationship between occupational self-direction and alienation reflects the disproportionate numbers of owners and of people high in the supervisory structure among those whose work is self-directed. We tested these possibilities by computing multiple-partial correlations between each set of occupational conditions and each type of alienation, in each instance statistically controlling the other set of occupational conditions.[5] Table 4.3 shows that, when occupational self-direction is statistically controlled, ownership and hierarchical position lose much of their explanatory power, implying that their effect is indirect, via occupational self-direction. Occupational self-direction, on the other hand, is related to alienation nearly as strongly when ownership and hierarchical position are statistically controlled as when they are not.[6] (Again, similar analyses, limited to the profit-making sector of the economy, yield identical results.) These findings suggest that the occupational conditions that directly affect feelings of alienation are those determinative of self-direction in one's work. Ownership and hierarchical position affect alienation mainly because owners and people high in the supervisory structure are able to be self-directed in their work.

Just as ownership and hierarchical position lose much of their explanatory power when the conditions determinative of occupational self-direction are statistically controlled, so might the conditions that make for occupational self-direction lose their explanatory power if *other* occupational conditions were controlled. Six occupational conditions are potentially pertinent: salary or wages, bureaucratization, pressure of time, and three types of job uncertainty—the risk of losing one's job or failing in one's business, the probability of being held responsible for things outside one's control, and the competitiveness of one's occupational situation (all of

---

[5] The multiple-partial correlation is a simple extension to multiple correlations of the logic of partial correlations (see Blalock, 1960: 350–351). It measures the magnitude of the relationship between a set of independent variables and some dependent variable when one or more other variables are statistically controlled.

[6] Alternatively, when ownership and position in the supervisory hierarchy are added to a multiple-regression equation already containing occupational self-direction, there is essentially no increment to the amount of variance explained for any type of alienation. When the conditions determinative of occupational self-direction are added to a multiple-regression equation already containing ownership and hierarchical position, the increment to the amount of variance explained is substantial, ranging from .08 for powerlessness to .21 for normlessness.

Table 4.3.   MULTIPLE-PARTIAL CORRELATIONS, ALIENATION
SCALES, BY OWNERSHIP AND HIERARCHICAL
POSITION, AND BY OCCUPATIONAL SELF-DIRECTION

Condition	Powerlessness	Self-Estrangement	Normlessness
1. Ownership and hierarchical position:			
Multiple correlation with the specified type of alienation	.13	.09	.09
Multiple-partial correlation, controlling:			
Occupational self-direction*	.04	.00	. . .§
Plus other pertinent occupational conditions†	.02	.02	. . .
Plus education	.03	.02	. . .
Plus other social characteristics‡	.04	.04	. . .
2. Occupational self-direction*:			
Multiple correlation with the specified type of alienation	.21	.18	.29
Multiple-partial correlation, controlling:			
Ownership and hierarchical position	.17	.16	.30
Plus other pertinent occupational conditions†	.12	.14	.25
Plus education	.08	.10	.15
Plus other social characteristics‡	.08	.12	.13

*Closeness of supervision, routinization, and substantive complexity.
†Specifically, salary or wages; bureaucratization; pressure of time; and the respondent's assessment of: the risk of his losing his job or failing in his business, the probability of his being held responsible for things outside of his control, and the competitiveness of his occupational situation.
‡Specifically, age, race, father's education and occupational status, intergenerational occupational mobility, the degree of urbanness of the place where the respondent lived longest as a child, the region in which that place was situated, religious background, and national background.
§When controlled for occupational self-direction, position in the supervisory hierarchy becomes *positively* related to normlessness, a reversal of direction from the zero-order correlation. This remains true when additional variables are brought into the equation.
N = 3101.

them as appraised by the respondent).[7] Using the same procedure as before, we additionally controlled all these facets of the job. Although the correlations between occupational self-direction and the various types of alienation are reduced, they remain appreciable (Table 4.3).

The next possibility to consider is that the conditions determinative of occupational self-direction might be related to alienation because men who are more self-directed are generally better educated, and education itself might affect alienation. To test this possibility, we added education to the

---

[7] These are the only occupational conditions included in the study that are related both to occupational self-direction and to one or more types of alienation, when education is statistically controlled. They are thus the only occupational conditions treated here that are potentially pertinent to explaining the relationship between occupational self-direction and alienation.

growing package of statistical controls. (This procedure may be overly stringent, for it ignores the possibility that education might affect, say, powerlessness only indirectly, by influencing the substantive complexity of work, but that substantive complexity directly affects feelings of powerlessness.) The correlations are further reduced (Table 4.3 again). Nevertheless, even using these stringent statistical procedures, which arbitrarily assign all shared variance to the control variables, the correlations between occupational self-direction and alienation are not trivial.

Several other social characteristics—age, race, father's education and occupational status, intergenerational occupational mobility, religious and national background, the degree of urbanness of the place where the respondent was raised, and the region in which that place was situated—are related both to the types of jobs men hold and to alienation. Thus, they might explain why occupational self-direction is related to alienation. However, adding these variables to the package of statistical controls does not appreciably change the picture. The relationships between occupational self-direction and alienation do not simply reflect differences between the social backgrounds of men who hold more self-directed and less self-directed jobs.[8] Moreover, having now simultaneously controlled virtually every social-structural variable that our own and previous investigators' analyses had found to be pertinent to alienation, we still find statistically significant, nontrivial relationships between occupational self-direction and the three types of alienation.[9]

---

[8] These multiple-regression analyses also permit specification of the relationships between alienation and social-structural conditions other than the occupational conditions on which this chapter focuses. Controlling all variables enumerated in the discussion above showed the following to be significantly related to powerlessness: a high risk (as appraised by the respondent) of losing one's job or business and low salary or wages. Significantly related to self-estrangement are a high risk of losing one's job or business, a high probability of being held responsible for things outside one's control, being older, and being white. Significantly related to normlessness are having a limited education, being young, being black, having predominantly southern or eastern European rather than northern or western European origins, having a "liberal" rather than a "fundamentalist" religious background, and having been upwardly mobile in occupational level, as compared to one's father's occupational level.

[9] This method of statistical analysis does not rule out the possibility that there may be differences, from one segment of the work force to another, in the degree to which the conditions determinative of occupational self-direction bear on one or another type of alienation. Tudor (1972), for example, found a pronounced relationship between the substantive complexity of work and powerlessness among men who have experienced little or no intergenerational occupational mobility and who have moderate to high incomes, but little or no relationship between substantive complexity and powerlessness among other employed men. The data used here do not confirm the existence of this particular pattern, nor do they reveal differences in the relationship of occupational self-direction and alienation between, e.g., employees of bureaucratic and nonbureaucratic firms and organizations, between white-collar and blue-collar workers, or between employees of profit-making firms and employees of government and nonprofit organizations. Nevertheless, there may be other differences between one segment of the work force and another that our relatively broad-gauge analyses have failed to detect (see also Bonjean and Grimes, 1970).

Two other possible interpretations of the relationships between occupational self-direction and alienation require different methods of analysis, which can be carried out only in part with the data at hand.

One interpretation is that alienation results not from occupational conditions as such, but from a discrepancy between workers' needs or values and their actual occupational experiences (see Argyris, 1973). A job of considerable substantive complexity, for example, might challenge some people and threaten others, with predictable consequences for their feelings of alienation. The available data, while pertinent to this interpretation, fall far short of what is needed for a definitive test, because they do not include measures of workers' needs, values, and capacities before they encountered their present occupational conditions. The data at hand concern only present occupational values, which of course have been influenced by occupational experiences. It is nevertheless notable that analysis of variance reveals no significant interaction between occupational values and the conditions determinative of occupational self-direction. Substantive complexity, for example, affects alienation regardless of how greatly the worker values intrinsic aspects of his work. This gives a hint that the effects of the occupational conditions in question may be considerable, no matter what the "fit" between job demands and values (but see Lofquist and Dawis, 1969). This conclusion implies, of course, not that men's needs and values are unimportant, but that the conditions determinative of occupational self-direction affect such basic needs and values as to apply to most workers, at least within the population studied.

The final substantive possibility that can be addressed with these data is that the correlations between occupational self-direction and alienation result, not from the effects of the job on feelings of alienation, but from selective recruitment or from men molding their jobs to match their feelings.[10] Self-estranged men, for example, might be unlikely to seek or to be

---

[10] Several technical possibilities must also be considered: (1) The findings might be an artifact of some deficiency in our indices, either of occupational conditions or of alienation. But there is evidence that our occupational indices are adequate (see Chapter 3). We have discussed most of the issues pertaining to the adequacy of our indices of alienation earlier in this chapter. (2) Respondents' tendencies to agree with "agree/disagree"-type questions, regardless of their content, and to answer in extremes (agreeing or disagreeing "strongly") might account for the relationships between occupational conditions and alienation. But statistically controlling "agree set" and an "extreme answer score" has only slight effect; these response tendencies do not explain our findings. (3) We might not have met the essential statistical assumptions of multiple-regression analysis. But analysis of variance has shown all the relationships between occupational conditions and alienation to be essentially linear. In extensive tests of possible interactions between education and the various occupational conditions, and among the occupational conditions themselves, we have found no interaction of any appreciable magnitude. Finally, the findings are not an artifact of treating the Guttman Scales as interval scales; we repeated the analyses, with essentially the same results, using indices based on factor analysis— a much closer approximation to interval scales—instead of Guttman Scales. Thus, the essential conditions of multiple-regression analysis—linearity and additivity of the independent variables, linearity of the dependent variables—appear to have been met.

selected for jobs of great substantive complexity; or if they hold such jobs, they might perform at the lowest level of complexity the jobs allow. Here, too, a definitive test requires longitudinal data. By borrowing from the methods of the econometricians, though, it is possible to make a tentative assessment of the degree to which our findings reflect the effects of job conditions on feelings of alienation and the degree to which they reflect the effects of alienation on job recruitment and performance. The particular method we employ is "two-stage least squares"; it is described in detail in Chapter 3 and the references cited therein. The models we test are directly analogous to that of Figure 3.1, with each of the facets of alienation, in turn, being substituted for ideational flexibility.

As we have seen, only for substantive complexity do we have the job-history data required for this type of analysis. Fortunately, though, substantive complexity is the most important of the three conditions determinative of occupational self-direction. Our analyses establish strong prima facie evidence that the substantive complexity of work has a causal impact on powerlessness, self-estrangement, and normlessness (see Table 4.4). For powerlessness and self-estrangement, the effects appear to be essentially unidirectional: Working at jobs of little substantive complexity leads people to feel powerless and self-estranged, but persons who feel powerless or self-estranged are not especially likely to be recruited into jobs of little substantive complexity. For normlessness, the relationship to job complexity appears to be reciprocal: Working at jobs of little substantive complexity is conducive to normlessness; it is also true that persons who do not take responsibility for their actions are more likely to be recruited into jobs

Table 4.4. ESTIMATED RECIPROCAL EFFECTS OF SUBSTANTIVE COMPLEXITY OF JOB AND ALIENATION

Type of Alienation	Effect of Specified Type of Alienation on Substantive Complexity†	Effect of Substantive Complexity on the Specified Type of Alienation	Exogenous Variables Included in the Equation for Alienation (All Others Nonsignificant)
Powerlessness	−.03	−.25*	Education (.06), region (−.04), age (.04).
Self-estrangement	.02	−.17*	Race (.09), age (−.05).
Normlessness	−.08*	−.16*	Education (−.18), religious background (.11), national background (−.10), race (.09), age (−.07), region of origin (−.04).

Note: Figures represent standardized β coefficients from the second stage of two-stage least squares regression equations.

† Substantive complexity of prior jobs, education, father's occupational level, maternal grandfather's occupational level, and religious background are always included in the equations.

* Statistically significant, $p < .05$.

of little substantive complexity. Although both processes occur, job complexity appears to have a greater impact on normlessness than does normlessness on job complexity.

In sum, there is substantial evidence that doing work of little substantive complexity is not only associated with, but actually results in, feelings of alienation. It seems a fair presumption that closeness of supervision and routinization also have a causal impact on alienation. In their principal thrust, then, the findings are entirely consonant with the basic Marxian analysis of the alienating effects of workers' loss of control over their essential job conditions. In this large-scale, capitalist economy, the type of control that is most important for alienation, though, is control, not over the product, but over the process, of one's work.

DISCUSSION

This chapter appraises two related hypotheses suggested by Marx's analysis of the occupational sources of alienation—one emphasizing control over the product of one's labor, the other emphasizing control over the work process. The analysis shows that, in this large-scale, capitalist system, control over the product of one's labor (ownership and hierarchical position) has only an indirect effect on alienation, whereas control over work process (closeness of supervision, routinization, and substantive complexity) has an appreciable direct effect on powerlessness, self-estrangement, and normlessness. Thus, the analysis clearly indicates that conditions of work that facilitate or deter the exercise of occupational self-direction bear meaningfully on three major types of alienation. Moreover, these findings provide evidence not only for an interconnection between these conditions of occupational life and men's orientations to nonoccupational social reality but even for a causal effect. We emphasize this because of the often-stated and widely accepted argument (see particularly Seeman, 1967, 1971, and 1972b) that there is little carryover from occupational experience to nonoccupational alienation. Our results indicate, to the contrary, that there *is* carryover from occupational experience to alienation in nonoccupational realms, and that this carryover is of the logically simplest type (see Breer and Locke, 1965)—the lessons of the job are directly generalized to nonoccupational realities. Occupational experiences that limit workers' opportunities to exercise self-direction in their work are conducive to feelings of powerlessness, self-estrangement, and even normlessness.

It must be emphasized that these findings, although derived from a large and representative sample, cannot safely be generalized beyond the United States or even beyond the time the data were collected. We do not know whether these occupational conditions would exert the same alienating effects in different cultural contexts or under different economic conditions.

This research was limited to the civilian population. We do not know whether, for example, closeness of supervision would have the same alienating effect in the presumably more authoritarian system of the military. Moreover, and more important, we do not know whether the conditions determinative of occupational self-direction would matter as much in other countries and cultures. In addition, the relative importance of the various occupational conditions may be affected by economic conditions: 1964 was a time of relatively great economic security in the United States; occupational self-direction might be less important and, say, job security more important at times of greater economic uncertainty.

Much of the theoretical literature attributes alienation to conditions stemming directly from capitalism or bureaucracy or both. The data used here are far from adequate for dealing with these issues; the research was limited to one country, capitalist and heavily bureaucratized. Yet the data do bear on these themes, and insofar as they do, they consistently imply that neither capitalism nor bureaucracy is the primary source of alienation in this industrial society. Within the United States, we have found that being or not being an owner is of, at most, minor importance for feelings of powerlessness, self-estrangement, and normlessness.[11] Moreover, admittedly within capitalist society, people employed in profit-making enterprises are no more alienated than are those who work for government or for non-profit enterprises. As for bureaucratization, as already noted, its effects are opposite to what would be expected by those who see bureaucratization as a source of alienation. Our findings point, instead, to occupational conditions that impinge more directly and immediately on the worker, in particular, to his opportunities to exercise self-direction in his work. Nevertheless, these very conditions are built into the class structure of this capitalist society. It is an open question, and one well worth investigating, whether these occupational conditions have the same effects in different social and economic structures.

---

[11] We should note, though, that when one selects a representative cross-section of the employed population, almost all the owners are necessarily owners of small to medium-sized enterprises—the petty bourgeoisie, certainly not the capitalists. So when we speak of ownership having little effect on alienation, we should more properly say that this is the case for the petty bourgeoisie, but we have no information about feelings of alienation among those who command sizeable amounts of property.

SECTION III

Job Conditions and Personality: Longitudinal Analyses

These three chapters are the heart of the book. Utilizing the data of a ten-year follow-up study of a subsample of the men interviewed in the original study, we attempt to deal straightforwardly with the issue of causal directionality. In so doing, we also develop a model of the overall relationship of occupational structure and personality and reconsider the interpretation of the relationships of social stratification to job conditions and to values and orientations developed in the first chapter of this book.

Chapter 5 presents the prototypic longitudinal assessment, focusing on the most pivotal job condition, the substantive complexity of work, and one crucial facet of psychological functioning, ideational flexibility. Using maximum-likelihood confirmatory factor analysis to separate measurement error from change, we develop measurement models for both substantive complexity and intellectual flexibility. These models show that, over the ten-year time span, the over-time correlations of both phenomena, shorn of measurement error, are high, that of ideational flexibility especially so. Nevertheless, a structural-equation causal analysis demonstrates that the effect of substantive complexity on ideational flexibility is real and remarkably strong—on the order of one-fourth as great as the effect of men's earlier levels of ideational flexibility on their present ideational flexibility. The reciprocal effect of ideational flexibility on the substantive complexity of work is even more pronounced. This effect, however, occurs more gradually over time.

In Chapter 6, we greatly enlarge this model of one job condition and one facet of psychological functioning, to consider not only the substantive complexity of the work, but all structural imperatives of the job, and not only ideational flexibility, but other major dimensions of personality as well. This model shows that the substantive complexity of work is of central importance to the interrelationship of job and personality. More generally, all the structural imperatives of the job affect and are affected by major dimensions of personality.

Building on these analyses, in Chapter 7 we reassess the interrelationship of social stratification, occupational self-direction, and psychological functioning, using longitudinal data and employing much more precise methods of analysis than those employed in Chapter 1. We find the magnitudes of the relationships between social stratification and psychological functioning to be much greater than the original estimates. These analyses also provide much stronger evidence that occupational self-direction plays a pivotal role in explaining the psychological impact of social stratification.

Then, we ask the same questions about social class as those we have asked about social stratification: Is social-class position consistently and strongly related to psychological functioning? If so, are these relationships to be explained in terms of the greater opportunity to be self-directed in one's work that is available to those who are more advantageously situated in the class structure? The positive answers to both questions provide strong empirical confirmation that occupational conditions—in particular, those that facilitate or impede the exercise of occupational self-direction—play an essential role in explaining the psychological effects, not only of social stratification but also of social class.

Sample and Methods of Data Collection

The analyses in this Section of the book are longitudinal. The baseline data come from the 1964 cross-sectional survey of men employed in civilian occupations throughout the United States. In 1974, the National Opinion Research Center (N.O.R.C.) carried out a follow-up survey for us, interviewing a representative sample of approximately one-fourth of those men who were then less than 65 years old. The age limitation was imposed to increase the probability that the men in the follow-up study would still be in the labor force. The method of sample selection is presented in Appendix A.

In this as in all longitudinal studies, the question of the representativeness of the follow-up sample is crucial for assessing the accuracy of any analyses we do. Of the 883 men whom we randomly selected for the follow-up study, N.O.R.C. succeeded in locating 820 (i.e., 93 percent) ten years after the original survey—in itself an interesting social fact. Apparently men who live their lives in the ordinary institutions of the society, although they may change residences a great deal, can be traced, given a modicum of cooperation from the post office, the telephone company, past employers, and unions.

Of the 820 men located, 35 had died. Of the remaining 785 men, N.O.R.C. actually reinterviewed 687, i.e., 78 percent of those originally selected and 88 percent of those located and found to be alive. In terms of current experience in survey research, these are certainly acceptable figures. We must nevertheless ask: Are the men who were reinterviewed representative of all those men whom we meant to interview? Can we generalize safely to the larger universe? We attempt to answer these questions empirically in Appendix A. These analyses give assurance that we can analyze the longitudinal data with confidence that whatever we find can be generalized to the larger population of employed men in the United States.

5

The Reciprocal Effects of the Substantive Complexity of Work and Intellectual Flexibility: A Longitudinal Assessment*

Melvin L. Kohn
and Carmi Schooler

From early Marx to "Work in America" (HEW Task Force, 1973) it has been argued that work affects such facets of personality as values, orientations, and intellectual functioning. From early Taylor to the most recent personnel selection manuals it has been argued—or at any rate assumed—that personality is formed before occupational careers begin, with people fitting into and perhaps molding their jobs, but not being affected by their jobs. The issue of whether jobs affect or only reflect personality is obviously crucial to occupational social psychology. More than that, the issue of the nature and direction of causal effects in the relationship between occupational conditions and psychological functioning provides a critical test of a theoretical question central to the entire field of social structure and personality—whether social structure affects personality only through

* This is a revised version of a paper of the same title originally published in the *American Journal of Sociology* (Kohn and Schooler, 1978). We are indebted to Virginia Marbley, Margaret Renfors, Mimi Silberman, Pearl Slafkes, and Erma Jean Surman for invaluable technical and editorial assistance; to Bruce Roberts and Carrie Schoenbach for complex computer programming; and to Robert M. Hauser for advice on measurement models. Most important of all, we are indebted to Duane F. Alwin for teaching us the concepts underlying confirmatory factor analysis, instructing us in the use of the ACOVS and LISREL computer programs, and making innumerable suggestions without which we might never have solved the intricate technical and theoretical problems encountered in developing the measurement models described in this chapter.

its influence on childhood socialization processes or also through a continuing influence during the entire life span.

In this chapter we address the issue of the nature and direction of effects in the relationship between occupational conditions and psychological functioning by attempting to assess the reciprocal relationship between one pivotal dimension of occupational structure, the substantive complexity of work, and one pivotal dimension of psychological functioning, intellectual flexibility. We choose the substantive complexity of work as the occupational condition to be assessed in this analysis for three reasons: Our previous analyses have shown substantive complexity to be a central element of occupational structure—an important determinant of occupational self-direction and an important structural imperative of the job (see Chapter 3). Moreover, substantive complexity is as strongly correlated with psychological functioning as is any other dimension of occupation we have examined. Finally, we have excellent descriptive information about the substantive complexity of work, which we have been able to validate by comparison to the objective job assessments of trained occupational analysts.

Our choice of intellectual flexibility to be the aspect of psychological functioning assessed in this analysis is made in part because it offers us the greatest challenge—intellectual flexibility obviously affects recruitment into substantively complex jobs, and there is every reason to expect it to be one of the most resistant to change of all facets of psychological functioning we have measured. Moreover, intellectual flexibility is so important a part of psychological functioning that we must not unthinkingly assume it to be entirely the product of genetics and early life experience. Rather, we should empirically test the possibility that intellectual flexibility may be responsive to the experiences of adult life.

In earlier analyses based on the data of the 1964 cross-sectional survey, we made provisional assessments of the reciprocal relationship between the substantive complexity of work and many facets of psychological functioning, including ideational flexibility (Chapters 3 and 4). In those analyses, we used a method called two-stage least squares, a relatively simple technique for estimating reciprocal causal models. Those findings constitute *prima facie* evidence that the substantive complexity of men's work does affect their psychological functioning, independently of the selection processes that draw men into particular fields of work and independently of men's efforts to mold their jobs to fit their needs, values, and capacities. Cross-sectional data, however, cannot provide definitive evidence of causality; only analysis of longitudinal data, measuring real change in real people, can be definitive.

Moreover, while the cross-sectional data provided retrospective information about the substantive complexity of past jobs, it could not provide information about men's psychological functioning at the times they held those jobs. Thus, we had no way of statistically controlling earlier levels of ideational flexibility in assessing the effect of substantive complexity (or anything else) on ideational flexibility. Nor could we examine lagged effects: for example, we could not assess the effects of earlier levels of ideational flexibility on the substantive complexity of later jobs. Our analyses were necessarily limited to assessing the contemporaneous reciprocal effects, as of 1964, of the men's then-current levels of substantive complexity and psychological functioning. Now we are able to assess the reciprocal effects of substantive complexity and ideational flexibility much more adequately, for we have conducted a ten-year follow-up survey of a representative portion of our original sample (see Appendix A).

We begin the chapter by explaining the concepts, substantive complexity and intellectual flexibility, and developing measurement models for both of them. These models are designed to deal with the most perplexing problem of longitudinal analysis—separating errors in measurement from change in the phenomena studied. Then we utilize the data provided by the measurement models to do a causal analysis of the reciprocal effects of substantive complexity and ideational flexibility.

UNRELIABILITY AND CHANGE

We now face the core technical problem in longitudinal analysis—how to separate unreliability of measurement from change in the phenomena studied. Measurement error is always problematic in causal analyses, because the magnitudes of regression coefficients are underestimated in direct proportion to the unreliability of the independent variables. Such error is particularly problematic in analyses of reciprocal effects, where each variable in a pair is an independent variable vis-a-vis the other. The problem is further exacerbated in longitudinal analyses because of the high probability that errors in the measurement of any indicator in the original data will be correlated with errors in the measurement of that same indicator at a later time. For example, any errors in the information obtained in a baseline survey about the complexity of men's work with things or in coding that information might well be correlated with errors in the same type of information in a follow-up survey. Such correlated errors in any pair of constituent items might make the overtime stability of the underlying concept—the substantive complexity of work—seem greater or less than it really is (see Bohrnstedt, 1969). Thus, before assessing changes in substantive complexity and the reasons for such changes, we must remove the effects of correlated errors in measurement of the indicators of this concept.

Confirmatory factor analysis provides an excellent method for accomplishing this difficult task. (See Joreskog, 1969, 1970, 1973a, 1973b; Joreskog, Gruvaeus, and van Thillo, 1970; Joreskog and van Thillo, 1972;

Joreskog and Sorbom, 1976a and b; Werts, Joreskog, and Linn, 1973; Werts, Linn, and Joreskog, 1971).[1] The essence of the method lies in the use of multiple indicators for each principal concept, inferring from the co-variation of the indicators the degree to which each reflects the underlying concept that they all are hypothesized to reflect and the degree to which each reflects anything else, which for measurement purposes is considered to be error. This method enables one explicitly to model correlations in the errors, i.e., the residuals. The test of one's success in differentiating underlying concepts from errors in the indicators is how well the hypothesized model reproduces the original variance-covariance matrix of the indicators.

The first step in the use of these procedures is to develop measurement models for the principal concepts—models that will later form the basis for a causal analysis. The measurement models must specify the relationships of indicators to concepts, take account of unreliability (or measurement error) in all the items that measure a concept, and allow for the possibility that measurement errors are correlated in repeated measurements of the same phenomena.

A MEASUREMENT MODEL FOR SUBSTANTIVE COMPLEXITY

By the substantive complexity of work we mean the degree to which the work, in its very substance, requires thought and independent judgment. Substantively complex work by its very nature requires making many decisions that must take into account ill-defined or apparently conflicting contingencies. Although, in general, work with data or with people is likely to be more complex than work with things, this is not always the case, and an index of the overall complexity of the work should reflect its degree of complexity in each of these three types of activity. Work with things can vary in complexity from ditch-digging to sculpting; similarly, work with people can vary in complexity from receiving simple directions or orders to giving legal advice; and work with data can vary from reading instructions to synthesizing abstract conceptual systems.

Our information about the substantive complexity of men's work in 1964 is derived from detailed questioning of each respondent about his work with things, with data or ideas, and with people (see Chapter 1). The same questions were repeated in the follow-up survey ten years later. These questions provided the basis for seven ratings: appraisals of the complexity of each man's work with things, with data, and with people (see Appendix B); an

---

[1] Other instructive discussions of the issues involved in separating unreliability from change are Alwin, 1973, 1976; Blalock, 1969; Burt, 1973; Hauser and Goldberger, 1971; Heise, 1969, 1970, 1975; Heise and Bohrnstedt, 1970; Lord and Novick, 1968; and Wheaton, et al., 1977. Informative applications of the technique are provided in Alwin, 1973; Bielby, Hauser, and Featherman, 1977; Mason, et al., 1976; and Otto and Featherman, 1975.

appraisal of the overall complexity of his work, regardless of whether he works primarily with data, with people, or with things (Appendix B); and estimates of the amount of time he spends working at each type of activity.

In earlier analyses (Chapter 3), we subjected these seven ratings to a one-dimensional exploratory factor analysis, which we then used as the basis for creating factor scores. Now, instead of using exploratory factor analysis to create a single composite score, we treat all seven ratings of the 1964 job as "indicators" of the underlying but not directly measured concept, the substantive complexity of that job (see Figure 5.1).[2] Each indicator is conceived to reflect the underlying concept, which it measures only imperfectly, and some degree of "error" in measurement. (See Alwin, 1973:259 and note 2; see also Lord and Novick, 1968:72.) The follow-up survey asks the same questions and makes the same seven ratings. Again, we treat these ratings as indicators of the underlying concept, in this instance the substantive complexity of the job held at the time of the 1974 interview. Again, we conceive of each indicator as reflecting the underlying concept, together with some degree of measurement error. We also allow for the possibility that errors of measurement are correlated over time—that whatever errors there may be in the measurement of complexity of work with things in the 1964 job, for example, may be correlated with errors in the measurement of complexity of work with things in the 1974 job.

We have information also about the complexity of each man's work in two of his earlier jobs, the first job he held for six months or longer and the job he held immediately before his 1964 job. Both of these measures are approximate scores, based on extrapolations from limited job history information (see Chapter 3). In our earlier analyses, we treated these as two separate variables. In the present analysis, we have no real need for measures of substantive complexity at two separate times before 1964. But the logic of our measurement model calls for using multiple indicators of concepts whenever it is possible to do so; it is the multiplicity of indicators that enables us to differentiate unreliability of measurement from change in true scores. We therefore treat these two measures as indicators of a single concept, "earlier" substantive complexity.

The overall fit of this model to the data, based on a chi-squared goodness-of-fit test, is fairly good: the total chi-square is 644.42, with 94 degrees of freedom, for a ratio of 6.86 per degree of freedom. (In this test, chi-square is a function of the discrepancies between the actual variance-covariance matrix and the variance-covariance matrix implied by the mea-

---

[2] In Figure 5.1, in all subsequent Figures, and in the text, all paths and correlations are expressed in standardized form. Standardized values are more easily comprehended than metric values when the metric is not inherently meaningful. Using standardized values makes it possible to compare indicators in the measurement models and causal paths in the structural-equation models (see Blalock, 1967). All computations have been based on unstandardized variance-covariance matrices.

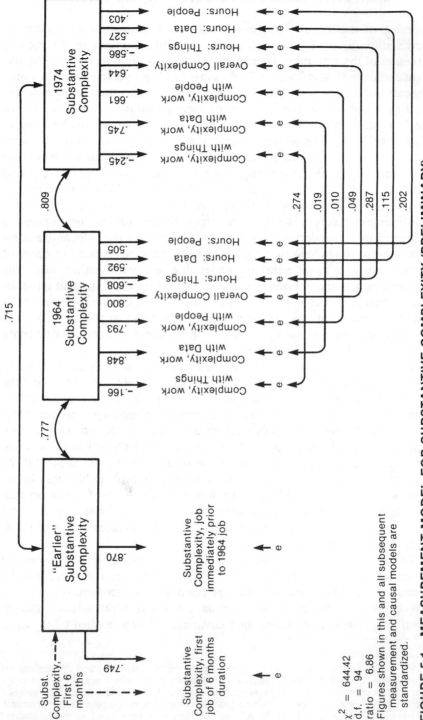

FIGURE 5.1 MEASUREMENT MODEL FOR SUBSTANTIVE COMPLEXITY (PRELIMINARY)

$\chi^2 = 644.42$
d.f. = 94
ratio = 6.86
Figures shown in this and all subsequent
measurement and causal models are
standardized.

108

surement model. For a sample of a given size, the smaller the chi-square per degree of freedom, the better the model fits the data.) An examination of the first-order partial derivatives of the maximum-likelihood function (see Costner and Schoenberg, 1973; Sorbom, 1975) indicates that the fit of model to data could be improved by taking into account other correlated errors of measurement—notably, the correlations between the residual for our overall rating of the complexity of each man's work and those for our specific ratings of the complexity of his work with things, with data, and with people. Allowing these residuals to correlate (modified model not shown) reduces the chi-square to 439.34, with 88 degrees of freedom, for a ratio of 4.99. (The difference between the initial chi-square and the chi-square in this modified model is 205.08. At 6 degrees of freedom, which is the difference between the degrees of freedom of the two models, this is clearly a statistically significant improvement.) All the parameters of this model are consistent with our earlier analyses. In particular, the complexity of work with data and with people and the overall complexity of the work are shown to bear a strong positive relationship to the underlying concept, while the amount of time spent working with things is shown to be strongly negatively related to the concept, in both 1964 and 1974. In these respects, the model accurately reflects both our theoretical intent (see Chapter 1) and the factor loadings of the earlier exploratory factor analysis (see Chapter 3).

There is, however, one flaw in this model, as well as in the earlier exploratory factor analysis: The complexity of men's work with things is depicted as being negatively related to the substantive complexity of their work. In principle, complexity of work in any realm—with things, as well as with data or with people—should contribute to the overall substantive complexity of the job. What our model actually reflects is that we had classified men who do not work with things into the lowest category of complexity of work with things; thus, men who work entirely with data or with people are classified together with unskilled laborers in the lowest category and are contrasted to men who do complex work with things.

To achieve a model fully congruent with our theoretical intent, we exclude all men who do not work with things from the computation of correlations involving this indicator, on the rationale that not working with things is qualitatively different from working with things at a low level of complexity.[3] (Concretely, we treat not working with things as if it were

---

[3] It is neither necessary nor desirable to follow a similar procedure for men who do not work with data or with people. For the measurement of substantive complexity, the logical implications of not working with things are different from those of not working with data or with people. Not working with things does not necessarily imply anything about the substantive complexity of the job; certainly it is possible to do substantively complex work that does not involve the direct manipulation of physical objects. On the other hand, not working with written materials or with people does imply a low level of substantive complexity; it is hard to imagine a substantively complex job that does not require some reading (e.g., of blueprints or specifications) and some discussion with supervisors, co-workers, or others.

"missing data" and use pairwise deletion in computing the correlations). Again, we allow the residual of each indicator to correlate with the residual of that same indicator ten years later. As with the earlier model, the fit of model to data is improved by taking into account other correlated residuals. In this model, the correlations of residuals that best improve the fit of model to data are those between the complexity of work with things and the amount of time spent working with things, with data, and with people, both intratime and over time.[4] With these residuals allowed to correlate (see Figure 5.2), the overall chi-square is 413.81, with 82 degrees of freedom, for a ratio of 5.05, which is nearly the same as that provided by the earlier model. What is more important, this model matches our theoretical intent exactly. The difference in the fit of model to data being minimal and the fit of model to theory being much better, we shall employ the model depicted in Figure 5.2 in our causal analyses. To be certain that the causal inferences we draw are not somehow an artifact of the choice of measurement model, we have also computed correlations for the alternative measurement model. Using this model would make no difference in the inferences we draw about the reciprocal effects of substantive complexity and intellectual flexibility.

The most interesting information provided by the measurement model depicted in Figure 5.2 is the estimates of the overtime correlations of job complexity. The correlations, as expected, are substantial; for example, the correlation between the substantive complexity of the 1964 job and that of the 1974 job is .77. The actual effect of earlier jobs on later jobs, as compared to the effect of other variables, can only be assessed in the causal analyses to come, when other independent variables are simultaneously considered. What the measurement model does tell us is that there has been considerable consistency in the substantive complexity of the men's jobs over the course of their careers.

A MEASUREMENT MODEL FOR INTELLECTUAL FLEXIBILITY

Our index of intellectual flexibility is meant to reflect men's actual intellectual performance in the interview situation. In the 1964 interview, we sampled a variety of indicators—including the men's answers to seemingly simple but highly revealing cognitive problems involving well-known issues, their handling of perceptual and projective tests, their propensity to "agree" when asked agree-disagree questions, and the impression they made on the interviewer during a long session that required a great deal of thought and reflection. None of these indicators is assumed to be completely

---

[4] It seems reasonable that these residuals might be correlated, because men's descriptions or evaluations of their work with things might well affect or be affected by their estimates of how much time they spend working in each type of activity. Moreover, measurement errors may be similar for both interviews.

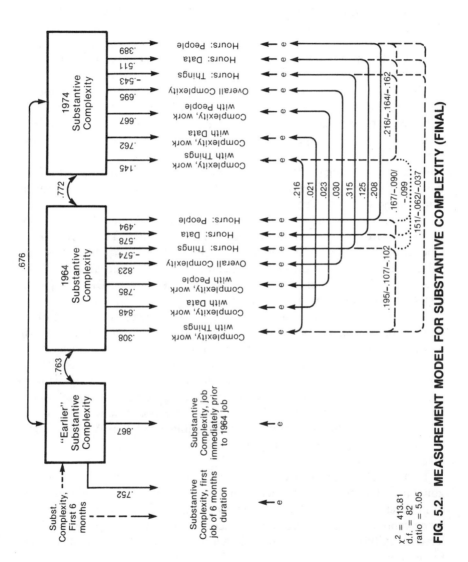

$\chi^2 = 413.81$
d.f. = 82
ratio = 5.05

FIG. 5.2. MEASUREMENT MODEL FOR SUBSTANTIVE COMPLEXITY (FINAL)

valid; but we do assume that all the indicators reflect, in some substantial degree, men's flexibility in attempting to cope with the intellectual demands of a complex situation.

We claim neither that this index measures innate intellectual ability nor that intellectual flexibility evidenced in the interview situation is necessarily identical to intellectual flexibility as it might be manifested in other situations; we do not have enough information about the situational variability of intellectual functioning to be certain. We do claim that our index reflects men's actual intellectual functioning in a non-work situation that seemed to elicit considerable intellectual effort from nearly all the respondents. That our index is not artifactual, and that it measures an enduring characteristic, is attested to by the evidence—to be presented shortly—of its remarkably high stability over time. Spaeth's (1976) analysis adds to the credibility of the index by showing that the correlations between an earlier variant of this index and various social phenomena are similar to those for more conventional indices of intellectual functioning.

More concretely and specifically, our index (see Figure 5.3) is based on seven indicators of each man's intellectual performance. These are: (1) The Goodenough estimate of his intelligence (see Witkin, et al., 1962), based on a detailed evaluation of the Draw-A-Person test; (2) the appraisal of Witkin et al. (1962) of the sophistication of body-concept in the Draw-A-Person test; (3) a summary score for his performance on a portion of the Embedded Figures test (see Witkin, et al., 1962); (4) the interviewer's appraisal of the man's intelligence; (5) the frequency with which he agreed when asked the many agree-disagree questions included in the interview; (6) a rating of the adequacy of his answer to the apparently simple cognitive problem: "What are all the arguments you can think of for and against allowing cigarette commercials on TV?" and (7) a rating of the adequacy of his answer to another relatively simple cognitive problem, "Suppose you wanted to open a hamburger stand and there were two locations available. What questions would you consider in deciding which of the two locations offers a better business opportunity?"

In the analyses described in Chapters 2 and 3, we performed an orthogonal principal components factor analysis of these various manifestations of intellectual flexibility. That analysis yielded two dimensions, one primarily perceptual, the other ideational. Since the ideational component of intellectual flexibility is of much greater theoretical interest, our analyses have focused on that dimension.

In the follow-up study, we secured entirely comparable data, after elaborate pre-testing to be certain that the cognitive problems had the same meaning in 1974 as in 1964. The measurement model we now employ for intellectual flexibility is similar to that for substantive complexity in most respects, with the following exceptions. First, following the logic of the two-factor model derived from the earlier exploratory factor analysis of intellec-

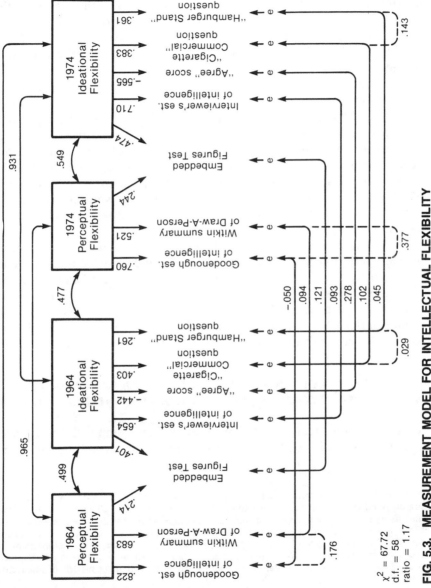

$\chi^2 = 67.72$
d.f. = 58
ratio = 1.17

FIG. 5.3. MEASUREMENT MODEL FOR INTELLECTUAL FLEXIBILITY

tual flexibility, we posit two concepts underlying the seven indicators.[5] Second, we have no assessments of intellectual flexibility prior to 1964, so there is nothing comparable to "earlier" substantive complexity. Third, to take into account that two of our indicators are based on the same task, the Draw-a-Person test, we allow their residuals to be correlated. Finally, following a lead provided by the first-order partial derivatives, we also allow for the possibility of the residuals of the two cognitive problems being correlated.

Figure 5.3 depicts the measurement model for intellectual flexibility, with the two underlying concepts allowed to correlate. The model shows that some of the indicators of intellectual flexibility are not especially reliable; this is the very reason we thought it necessary to construct a measurement model that would differentiate unreliability of measurement from actual intellectual functioning. Judging by the goodness-of-fit test, the model is successful in achieving this objective: the overall chi-square is 67.72, with 58 degrees of freedom, for a ratio of 1.17, which means that the model provides a very good approximation to the actual variances and covariances of the indicators.

In the causal analyses, we shall focus on the ideational component of intellectual flexibility. From the measurement model, we learn that the correlation between men's levels of ideational flexibility in 1964 and their levels of ideational flexibility in 1974, shorn of measurement error, is a very substantial .93. Clearly, there has been great consistency in men's levels of ideational flexibility over the ten year period.[6] The question for causal analysis is whether job conditions have nevertheless had some effect.

CAUSAL ANALYSIS: THE RECIPROCAL EFFECTS OF SUBSTANTIVE COMPLEXITY AND IDEATIONAL FLEXIBILITY

To do structural-equation causal analyses, we have computed the variances and the (unstandardized) covariances for the "true scores" for job com-

---

[5] We get slightly different estimates of the parameters of the measurement model, depending on whether we posit (as in the exploratory factor analysis of Chapter 2) that the two underlying concepts are necessarily orthogonal to each other or that they are possibly correlated with one another. Because the nonorthogonal model provides a significantly better fit to the data, we shall employ it in the causal analyses that follow. (In any event, estimates of the reciprocal effects of substantive complexity and ideational flexibility prove to be virtually identical whether based on orthogonal or on nonorthogonal measurement models of intellectual flexibility.)

[6] Parenthetically, the correlation between an index of ideational flexibility based on factor scores derived from exploratory factor analysis of the 1964 data and a similar index based on the same factor loadings for 1974 is a much lower .59. This finding dramatically illustrates a moral that methodologists have long been preaching—that correlations may be radically understated when they are not corrected for the attenuation that results from unreliability of measurement.

plexity at the various stages of career, ideational flexibility in 1964 and in 1974, and all the other variables that will enter into the analyses.[7] These variances and covariances are the data on which the causal models of the reciprocal relationship between substantive complexity and ideational flexibility are based.[8]

A reciprocal relationship can occur contemporaneously (albeit not necessarily instantaneously) or more gradually over time. Our earlier analyses, using cross-sectional data, could consider only contemporaneous effects. There is, however, no reason in principle why substantive complexity and ideational flexibility might not affect each other both contemporaneously and more gradually over time. We shall therefore assess causal models that allow the possibility of both contemporaneous and "lagged" reciprocal effects (see Figure 5.4).

The model depicted in Figure 5.4 includes as potentially pertinent exogenous variables all social characteristics that prior research literature and our own earlier analyses give us any reason to believe might affect either substantive complexity or ideational flexibility. We thus include in the model the respondent's own age and level of education, his mother's and his father's levels of education, his father's occupational level, his maternal and paternal grandfathers' occupational levels, his race, national background, and religious background, the urbanness and region of the country of the principal place where he was raised, and even the number of brothers and sisters he had. We also include as exogenous variables the respondent's 1964 levels of substantive complexity and ideational flexibility, as well as the substantive complexity of his "earlier" (pre-1964) jobs.

In contemporaneous-effects models (and other "nonrecursive" models), the number of parameters to be estimated will be greater than the amount of information provided by the intercorrelations among the variables, unless some assumptions are imposed on the model, usually by setting some path(s) to zero. (Alternatively, one can impose other restrictions on the model, e.g., as we have in fact done, by not allowing the residuals to be correlated.) The problem of insufficient information is generally referred to as the "identification" problem. A variable that identifies an equation by not being allowed to have a direct effect on the dependent variable of that equation is called an instrument. For an instrument to identify an equation meaningfully, there must be good theoretical justification that its effect

---

[7] Our procedure has been to develop measurement models independently for each concept, compute the covariances among "true scores", and use these covariances as the data for causal analysis.

[8] In developing the causal (i.e., linear structural equation) models, we employed the LISREL computer program (Joreskog and van Thillo, 1972), as subsequently modified by Ronald Schoenberg. Pertinent writings on the strategy of this type of causal analysis are Burt, 1976; Duncan, 1975; Heise, 1970, 1975; Joreskog, 1973b, 1977; Joreskog and Sorbom, 1976a; Werts, Joreskog, and Linn, 1973; and Werts, Linn, and Joreskog, 1971.

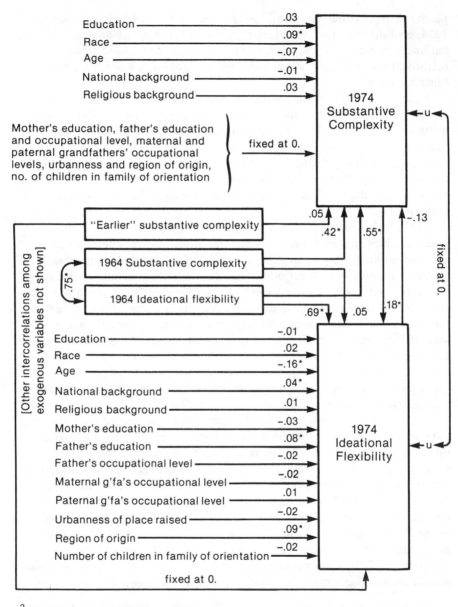

Education ——————————— .03
Race ——————————————— .09*
Age ——————————————— -.07
National background ——————— -.01
Religious background ——————— .03

1974
Substantive
Complexity

Mother's education, father's education
and occupational level, maternal and
paternal grandfathers' occupational
levels, urbanness and region of origin,
no. of children in family of orientation } fixed at 0.

—u—

[Other intercorrelations among exogenous variables not shown]

"Earlier" substantive complexity ———— .05
.42*
1964 Substantive complexity ————————
.75*
1964 Ideational flexibility ————————
.69*
.55*
.05
.18*
-.13

fixed at 0.

Education ——————————— -.01
Race ——————————————— .02
Age ——————————————— -.16*
National background ——————— .04*
Religious background ——————— .01
Mother's education ——————— -.03
Father's education ——————— .08*
Father's occupational level ———— -.02
Maternal g'fa's occupational level — -.02
Paternal g'fa's occupational level — .01
Urbanness of place raised ———— -.02
Region of origin ——————————— .09*
Number of children in family of orientation — -.02

1974
Ideational
Flexibility

—u—

fixed at 0.

χ^2 (for the causal model) = 10.42
d.f. = 144
ratio = 0.07
* = Statistically significant, $p \leq .05$.

**FIG. 5.4. RECIPROCAL EFFECTS OF SUBSTANTIVE COMPLEXITY AND
IDEATIONAL FLEXIBILITY: FULL MODEL**

should only be indirect and the instrument must be correlated with the variable it is not allowed to affect directly. The stronger the correlation between the instrument and the dependent variable, the more efficacious the instrument for identifying the equation. (For lucid discussions of this complex topic, see Duncan, 1967 and 1975:81-90; and Heise, 1975:160–181. Still pertinent is Simon's (1957) now-classic essay on the subject.)

Thus, for our model to be adequately identified, the direct effects of one or more exogenous variables on 1974 ideational flexibility must be fixed at some value, e.g., zero; similarly, the direct effects of one or more exogenous variables on 1974 substantive complexity must also be fixed at zero or some other value; otherwise there will be too little empirical information to solve the equations unequivocally. To identify the equation for 1974 substantive complexity, we posit that social background characteristics that would not be interpreted as job credentials by employers (even by discriminatory employers) do not directly affect the substantive complexity of the 1974 job; these variables are thus used as instruments to identify the equation. The rationale is that these variables—maternal and paternal education, paternal occupational level, maternal and paternal grandfathers' occupational levels, urbanness and region of origin, and number of children in the parental family—may very likely have affected men's job placement earlier in their careers. By the time that men are at least ten years into their careers, though, these variables should no longer have any direct effect on the substantive complexity of their jobs, certainly not when the substantive complexity of their "earlier" and 1964 jobs are statistically controlled. Similarly, we posit that the substantive complexity of "earlier" jobs should have no direct effect on the men's ideational flexibility in 1974, when the substantive complexity of their 1964 and 1974 jobs are statistically controlled.[9]

As Figure 5.4 shows, the substantive complexity of the jobs the men held in 1964 is an important determinant of the substantive complexity of the jobs they held ten years later; their ideational flexibility in 1964 is an even more important determinant of their ideational flexibility at the later time. The stabilities of both phenomena, particularly of ideational flexibility, are high. Nevertheless, the reciprocal effects of substantive complexity and ideational flexibility are considerable.

---

[9] These overidentifying restrictions raise a question as to whether the number of degrees of freedom computed by LISREL and presented in Figures 5.4 and 5.5 is correct. Some contend that the correct number of degrees of freedom for an overidentified model based on a covariance matrix of "true scores" should exclude those degrees of freedom deriving from the overidentifying restrictions. We do not find this argument convincing. In any event, the number of degrees of freedom in structural-equation models is important primarily for giving a comparative basis for evaluating the magnitudes of the chi-squares of alternative models. What really matters in making these comparative judgments is that the procedures be consistent.

The effect of substantive complexity on ideational flexibility is approximately one-fourth as great as the effect of men's ten year earlier levels of ideational flexibility. This effect is essentially contemporaneous: The lagged path from 1964 substantive complexity to 1974 ideational flexibility is a statistically nonsignificant .05, while the contemporaneous path from 1974 substantive complexity is, at .18, more substantial and statistically significant.[10]

A path of .18 might not in ordinary circumstances be considered especially striking; but a continuing effect of this magnitude on so stable a phenomenon as ideational flexibility is impressive, for the cumulative impact is much greater than the immediate effect at any one time. Continuing effects, even small-to-moderate continuing effects, on highly stable phenomena become magnified in importance. The effect of the substantive complexity of work on ideational flexibility is especially noteworthy when we take into account that we are dealing with men no younger than 26 years of age, who are at least ten years into their occupational careers.

The reciprocal effect of ideational flexibility on substantive complexity is even more impressive—surpassing that of the substantive complexity of the 1964 job. This effect is entirely lagged, i.e., it is the men's ideational flexibility in 1964, not contemporaneously, that significantly affects the substantive complexity of their 1974 jobs. The longitudinal analysis thus demonstrates that, over time, the relationship between substantive complexity and ideational flexibility is truly reciprocal. The effect of substantive complexity on ideational flexibility is more rapid: the demands of the current job affect current thinking processes. Ideational flexibility, by contrast, has a delayed effect on substantive complexity: current ideational flexibility does not affect current job demands, but it will have a sizeable effect on the further course of one's career.

Have we somehow misspecified the equations, leaving out some important variables that might alter the overall picture or in some other way misconceiving the true picture? Since no structural model can ever be "proved" (Duncan, 1975), but can only be compared to other plausible models, all reasonable alternatives must be considered.

One indication that the equations have not been seriously misspecified is that if we allow the residuals for 1974 substantive complexity and 1974 ideational flexibility to be correlated, the correlation proves to be nonsignificant and the estimates of all parameters remain essentially unchanged. Thus, it

---

[10] A cautionary note is in order here. Our analysis does not take into account the length of time the men have been in their present jobs; thus, all we mean by "contemporaneous" is that the effect results from the job currently held (however long it has been held, short of ten years), not from any previous job. A more exact appraisal of the timing of job effects would be exceedingly difficult to accomplish without measurements of both substantive complexity and ideational flexibility at more frequent intervals than we have made.

seems unlikely that some important variable affecting both substantive complexity and ideational flexibility has been left out of the model. More-over, the results do not depend on our choice of instruments, for using a variety of other instruments does not appreciably change the results. Nor do our findings result from the presence of statistically nonsignificant social background characteristics in the model, for deleting the nonsignificant so-cial characteristics from the predictive equations does not affect our conclu-sions. In particular, the effect of substantive complexity on ideational flexibility is slightly strengthened by the deletion of social characteristics that do not have statistically significant effects. The model is robust, what-ever reasonable modifications we try.

Finally, our findings do not result from our having fixed the values of the measurement models before estimating the causal model (see Burt, 1973). We have confirmed the causal model by developing a model in which both measurement and causal parameters are estimated simultaneously. This model confirms both the measurement models and the causal model de-picted in Figure 5.4. In particular, it shows the effect of substantive com-plexity on ideational flexibility to be contemporaneous and of the same magnitude as previously shown. The effect of ideational flexibility on sub-stantive complexity is again shown to be lagged. The magnitude of this path, too, is exactly the same as in Figure 5.4.

The one anomaly in the model shown in Figure 5.4 is that the path from 1974 ideational flexibility to 1974 substantive complexity is not just statisti-cally nonsignificant, it is negative. Despite its statistical nonsignificance, the existence of such a negative path suggests a problem of multicollinearity (see Blalock, 1963; Farrar and Glauber, 1967; and Gordon, 1968), probably resulting from the very high correlation ($r = .93$) between 1964 and 1974 ideational flexibility. When we use indices of both 1964 and 1974 ideational flexibility as independent variables vis-a-vis substantive complexity, we probably exaggerate the importance of 1964 ideational flexibility while creating an artificially negative effect for 1974 ideational flexibility. A more clearcut assessment of the effect of ideational flexibility on substantive complexity requires our dropping the statistically nonsignificant contempo-raneous path from the model. Similarly, a clearcut assessment of the effect of substantive complexity on ideational flexibility requires our dropping the statistically nonsignificant lagged path from the model. Therefore, in Fig-ure 5.5 we delete these (and all other) nonsignificant paths and re-estimate the model. This, we believe, represents a more accurate assessment of the overall effects of substantive complexity and ideational flexibility on each other.

This model shows the contemporaneous effect of substantive complexity on ideational flexibility to be of virtually the same magnitude (a path of .17) as that shown in Figure 5.4. Even with a slightly higher estimate of the

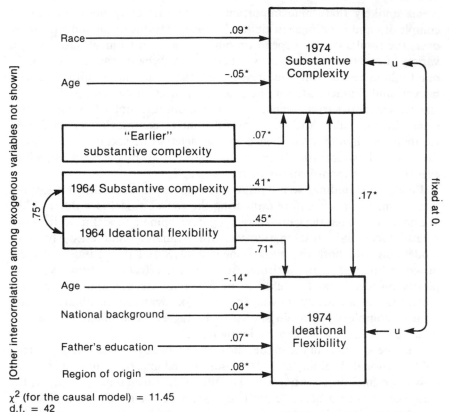

χ^2 (for the causal model) = 11.45
d.f. = 42
ratio = 0.27
* = Statistically significant, $p \leq .05$.

**FIGURE 5.5 RECIPROCAL EFFECTS OF SUBSTANTIVE COMPLEXITY
AND IDEATIONAL FLEXIBILITY: SIGNIFICANT PATHS ONLY**

stability of ideational flexibility (at .71), the effect of substantive complexity on ideational flexibility remains nearly one-fourth as great as that of the men's 10-year earlier levels of ideational flexibility.

The lagged effect of ideational flexibility on substantive complexity (a path of .45) is not quite so great as it had appeared to be before we removed the nonsignificant, negative contemporaneous path in Figure 5.4, but by any other standard it is very large. Ideational flexibility surpasses even the substantive complexity of men's 1964 jobs as a determinant of the substantive complexity of their 1974 jobs.

Just as we did for the model depicted in Figure 5.4, we have confirmed Figure 5.5 by developing a model in which measurement and causal parameters are simultaneously estimated.[11] All parameters of the measurement models for both substantive complexity and ideational flexibility are very close to those shown in Figures 5.2 and 5.3, most of them nearly identical. The causal model, too, is confirmed, the contemporaneous path from substantive complexity to ideational flexibility being exactly as we had found it to be in Figure 5.5 (.17), the lagged path from ideational flexibility to substantive complexity being slightly lower (.41 instead of .45). All other causal parameters are very close to those shown in Figure 5.5.

The data thus demonstrate, beyond reasonable doubt, what heretofore could be stated as only a plausible thesis buttressed by presumptive evidence—that the substantive complexity of men's work both considerably affects, and is considerably affected by, their ideational flexibility.

DISCUSSION

There are several limitations to the analyses reported in this chapter: some, we remedy in later chapters; others may be beyond our ingenuity or the scope of our data.

One obvious limitation is that our analysis has thus far been restricted to substantive complexity and ideational flexibility. In Chapter 6, we shall develop a more general model of job structure and measurement models for other facets of psychological functioning; we shall also develop a causal model of the overall relationship between job structure and psychological functioning.

Second, the present analysis, as was true of all our previous analyses of occupational conditions, deals only with men. This lack will be remedied in Chapter 8.

A third limitation is that, although our measurement models take account of unreliability in indicators of the two central concepts, they have not dealt with possible unreliability of measurement for education, race, age, or any other aspect of social background. Our own data do not provide any solid basis for assessing reliability of measurement of these variables, and we are dubious about using reliability coefficients derived from other bodies of data as the basis for correcting correlations for attenuation. It would probably not make any real difference in the causal analysis; without evidence, however, the issue must be left unresolved.

Fourth, conspicuously lacking in our treatment of these data is a systematic analysis of "career" patterns. We have treated prior jobs (and even the

---

[11] The chi-square for the combined measurement-causal model comparable to Figure 5.4 is 1035.23, with 546 degrees of freedom, for a ratio of 1.90, a remarkably good fit of model to data for so complex a model based on so large a number of cases. The chi-square for the combined model comparable to Figure 5.5 is nearly the same—1036.68, with 548 degrees of freedom, for a ratio of 1.89. Nothing is lost in the fit of model to data in simplifying the model.

same job, held ten years earlier) as if all series of jobs were equally continuous or discontinuous along some meaningful career line. A more realistic conceptualization would have to take account that some job changes represent logical progressions in a meaningful sequence, while others represent shifts out of one career sequence, perhaps into another. We know of no really satisfactory way of dealing with this issue, despite early efforts by Wilensky (1961) and several more recent efforts by others (e.g., Ladinsky, 1976) at classifying career patterns.

Fifth, both our measurement models and our causal models assume that relationships among variables are essentially the same for all segments of the work force. The assumption is obviously testable, although we recognize that a thorough assessment may require a much larger body of data than ours. It would be especially desirable to examine these models separately for workers at different ages and at different stages of career.

Sixth, as must be apparent to the reader, changes in occupational circumstances are not the only changes that people experience in a ten-year interval: some marry, or divorce, or become widowed; traumas and joyous events occur; these and other occurrences may exacerbate, mitigate, or deflect the processes our models depict. We have information about these events, but the depth of the data and the size of the sample may not be adequate for causal analysis of so complex a process.

Despite these limitations, we believe that we have shown, more definitively than has ever been shown before, that the relationship between occupational conditions and psychological functioning is reciprocal: Occupational conditions both affect and are affected by psychological functioning.

These findings come down solidly in support of those who see occupational conditions as affecting personality and in opposition to those who see the relationship between occupational conditions and personality as resulting solely from selective recruitment and job-molding. We do not deny that personality has great importance in determining who go into what types of jobs and how they perform those jobs; in fact, our analyses underline the importance of these processes. That has never been seriously at issue. What has been disputed is whether the reverse phenomenon—of job conditions molding personality—also occurs. The evidence of our study unequivocally supports the position that it does occur. Thus our findings bear directly on an issue central to the field of social structure and personality—whether social-structural conditions affect personality only during childhood socialization or continue to affect personality throughout adulthood. Here is clear evidence that one important facet of social structure—the substantive complexity of work—directly affects adult personality.

In particular, this study adds to and helps specify the growing evidence that the structure of the environment has an important effect on cognitive development (see Rosenbaum, 1976) and that cognitive processes do not become impervious to environmental influence after adolescence or early adulthood, but continue to show "plasticity" throughout the life span (see Baltes, 1968; Baltes and Schaie, 1976; but see Horn and Donaldson, 1976). Our findings reinforce this conclusion by showing that ideational flexibility continues to be responsive to experience well into mid-career and probably beyond. In fact, it appears that the remarkable stability of ideational flexibility reflects, at least in part, stability in people's life circumstances. Ideational flexibility is ever-responsive to changes in the substantive complexity of people's work; for most people, though, the substantive complexity of work does not fluctuate markedly.

This study demonstrates as well the important impact of ideational flexibility on substantive complexity. We think it noteworthy that this effect appears to be lagged, rather than contemporaneous. The implication is that the structure of most jobs does not permit any considerable variation in the substantive complexity of the work: job conditions are not readily modified to suit the needs or capacities of the individual worker. Over a long enough time, though—certainly over a period as long as ten years—many men either modify their jobs or move on to other jobs more consonant with their intellectual functioning. Thus, the long-term effects of ideational flexibility on substantive complexity are considerable, even though the contemporaneous effects appear to be negligible.

Our models, of course, start in mid- or later career. There is every reason to believe that men's levels of ideational flexibility in childhood, adolescence, and early adulthood may have had an important effect on their educational attainments, and our data show that educational attainment has had an extremely important effect on the substantive complexity of the early jobs in men's careers. Since the substantive complexity of early jobs is a primary determinant of the substantive complexity of later jobs, it seems safe to infer that ideational flexibility's long-term, indirect effect on the substantive complexity of later jobs has been even greater than our analysis depicts.[12]

In the broadest sense, our findings support our general strategy for stu-

---

[12] The reciprocal relationship between substantive complexity and ideational flexibility implies also an internal dynamic by which relatively small differences in substantive complexity at early stages of a career may become magnified into larger differences in both substantive complexity and ideational flexibility later in the career. If two men of equivalent ideational flexibility were to start their careers in jobs differing in substantive complexity, the man in the more complex job would likely outstrip the other in further intellectual growth. This, in time, might lead to his attaining jobs of greater complexity, further affecting his intellectual growth. Meantime, the man in the less complex job would develop intellectually at a slower pace, perhaps not at all, and in the extreme case might even decline in his intellectual functioning. As a result, small differences in the substantive complexity of early jobs might lead to increasing differences in intellectual development.

dying the relationship between social structure and personality. We have consistently argued that, in interpreting the relationship between social structure and individual psychological functioning, one should always ask how a person's position in the larger social structure affects the conditions of life that directly impinge on him (see Chapters 1, 3, and 11; see also Kohn, 1963, 1969, 1977; Schooler, 1972; and Olsen, 1974). Thus, in attempting to interpret the relationship of social stratification with values and orientations, we saw stratification-related differences in occupational conditions as a potentially important bridge between position in the hierarchical ordering of society and conceptions of reality (Chapter 1). Substantive complexity is particularly important for, on the one hand, the substantive complexity of work is closely linked to the job's location in the stratification system and, on the other, the substantive complexity of people's work is correlated with their values and orientations. Our past research demonstrated that the relationship of social stratification with values and orientation could reasonably be attributed, in large degree, to differences in such occupational conditions as substantive complexity. But not even our two-stage least squares analysis (Chapter 3) demonstrated conclusively that substantive complexity has an actual causal effect on values, orientations, or any other psychological phenomenon. The present analysis buttresses our analytic strategy by showing that substantive complexity actually does have a causal impact on one pivotal aspect of psychological functioning, ideational flexibility.

Admittedly, the present analysis has not demonstrated that substantive complexity directly affects values or self-conceptions or social orientations —in fact, anything other than ideational flexibility. Still, ideational flexibility is a crucial test. Because of its remarkable stability, ideational flexibility offers the most difficult challenge to the hypothesis that substantive complexity actually affects some important aspect of psychological functioning. Moreover, ideational flexibility is tremendously important in its own right. Finally, we see ideational flexibility as intimately related to values, self-conceptions, and social orientations. Thus, demonstrating the causal impact of substantive complexity on ideational flexibility gives us every reason to expect substantive complexity to have a causal impact on values and orientations, too. In subsequent chapters, we shall assess the hypothesized causal impact of substantive complexity—and of other structural imperatives of the job—on values, self-conceptions, and social orientations. For now, one crucial causal link in the relationship between social structure and psychological functioning has been conclusively demonstrated.

Job Conditions and Personality: A Longitudinal Assessment of Their Reciprocal Effects*

Melvin L. Kohn and Carmi Schooler

In this chapter, we continue to assess the effects of men's working conditions on their personalities and the effects of their personalities on their
working conditions.[1] In Chapter 5, using confirmatory factor analysis and
linear structural-equations causal analysis, we did a prototypic longitudinal
analysis of the reciprocal effects of the substantive complexity of work and
ideational flexibility. That analysis yielded convincing evidence that the
substantive complexity of work both affects and is affected by this ob-

* This is a revised version of a paper of the same title originally published in the *American
Journal of Sociology* (Kohn and Schooler, 1982). We are indebted to several people for essential help: to Ronald Schoenberg for repeatedly and ingeniously modifying the computer program to meet our ever-increasing needs and for advice on identifying complex
reciprocal-effects models; to Carrie Schoenbach, Bruce Roberts, and Margaret Renfors for
conscientious and thoughtful computer programming and data-analysis; and to Virginia
Marbley for uncomplainingly and effectively transcribing innumerable revisions of this chapter. The models in this chapter were estimated by MILS, an advanced version of LISREL
(Joreskog and van Thillo, 1972) developed by Ronald Schoenberg.

[1] Other evidence of job conditions affecting critical aspects of personality is provided by
studies done subsequent to the publication of the papers that have become Chapters 3 and 4 of
this book. Many of these studies are reviewed in Kohn (1977; 1981b) and in Chapter 12 of this
book. The most pertinent are the longitudinal studies by Mortimer and Lorence (1979a, b).
Also pertinent are the longitudinal studies by Andrisani and Abeles (1976), Andrisani and
Nestel (1976), and Brousseau (1978), and the cross-sectional studies by Coburn and Edwards
(1976), Grabb (1981a), Hoff and Gruneisen (1978), St. Peter (1975), and our colleagues' and
our study of women's job conditions and psychological functioning (Chapter 8 of this book).

viously important facet of psychological functioning. In the present analysis, we enlarge the causal model to take into account not only a broader range of job conditions, but also a broader range of psychological variables. The goal of this chapter is to develop and assess a general model of the reciprocal effects of job conditions and major dimensions of personality.

JOB CONDITIONS

The present analysis focuses on fourteen job conditions that have substantial impact on men's psychological functioning, independent of each other and of education. Together, they identify a man's place in the organizational structure, his opportunities for occupational self-direction, the principal job pressures to which he is subject, and the principal extrinsic risks and rewards built into his job.

Specifically, the aspects of an individual's place in the organizational structure that we consider are ownership, bureaucratization, and hierarchical position. The facets of occupational self-direction that we measure are the substantive complexity of the work, the closeness of supervision, and the degree of routinization. The job pressures are time-pressure, heaviness, dirtiness, and the number of hours worked in the average week. The extrinsic risks and rewards are the probability of being held responsible for things outside one's control, the risk of losing one's job or business, job protections, and job income. As we did with a similar but not identical set of job conditions in Chapter 3, we call these fourteen conditions the *structural imperatives* of the job.[2] They are "structural" in two senses: They are built into the structure of the job and they are a function of the job's location in the structures of the economy and the society. These job conditions are "imperatives" in that they define the occupational realities that every worker must face.

---

[2] In Chapter 3, we used the term, structural imperatives of the job, to describe a set of twelve job conditions. Three job conditions have been added to those we then called the structural imperatives of the job and one has been deleted. We add job protections and job income because an analysis of bureaucratization (Chapter 2) suggested that these, along with the substantive complexity of work, might be important mediating conditions through which the individual's position in the organizational structure affects his psychological functioning. Hours worked per week is added because our analysis of women's job conditions and psychological functioning (Chapter 8) indicates that for women, where hours of work are highly variable, this is an important job condition; for comparability, we now include it in the analysis of men. Deleted from the set is the respondent's estimate of the probability, in his field, of a "sudden and dramatic change in income, reputation, or position." There are two reasons for doubting that this is really a job condition. The question refers to a career contingency rather than a job condition. Moreover, we have only limited information about whether the individual believes that the "sudden and dramatic change" might result from externally imposed conditions or from his own achievements or failures.

A Measurement Model of Occupational Self-direction

We begin with a measurement model of *occupational self-direction,* by which we mean the use of initiative, thought, and independent judgment in work. Since the three job conditions that facilitate or inhibit the exercise of occupational self-direction—substantive complexity, closeness of supervision, and routinization—reflect one overarching concept, and since we have multiple indicators of two of them, we have developed a combined model, presented in Figure 6.1, that encompasses all three.

We define the *substantive complexity of work* as the degree to which performance of the work requires thought and independent judgment. Substantively complex work by its very nature requires making many decisions that must take into account ill-defined or apparently conflicting contingencies. Substantive complexity of work is measured as in Chapter 5; the measurement model there developed is now incorporated into a larger model of occupational self-direction.

Closeness of supervision limits one's opportunities for occupational self-direction: A worker cannot exercise occupational self-direction if he is closely supervised, although not being closely supervised does not necessarily mean that he is required or even free to use initiative, thought, and independent judgment. Closeness of supervision is measured by a worker's subjective appraisals of his freedom to disagree with his supervisor, how closely he is supervised, the extent to which his supervisor tells him what to do rather than discussing it with him, and the importance in his job of doing what one is told to do (see Chapter 1).

Routinization is the final facet of occupational self-direction. Highly routinized (repetitive and predictable) jobs restrict possibilities for exercising initiative, thought, and judgment, while jobs with a variety of unpredictable tasks may facilitate or even require self-direction. Respondents' work was coded from most variable (the work involves doing different things in different ways and one cannot predict what may come up) to least variable (the work is unvaryingly repetitive).[3]

The measurement model for occupational self-direction, including the correlations of residuals depicted in Figure 6.1, provides a good fit to the

---

[3] Our present treatment of routinization differs from earlier analyses, where we indexed routinization by two questions, one about the repetitiveness of the work tasks, the other about the complexity of the "units" of which the work is comprised. Confirmatory factor analysis reveals that the nature of the units of work reflects not only routinization but also substantive complexity and even how closely the work is supervised. Faced with the choice of a single indicator of routinization or a needlessly complex measurement model, we elect to use the single indicator. We are, however, adding to the index of repetitiveness by including further information from the interviews about the predictability of non-repetitive work.

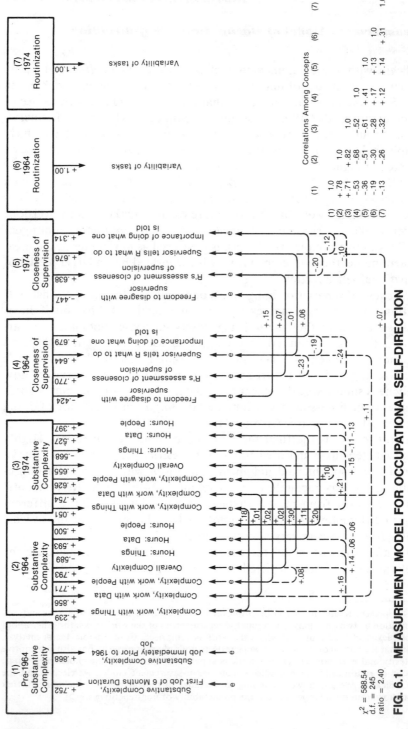

FIG. 6.1. MEASUREMENT MODEL FOR OCCUPATIONAL SELF-DIRECTION

$\chi^2 = 588.54$
d.f. = 245
ratio = 2.40

128

variance-covariance matrix of the indicators. The chi-square is 588.54, with 245 degrees of freedom, for a ratio of 2.40.

A Model of Job Structure

Now we expand the measurement model of occupational self-direction into a causal model of job structure. As illustrated in Figure 6.2, this model includes all fourteen structural imperatives of the job.[4] Since we do not have multiple indicators of job conditions other than those involved in occupational self-direction, it is not possible to develop measurement models for any of them. Nor do we wish to use the specific job conditions as indicators in more general measurement models of organizational structure, job pressures, and extrinsic risks and rewards, because to do so would take away our ability to assess the separate effects of particular job conditions. For example, if we used time pressure, heaviness, dirtiness, and number of hours worked as indicators in a measurement model of job pressure, we would no longer be able to examine the separate effects of each of the four types of job pressures.[5] We therefore use single-indicator measures of these job conditions, recognizing that each is subject to some unknown degree of measurement error. Using single-indicator measures may result in our underestimating the effects of these job conditions on each other, on other job conditions, and in later models, on personality.

The causal model includes as potentially pertinent exogenous variables not only the pre-1974 job conditions but also those social characteristics that the research literature and our own earlier analyses give us reason to believe might have affected the job placement of men who are at least ten

---

[4] Of the three aspects of a man's position in the organizational structure that we measure, bureaucratization of the firm or organization in which he is employed is indexed on the basis of the number of formal levels of supervision and the size of the organization (see Chapter 2); ownership/nonownership is based on his self-report; and position in the supervisory hierarchy is measured in terms of the number of people over whom he says he has direct or indirect supervisory authority. Of the four job pressures, three are measured by the respondent's appraisals—frequency of time pressure, how dirty he gets in his work, and the number of hours he works in an average week. The fourth, heaviness of work, is our appraisal, based on his description of his work with things. Extrinsic risks and rewards are measured by the individual's perceptions of the likelihood of being held responsible for things outside his control and of the risk of losing his job or business, his reported income, and a simple additive index of whether or not his job provides such benefits as job security and sick leave. These measures are described more fully in Chapter 3.

[5] We faced a similar dilemma in measuring the substantive complexity of work, where the choice was between preserving the distinction, for example, between the complexity of work with data and the complexity of work with things, or developing an index of the more encompassing concept, the substantive complexity of work. There we opted against preserving the distinctions and in favor of the more encompassing concept. Here we take the opposite choice, since we regard the distinction, for example, between time-pressure and heaviness, as potentially important and the more encompassing term, job pressures, as more a rubric than a true concept.

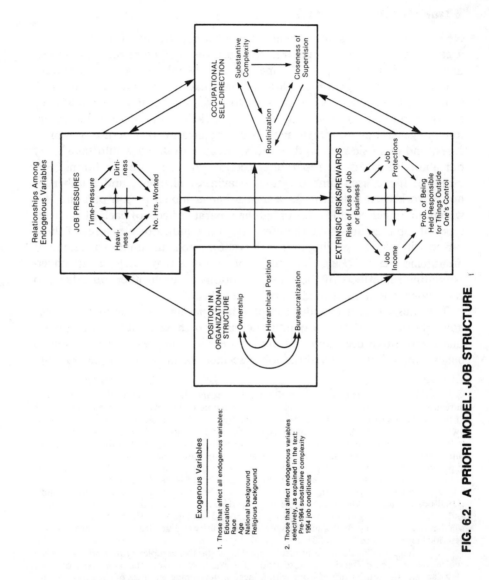

Relationships Among Endogenous Variables

JOB PRESSURES
Time-Pressure
Dirti-ness
Heavi-ness
No. Hrs. Worked

OCCUPATIONAL SELF-DIRECTION
Substantive Complexity
Closeness of Supervision
Routinization

POSITION IN ORGANIZATIONAL STRUCTURE
Ownership
Hierarchical Position
Bureaucratization

EXTRINSIC RISKS/REWARDS
Risk of Loss of Job or Business
Job Protections
Prob. of Being Held Responsible for Things Outside One's Control
Job Income

Exogenous Variables

1. Those that affect all endogenous variables:
Education
Race
Age
National background
Religious background

2. Those that affect endogenous variables selectively, as explained in the text:
Pre-1964 substantive complexity
1964 job conditions

FIG. 6.2. A PRIORI MODEL: JOB STRUCTURE

130

years into their occupational careers. These are the respondent's level of education, race, age, national background, and religious background. Our model should therefore be thought of as a depiction of men-in-jobs rather than as an abstract picture of job structure, per se. We deliberately omit other social characteristics (e.g., parental socio-economic characteristics) that might have affected job placement at earlier career stages but should not directly affect job placement once men are well into their careers.

With some exceptions, to be discussed below, there is no reason in principle why the fourteen job conditions might not affect each other both contemporaneously (albeit not necessarily instantaneously) and over time. We therefore should prefer to assess causal models that simultaneously allow both "contemporaneous" effects, i.e., the effects of present job conditions on each other, and "cross-lagged" effects, i.e., the effects of each of the conditions of work in the job held ten years earlier on the other conditions of the present job—as we did in our analysis of the reciprocal effects of substantive complexity of work and ideational flexibility in Chapter 5. Unfortunately, if our model were to allow both contemporaneous and cross-lagged effects, the number of parameters to be estimated would surpass what is possible with the information available.

To identify the equations, we must assume that some effects cannot be direct, but only indirect. If we had pre-1964 measures of all structural imperatives of the job—as we have for substantive complexity—those measures would provide the instrumentation for simultaneous assessment of the contemporaneous and cross-lagged effects of job conditions on one another.[6] Lacking such instrumentation, we must give priority to testing either contemporaneous or cross-lagged effects. Our choice is to give priority to contemporaneous effects, using the 1964 job conditions as instruments to identify the effects of 1974 job conditions on one another.

We give priority to contemporaneous effects for two reasons: First, we must take seriously the structural integrity of the job. It would deny the reality of job structure to assume, for example, that the likelihood of being held responsible for things outside one's control depends more on the time pressure experienced in some past job than on the time pressure experienced in the present job. Second, the simultaneous assessment of contemporaneous effects provides a straightforward way of accomplishing our principal intent—to decompose the correlation between, for example, the substantive complexity of men's current jobs and how closely men are supervised in

---

[6] Even though we could use pre-1964 substantive complexity as an instrument to test the contemporaneous and cross-lagged effects of substantive complexity simultaneously, we deliberately do not do so, because this would make substantive complexity noncomparable to the other job conditions. In fact, we get essentially the same results whether we treat substantive complexity as we do other job conditions or allow it to have simultaneous contemporaneous and lagged effects on other job conditions.

these jobs. Testing the effects of 1964 substantive complexity on 1974 closeness of supervision and of 1964 closeness of supervision on 1974 substantive complexity—while clearly pertinent—does not deal as directly with the critical correlation. If the interval between measurements were ten days or even ten weeks, giving priority to lagged effects might very well be justified. But with a ten-year interval between measurements, an unequivocal test of reciprocity can be accomplished only by allowing contemporaneous reciprocal effects.[7]

When in a model that tests only contemporaneous effects we find that some job condition (say, closeness of supervision) significantly affects some other job condition (say, substantive complexity), we can reasonably assume that the effect is real, although we do not know whether it is entirely contemporaneous. When, however, that effect proves not to be statistically significant in such a model, we have no basis for concluding that supervision really has no impact on substantive complexity. A full model, depicting both contemporaneous and lagged effects, might show that 1964 closeness of supervision has had a significant lagged effect on 1974 substantive complexity; a full model might even reveal a significant contemporaneous effect that was not previously apparent.

Being unable to test a full model, we search for effects that we may have missed, by now fixing at zero the paths that were nonsignificant in the contemporaneous-only model and estimating the corresponding lagged paths.[8] If we again find that closeness of supervision has no statistically significant effect on substantive complexity, we can conclude that closeness of supervision would not affect substantive complexity even in a full model. If we now find a significant lagged effect, though, we can be reasonably confident that closeness of supervision does affect substantive complexity. Even so, we cannot be certain that this effect is entirely lagged, for in a model

---

[7] We have systematically tested "reduced-form" models (i.e., models that do not test contemporaneous effects but simply allow each endogenous variable to be affected by the entire set of exogenous variables) designed to be comparable to all of the models presented in this chapter. In a reduced-form job-structure model, each current job condition would be affected by all past job conditions and all pertinent social characteristics. Reduced-form models do capture many of the effects depicted in the models presented in this chapter. But because reduced-form models test, not the effect of, say, current routinization on current substantive complexity, but the effect of 1964 routinization on 1974 substantive complexity, they fail to capture the effects of variables that do not have pronounced lagged effects or are not highly stable over time. Because reduced-form models do not test contemporaneous effects, they are of only limited utility for our purposes.

[8] Fixing the nonsignificant contemporaneous paths at zero in no way distorts the models presented here. In all instances, those paths are so small that removing them from the models does not change the magnitudes of the remaining parameters to more than a trivial extent. Nor does adding lagged paths affect the magnitudes of the contemporaneous paths in any of our models.

that does not simultaneously allow a contemporaneous effect, a lagged effect has two components. One is the truly lagged effect of 1964 closeness of supervision on 1974 substantive complexity. The other is the combination of the lagged effect of 1964 closeness of supervision on 1974 closeness of supervision and the contemporaneous effect of 1974 closeness of supervision on 1974 substantive complexity. Thus, we cannot be confident that what appear to be lagged effects of job conditions on one another are truly lagged, but, whether they in fact are lagged, contemporaneous, or both, they are real.

In assessing the model of job structure, we must recognize that the individual's place in the organizational structure—as defined by ownership, bureaucratization, and hierarchical position—cannot be contemporaneously affected by any other job condition. This is definitionally true, for a change from ownership to nonownership or the reverse, or from a more bureaucratic to a less bureaucratic firm or organization, or the reverse, or from a higher to a lower position in the supervisory hierarchy, or the reverse, signifies a change in job. It is not even possible for the three aspects of organizational structure to affect each other without the job becoming a different job; but if there can be no contemporaneous effects of job conditions on ownership, bureaucratization, or hierarchical position, then all lagged effects on ownership, bureaucratization, and hierarchical position are identified and can be tested.[9]

The model, thus identified, is summarized in Table 6.1. From this Table, we learn:

1. On the most general level: Job conditions are intricately linked; all structural imperatives of the job affect and are affected by one or more of the others.
2. Position in the organizational structure has a widespread impact on other conditions of work. Ownership results in doing substantively more complex work, at higher levels of income, but with a greater risk of losing one's job or business. Bureaucratic firms and organizations provide substantively more complex work, more extensive job protections, higher income, physically lighter work, and a shorter work week. Higher position in the supervisory hierarchy results in substantively more complex, less routine, less closely supervised, and physically lighter work; higher levels of pay; and longer hours of work. In sum, the three facets of position in the

---

[9] Because we do not allow ownership, bureaucratization, and hierarchical position to affect each other, we allow their residuals to correlate.

Table 6.1. A MODEL OF JOB STRUCTURE

Statistically Significant Effects of: On 1974:	Substantive Complexity	Routinization	Closeness of Supervision	Ownership	Bureau-cratization	Position in Hierarchy	Time pressure
Occupational Self-direction							
Substantive complexity	.36(L)[a]	-.11(C)	-.24(C)	.09(C)	.13(C)	.18(C)	.06(C)
Routinization	.0[b]	.27(L)	.0	.0	.0	-.09(C)	.0
Closeness of supervision	-.31(L)	.0	.08(L)	.0	.0	-.15(C)	.0
Position in Organizational Structure							
Ownership	.08(L)	.0	.0	.55(L)	.0	.0	.0
Bureaucratization	.0	.0	.0	-.13(L)	.48(L)	.0	.0
Position in hierarchy	.20(L)	.0	.0	.0	.0	.30(L)	.10(L)
Job Pressures							
Time pressure	.11(C)[a]	.0	.0	.0	.0	.0	.30(L)
Heaviness	.0	-.12(C)	.0	.0	-.09(C)	-.10(C)	.0
Dirtiness	-.40(C)	-.11(C)	.0	.0	.0	.0	.0
Hours of work	.10(C)	.0	.0	.0	-.23(C)	.06(C)	.0
Extrinsic Risks and Rewards							
"Held Responsible"	.17(C)	-.08(L)	.0	.0	.0	.0	.17(C)
Risk of loss of job or business	.0	.0	.0	.32(C)	.0	.0	.0
Job protections	.0	.11(L)	.0	.0	.35(C)	.0	.0
Job income	.17(C)	.0	.0	.20(C)	.18(C)	.15(C)	.0

	Heaviness	Dirtiness	Hours of Work	"Held Responsible"	Risk of Loss of Job	Job Protections	Job Income
Occupational Self-direction							
Substantive complexity	.0	.0	.0	.0	.0	.08(L)	.0
Routinization	.0	.0	.0	.0	.0	.0	−.10(L)
Closeness of supervision	−.11(C)	.10(L)	.0	.11(C)	.19(C)	.06(C)	−.12(L)
Position in Organizational Structure							
Ownership	.0	.0	.0	.0	.0	−.09(L)	.0
Bureaucratization	.0	.0	.0	−.05(L)	.0	.0	.0
Position in hierarchy	.0	.0	.0	.0	.0	.0	.0
Job Pressures							
Time pressure	.0	.0	.0	.0	.0	.0	.14(C)
Heaviness	.21(L)	.26(C)	.09(L)	−.07(C)	.0	.0	.0
Dirtiness	.0	.39(L)	.15(C)	.0	.0	.0	.0
Hours of work	.0	.15(L)	.16(L)	.0	.0	.0	.24(C)
Extrinsic Risks and Rewards							
"Held responsible"	.0	.0	.08(C)	.24(L)	.0	.0	.0
Risk of loss of job or business	.0	.0	.0	.0	.21(L)	.0	.0
Job protections	.13(C)	.0	.0	.0	.0	.34(L)	.0
Job income	.0	−.11(C)	.0	.0	.0	.0	.34(L)

[a](L) means a lagged effect (e.g., of 1964 substantive complexity on 1974 substantive complexity); (C) means a contemporaneous effect (e.g., of 1974 substantive complexity on 1974 time pressure).

[b].0 means a nonsignificant effect that has subsequently been fixed at zero.

Note: Paths from pre-1964 substantive complexity and from social background characteristics are not shown in this table.

135

organizational structure have similar effects on substantive complexity and job income, but they have decidedly different effects on the number of hours worked and on job protections and job risks, with ownership maximizing risk and bureaucratization maximizing job protections.

3. The substantive complexity of work stands out as the keystone of the entire job structure—affected by and, in turn, affecting many other job conditions. Not only do ownership, bureaucratization, and hierarchical position increase the substantive complexity of work, but so, too, do nonroutinized working conditions, freedom from close supervision, greater time pressure, and, over time, job protections. The substantive complexity of work, in turn, affects several other aspects of work: Doing substantively more complex work results in doing work that is less dirty, and increases the probability of being held responsible for things outside one's control, of receiving higher income, working under greater time pressure, and working longer hours; over time, doing substantively more complex work results also in being less closely supervised, rising in the supervisory hierarchy, and becoming an owner. In short, substantively complex work is at the core of highly placed, responsible, demanding but rewarding jobs. It is the key link between the position of a job in the organizational structure and other, more proximate, conditions of work. No other job condition is as intricately bound to the entire set of structural imperatives of the job as is substantive complexity.

4. Finally, with only one possible exception, all the statistically significant effects of job conditions on one another are consonant with past knowledge about the organization of work. They can be seen as the outcomes either of direct processes (e.g., close supervision decreasing substantive complexity) or of well-known indirect processes (e.g., routinization decreasing heaviness and dirtiness through mechanization). The only finding that may contradict expectations is that heavy work results in more freedom from supervision; but, then, the expectation may be stereotypic, based perhaps on our not distinguishing heavy from dirty work. It is pertinent that jobs requiring heavy work tend to be performed out of sight of supervisors—jobs such as farming, construction carpentry, and long-haul trucking (see Chapter 3, Table 3.2).

Overall, then, the model demonstrates that job conditions are linked intricately and meaningfully, with position in the organizational structure having widespread effects on other job conditions, and with the substantive complexity of work pivotal to the entire job structure.

JOB CONDITIONS AND IDEATIONAL FLEXIBILITY

By enlarging the model of job structure to include one or another facet of personality, we can assess the reciprocal effects of job conditions and each facet of personality. We begin by assessing the reciprocal effects of job conditions and ideational flexibility.[10]

Identifying the effects of job conditions on ideational flexibility poses the same problems that we faced in the model of job structure and we follow the same procedures. Identifying the effects of ideational flexibility on job conditions, however, is greatly facilitated if we posit that social characteristics that employers (even discriminatory employers) would not interpret as job credentials do not directly affect the job conditions of men who are at least ten years into their work careers (see Chapter 5). The rationale is that maternal and paternal education, paternal occupational status, maternal and paternal grandfathers' occupational statuses, urbanness and region of origin, and number of children in the parental family may have affected job placements earlier in the men's careers, but that by the time of the follow-up study these noncredentialing social characteristics would no longer have any direct bearing on job placement. They can thus be used as instruments to identify the contemporaneous effects of ideational flexibility on job conditions, a procedure that permits us to test the lagged effects of ideational flexibility even when its contemporaneous effects are statistically significant. We can therefore be much more confident about distinguishing the contemporaneous from the lagged effects of ideational flexibility on job conditions than we can about distinguishing the contemporaneous from the lagged effects of job conditions on other job conditions or on ideational flexibility.

---

[10] In an analysis that includes the three job conditions determinative of occupational self-direction (Kohn and Schooler, 1981), we arrived at a causal model similar to, but richer than, the one depicted in Chapter 5 for the reciprocal effects of substantive complexity and ideational flexibility. This model shows the contemporaneous effect of substantive complexity on ideational flexibility to be as great as it appeared to be in the more limited analysis of Chapter 5; at .17, it is approximately one-fourth as large as the direct effect of men's earlier levels of ideational flexibility. To this impressive effect of substantive complexity on ideational flexibility are now added small but statistically significant direct effects of routinization and closeness of supervision, the former lagged, the latter contemporaneous. Routinization and closeness of supervision also have indirect contemporaneous effects on ideational flexibility, in that both affect substantive complexity. Thus, substantive complexity is important not only in its own right, but also as a mechanism by which the other aspects of occupational self-direction affect ideational flexibility.

The effect of ideational flexibility on substantive complexity, in the occupational self-direction model as in the analysis of Chapter 5, is entirely lagged. With routinization and closeness of supervision allowed to affect substantive complexity, the effect of ideational flexibility on substantive complexity is somewhat reduced (.36 instead of .41), but it is still very substantial indeed. Ideational flexibility is also shown to have a moderately strong lagged effect on closeness of supervision. Thus, the model confirms that the effects of ideational flexibility on job conditions, while entirely lagged, are appreciable.

As in the model of job structure, we must recognize that ownership, bureaucratization, and hierarchical position cannot be contemporaneously affected by anything else. This poses a dilemma: how best to model the effects of ownership, bureaucratization, and hierarchical position on ideational flexibility. The logic of assessing the directions of effects in the relationships between job conditions and ideational flexibility requires the simultaneous testing of pairs of reciprocal paths—from some job condition to ideational flexibility and from ideational flexibility to that same job condition. Since ideational flexibility cannot have direct contemporaneous effects on ownership, bureaucratization, and hierarchical position, allowing these job conditions to have direct contemporaneous effects on ideational flexibility would assume the very unidirectionality of effects that our entire analysis is designed to transcend. We would be prejudging the issue we are trying to evaluate. Fortunately, there is nothing to preclude our allowing ownership, bureaucratization, and hierarchical position to have either direct lagged effects or indirect contemporaneous effects on ideational flexibility.[11] Still, to say that ownership, bureaucratization, and hierarchical position may have direct lagged or indirect contemporaneous effects on ideational flexibility does not necessarily prove that, in reality, they do not also have direct contemporaneous effects. We deal with the dilemma by testing and comparing two alternative models—initially, a model that allows position in the organizational structure to have only indirect contemporaneous and direct lagged effects, later a model that allows organizational position to have direct contemporaneous effects on ideational flexibility.

The model of job conditions and ideational flexibility that does not allow position in organizational structure to have direct effects is presented in Table 6.2. Since the effects of job conditions on one another are essentially unchanged by adding ideational flexibility (or any other facet of personality) to the model of job structure, we do not repeat in Table 6.2 that part of the model already presented in the previous Table.[12] Three things stand out in this model:

---

[11] The cross-sectional analysis of Chapter 2 found that bureaucratization's effects on ideational flexibility are primarily indirect, mediated principally through substantive complexity, income, and job protections. Extending the logic of that analysis, we hypothesize that not only bureaucratization, but also ownership and hierarchical position, exert their primary psychological impact indirectly, through more proximate job conditions.

[12] Although adding ideational flexibility or any other facet of personality to the model of job structure never greatly affects the estimates of job effects on one another or the effects of social characteristics on job conditions, in a few instances an effect does become statistically nonsignificant. When this happens, we follow a practice used throughout this chapter, fixing the nonsignificant effect at zero. We do so primarily to keep the number of estimated parameters within the capacity of the computer program. With a sample size of 687 and a robust model, statistically nonsignificant paths are ordinarily so small that it makes no difference to the remainder of the model whether they are left in or fixed at zero.

Table 6.2. THE RECIPROCAL EFFECTS OF JOB CONDITIONS AND IDEATIONAL FLEXIBILITY

	Statistically Significant Effects of:	
	Job Conditions (and Background Variables) on Ideational Flexibility	Ideational Flexibility on Job Conditions[a]
Job Conditions:		
Occupational Self-direction		
Substantive complexity	.13(C)[b]	.31(L)
Routinization	−.04(L)	.0[c]
Closeness of supervision	−.03(C)	−.17(L)
Position in Organizational Structure		
Ownership	.0	.07(L)
Bureaucratization	.0	.07(L)
Position in hierarchy	.0	.0
Job Pressures		
Time pressure	.10(L)	.0
Heaviness	−.07(C)	.0
Dirtiness	.0	.0
Hours of work	.0	−.23(L)
Extrinsic Risks and Rewards		
"Held responsible"	−.06(C)	.0
Risk of loss of job or business	.03(C)	.0
Job protections	−.09(L)	−.14(L)
Job income	.06(C)	.0
Background Variables:		
Education	.0	
Race	.0	
Age	−.14	
National background	.04	
Religious background	.0	
Number of siblings	.0	
Region of origin	.08	
Urbanness of place raised	−.03	
Mother's education	−.03	
Father's education	.07	
Father's occupational status	.0	
Maternal grandfather's occupational status	−.03	
Paternal grandfather's occupational status	.0	
Stability of ideational flexibility	.70(L)	

[a]Effects of social characteristics and other job conditions on job conditions are not shown in this table.
[b](C) means a contemporaneous effect; (L) means a lagged effect.
[c].0 means a nonsignificant effect that has subsequently been fixed at zero.

1. Several conditions of the current job have statistically significant effects on current ideational flexibility, even with earlier ideational flexibility, pertinent social characteristics, and other job conditions statistically controlled. Doing substantively complex work, receiving higher income, and being at risk of losing one's job or business all increase ideational flexibility, whereas being closely supervised, doing heavy work, and thinking that one may be held responsible for things outside one's control tend to decrease ideational flexibility. In addition, time pressure in the job held ten years ago increases one's current ideational flexibility, while routinization and job protections in the earlier job decrease one's current ideational flexibility. The magnitudes of these effects are only small to moderate (ranging from .03 to .13), but it is nevertheless impressive that so many of the structural imperatives of the job significantly affect ideational flexibility, even under such stringent statistical controls. Overall, job conditions that facilitate or require intellectual alertness seem to increase ideational flexibility as measured in a non-work situation; job conditions that minimize the necessity or desirability of intellectual alertness seem to decrease ideational flexibility. It is noteworthy that the substantive complexity of work, which we found to be central to the entire job structure, has the strongest direct effect on ideational flexibility of any job condition.

2. Although this model does not permit ownership, bureaucratization, and hierarchical position to have direct contemporaneous effects on ideational flexibility, and although we find that none of the three has a statistically significant lagged effect on ideational flexibility, they do have modest indirect effects, since all three aspects of position in the organizational structure affect conditions of work that bear on ideational flexibility. In particular, all three affect the substantive complexity of work. The alternative model—which permits position in the organizational structure to have direct, uni-directional effects on ideational flexibility—sets upper limits for our estimates of the direct effects of ownership, bureaucratization, and hierarchical position on ideational flexibility and lower limits for our estimates of the direct effects of all other job conditions on ideational flexibility. Such a model shows that neither ownership nor bureaucratization would have a statistically significant direct effect on ideational flexibility. Hierarchical position would have a statistically significant direct effect, a path of .09. The direct contemporaneous effects of other job conditions would be somewhat reduced; in particular, the direct effect of substantive complexity on ideational flexibility would be reduced from .13 to

.10. Juxtaposing the two models, we conclude that hierarchical position has a direct contemporaneous effect on ideational flexibility of no more than .09, while substantive complexity has a direct contemporaneous effect on ideational flexibility of no less than .10 and no more than .13. The unresolved issue is simply the degree to which the effect of hierarchical position is mediated through substantive complexity. In any case, both substantive complexity and hierarchical position are clearly pertinent to ideational flexibility.

3. The effects of ideational flexibility on job conditions are impressive, albeit entirely lagged, suggesting that the process by which ideational flexibility affects conditions of work is primarily one of selective recruitment and retention, rather than of job-molding, which we would expect to be more contemporaneous. Greater ideational flexibility in 1964 is conducive to working at jobs of greater substantive complexity in 1974, with less supervision, fewer hours of work, and fewer job protections. Greater ideational flexibility also increases the probability of becoming an owner or working in a bureaucratic firm or organization. In sum, the long-term consequence of greater ideational flexibility is the increased likelihood of attaining a self-directed position. Although this process occurs only gradually, over the course of time its cumulative impact is far from negligible.

JOB CONDITIONS AND ORIENTATIONS TO SELF AND SOCIETY

Do job conditions affect, and are they affected by, other facets of personality in the same way that they affect and are affected by ideational flexibility? Does the substantive complexity of work play a pivotal role vis-a-vis self-conceptions and social orientations? Alternatively, might time pressure or job protections or dirtiness be more important than substantive complexity for such facets of personality as anxiety or self-esteem? To answer these questions, we substitute for ideational flexibility each of several aspects of self-conception and social orientation that a priori logic and our past research give us reason to think might influence job recruitment and retention or might be affected by job experience. Specifically, we consider authoritarian conservatism, anxiety, trust, self-confidence, self-deprecation, idea conformity, fatalism, and standards of morality.[13] The measurement models for these concepts are summarized in Appendix C.

---

[13] We attempted also to assess the relationships between job conditions and receptiveness or resistance to change, but were unable to produce a statistically meaningful model. The over-time stability of receptiveness to change was consistently greater than 1.0 (standardized).

The findings derived from the causal models for the several facets of self-conception and social orientation are summarized in Table 6.3, which shows:

1. All of the proximate conditions of work except heaviness directly affect one or more aspects of self-conception and social orientation. With only a few exceptions (to be discussed below), the effects of job conditions on personality are readily interpretable as a learning-generalization process—learning from the job and generalizing those lessons to off-the-job realities. In particular, occupational self-direction leads to self-directed orientations to self and society: Men who are self-directed in their work are consistently more likely to become nonauthoritarian, to develop personally more responsible standards of morality, to become more trustful, more self-confident, less self-deprecatory, less fatalistic, less anxious, and less conformist in their ideas. Job pressures are much less consistent in their impact on self-conception and social orientation: Heaviness has no statistically significant effects; dirtiness is demoralizing; time pressure is in the main self-enhancing; and working longer hours tends, in the long run, to be reassuring. Certainly, one cannot conclude that job pressures, as we have measured them, are uniform in their psychological import.[14] Extrinsic risks have predictable consequences—they are threatening. Rewards can be reassuring. Here, however, we encounter the few real anomalies: Higher income leads over time to less self-confidence and to greater self-deprecation; job protections are conducive to authoritarian conservatism and to distrustfulness.[15] It is noteworthy that the anomalies involve risks and rewards attached to the job, rather than the actual conditions of work. Overall, the results are most clearcut for those job conditions that are most central to the work itself; in particular, they demonstrate the importance for self-conceptions and social orientations of occupational self-direction.

2. Some of the job conditions affected by ownership, bureaucratization, and position in the supervisory hierarchy—namely, substan-

---

[14] Since all these job pressures might be regarded as "stressful", these findings cast doubt on any interpretation that the effects of stress are necessarily deleterious.

[15] We have resolved a few other minor anomalies that we think are based on inadequate identification. In particular, when the reciprocal paths between some job condition and some facet of self-conception or social orientation were both statistically significant but of opposite sign, we tested each path alone, fixing the other path at zero. The tested path was generally reduced in magnitude, usually to statistical nonsignificance, in which case it, too, was fixed at zero. In a few instances, one or the other path (never both) remained statistically significant, and we kept it. This procedure may have resulted in our losing some real, opposite-signed effects, but since the identification on which the model is based is not strong enough to ensure that such effects are not simply a statistical artifact, we prefer to lose them than to claim effects that may not be real and risk distorting the rest of the model.

tive complexity, closeness of supervision, job protections, and job income—have widespread effects on self-conception and social orientation. Thus, organizational structure does have indirect effects on orientation. If position in the organizational structure were also allowed to have direct contemporaneous effects on the several facets of self-conception and social orientation, both ownership and bureaucratization would negatively affect trustfulness. Bureaucratization would have a contemporaneous negative, rather than a lagged negative, effect on self-deprecation. Nevertheless, the effects of proximate job conditions depicted in Table 6.3 would be unchanged.

3. Almost every facet of self-conception and social orientation we have examined affects at least one job condition. These effects appear to be preponderantly lagged. Although there are a few contemporaneous effects of self-conceptions and social orientations on job conditions, we cannot be altogether sure of their reality, because some of them may reflect, not personality affecting actual conditions of work, but personality affecting one's perceptions of those conditions. Thus, for example, seeing oneself as being held responsible for things outside one's control is a highly subjective appraisal. Similarly, although anxious people may behave in ways that result in greater pressure of time, perhaps anxious people simply feel more time-pressured. Still, some of the affected job conditions—notably, the heaviness of work, job protections, and closeness of supervision—are based on more objective indices. In any case, there is no reason to doubt the validity of the lagged effects, which pertain primarily to more objectively measured characteristics of the job, such as hours of work, the substantive complexity of work, and closeness of supervision. These lagged effects are not dramatic in magnitude, but they demonstrate that the personalities of workers sooner or later do affect their conditions of work. In particular, men who have self-directed orientations—who take personal responsibility for their own moral standards, who are open-minded, who are not fatalistic, who are not conformist in their ideas—are more likely over the course of time to attain responsible, self-directed positions.

TOWARD AN OVERALL MODEL OF JOB CONDITIONS AND PERSONALITY

An obvious limitation of the analysis thus far is that, while we have considered a number of job conditions simultaneously, we have dealt with ideational flexibility and the several facets of self-conception and social orientation only in separate models. A full assessment requires a model of

Table 6.3. THE RECIPROCAL EFFECTS OF JOB CONDITIONS AND EACH OF SEVERAL FACETS OF SELF-CONCEPTION AND SOCIAL ORIENTATION[a]

Statistically Significant Effects of Job Conditions on Self-Conception and Social Orientation[a]

	Substantive Complexity	Routinization	Closeness of Supervision	Ownership[b]	Bureaucratization[b]	Position in Hierarchy[b]	Time-Pressure	Heaviness
Authoritarian-conservatism	-.11(C)							
Personally responsible standards of morality	.27(C)							
Trustfulness		-.08(C)	-.07(C)				-.05(C)	
Self-confidence			-.14(L)				.10(C)	
Self-deprecation	-.25(C) -.12(L)				-.07(L)			
Fatalism								
Anxiety			.18(C)					
Idea-conformity		.10(C)	.12(C)				-.10(L)	

	Dirtiness	Hours of Work	"Held Responsible"	Risk of Loss of Job	Job Protections	Job Income	Overtime Stability
Authoritarian-conservatism			.07(C)		.06(C)		(.59)
Personally responsible standards of morality		-.08(L)	-.08(L)				(.53)
Trustfulness				-.08(L)	-.09(C)	.11(C)	(.70)
Self-confidence	-.05(C)				.13(C)	-.08(L)	(.50)
Self-deprecation						.07(L)	(.54)
Fatalism		-.11(L)				-.09(C)	(.57)
Anxiety	.12(C)				-.13(C)		(.51)
Idea-conformity		-.08(L)			-.10(C)		(.35)

Statistically Significant Effects of Each Facet of Self-conception and Social Orientation on Job Conditions:[c]

	Substantive Complexity	Routiniz-ation	Closeness of Supervision	Ownership[b]	Bureau-cratization[b]	Position in Hierarchy[b]	Time-Pressure	Heaviness
Authoritarian-conservatism			.09(L)	−.09(L)				
Personally responsible standards of morality	.05(L)		−.09(L)					
Trustfulness					.10(C)			
Self-confidence								
Self-deprecation								
Fatalism			.18(L)			−.07(L)		.10(C)[d]
Anxiety	−.05(L)		.12(C)				.09(C)	
Idea-conformity								

	Dirtiness	Hours of Work	"Held Responsible"	Risk of Loss of Job	Job Protections	Job Income
Authoritarian-conservatism						
Personally responsible standards of morality						
Trustfulness		−.15(L)	−.09(L)			
Self-confidence	−.06(L)	.10(L)	−.13(C)			
Self-deprecation		.12(L)				
Fatalism						
Anxiety			.10(C)			
Idea-conformity			−.15(C)			

[a]Controlling other job conditions, the 1964 level of that facet of self-conception or social orientation, and all background variables.
[b]The effects on and by ownership, bureaucratization, and position in the supervisory hierarchy can only be lagged in these models.
[c]Controlling other job conditions, including the 1964 analogue of that particular job condition, and "credentialling" background variables.
[d]There is also a lagged effect of .08.

several job conditions and several dimensions of personality. Such a model would permit us to consider whether some aspects of personality play a mediating role between job conditions and other aspects of personality (as hypothesized about intellectual flexibility in Kohn, 1980), whether job conditions continue to affect particular aspects of personality even when other aspects of personality are statistically controlled, and whether particular aspects of personality continue to affect job conditions even with other aspects of personality statistically controlled.

Attempting to deal with all eight facets of self-conception and social orientation in one causal model would not only be unduly complex but would also result in serious problems of linear dependency. Instead, we have performed a "second-order" confirmatory factor analysis, based on the hypothesis that there are two principal underlying dimensions, self-directedness versus conformity to external authority and a sense of distress versus a sense of well-being.[16]

Self-directedness implies the beliefs that one has the personal capacity to take responsibility for one's actions and that society is so constituted as to make self-direction possible. In our earlier work (see Chapter 1; see also Kohn, 1969, Chapters 5 and 11), we interpreted the relationships of social stratification with self-conceptions and social orientations as reflecting the propensity of men in higher social-stratification positions to believe that their own capacities and the nature of the world around them make self-direction seem both possible and efficacious. Men of lower stratification position, on the contrary, are more likely to believe that conformity to external authority is all that their own capacities and the exigencies of the world allow. Implicit in these interpretations is the hypothesis that several of the facets of self-conception and social orientation measured in this study reflect self-directedness or conformity to external authority, albeit imperfectly and to varying degree.

The hypothesis that a sense of well-being or of distress constitutes a second principal dimension underlying the several facets of self-conception and social orientation is based in the main on our original intent, to index all major aspects of psychological functioning that might affect job placement or be affected by job conditions. We strove to measure not only a man's assessment of personal efficacy, but also his feelings of comfort or pain. Self-directedness and conformity may each have distinct psychic costs and rewards.

The second-order model, presented in Figure 6.3, confirms our expecta-

---

[16] We put quotation marks around "second-order" to indicate that this is not a model based on all 57 indicators of self-conception and social orientation, but an approximation thereto, in which we use Bartlett-type factor scores of the eight first-order factors as the input variables to a confirmatory factor analysis.

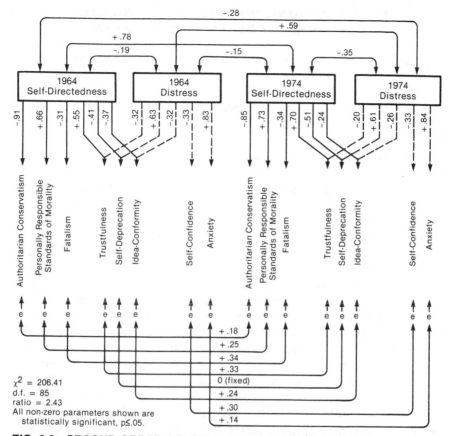

FIG. 6.3. SECOND-ORDER CONFIRMATORY FACTOR ANALYSIS OF SELF-CONCEPTION AND SOCIAL ORIENTATION

tions. Self-directedness is reflected in not having authoritarian conservative beliefs, in having personally responsible standards of morality, in being trustful of others, in not being self-deprecatory, in not being conformist in one's ideas, and in not being fatalistic—all of which is certainly in accord with our premises. Distress is reflected in anxiety, self-deprecation, lack of self-confidence, nonconformity in one's ideas, and distrust—which certainly appears valid. This model, which allows over-time correlations of the residuals of the first-order concepts but deliberately does not permit any intra-time correlated residuals, fits the data reasonably well: the chi-square is 206.41, with 85 degrees of freedom, for a ratio of 2.43. Together with ideational flexibility, the two dimensions of orientation defined by this model provide a partial but useful conceptualization of personality.

JOB CONDITIONS, IDEATIONAL FLEXIBILITY, SELF-DIRECTEDNESS, AND DISTRESS

Treating personality in terms of three basic dimensions—ideational flexibility, self-directedness of orientation, and distress—enables us to develop a general model of job conditions and multiple dimensions of personality.[17] In testing this model, we face a new problem of identification: how best to identify the effects of the three dimensions of personality on one another. We use the same procedure as for identifying the effects of job conditions on one another and on personality, namely, giving priority to contemporaneous effects and using the cross-lagged effects as instruments. As it turns out, there are two nonsignificant contemporaneous intrapsychic effects (those relating distress and ideational flexibility) and their lagged analogues are also nonsignificant.

The causal model (see Table 6.4) depicts a dynamic system in which job conditions affect all three dimensions of personality, all three dimensions of personality affect job conditions, and the three dimensions of personality affect one another. More concretely: The effects of job conditions on personality are essentially the same as those we have seen in the separate analyses of job conditions with ideational flexibility and with each of the eight facets of self-conception and social orientation. Thus, ideational flexibility is increased by job conditions that facilitate intellectual alertness, with substantive complexity having the strongest effect of any proximate condition of work. The main job determinant of self-directedness, too, is substantive complexity. Job conditions that sooner or later result in feelings of distress are lack of job protections, dirty work, close supervision, a low position in the supervisory hierarchy, and fewer hours of work—all but the last suggesting oppressive working conditions, and the entire set typical of unskilled employment in the secondary labor market.[18] These findings support a learning-generalization model: Self-directed work leads to ideational flexibility and to a self-directed orientation to self and society; oppressive working conditions lead to distress.

The effects of these basic dimensions of personality on job conditions

---

[17] One of the indicators of ideational flexibility is the respondent's propensity to agree with "agree-disagree" questions. Because such questions are built into the mode of inquiry used in assessing self-conception and social orientation, there is linear dependence between ideational flexibility and self-directedness. We solve the problem by using a modified measurement model of intellectual flexibility that does not include the "agree score" as an indicator. Factor scores of ideational flexibility based on the two models correlate .94.

[18] There is also an anomalous positive lagged path from 1964 job income to 1974 distress, a path opposite in sign to the zero-order correlation. This path may be artifactual; it is not statistically significant unless all the paths from current job conditions to distress present in the final model are allowed. Including or excluding this path does not affect the magnitudes of other paths in the model.

THE RECIPROCAL EFFECTS OF JOB CONDITIONS, IDEATIONAL FLEXIBILITY, SELF-DIRECTEDNESS/CONFORMITY, AND DISTRESS/WELL-BEING

Statistically Significant Effects of:[a]

	Job Conditions On:			On Job Conditions		
	Ideational Flexibility	Self-directedness	Distress	Ideational Flexibility	Self-directedness	Distress
Job Conditions						
Occupational Self-direction						
Substantive complexity	.11(C)[b]	.12(C)	.0	.26(L)	.0	.0
Routinization	−.03(L)	.0	.0	.0	.0	.0
Closeness of supervision	.0[c]	.0	.09(C)	.0	−.13(L)	.0
Position in Organizational Structure						
Ownership	.0	.0	.0	.06(L)	.0	.0
Bureaucratization	.0	.0	.0	.07(L)	.0	.0
Position in hierarchy	.0	.0	−.10(L)	.0	.0	.0
Job Pressures						
Time pressure	.05(C)	.0	.0	.0	.0	.11(C)
Heaviness	−.07(C)	.0	.10(C)	.0	−.11(L)	−.07(L)
Dirtiness	.0	.0	−.08(C)	.0	.0	.0
Hours of work	.0	.0	.0	−.22(L)	.0	.0
Extrinsic Risks and Rewards						
"Held responsible"	−.04(C)	−.06(C)	.0	.0	.0	.11(C)
Risk of loss of job or business	.0	−.04(L)	.0	.0	.0	.0
Job protections	−.08(L)	−.05(C)	−.16(C)	−.14(L)	.0	.0
Job income	.07(C)	.0	.11(L)	.0	.08(L)	.0

Statistically Significant Effects of:

On:	Ideational Flexibility	Self-directedness	Distress
Ideational Flexibility	.57(L)	.24(C)	.0
Self-directedness	.13(C)	.43(L)	−.08(C)
Distress	.0	−.25(C)	.54(L)

[a] Controlling pertinent social characteristics.
[b] (C) means a contemporaneous effect; (L) means a lagged effect.
[c] .0 means a nonsignificant effect that has subsequently been fixed at zero.

also are essentially the same as those found in the prior analyses. Ideationally more flexible men are more likely to achieve, in time, self-directed positions. A self-directed orientation results, over time, in being less closely supervised, having greater income, and doing physically lighter work, in short, in more advantageous jobs. Psychic distress results in working under greater time pressure and in a greater likelihood of being held responsible for things outside one's control. (Both of these subjective appraisals may of course be objectively inaccurate.) In time, distress leads also to doing physically lighter work. The only discrepancy between these findings and what we have seen before is that self-directedness does not have quite as wide a range of direct effects on job conditions as one might have expected. The explanation becomes clear when we examine intrapsychic effects: Self-directedness affects some job conditions, not directly, but indirectly through ideational flexibility.

The intrapsychic effects, the heretofore-missing component of the job-personality system, are impressive. Ideational flexibility both positively affects and is positively affected by self-directedness. Self-directedness negatively affects and is negatively affected by distress. Noteworthy among these intrapsychic effects are the strong effects of self-directedness on ideational flexibility and distress. Self-directedness affects both ideational flexibility and distress decidedly more strongly than they affect self-directedness or than they affect each other. If one of the three dimensions of personality is pivotal, it is self-directedness.[19]

DISCUSSION

Before summarizing the findings of these analyses and discussing their theoretical and practical import, it is necessary to point out the principal limitations of our data and methods of analysis.

The most important limitation of the analysis is one that we did not fully comprehend before actually doing longitudinal analysis—namely, that we have measurements at only two times and that there is a long interval between them. Both aspects pose serious problems. Identifying the models would be simpler and more certain with measurements at three times, because three measurements would provide instruments for assessing contem-

---

[19] We must again ask: What would be the consequence of allowing ownership, hierarchical position, and bureaucratization to directly affect the three dimensions of personality? Their effects on ideational flexibility would be as shown earlier. None of them would significantly affect self-directedness. Bureaucratization would increase distress and hierarchical position would decrease it, neither to any great extent, and the direct effect of bureaucratization would be opposite to its indirect effect through job protections. Most important, the effects of other job conditions on personality would not be greatly affected, the principal difference (as before) being a diminished, but still substantial, effect of substantive complexity on ideational flexibility.

poraneous and lagged effects simultaneously.[20] The ten-year time interval between interviews poses related yet different problems. Even in determining the effects of personality on job conditions, a process in which we could test contemporaneous and lagged effects simultaneously, we had to hedge the meaning of "contemporaneous" and "lagged". To appraise the actual timing of effects, we should ideally have measurements at frequent intervals (for this purpose, three is probably not enough). Only then would we be able to sharply differentiate truly contemporaneous from truly lagged effects.

Another limitation of our analysis is the inadequacy, particularly the subjectivity, of several of our indices of job conditions. We are fearful, for example, that we may have given short shrift to routinization, which is measured by a single, rather subjective indicator, in contrast to the substantive complexity of work, the best indexed of the job conditions we have studied. Clearly, multiple-indicator measures of all job conditions are needed. As for the issue of subjectivity, the solution is not readily apparent. What is the best way to measure time pressure? Should the ideal index of time pressure include a subjective component or should it be, insofar as possible, a measure solely of the external requirements of the job?

There are other limitations, some of them discussed at sufficient length in previous chapters (in particular, Chapters 3 and 5) that they need only be enumerated here: We have not been able to measure the organizational, technological, and interpersonal contexts of work as well as we have the actual conditions of work; we have done no systematic analysis of career patterns; we do not know whether the effects we have found are essentially the same for all age-cohorts and for all segments of the work force; and we have not taken into account other important events that may have occurred in the lives of these men during the ten-year interval between the baseline and the follow-up interviews. There is a final issue that seems to us even more important than we had earlier recognized it to be—the desirability of validating our interview-based methods and findings with observation-based studies.

These limitations notwithstanding, this analysis does take us considerably beyond our original approach (Chapter 1 and Kohn, 1969), which allowed us only to assume that stratification-related conditions of life affect

---

[20] Even with measurement at three times, identification is still somewhat problematic, for it rests on the belief that some variable measured at time one can directly affect its analogue at time three, but cannot directly affect some other variable at time three. The belief is plausible—certainly more so than the belief that there can be no cross-lagged effects from time one to time two—but hardly certain. Is identification ever certain? It is nonetheless clear that three measurements are preferable to two, as can be readily seen in the effective instruments we were able to employ in our analysis of the reciprocal effects of substantive complexity and ideational flexibility (in Chapter 5), where we had three measurements of substantive complexity, even if not of ideational flexibility.

the psychological functioning of individuals. We now have strong evidence that job conditions actually do affect personality, and also that personality affects job conditions. Moreover, these reciprocal processes are embedded in an intricate and complex web in which job conditions also affect each other and some aspects of personality affect others.

Our longitudinal analysis repeatedly demonstrates the importance for personality of occupational self-direction—especially, the substantive complexity of work, the job condition most strongly related to social stratification in our earlier analyses. Jobs that facilitate occupational self-direction increase men's ideational flexibility and promote a self-directed orientation to self and to society; jobs that limit occupational self-direction decrease men's ideational flexibility and promote a conformist orientation to self and to society. The analysis further demonstrates that opportunities for exercising occupational self-direction—especially, for doing substantively complex work—are to a substantial extent determined by the job's location in the organizational structure, with ownership, bureaucratization, and a high position in the supervisory hierarchy all facilitating the exercise of occupational self-direction. These findings provide strong empirical support for the interpretation that stratification-related conditions of work actually do affect personality. The longitudinal analysis also provides evidence of other job-to-personality effects, the most important being that oppressive working conditions produce a sense of distress. Implicit in all these findings is the consistent implication that the principal process by which a job affects personality is one of straightforward generalization from the lessons of the job to life off-the-job, rather than such less direct processes as compensation and reaction-formation.

The longitudinal analysis demonstrates also that, over time, personality has important consequences for the individual's place in the job structure. Both ideational flexibility and a self-directed orientation lead, in time, to more responsible jobs that allow greater latitude for occupational self-direction. Feelings of distress lead to actual or perceived time pressure and uncertainty. We think it noteworthy that so many of the personality-to-job effects—particularly the effects of personality on the most objectively measured conditions of work—are lagged rather than contemporaneous. The implication is that job conditions are not readily modified to suit the needs or capacities of the individual worker. Over a long enough time, though, many men either modify their jobs or move to other jobs more consonant with their personalities. Thus, the long-term effects of personality on job conditions are considerable. The process of job affecting man and man affecting job is truly reciprocal throughout adult life.

Finally, this analysis depicts a set of intrapsychic effects, which contribute to the dynamic impact of the entire system. Ideational flexibility increases and is increased by a self-directed orientation; a self-directed orientation decreases and is decreased by distress. Self-directedness has particularly strong effects on the other two dimensions of personality.

However complex the system and however diverse the effects, the findings highlight the centrality for job and personality of a mutually reinforcing triumvirate—ideational flexibility, a self-directed orientation to self and society, and occupational self-direction. Ideational flexibility is both responsive to and productive of occupational self-direction. A self-directed orientation increases ideational flexibility and decreases a sense of distress. Occupational self-direction—especially substantive complexity, the keystone of the job structure—decidedly affects both ideational flexibility and a self-directed orientation.

The interrelationship of ideational flexibility, a self-directed orientation, and occupational self-direction is integral to the stratification system of the society. Occupational self-direction is substantially determined by such stratification-linked aspects of organizational position as ownership and hierarchical level; ideational flexibility and a self-directed orientation, in turn, affect the likelihood of an individual achieving a highly placed organizational and social position. In short, occupational self-direction, ideational flexibility, and a self-directed orientation are intertwined in a dynamic process through which the individual's place in the stratification system both affects and is affected by his personality.

Class, Stratification, and Psychological Functioning[*]

Melvin L. Kohn
and Carrie Schoenbach

In this chapter we re-evaluate the role of occupational self-direction in explaining the effects of social stratification on values, orientations, and cognitive functioning. We ask essentially the same questions as in Chapter 1: What is the relationship of social stratification to psychological functioning? To what extent does this relationship result from the greater opportunity to exercise occupational self-direction enjoyed by men of higher social position? To answer these questions, we now use the longitudinal data of

---

[*] This chapter was prepared especially for this book, but its origins go back to two earlier papers. The measurement models for social-stratification position and for parental values were developed in Kohn and Schoenbach (1980). The method for assessing the reciprocal effects of occupational position and occupational self-direction was developed in Slomczynski, Miller, and Kohn (1981), as was the method for disaggregating occupational position and occupational self-direction into their component first-order concepts, thereby making possible the assessment of their independent effects on values and orientations. The analyses presented in this chapter differ from those in Slomczynski, Miller, and Kohn (1981), not only in that we here examine facets of psychological functioning not considered in that paper, but also in that the models developed for that paper were constrained to be as close as possible to those that could be estimated with cross-sectional comparative data from Poland; here, though, we can take full advantage of the longitudinal nature of the U.S. data.

We are indebted to Ronald Schoenberg for statistical advice, to Bruce Roberts for conscientious and thoughtful computer programming, and to Virginia Marbley for accurately and expeditiously transcribing the many revisions of this chapter. The models in this chapter were estimated by MILS, an advanced version of LISREL developed by Ronald Schoenberg.

the follow-up study and the method of linear structural-equations analysis. We treat as reciprocal the relationships between social-stratification position and occupational self-direction and between occupational self-direction and psychological functioning, testing empirically issues that previously were treated only by a priori argument.

A second purpose of this chapter is to address questions about social class similar to those we ask about social stratification. We have throughout this book deliberately used the term, social stratification, when discussing the hierarchical ordering of society and have reserved the term, social classes, to mean groups defined in terms of their relationship to ownership and control of the means of production. Thus far, our analyses have been limited to social stratification. Since social class represents a theoretically powerful alternative conceptualization of the socioeconomic organization of industrial society, we now ask the same questions about social class that we ask about social stratification: What is the relationship of social class to values, orientations, and cognitive functioning? To what extent does this relationship result from the greater opportunity to exercise occupational self-direction enjoyed by those who are more advantageously situated in the class structure?

THE RELATIONSHIP OF SOCIAL-STRATIFICATION POSITION TO PSYCHOLOGICAL FUNCTIONING

A Measurement Model of Social-stratification Position

A measurement model for social-stratification position can deal not only with measurement error but also with the perplexing issue of what are the appropriate weights to assign to education, occupational status, and income. The two-factor Hollingshead Index, used in Chapter 1, gives occupational status a weight of seven, gives educational level a weight of four, and excludes income. An often-employed alternative to a composite index of social stratification is to use education, occupational status, and perhaps income as independent variables in multiple-regression analyses. But that procedure simply gives occupational status, education, and (where included in the equations) income whatever weights maximize their multiple correlation with whatever facet of psychological functioning is the dependent variable in a particular equation. Such a procedure results in a different linear combination for each facet of psychological functioning and may exaggerate the magnitudes of the correlations. It would be more meaningful to combine the components of social-stratification position by some theoretically appropriate internal criterion than by so atheoretical and inconstant an external criterion.

Confirmatory factor analysis weights the components of social-stratification position by assessing and building on their shared variance. Thus, the rationale for our measurement model is that we conceive of social-stratification position as best inferred from the covariation of occupational status, education, and income. Our measurement model of social-stratification position (see Figure 7.1) is an extension of a model of occupational status developed by Schooler (1980). He uses as indicators of occupational status not only the Hollingshead occupational classification employed in the original analysis, but also the indices later developed by Duncan (1961), by Hodge, Siegel, and Rossi (1964; Siegel, 1971), and by Treiman (1977).[1] In our model of social-stratification position, occupational status becomes one of three "indicators" of the second-order concept, social-stratification position, the other two indicators being education and job income. This model fits the data quite well: The chi square is 90.48 with 34 degrees of freedom, for a ratio of 2.66.

In this model, education and occupational status appear to be equally powerful indicators of social-stratification position, with income of decidedly lesser importance. It could be argued, however, that the importance of occupational status, relative to that of education and of income, is exaggerated. Since all four classifications of occupational status explicitly or implicitly take into account the educational requirements and income levels of occupations, the model may overestimate the magnitudes of the correlations of occupational status with education and with income and, as a consequence, may overestimate the magnitude of the path from social-stratification position to occupational status. In any case, the possible redundancy of measurement does not affect the basic rationale of the measurement model. The model, of course, does not deal with the *causal* relationships of education, occupational status, and income, only with their covariations.

At several points in the analysis, it will be useful to separate education from occupational status and job income and to treat the latter two as "indicators" of a different second-order concept, which we call occupational position. To this end, we develop a second-order measurement model of occupational position (Figure not shown). Its parameters are very similar to those of the social-stratification model; the fit of this model to the data is necessarily the same as is that of the model of social-stratification position.

Measurement Models of Psychological Functioning

In evaluating the relationships between social-stratification position and psychological functioning, we examine nearly all facets of values and orien-

---

[1] The Hollingshead occupational classification proves to be as reliable a measure of occupational status as is any of the newer classificatory methods, reflecting the underlying concept almost perfectly. The Hollingshead classification was, and remains, a thoroughly serviceable measure of occupational status.

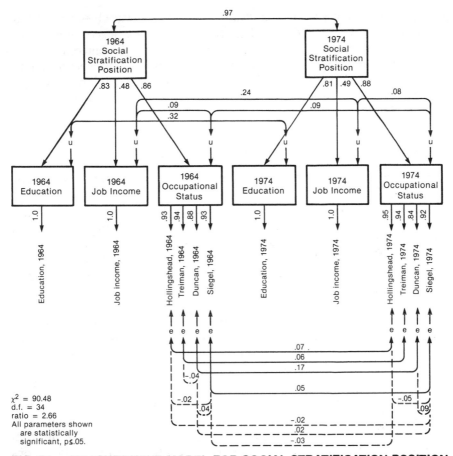

FIG. 7.1. MEASUREMENT MODEL FOR SOCIAL-STRATIFICATION POSITION

tations considered in Chapter 1. (The exceptions are judgments about work—a concept tangential to our focus on off-the-job psychological functioning—and one facet of social orientation, receptivity to change, for which we were unable to develop a satisfactory longitudinal model.) In addition to the several discrete facets of orientation, we now consider their two underlying dimensions—self-directedness and distress. We also consider alienation, even though it is indexed by many of the same questions as are self-directedness and distress, because it provides an alternative conceptualization of orientation. Finally, we include ideational flexibility, which we now see both as a possible intervening mechanism through which education might affect values and orientations and also as a central facet of psychological functioning of great importance in its own right. The focus of attention is on valuation of self-direction, self-directedness of orientation, distress, alienation, and ideational flexibility.

Many of the measurement models of psychological variables required for this chapter have been developed in previous chapters. Specifically, we utilize the measurement model for ideational flexibility, presented in Chapter 5, and those for the several dimensions of orientation, presented in Chapter 6 and Appendix C. For this analysis, we need measurement models also for parental values, values-for-self, and alienation. These, too, are presented in Appendix C.

Social Stratification and Psychological Functioning

The correlations of social-stratification position with values and orientations (see Table 7.1) are appreciably stronger than the analyses of Chapter 1 had indicated. To take a pivotal example: The correlation of social-stratification position with parental valuation of self-direction, as originally calculated from cross-sectional data, using Hollingshead's two-factor Index of Social Position and measuring parental valuation of self-direction on the basis of exploratory factor analysis, was .34. Now, using longitudinal data and confirmatory factor-analytic measurement models, we find the correlation to be .56 for 1964, when the children were three to fifteen years old, and .66 ten years later, when the children were thirteen to twenty-five years old.[2] If, as we think, values are a crucial link in the interpretive chain from social-stratification position to behavior (see Kohn, 1977 and 1981b), the magnitude of this correlation is of more than trivial import.

Just as with fathers' valuation of self-direction or conformity for their children, the correlations of social-stratification position with men's valuation of self-direction or conformity for themselves are now found to be substantially larger than the original analysis had shown, increasing from .17 to .37 in 1964 and to .40 in 1974. The magnitudes of these correlations are not as great as are those for parental values, perhaps because the improved question about values-for-self used in the follow-up survey cannot fully compensate for the imperfections of the 1964 question (see the discussion in Appendix C). At any rate, correlations of .37 and .40 are of a magnitude substantial enough to be consonant with our interpretation that values provide an important link between social structure and behavior.

As with parental values and values-for-self, the correlations of social-stratification position with the several facets of orientation are in all instances larger, in the main considerably larger, than had earlier seemed to be the case. This is especially true for those facets of orientation indicative of self-directedness versus conformity to external authority, i.e., authoritar-

---

[2] Our interpretation does not predict whether parents' social-stratification positions will be related to their valuation of striving for success. In fact, this correlation is a statistically nonsignificant + .07 in 1964 and a statistically significant − .18 in 1974.

Table 7.1. ZERO-ORDER CORRELATIONS OF SOCIAL-STRATIFICATION POSITION AND PSYCHOLOGICAL FUNCTIONING; REGRESSION COEFFICIENTS FOR EDUCATION AND OCCUPATIONAL POSITION

	Zero-order Correlations	Standardized Regression Coefficients	
	Social-stratification Position	Education	Occupational Position
Values			
Parental valuation of self-direction			
1964	.56*	.37*	.21*
1974	.66*	.52*	.17*
Valuation of self-direction for oneself			
1964	.37*	.34*	.06
1974	.40*	.34*	.07
Intellectual Functioning			
Ideational flexibility			
1964	.87*	.54*	.34*
1974	.85*	.48*	.40*
Second-order Dimensions of Orientation			
Self-directedness			
1964	.68*	.48*	.21*
1974	.70*	.47*	.25*
Distress			
1964	−.09*	.10	−.19*
1974	−.18*	.03	−.22*
Alienation			
1964	−.31*	.03	−.35*
1974	−.41*	−.14*	−.28*
First-order Dimensions of Orientation			
Authoritarian-conservatism			
1964	−.65*	−.47*	−.19*
1974	−.64*	−.49*	−.17*
Standards of morality			
1964	.41*	.20*	.23*
1974	.47*	.19*	.28*
Trustfulness			
1964	.49*	.37*	.15*
1974	.56*	.35*	.22*
Self-confidence			
1964	.25*	.16*	.08
1974	.22*	.16*	.06
Self-deprecation			
1964	−.24*	−.16*	−.08
1974	−.40*	−.16*	−.26*

Table 7.1. (*continued*)

	Zero-order Correlations	Standardized Regression Coefficients	
	Social-stratification Position	Education	Occupational Position
Fatalism			
1964	−.24*	−.13*	−.10
1974	−.34*	−.08	−.25*
Anxiety			
1964	−.11*	.12*	−.24*
1974	−.21*	−.01	−.20*
Idea-conformity			
1964	−.30*	−.31*	.00
1974	−.18*	−.17*	.00

N = 687, except for parental valuation of self-direction, where N = 399.
* = Statistically significant, .05 level or better.

ian conservatism, standards of morality, and trustfulness. As a result, the relationship between social-stratification position and the second-order factor, self-directedness, is strong—correlations of .68 and .70 for 1964 and for 1974, respectively. In contrast, the correlations of social stratification with distress are only − .09 and − .18. Clearly, social-stratification position is much more important for self-directedness than for distress. Alienation, which has components of both self-directedness and distress, falls midway, its correlations with social-stratification position being − .31 in 1964 and − .41 in 1974.

Even more dramatic than the relationship between social-stratification position and self-directedness is that between social-stratification position and ideational flexibility—a correlation of .87 in 1964 and .85 in 1974. Ideational flexibility clearly deserves an important place in our analysis of the psychological concomitants of social-stratification position.

In sum, social-stratification position is strongly related to cognitive functioning, to self-directedness of orientation, and to parental valuation of self-direction; it is somewhat less strongly, but still appreciably, related to men's valuation of self-direction for themselves and to alienation; it is least strongly, but nonetheless significantly, related to distress.

Multiple-regression analysis provides an approximate way to assess the relative contributions of education and of occupational position to the correlations of social-stratification position with psychological functioning (again see Table 7.1). The findings must be interpreted cautiously, both because education and occupational position are rather highly correlated (.75 in 1964 and .74 in 1974) and because these analyses do not yet take into account that education's effects may be partly indirect, through education affecting occupational position. Still, multiple-regression analyses using education and occupational position as independent variables vis-a-vis the several facets of psychological functioning do tell us something about the relative importance of these two major components of social stratification. Occupational position is more important than is education for distress and for alienation. Education is more important for cognitive functioning, for valuing self-direction, and for having a self-directed orientation. Still, even with education statistically controlled, the relationships of occupational position with cognitive functioning, values, and self-directedness of orientation are generally statistically significant and nontrivial in magnitude.

Despite the greater importance of education than of occupational position vis-a-vis ideational flexibility, values, and some facets of orientation, it would be unwarranted to conclude that formal education, per se, explains the relationships between social stratification and these facets of psychological functioning. The analyses of Chapters 3, 5, and 6 strongly suggest that occupational self-direction may explain some substantial part of the psychological impact, not only of occupational position, but also of education.

RECONCEPTUALIZING THE RELATIONSHIP BETWEEN SOCIAL STRATIFICATION AND OCCUPATIONAL SELF-DIRECTION

Chapter 1 asked whether substantive complexity, closeness of supervision, and routinization might explain—at least in substantial part—the relationships of social-stratification position with values and orientations. The method then used to answer the question was to statistically control these three job conditions, to see how much the correlations of social-stratification position with values and orientations would thereby be reduced. Such an analytic procedure, however, assumes unidirectional causality, from social-stratification position to occupational self-direction. This seems an appropriate assumption for education, because formal education ends for most men in the United States before their occupational careers get underway.[3] The appropriate assumption for occupational position, however, is that it may both affect and be affected by occupational self-direction. Since occupational position signifies a job's placement in the system of social stratification, it can affect the actual conditions of work experienced in that job. But since occupational position—and, in particu-

---

[3] Our data show a correlation of .97 between men's educational levels at the time of the first interview, in 1964, and at the time of the follow-up interview, ten years later. The correlation is of essentially the same magnitude for the oldest, intermediate, and youngest segments of the work force.

lar, the indicators we use to measure occupational position, i.e., status and income—is a reward, distributed in accordance with critical aspects of the work performed, it can be affected by job conditions.[4]

We therefore consider the relationship between occupational position and occupational self-direction to be reciprocal, as depicted in the combined measurement and causal model of Figure 7.2. Occupational self-direction is a second-order concept, the first-order concepts being substantive complexity, routinization, and closeness of supervision.[5] Occupational position also is a second-order concept, with job income and occupational status as its first-order concepts. Education is exogenous to both occupational position and occupational self-direction and is permitted to affect both, in 1964 and also in 1974.

To provide identification for assessing the reciprocal effects of occupational position and occupational self-direction, we permit the occupational position of the job held in 1964 to directly affect the present job's occupational position but not its occupational self-direction; correspondingly, the occupational self-direction of the 1964 job is allowed to directly affect the present job's degree of occupational self-direction but not its occupational position. (For a discussion of the rationale and also the dangers of this procedure, see Heise, 1975:184–185.) The contemporaneous relationship between occupational position and occupational self-direction is undoubtedly the outgrowth of longer-term processes of selective recruitment into and retention in particular jobs, individual career mobility, and changes in how work is organized in this society. Our model depicts the outcomes of these ongoing processes.[6]

Those social characteristics that might be pertinent to the job placement of men who are well into their careers are permitted to affect both occupational position and occupational self-direction. The relevant characteristics are age, race, national background, and religious background. We include these social characteristics primarily as statistical controls.

We find that much of education's effect on occupational self-direction occurs during earlier stages of career—certainly by the time of the 1964

---

[4] Even though our measures of occupational status refer to the occupation generally, we are treating them as proxies for the status of an individual's own job. Job income is of course specific to the particular job. Since we are treating occupational status and income as attributes of a job, it is reasonable to think of them as subject to the effects of other job conditions.

[5] A second-order measurement model of occupational self-direction is presented in Appendix C. All of the parameters of this model, including the correlations of the residuals of the indicators and of the first-order concepts, are retained in our assessment of the relationship between social-stratification position and occupational self-direction.

[6] If we had measurements at much closer intervals than ten years (and if we had the necessary instruments to do so), we would model the effect of occupational position on occupational self-direction as both contemporaneous and lagged, that of occupational self-direction on occupational position as only lagged.

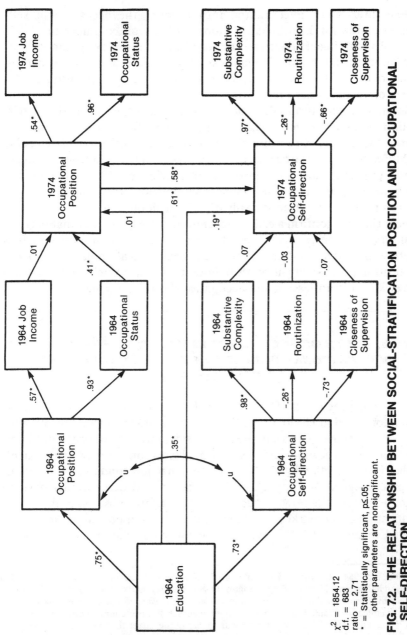

$\chi^2 = 1854.12$
d.f. = 683
ratio = 2.71
* = Statistically significant, p≤.05;
other parameters are nonsignificant.

FIG. 7.2. THE RELATIONSHIP BETWEEN SOCIAL-STRATIFICATION POSITION AND OCCUPATIONAL SELF-DIRECTION
(First-measurement parameters, paths from social characteristics to endogenous variables, and some correlations among residuals not shown.)

baseline interviews.[7] Even taking into account the occupational self-direction of the job held in 1964, though, education continues to have a statistically significant, nontrivial direct effect (.19) on occupational self-direction in the 1974 job. The cumulative effect of education on current occupational self-direction is .72, most of this effect indirect, through education's effect on earlier jobs.[8]

Despite our statistically controlling education, prior occupational self-direction, and relevant social characteristics, the effect of occupational position on occupational self-direction is substantial, the direct effect being .61. Moreover, the reciprocal effect of occupational self-direction on occupational position is also substantial, a direct effect of .58. These mutually reinforcing processes between occupational position and occupational self-direction result in an extraordinarily high correlation: .96.

These findings confirm a central tenet of our interpretation, that occupational self-direction is closely linked to social-stratification position. It is therefore plausible to think that the psychological impact of social-stratification position might result in good part from the close relationship between social stratification and occupational self-direction.

THE EFFECTS OF SOCIAL-STRATIFICATION POSITION AND OCCUPATIONAL SELF-DIRECTION ON VALUES AND ORIENTATIONS

Distinguishing the direct effects of social-stratification position on values, orientations, and intellectual flexibility from its indirect effects through occupational self-direction is a matter of considerable importance to our interpretation. Do education and occupational position directly affect men's psychological functioning? Or is it, rather, that job conditions directly affect psychological functioning, with education and occupational position mattering not for their own sakes but because a job's position in the social-stratification order markedly influences a worker's opportunities to be self-directed in his work? Not even a near-unity correlation between occu-

---

[7] Since the 1964 job is the earliest job depicted in this model, the model makes it appear that education has strong effects on the occupational self-direction and occupational position of the job held in that particular year. But, if our causal model were to include pre-1964 jobs, the effects of education would be shown to occur even earlier. For present purposes, the important point is that education's greatest effects occur earlier in the career than the present job.

[8] Calculating direct, indirect, and total effects in nonrecursive models is more difficult than in recursive models because of feedback effects. The MILS computer program calculates total and indirect effects, following Fox (1980). This information makes posssible the straightforward computation of particular indirect effects, e.g., the indirect effect of education on the occupational self-direction of the 1974 job via the occupational self-direction of the 1964 job.

pational position and occupational self-direction necessarily means that social-stratification position and occupational self-direction have the same causal dynamics vis-a-vis other variables.

Because of the almost perfect correlation between occupational position and occupational self-direction, a causal model that permitted both of them to directly affect some facet of psychological functioning would be afflicted with overwhelming problems of multicollinearity. To side-step such problems, we disaggregate occupational position and occupational self-direction into their components and allow these components to affect one or another facet of current psychological functioning.[9] This is accomplished by extending the model depicted in Figure 7.2 to allow education, occupational status, income, substantive complexity, routinization, and closeness of supervision to directly affect some specified facet of psychological functioning. It must be emphasized that this analysis does not yet take into account the stability of psychological functioning. Nor does it model as reciprocal the relationship either of occupational position or of occupational self-direction with psychological functioning. The immediate objective is to disaggregate the relationships of social-stratification position and occupational self-direction with psychological functioning. The next step in the analysis will be to go beyond disaggregation of correlations to analyze reciprocal effects.

Figure 7.3 provides an example that shows the unidirectional "effects" of education, occupational position, and occupational self-direction on fathers' valuation of self-direction for children.[10] In this model, too, we allow social characteristics that might be pertinent to current job placement to affect both occupational position and occupational self-direction. These social characteristics, as well as others that might affect psychological functioning, are also allowed to affect whichever facet of psychological

---

[9] This procedure is feasible because the correlations among the components of occupational position and of occupational self-direction, although high, are not quite as high as that between the second-order concepts; the strongest correlation is .90, between occupational status and the substantive complexity of work. In these analyses, we follow essentially the same procedures as in Slomczynski, Miller, and Kohn (1981), except that here we use the follow-up data, the sample being the subsample of men in the follow-up study and the indices of psychological functioning being those of 1974, not 1964.

[10] Since it would be exceedingly cumbersome and would serve no important purpose to estimate anew a combined measurement and causal model for each facet of psychological functioning, we now impose the (unstandardized) parameters of the model depicted in Figure 7.2 on causal models that use factor scores to index first-order concepts. Because factor scores are not entirely reliable, we correct the correlations of factor scores with each other and with other variables, using information provided by MILS about the correlations of the factor scores with the "true" scores for the constructs. We fix the paths from concepts to indicators and the principal causal paths at the (unstandardized) values found in the more detailed model but (to put no undue constraints on the model) re-estimate the residuals and the correlations among residuals.

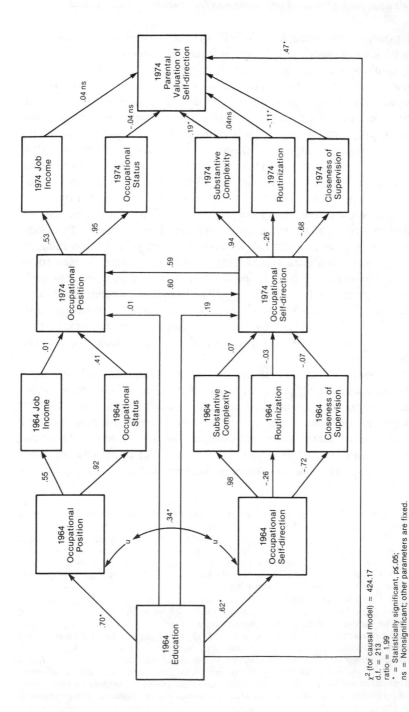

χ^2 (for causal model) = 424.17
d.f. = 213
ratio = 1.99
* = Statistically significant, $p \leq .05$;
ns = Nonsignificant; other parameters are fixed.

FIG. 7.3. THE EFFECTS OF EDUCATION, OCCUPATIONAL POSITION, AND OCCUPATIONAL SELF-DIRECTION ON PARENTAL VALUATION OF SELF-DIRECTION
(Paths from social characteristics to endogenous variables and correlations among residuals not shown.)

functioning is being assessed in the particular model—in this case, parental valuation of self-direction.[11]

Education has a sizeable and statistically significant direct effect (.47) on parental valuation of self-direction, while two components of occupational self-direction, substantive complexity and closeness of supervision, have smaller but nonetheless statistically significant effects (.19 and -.11, respectively). Thus, education and occupational self-direction significantly affect parental valuation of self-direction, independent of each other and of occupational position. Similar models for values-for-self, ideational flexibility, and the several facets of orientation (see Table 7.2) yield the general conclusion that one or another component of occupational self-direction significantly affects every aspect of psychological functioning we examine, despite education and occupational position being statistically controlled. In particular, substantive complexity has a statistically significant effect on valuation of self-direction, both for one's children and for oneself; on ideational flexibility; on self-directedness, distress, and alienation; and on four of the eight first-order dimensions of orientation—authoritarian conservatism, standards of morality, self-confidence, and self-deprecation. Where substantive complexity does not have a significant effect—vis-a-vis trustfulness, fatalism, anxiety, and idea-conformity—closeness of supervision fills the breach. In short, occupational self-direction, particularly the substantive complexity of work, is of considerable importance for psychological functioning, independent of its close association with education and with occupational position.

It is equally clear, though, that occupational self-direction does not completely explain the impact of social-stratification position, particularly of education, on psychological functioning. Education has a statistically significant effect on values, on cognitive functioning, and on self-directedness and its component facets of orientation, above and beyond that exerted through education's affecting occupational self-direction. Income, too, affects some aspects of orientation, namely self-directedness, trustfulness, self-confidence, and fatalism. Occupational status, however, is overwhelmed by the other independent variables in the equations, its regression coefficients being either nonsignificant or reversed in sign.

It would appear, then, that the answer to our question, does social-stratification position affect values, orientations, and intellectual flexibility because of, or independent of, its close association with occupational self-direction is: both. Education and job income continue to affect several

---

[11] The pertinent social characteristics are age, race, national background, religious background, parental family socioeconomic status (a construct based on mother's and father's education, father's occupational status, and maternal and paternal grandfathers' occupational statuses), the urbanness and region of the country of the principal place where the respondent was raised, and the number of brothers and sisters he had.

Table 7.2. THE EFFECTS OF SOCIAL-STRATIFICATION
POSITION AND OCCUPATIONAL SELF-DIRECTION
ON PSYCHOLOGICAL FUNCTIONING

| | Standardized Regression Coefficients | | | | | |
| | Social-stratification Position | | | Occupational Self-direction | | |
	Educa-tion	Job Income	Occ. Status	Subst. Complex.	Close. Super.	Routin-ization
Values						
Parental valuation of self-direction	.47*	.04	−.04	.19*	−.11*	.04
Valuation of self-direction for oneself	.20*	.00	−.14	.27*	.01	−.04
Intellectual Functioning						
Ideational flexibility	.29*	.03	−.08*	.53*	−.02	.06*
Second-order Dimensions of Orientation						
Self-directedness	.36*	.06*	−.13*	.37*	−.03	.03
Distress	.05	−.01	.06	−.30*	.05	.02
Alienation	−.06	.02	.00	−.37*	.01	.02
First-order Dimensions of Orientation						
Authoritarian-conservatism	−.37*	−.01	.06	−.23*	.04	−.02
Standards of morality	.18*	.04	−.19*	.50*	−.01	.09*
Trustfulness	.33*	.07*	.05	−.09	−.13*	−.06
Self-confidence	.09	.09*	−.13	.25*	.04	.02
Self-deprecation	−.07	−.03	.12	−.49*	−.05	.00
Fatalism	−.07	−.12*	−.08	.00	.14*	−.04
Anxiety	−.01	.00	−.01	−.15	.15*	.02
Idea-conformity	−.09	−.02	.09	−.05	.25*	.10*

* = Statistically significant, .05 level or better.

facets of psychological functioning even when occupational self-direction is statistically controlled. Thus, the psychological effects of social-stratification position cannot be entirely explained in terms of the greater opportunities for occupational self-direction available to people of higher educational and occupational position. On the other hand, occupational self-direction does have impressive independent effects on all the psychological phenomena we have studied, implying that some part of the effect of social-stratification position on psychological functioning is indirect, via occupational self-direction. The question becomes, then, what proportions of the total effects of social-stratification position are indirect, via its impact on occupational self-direction?

From the analyses summarized in Table 7.2, it is possible to assess the degree to which the effects of social-stratification position occur indirectly via occupational self-direction (see Table 7.3). To make this assessment, we note the total effects of social-stratification position on the several facets of values, orientation, and cognitive functioning; we calculate the indirect effects of social-stratification position via occupational self-direction; and, finally, we calculate the proportions of the total effects that are attributable to occupational self-direction.[12] We make the same assessment for the two components of social-stratification position—education and occupational position.

As shown in Table 7.3, the psychological effects of *social-stratification position* are very substantially attributable to occupational self-direction, the proportions generally ranging from one-half to two-thirds or more. More specifically, for almost all facets of psychological functioning, the effects of *occupational position* are entirely attributable to occupational self-direction. The psychological effects of *education* are in varying degree attributable to occupational self-direction, ranging from a low of 15 percent for trustfulness to a high of 100 percent for distress, with a median of about 60 percent. Thus, we have much firmer evidence than in Chapter 1 that the psychological impact of social-stratification position—and of its two principal components—are substantially attributable to occupational self-direction.

THE RECIPROCAL EFFECTS OF OCCUPATIONAL SELF-DIRECTION AND PSYCHOLOGICAL FUNCTIONING

We have to this point followed the logic of Chapter 1 in implicitly assuming that occupational self-direction affects but is not affected by values, orientations, and cognitive functioning. Now, following the logic of subsequent chapters, we abandon the assumption of unidirectionality, recognizing that men's values, orientations, and intellectual flexibility may affect their conditions of work. In a new set of causal models, we assess the reciprocal effects of occupational self-direction and each facet of psychological func-

---

[12] The analyses of Chapter 1 assessed the proportional reduction in the *correlations* of social stratification with values and orientations; now we assess the proportion of the total *effect* of social stratification that is indirect, via occupational self-direction. In causal terms, the latter is far more meaningful (see Duncan, 1970).

The direct and indirect effects of education and of occupational position are provided by the MILS program, and from this information we calculate those indirect effects that are attributable to occupational self-direction. Social-stratification position is not explicitly included in the model, but the MILS program does provide the intercorrelations of 1964 education, 1974 occupational status, and 1974 job income implied by the model. Using this information, we derive the paths from an implicit second-order social-stratification construct to these three first-order constructs and, alternatively, to education and occupational position. This provides the data for computing the total and indirect effects of social-stratification position on any particular facet of psychological functioning.

Table 7.3. THE TOTAL EFFECTS OF SOCIAL-STRATIFICATION POSITION, EDUCATION, AND OCCUPATIONAL POSITION AND INDIRECT EFFECTS ATTRIBUTABLE TO OCCUPATIONAL SELF-DIRECTION

	Social-stratification Position			Education			Occupational Position		
	Total Effect	Indirect Effect	Indirect As %	Total Effect	Indirect Effect	Indirect As %	Total Effect	Indirect Effect	Indirect As %
Values									
Parental valuation of self-direction	.67	.34	50%	.63	.16	26%	.20	.21	100%
Valuation of self-direction for oneself	.28	.27	95%	.28	.12	43%	.04	.17	100%
Intellectual Functioning									
Ideational flexibility	.82	.67	81%	.59	.32	54%	.37	.43	100%
Second-order Dimensions of Orientation									
Self-directedness	.63	.46	73%	.54	.22	40%	.19	.29	100%
Distress	−.34	−.43	100%	−.14	−.20	100%	−.23	−.27	100%
Alienation	−.53	−.50	94%	−.30	−.24	80%	−.31	−.33	100%
First-order Dimensions of Orientation									
Authoritarian-conservatism	−.52	−.30	57%	−.50	−.14	28%	−.14	−.19	100%
Standards of morality	.49	.52	100%	.38	.24	64%	.16	.33	100%
Trustfulness	.45	.11	25%	.41	.06	15%	.16	.07	43%
Self-confidence	.22	.24	100%	.17	.12	68%	.06	.14	100%
Self-deprecation	−.49	−.54	100%	−.30	−.25	85%	−.24	−.34	100%
Fatalism	−.43	−.24	56%	−.21	−.13	60%	−.29	−.15	52%
Anxiety	−.38	−.36	96%	−.18	−.17	94%	−.25	−.24	96%
Idea-conformity	−.27	−.28	100%	−.20	−.13	65%	−.10	−.18	100%

tioning. We have assessed similar models in Chapter 6, but then for job conditions generally. Now we limit the analysis to substantive complexity, routinization, and closeness of supervision, treating these three job conditions as indicators of a second-order concept, occupational self-direction.

In these causal models (illustrated for parental valuation of self-direction in Figure 7.4), occupational self-direction in the job held ten years earlier is permitted to affect occupational self-direction in the current job, and the particular facet of psychological functioning ten years earlier is permitted to affect that facet of psychological functioning currently. Cross-lagged effects, however, are fixed at zero—they are used as instruments. Since nearly all the men had completed their formal educations before 1964, education is necessarily modelled as having unidirectional effects on both occupational self-direction and psychological functioning. (This may exaggerate the effect of education on psychological functioning; at some earlier time, psychological functioning must also have affected education.) Because nearly all of the effects of occupational position have been shown to be attributable to occupational self-direction, it is unnecessary to include occupational position in the models. As before, other social characteristics that might affect current psychological functioning are permitted to have such effects and a subset of those social characteristics, which might be seen by an employer as credentials for a job, are allowed to affect current occupational self-direction.[13]

As Figure 7.4 shows, occupational self-direction both affects and is affected by parental valuation of self-direction. Moreover, education significantly affects parental valuation of self-direction in 1974, even though parental valuation of self-direction ten years earlier is statistically controlled. For no other facet of psychological functioning, though, not even for values-for-self, does education have a statistically significant effect on current functioning consistent in sign with its zero-order correlation. For the effects of education to be rendered nonsignificant, in most instances to be reversed in sign, seems so implausible as to suggest that the model be respecified when applied to facets of psychological functioning other than parental values—that education be permitted to have only an indirect effect on current psychological functioning, via its almost invariably strong effect on ten-year earlier psychological functioning.[14] Otherwise, the effect of oc-

---

[13] These models impose the parameters from the measurement model of occupational self-direction on causal models that use factor scores as their indices of first-order concepts. The residual of occupational self-direction is allowed to correlate with the residual of the facet of psychological functioning being examined in the particular model. This correlation is retained if statistically significant; otherwise, it is fixed at zero.

[14] Respecifying the models to permit education to have only an indirect effect on current psychological functioning, via its effect on earlier psychological functioning, does not reduce the total effect of education on current psychological functioning. It simply depicts differently the process by which this comes about.

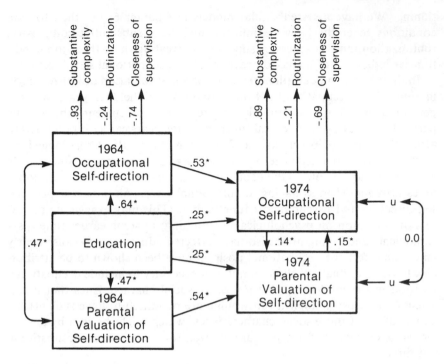

χ^2 (for the causal model) = 295.02
d.f. = 166
ratio = 1.78
* = Statistically significant, p≤.05; all other
    parameters are fixed.

**FIG. 7.4. THE RECIPROCAL EFFECTS OF OCCUPATIONAL
SELF-DIRECTION AND PARENTAL VALUATION OF
SELF-DIRECTION**
(Paths from social characteristics to endogenous variables and
correlations among residuals not shown.)

cupational self-direction on psychological functioning might be exaggerated. We think that education continues to have a direct effect on parental values (and only on parental values) because changes in parents' values for their children reflect not only changes in the parents' own psychological functioning but also differences in what a parent deems appropriate for younger and for older children—differences that are linked to parents' educational levels.

The models, thus specified, show occupational self-direction to have statistically significant, generally substantial, effects on all facets of psychological functioning included in our analysis (see Table 7.4).[15] In many instances, the relationship is reciprocal, with psychological functioning affecting, as well as being affected by, occupational self-direction.

Since these models test only contemporaneous, but not cross-lagged, effects, they do not tell us whether the effects of occupational self-direction on values, orientations, and intellectual flexibility are ongoing and continuous or occur only after some lapse of time. Nor do they tell us whether the effects of values, orientations, and intellectual flexibility on occupational self-direction result primarily from men molding their jobs to fit their values (primarily a contemporaneous process) or from the selection of men into jobs for which they are suited and out of jobs for which they are not suited (a lagged process).

We have attempted to estimate models that simultaneously assess the contemporaneous and lagged reciprocal effects of occupational self-direction and psychological functioning, but have been only partially successful.[16] A model of the reciprocal effects of occupational self-direction and ideational flexibility clearly and unambiguously shows that the effect of occupational self-direction on ideational flexibility is contemporaneous, while that of ideational flexibility on occupational self-direction is lagged. A similar model for self-directedness of orientation is somewhat equivocal (there is a negative, albeit statistically nonsignificant, contemporaneous effect of self-directedness on occupational self-direction), but the results are consonant: Occupational self-direction has a significant contemporaneous effect on self-directedness of orientation, while a self-directed orientation

---

[15] The effects of occupational self-direction on psychological functioning shown in Table 7.4 are stronger than those shown in Table 7 of Slomczynski, Miller, and Kohn (1981), even though based on the same data. This is primarily because we now utilize a more complete measurement model of occupational self-direction, one that includes all those correlations among the residuals of early substantive complexity, 1964 and 1974 substantive complexity, 1964 and 1974 closeness of supervision, and 1964 and 1974 routinization that are included in the second-order measurement model described in Appendix C. In the Slomczynski, Miller, and Kohn (1981) analysis, none of these correlations of residuals was included.

[16] To identify such models, we treat early substantive complexity as a proxy for early occupational self-direction, allowing it to affect 1974 occupational self-direction directly but to affect 1974 psychological functioning only indirectly. Using early substantive complexity as a proxy for early occupational self-direction is, in itself, a not-unreasonable procedure. This usage does, however, require some distortion of the measurement model of occupational self-direction, for we can no longer allow early substantive complexity to be correlated with the residual of 1974 occupational self-direction; to do so would destroy its value as an instrument. Nor is it appropriate to allow early substantive complexity to be correlated with the residuals of 1964 and 1974 substantive complexity (but not of 1964 and 1974 routinization and closeness of supervision) for, if early substantive complexity is a proxy for early occupational self-direction, then it is no more reasonable to allow it to be correlated with the residuals of 1964 and 1974 substantive complexity than with the residuals of 1964 and 1974 closeness of supervision or routinization. Still, such a model involves no very strong assumptions and is worth testing for what it can tell us.

Table 7.4.   THE RECIPROCAL EFFECTS OF OCCUPATIONAL
SELF-DIRECTION AND PSYCHOLOGICAL
FUNCTIONING

	Standardized Path Coefficients		
	Occupational Self-direction to Psychological Variable	Psychological Variable to Occupational Self-direction	Education to Psychological Variable[a]
Values			
Parental valuation of self-direction	.14*	.15*	.25*
Valuation of self-direction for oneself	.32*	−.05	.28*
Intellectual Functioning			
Ideational flexibility	.27*	.63*	.64*
Second-order Dimensions of Orientation			
Self-directedness	.43*	.28*	.53*
Distress	−.21*	−.04	−.06
Alienation	−.30*	−.12*	−.23*
First-order Dimensions of Orientation			
Authoritarian-conservatism	−.29*	−.21*	−.50*
Standards of morality	.32*	.17*	.40*
Trustfulness	.22*	.01	.40*
Self-confidence	.12*	.15*	.23*
Self-deprecation	−.27*	−.15*	−.23*
Fatalism	−.21*	−.19*	−.12*
Anxiety	−.23*	−.02	−.09*
Idea-conformity	−.12*	−.18*	−.28*

[a] Effect of education on 1964 psychological variable, except for parental valuation of self-direction, where we show effect of education on 1974 valuation of self-direction.
* = Statistically significant, .05 level or better.

has a significant lagged effect on occupational self-direction. Unfortunately, the identification of this type of model is not strong enough for us to reach statistically sensible solutions for other facets of psychological functioning. It would appear, then, that the effects of ideational flexibility and of a self-directed orientation on occupational self-direction are probably lagged rather than contemporaneous; for other aspects of psychological functioning we cannot say. Whatever the timing, though, the relationship between occupational self-direction and psychological functioning is quintessentially reciprocal.

In sum, as was clearly foreshadowed in Chapter 6, occupational self-direction has a causal impact on every facet of values, orientation, and cognitive functioning that we have examined. Our models also suggest that, except in the case of parental values, the psychological effects of education are indirect, in part through occupational self-direction, in part through education's having affected psychological functioning at an earlier time—in this model, 1964. What our model cannot assess is the degree to which education's effect on 1964 psychological functioning results from education's having affected occupational self-direction at some earlier stage of career. In any event, it is clear that occupational self-direction plays a major part in explaining the psychological effects not only of occupational position but also of education.

THE ROLE OF IDEATIONAL FLEXIBILITY IN MEDIATING THE EFFECTS OF EDUCATION AND OCCUPATIONAL SELF-DIRECTION ON VALUES AND ORIENTATIONS

Even though occupational self-direction is of considerable importance in explaining the psychological impact of education, it does seem that education has an appreciable impact on psychological functioning above and beyond what can reasonably be attributed to occupational self-direction. Why? In Chapter 1, it was hypothesized that education is pertinent to values and orientations, not only because of education's role in job placement, but also because education may provide the intellectual flexibility and breadth of perspective that are essential for self-directed values and orientations; lack of education must seriously interfere with men's ability to be self-directed. This hypothesis was originally tested by statistically controlling a measure of intellectual flexibility, with the result that the partial correlations of education with values and orientations were substantially reduced. It would be desirable to retest this hypothesis with methods that do not assume unidirectional effects of intellectual flexibility on other facets of psychological functioning—an assumption clearly inconsistent with the analyses of Chapter 6. Such a test requires that we extend the model of occupational self-direction and ideational flexibility to include at least one other facet of psychological functioning. Even in such models, though, we must continue to make the strong assumption that education has had unidirectional effects on psychological functioning, an assumption contrary to our belief that educational attainment must have been reciprocally related to psychological functioning at earlier stages of the men's lives. Although our models may exaggerate the total effects of education on psychological functioning, they do tell us a great deal about process.

Such models can test the further hypothesis, previously advanced for substantive complexity (Kohn, 1980: 205) and easily extended to occupational self-direction: "[T]he process by which [occupational self-direction] affects values and orientation may be mediated, at least in part, through intellectual flexibility. Increased intellectual flexibility may, for example, increase one's valuation of self-direction and one's tolerance of different beliefs; decreased intellectual flexibility may result in greater valuation of conformity to external authority and increased authoritarian conservatism. What makes this causal chain . . . plausible . . . is that intellectual flexibility is qualitatively different from . . . other psychological phenomena: it represents not content of thought, but process of thought. Many of the psychological processes affected by [occupational self-direction] involve thinking: valuing thinking for oneself, being tolerant of other people's thinking for themselves, and thinking through one's own moral standards. The hypothesis that intellectual flexibility plays a strategic intermediary role in explaining the effects of [occupational self-direction] on values and orientation is in principle testable, and we shall try to test it with our longitudinal data.'' The crux of the matter is whether ideational flexibility significantly and substantially affects other facets of psychological functioning.

A set of models (Figures not shown) that includes ideational flexibility and one other dimension of psychological functioning consistently fails to support either hypothesis.[17] That is, ideational flexibility does not have a statistically significant effect on parental values, values-for-self, self-directedness, distress, or alienation.[18] Instead, self-directedness of orientation and valuation of self-direction (for oneself) significantly affect ideational flexibility. This suggests that self-directed values and orientation may play the type of role we had hypothesized for ideational flexibility.

A parallel set of models that includes self-directedness of orientation (instead of ideational flexibility) and one other dimension of psychological functioning shows self-directedness of orientation to significantly affect not only ideational flexibility, but also values-for-children, values-for-self, and distress. Values-for-self and distress reciprocally affect self-directedness.

---

[17] The index of ideational flexibility used in these models is the one developed in Chapter 6 that does not include the "agree score" as an indicator and thus does not involve linear dependency with those psychological indices that are based on agree-disagree questions. The specification of the models is essentially the same as that used for models of the reciprocal effects of occupational self-direction and any one facet of psychological functioning. Thus, wherever statistically significant, all pertinent social characteristics are allowed to affect current psychological functioning and earlier occupational self-direction, but only those characteristics that might be interpreted as "credentialling" are allowed to affect 1974 occupational self-direction. The residual of 1974 occupational self-direction is permitted to correlate with the residuals of the 1974 psychological variables wherever statistically significant. In addition, the residuals of the psychological variables are allowed to correlate with each other. Finally, in the model of ideational flexibility and self-directedness, we depict the effects of occupational self-direction on psychological functioning as contemporaneous, those of psychological functioning on occupational self-direction as lagged.

[18] Now that we have gone beyond the analyses of Chapter 1, we no longer include the first-order dimensions of orientation; little would be learned from their inclusion that is not provided by the second-order dimensions.

(We do not assess the relationship between self-directedness and alienation, since they are based on overlapping indicators.) Thus, ideational flexibility cannot play its hypothesized intervening role because it does not significantly affect values and orientations; self-directedness of orientation, however, does appear to play such a role.

A more general model, depicted in Figure 7.5, shows the causal interrelationship of education, occupational self-direction, ideational flexibility, self-directedness of orientation, and distress. We are unable to estimate this entire model *de novo;* we have therefore re-estimated only those parameters that were statistically significant in either the set of models for ideational flexibility or the set of models for self-directedness of orientation and have fixed at zero all parameters that were consistently nonsignificant. In this sense, Figure 7.5 is more heuristic than definitive, even though the model does allow all paths and all correlations of residuals that had proved to be statistically significant in any simpler model.

The most powerful direct effect of occupational self-direction is on self-directedness of orientation, which in turn substantially affects ideational flexibility and also affects and is affected by distress. From a psychological point of view, self-directedness of orientation is at the heart of this system of mutual effects of occupational self-direction and psychological functioning. We had earlier hypothesized that occupational experience affects an individual's sense of self and of the world through its effect on his cognitive functioning. Instead, we now learn that occupational experience *directly* affects an individual's view of himself and the world and that—to some degree—occupational experience indirectly affects an individual's cognitive functioning through its effect on his sense of self and the world.

The model also clarifies the processes by which education affects psychological functioning. Its effect on distress is minimal. As has been evident throughout our analyses, some considerable proportion of education's effects on both ideational flexibility and self-directedness of orientation is "direct", in the sense that education directly affects both 1964 ideational flexibility and 1964 self-directedness, both of which strongly affect their 1974 counterparts.[19] As has also been evident throughout our analyses, some proportion of education's effects on both ideational flexibility and

---

[19] Figure 7.5 exaggerates the direct effects of education on 1964 ideational flexibility and 1964 self-directedness, not only because it models education as having unidirectional effects on 1964 psychological functioning, but also because it takes no account of 1964 occupational self-direction affecting psychological functioning. Education faces little competition in this model. (If we had the instruments, we would model a reciprocal relationship between 1964 occupational self-direction and 1964 psychological functioning. Some of what appears in Figure 7.5 to be the direct effect of education would undoubtedly be shown to be indirect, via 1964 occupational self-direction.) Still, we believe that a substantial component of education's effect on psychological functioning is not mediated through occupational self-direction, but results from the educational process itself.

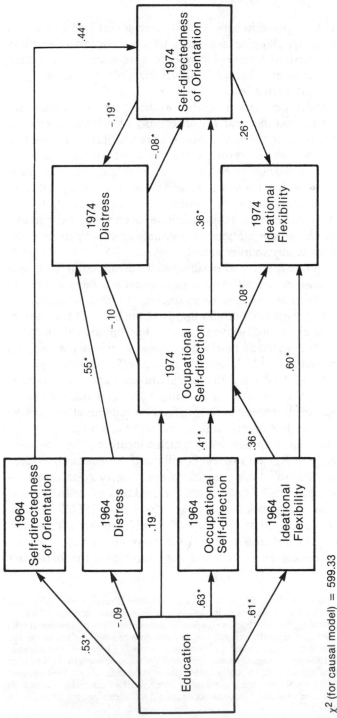

χ^2 (for causal model) = 599.33
d.f. = 186
ratio = 3.22

* = Statistically significant, p≤.05; other parameters are nonsignificant.

FIG. 7.5. OCCUPATIONAL SELF-DIRECTION, IDEATIONAL FLEXIBILITY, SELF-DIRECTEDNESS OF ORIENTATION, AND DISTRESS

(Correlations among 1964 variables, correlations among residuals, and paths from social characteristics to endogenous variables not shown.)

self-directedness of orientation is indirect, through occupational self-direction. What is newly illustrated in this model is education's indirect effect on ideational flexibility through self-directedness of orientation. This effect, approximately .09, represents only about sixteen percent of education's total effect on ideational flexibility, a modest proportion but important nonetheless, because self-directness of orientation probably continues to affect ideational flexibility throughout men's occupational careers and, in all likelihood, throughout their lives.

These conclusions obviously depend in part on our having fixed at zero the paths from ideational flexibility to self-directedness and to distress, because those paths were statistically nonsignificant in simpler models. We are able to modify the model in a crucial respect, by reopening the path from ideational flexibility to self-directedness of orientation. In a model thus modified, the effect of self-directedness on ideational flexibility remains positive and statistically significant, while the effect of ideational flexibility on self-directedness is negative but statistically nonsignificant. Thus, in the modified model, too, ideational flexibility does not significantly affect self-directedness.

The absence of a significant effect of ideational flexibility on self-directedness is discrepant with the model of job structure and personality (Table 6.4), where ideational flexibility has a modest but nonetheless statistically significant positive effect on self-directedness. The one notable difference between the two models is that, in the job-structure model (Table 6.4), education is permitted to directly affect 1974 self-directedness of orientation. In the occupational self-direction model (Figure 7.5), education is permitted to affect 1974 self-directedness only indirectly, through 1964 self-directedness—on the basis of our having found in a model of occupational self-direction and self-directedness of orientation that the direct effect of education on 1974 self-directedness would be negative and nonsignificant. In the model of occupational self-direction and three dimensions of personality, however, a path from education to self-directedness of orientation would be significant and positive. The presence of such a path would reduce the magnitude of the path from occupational self-direction to self-directedness of orientation from .36 to .24. But, crucially, the path from ideational flexibility to self-directedness of orientation would remain statistically nonsignificant, a trivial .01. All models are consistent on the main point: Whether examined in context of a model of job conditions and personality or in context of a model of occupational self-direction and personality, the predominant effect in the relationship between ideational flexibility and self-directedness of orientation is *from* self-directedness *to* ideational flexibility.

We do not deny the importance of ideational flexibility, which has a considerable (in the present models, lagged) effect on occupational self-direction. Ideationally flexible men tend, over time, to be self-directed in their work; doing self-directed work encourages a self-directed orientation; and a self-directed orientation facilitates greater ideational flexibility. In a general sense, the hypothesis that ideational flexibility plays a key role in the interrelationship of education, occupational self-direction, and values and orientations is confirmed, but the specific hypothesis about how ideational flexibility enters into the process was certainly wide of the mark. The importance of ideational flexibility lies not in its contemporaneous effects on values and orientations, but in its long-term effect on occupational self-direction.

SOCIAL CLASS

We have thus far focused on social stratification to the exclusion of social class. What of social class? Does it bear a relationship to psychological functioning similar to that of social stratification? If so, does occupational self-direction play a similar role in explaining the relationship?

Answering these questions requires that we face the difficult issues of how best to conceptualize and index social class. The classic bourgeoisie-proletariat distinction is clearly insufficient as a depiction of the class structure of modern industrial society. The question is, what further distinctions are essential and how should they be drawn? In postulating a petty bourgeoisie, which like the true bourgeoisie owns the means of production, but which like the proletariat performs labor rather than controlling the labor power of others, Marx proposed both a further distinction and a rationale for making additional distinctions. Nearly all subsequent theorists have followed Marx's example, making distinctions that attempt to "disaggregate" the two large composites, owners and workers, into a greater number of more homogeneous categories. We do the same, borrowing from Erik Wright (1976, 1978a, 1978b, 1979; Wright and Perrone, 1977), Robinson and Kelley (1979), and Gagliani (1981).

In his provocative analyses of the class structure of American society, Wright argues that there exist in this and other advanced capitalist societies three basic class locations—a bourgeoisie, whose members control investments and the accumulation process, the physical means of production, and the labor power of others; a petty bourgeoisie, whose members control investment and the means of production, but not the labor power of others; and a proletariat, whose members control none of these essential elements of production. Wright argues that there are, in addition, groups whose situations are more complex, to which he applies the evocative term, contradictory locations within class relations. Between the proletariat and the bourgeoisie is management, a group that he subdivides into top managers, middle managers, technocrats, and foremen and line supervisors (both of the latter caught between management and the workers they supervise). The "contradictory location" between the proletariat and the petty bourgeoisie is a group he terms "semi-autonomous employees", mainly white-collar technical employees and certain highly skilled craftsmen who have control over how they do their work and have at least some control over what they produce, but who do not enjoy the degree of autonomy of the self-employed. The "contradictory location" between the petty bourgeoisie and the bourgeoisie is composed of small employers, a group of considerable importance to our analyses, since almost all employers interviewed in any cross-sectional survey have only a few employees.

Although no study embodies all the distinctions Wright makes, the evidence is considerable that his conceptualization is empirically potent. This is shown both in Wright's own research (see, in particular, Wright and Perrone, 1977) and in the work of others (e.g., Kalleberg and Griffin, 1980; Robinson and Kelley, 1979). We cannot, however, accept his entire analysis as the basis for our classification. We find problematic Wright's use of "autonomy" (which is similar to our "occupational self-direction") as the criterion for distinguishing semi-autonomous employees from the proletariat. In our view, autonomy, although closely linked to the job's location in the class structure, is not itself definitional of class. The fact of being subject to the supervisory authority of an employer or his agent may be indicative of one's class situation, but the degree of autonomy one enjoys in one's work seems to us to be more a consequence than a criterion of class. A further difficulty for us, even if not for Wright, is that if we were to use autonomy as a criterion for indexing social class, it would be logically inconsistent to then ask whether the psychological effects of social class are attributable to occupational self-direction. We therefore do not use Wright's distinction between the proletariat and semi-autonomous workers.

We do, however, accept Wright's argument that control over the work of others is a valid criterion of class. Here we follow also the logic of Robinson and Kelley (1979), who would merge Marx and Dahrendorf to define classes in terms both of control over the means of production and of control over subordinates. The major import of their argument for our purposes is that the principal distinction among employees would be in terms of their control over other persons. We find this argument attractive, both because it seems to us that control over the work of others is integral to class and because there is no logical contradiction between using authority over others as a criterion of class and then asking whether the psychological impact of class is attributable to occupational self-direction.[20]

---

[20] A problem for us, though, is that our index of occupational self-direction includes as one of its first-order indicators information about authority over others. Specifically, complexity of work with people, an indicator of substantive complexity, uses supervisory responsibility as one of its criteria. But since supervision is only one of several criteria for evaluating complexity of work with people, and complexity of work with people is only one of seven indicators of substantive complexity, this can hardly have much consequence for our analysis.

Unless we find some substitute for Wright's distinction between the proletariat and semi-autonomous workers, we may treat as relatively homogeneous a large and heterogeneous segment of the work force: all non-supervisory employees. As a potential way of differentiating possibly important class interests within this segment, we follow Gagliani (1981), Vanneman and Pampel (1977), and Poulantzas (1975), in treating the distinction between manual and nonmanual work, at least tentatively, as a further criterion of class. This distinction is certainly time-honored, going back to Marx's discussion of the "mental production" of intellectuals and the "physical production" of workers. Gagliani argues that even in modern capitalist economies, nonmanual workers enjoy a privileged position in conditions of work and in income, privileges great enough to make their interests more akin to those of management than to those of manual workers. We find the argument convincing, as applied to male nonsupervisory workers; we do not think it valid for females, nor do we think it applicable to supervisory employees. Since our analysis is limited to males, we do employ the white-collar/blue-collar distinction, using it, not as an alternative to Wright's distinction between first-line supervisors and the proletariat, but as an alternative to Wright's division of non-supervisory employees into the proletariat and semi-autonomous employees. We take it as a working hypothesis that nonmanual male workers play a role in the productive process sufficiently different from that of manual male workers that they occupy a distinctive class position.

On the basis of these considerations, we divide the population of men employed in civilian occupations into six categories, which, whether we term them "social classes", "locations" within the class structure, or class categories, are distinguished on the basis of their differential relationships to ownership and control over the physical resources and the people involved in production.

Our classification is necessarily imprecise in establishing class boundaries. There is, for example, no theoretically compelling reason to decide whether having a five- or a fifteen- or a fifty-percent investment in a firm constitutes ownership. After examining the interview reports, we draw the line at twenty percent, which seems to differentiate men whose on-the-job roles are more like those of owners than like those of employed management or first-line supervisors. More problematic and more important: Does having a single employee distinguish a small employer from a petty bourgeois? Two? Three? On the basis of a case-by-case examination of the interview records, we draw the line between three non-family employees and four or more. Having four non-family employees seems to differentiate firms where the work role of the owner is more that of supervisor than that of primary producer.

A further problem is that we cannot make all the distinctions we would wish to make, because the sample does not contain sufficient numbers of men in some of the categories. Thus, we have too few men in managerial positions to be able to distinguish between higher and lower management. Furthermore, the category, large employers, however important it may be for social theory, is for us an almost empty cell. The one employer of 100 or more workers in our sample will be combined with other employers in a category that is overwhelmingly comprised of employers of fewer than 25 workers. Still, a serviceable classification is possible:

1. Employers: owners who employ four or more non-family workers [in our sample, overwhelmingly small employers]. N = 32
2. Self-employed ["petty bourgeoisie"]: owners who employ no more than three non-family workers. N = 82
3. Management: employees who have less than a 20 percent share in the ownership of the enterprise that employs them and who have at least two hierarchical levels beneath them.[21] N = 65
4. First-line supervisors: employees who have direct supervisory authority over three or more workers and have only non-supervisory workers beneath them.[22] N = 122
5. White-collar workers: nonmanual, non-supervisory employees. N = 105
6. Blue-collar workers: manual, non-supervisory employees. N = 219

As is evident from the number of men in each class category, this classification yields a meaningful distribution. Moreover, descriptive statistics (Table 7.5) demonstrate the validity of the argument of class-theoreticians that, although social class and social stratification have much in common, they are far from identical. This is so despite the distinction between white-collar and blue-collar workers being integral to our indices of both stratification and class. The correlation between social class and social stratification (expressed in terms of *eta,* a correlation coefficient appropriate to the non-

---

[21] We did not ask how many hierarchical levels are below the respondent, but we can infer whether there are at least two such levels from answers to two questions, one asking how many employees are "under you, either because they are directly under you or because they are under people you supervise," the other asking "how many of these are directly under you, with nobody in between." If the total number "under" the respondent is larger than the number who are "directly under" him, we infer that there are at least two levels beneath him. The inference is then checked against the detailed interview record.

[22] The interview records show that employees who supervise one worker are without exception "doers", assisted by a helper, secretary, or trainee. Most employees who have two subordinates are similarly situated, but some actually are first-line supervisors of very small work crews—in most cases, a work crew that is seasonally or situationally smaller than usual. Those men who supervise only two others but who actually function as first-line supervisors have been thus categorized. Those who supervise three others in all instances prove to be first-line supervisors.

Table 7.5. RELATIONSHIP OF SOCIAL CLASS TO
SOCIAL STRATIFICATION AND
OCCUPATIONAL SELF-DIRECTION

	N's	Means[a]			
		Social Strat.	Education	Job Income[b]	Occ. Status
1 Employers	(32)	1.33	.96	14.68	9.48
2 Petty bourgeoisie	(82)	.26	−.24	2.59	4.20
3 Management	(65)	1.51	1.45	9.39	9.69
4 First-line supervisors	(122)	.23	.06	−0.46	2.29
5 White-collar	(106)	1.48	1.52	−1.40	8.93
6 Blue-collar	(219)	−1.58	−1.25	−4.91	−11.43
Eta[c] =		.72	.51	.47	.71
F =		98.53	44.05	33.98	123.50

	N's	Occ. Self-Direction	Substantive Complexity	Close. of Supervision	Routin-ization
1 Employers	(32)	.51	1.02	.xx[d]	− .36
2 Petty bourgeoisie	(82)	− .02	− .03	.xx	− .19
3 Management	(65)	1.15	1.34	− .33	− .49
4 First-line supervisors	(122)	.43	.45	− .13	− .10
5 White-collar	(106)	.71	.99	− .14	.02
6 Blue-collar	(219)	−1.00	−1.26	.24	.32
Eta[c] =		.74	.74	.41	.19
F =		79.43	94.08	17.44	4.48

[a]Expressed as differences from grand mean.
[b]The metric for job income is thousands of dollars annual income.
[c]Corrected for unreliability of measurement.
[d]Irrelevant.

ordinal classification of social class) is .72—much below unity.[23] Moreover, the relationships of social class with social stratification and with the components of social stratification are not linear or even ordinal. Employers do not rank highest in social-stratification position; managers do, followed closely by white-collar workers—a category that includes professionals. The one respect in which employers clearly rank first is in job income, which should hardly surprise anyone of Marxist persuasion. In general, these descriptive data justify the contention that social classes are discrete categories. Moreover, the sharp break between blue-collar workers and others justifies the decision to differentiate manual from nonmanual, nonsupervisory workers.

These findings show also a sizeable relationship between social-class po-

---

[23] *Eta* represents the square root of the proportion of the variance in a dependent variable that is attributable to some independent variable(s). All correlations and partial correlations based on *eta* have been corrected for measurement error, to make the statistics presented for social class comparable to those earlier presented for social stratification.

sition and occupational self-direction—a correlation of .74. Again, it is not employers but managers who are most self-directed in their work, and this by a substantial margin. Next most self-directed in their work are nonmanual, non-supervisory workers, followed by employers and then by first-line supervisors. The petty bourgeoisie rank relatively low and manual workers lowest of all.

The correlations between social-class position and values, orientations, and intellectual functioning are substantial, even if generally not as large as those between social-stratification position and these same facets of psychological functioning (see Table 7.6). The correlation between social-class position and ideational flexibility, for example, is .58, with managers and employers ranking highest, followed by white-collar employees, supervisors, the petty bourgeoisie, and, at some distance, manual workers. The correlation between social-class position and self-directedness of orientation is .43, with employers ranking highest, managers and white-collar workers next, and manual workers lowest. The findings are similar with respect to men's valuing self-direction, both for children and for self: Managers and employers rank high in their valuation of self-direction; manual workers have the most conformist values. Where manual workers rank high is in distress and alienation.

Since there are sizeable differences between white-collar and blue-collar non-supervisory employees, one must wonder whether our building this distinction into the index of social class has produced artifactually high correlations between social class and psychological functioning. The question is easily answered: If we combine white-collar and blue-collar employees into a single category—the proletariat—thereby making a five-category schema for social class, the correlations between social class and psychological functioning remain virtually unchanged. Thus, a class index based entirely on ownership and control over the means of production and the labor power of others yields the same conclusion: Class is consistently and substantially related to values, orientations, and intellectual functioning.

Are the class-correlations attributable to occupational self-direction? In analyzing the relationship between social class and occupational self-direction, we revert to unidirectional models, testing whether the correlations between social class and psychological functioning are reduced when occupational self-direction is statistically controlled. We find that the correlations are markedly reduced, albeit not to zero, regardless of whether we use the index of social class that makes the white-collar/blue-collar distinction or the index that ignores this distinction (again see Table 7.6). Moreover, we find no statistically significant interaction between social class and occupational self-direction vis-a-vis any facet of psychological functioning, indicating that the relationships between occupational self-direction and psychological functioning are essentially the same in all social classes. Given

Table 7.6.   RELATIONSHIP OF SOCIAL CLASS TO VALUES, ORIENTATIONS, AND INTELLECTUAL FLEXIBILITY

	N's	Parental Valuation of Self-dir.	Valuation of Self-dir. for Self	Ideational Flexibility	Self-Directed Orientation	Distress	Alienation
		Means[a]					
1 Employers	(32)	.11	.11	.32	.54	−.14	−.19
2 Petty bourgeoisie	(82)	.02	−.10	.01	−.04	−.06	.01
3 Management	(65)	.12	.29	.33	.42	−.11	−.18
4 First-line supervisors	(122)	.04	.04	.13	.12	−.11	−.10
5 White-collar	(106)	.07	.12	.25	.42	.03	−.10
6 Blue-collar	(219)	−.12	−.14	−.34	−.46	.13	.19
		Correlations					
Eta[b] =		.47	.23	.58	.43	.18	.31
F =		21.73	7.00	61.36	28.00	4.18	13.40
Eta, controlling occ. self-direction =		.13	.12	.15	.16	.13	.07
Proportional reduction =		72%	49%	74%	62%	29%	79%
		Correlations for Social Class when White-collar and Blue-collar Employees are Combined					
Eta[b] =		.47	.23	.57	.43	.17	.31
F =		26.76	8.77	76.37	34.89	4.69	16.50
Eta, controlling occ. self-direction =		.10	.12	.11	.15	.11	.03
Proportional reduction =		79%	49%	82%	65%	38%	90%

[a]Expressed as differences from grand mean.
[b]Corrected for unreliability of measurement.

what we have previously learned about the causal impact of occupational self-direction on values, orientations, and intellectual functioning, we conclude that the psychological impact of social class, like that of social stratification, is to a very substantial degree indirect: Social-class position markedly affects men's opportunities to exercise occupational self-direction; the exercise of occupational self-direction in turn markedly affects men's psychological functioning.

CONCLUSION

In this chapter, we have assessed the interrelationships of both social stratification and social class with occupational self-direction and psychological functioning. In dealing with social stratification, we have addressed essentially the same questions as those with which this book began, now testing empirically several crucial parts of the interpretation. In these analyses, we have used the longitudinal data provided by the follow-up study and have employed much more exact and rigorous methods than were heretofore available.

Still, many limitations of data and of method discussed in previous chapters apply as well to these analyses. In addition, we must be cautious in drawing conclusions from models that disaggregate such extremely high correlations as that between occupational position and occupational self-direction. We must also be cautious in drawing conclusions from causal models that include two or more facets of psychological functioning, because some of these models suffer problems of identification and the most complete model cannot be estimated de novo. Nevertheless, crucial analyses—e.g., of the reciprocal effects of occupational self-direction and each of the several facets of psychological functioning—do not require such tentativeness. There are firm conclusions of fundamental importance to the thesis of this book to be drawn from these analyses.

The findings could hardly be more supportive of our thesis. We find consistent relationships between social-stratification position and values and orientations: The higher men's social-stratification positions, the more likely they are to value self-direction, for themselves and for their children, and the more likely they are to hold self-directed orientations to self and society. We can now add to those original conclusions that the magnitudes of the correlations are considerably larger than the earlier methods of analysis had indicated and that the basic pattern of correlations holds not only for values and the first-order facets of orientation originally examined, but also for self-directedness of orientation, distress, alienation, and ideational flexibility.

We confirm, too, that the psychological impact of social-stratification position is substantially attributable to occupational self-direction. This conclusion is based on an empirical assessment of the reciprocal relationship between occupational position and occupational self-direction. We find each to affect the other strongly, with education affecting both. As a result, the correlation of occupational position with occupational self-direction is near unity. Thus, a basic tenet of our interpretation, that there is a close relationship between social-stratification position and occupational self-direction, is confirmed. Despite this high correlation, though, it is possible (by disaggregating social stratification and occupational self-direction into their component concepts) to distinguish the psychological effects of social-stratification position from those of occupational self-direction. These analyses show—subject to the cautions expressed above—that the psychological impact of social-stratification position (and of its components, education and occupational position) is attributable, in very substantial degree, to occupational self-direction.

The original analysis posited that the experience of occupational self-direction must actually affect values and orientation. That proposition was both the crucial element in the entire interpretation and—since it was based only on a priori argument—the most questionable. A major focus in nearly every succeeding chapter of this book has been the empirical test of this argument, at first with cross-sectional data and two-stage least squares, then with longitudinal data and linear structural-equations models, developing the models further in each succeeding analysis. Now we have brought the method to bear most directly on the critical reciprocal relationships, those between occupational self-direction and the several facets of values, orientation, and cognitive functioning. In every instance, we find that occupational self-direction does have a causal impact on psychological functioning. In most instances, the relationship is reciprocal, with values, orientations, and cognitive functioning also affecting the exercise of self-direction in work. The interpretive chain is now complete: Social-stratification position affects and is affected by occupational self-direction; occupational self-direction affects and is affected by psychological functioning. Moreover (as was argued in Chapter 6), occupational self-direction, ideational flexibility, and a self-directed orientation are intertwined in a dynamic process through which the individual's place in the stratification system both affects and is affected by his personality.

In the analyses of this chapter, we have also re-evaluated the processes by which education affects values and orientation. Our models, as noted, continue to treat the effects of education on psychological functioning as unidirectional, undoubtedly exaggerating those effects. Still, the models tell us a great deal about process. Contrary to the hypothesis advanced in Chapter 1, ideational flexibility does not play a substantial intervening role in the process by which education affects values and orientation. Instead, ideational flexibility is more affected by, than a determinant of, self-directed values and orientations. This being the case, another hypothesis—that ideational flexibility plays an intervening role in the process by which occupational self-direction affects values and orientations—also falls by the wayside. We conclude instead that the effects of both education and occupational self-direction on self-directed values and orientations are predominantly direct; and, furthermore, that the effects of education and of occupational self-direction on ideational flexibility are in part indirect, through self-directed values and orientations.

Finally, we learn that occupational self-direction plays a crucial role in explaining the psychological impact of social class, just as it does in explaining the psychological impact of social stratification. The psychological effects of social class examined in our analyses prove to be mainly a function of the varying degrees of occupational self-direction enjoyed by men at various locations in the class system. Perhaps occupational self-direction does not play so pivotal a role in explaining the impact of social-class position on such things as social-class identification and political ideology. But, for the psychological phenomena we have examined, occupational self-direction clearly plays a major part in explaining the impact of social class.

Whether we look through the prism of the stratification system or of the class system of this society, we find that men's positions in the larger socio-economic structure affect their values, orientations, and cognitive functioning, in large part because of the close link between socioeconomic position and the opportunity to be self-directed in one's work.

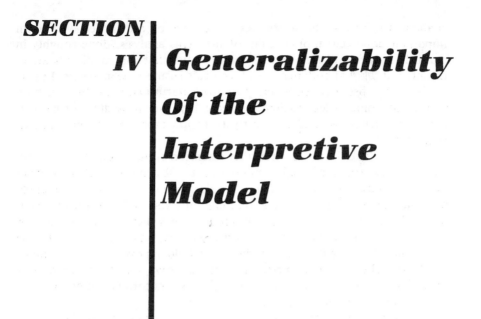

SECTION IV Generalizability of the Interpretive Model

All the empirical analyses presented to this point have focused on the relationships between men's job conditions and men's psychological functioning. In this Section of the book, we expand the interpretive model greatly, to deal not only with men's, but also with women's, job conditions and psychological functioning; not only with intrapsychic functioning, but also with behavior; not only with the conditions of work experienced in paid employment, but also with those experienced in housework; and not only with current job conditions, but also with the historical residue of job conditions experienced by one's forebears.

Chapter 8 uses interviews with the wives of the men in the follow-up study to ask whether job conditions affect women similarly to men. We find that, although woman's job conditions are quite different from those of men, the psychological effects of particular job conditions are much the same for women as for men. Moreover, the magnitudes of the relationships between job conditions and psychological functioning are as large for women as for men. We conclude that our interpretation is fully applicable to women.

Chapter 9 extends the interpretation from intrapsychic phenomena to behavior, specifically, to the intellectuality of leisure-time pursuits. Admittedly, our data are derived from respondents' *reports* about their behavior, not from observations by some other person. Admittedly, too, the intellectuality of leisure-time activity is but one small segment of behavior; still, it enables us to assess whether the lessons of the job are carried over to an important non-occupational realm of life. This analysis, done roughly in parallel for men and for women, demonstrates that job conditions affect the intellectuality of both men's and women's leisure-time activities. In particular, the substantive complexity of work has a marked effect on both men's and women's leisure-time intellectuality, thus providing further evidence that people generalize directly from job experience to nonoccupational activities.

Chapter 10 provides an even further extension of the model, from the job conditions experienced in paid employment to the conditions of work experienced in housework. This analysis, too, is done more or less in parallel for men and women—on the expectation that housework will affect people similarly, albeit perhaps not to equal degree, whatever their sex and whether or not they are employed outside the home. This expectation is not met. The conditions of work experienced in housework do appear to affect women's psychological functioning in essentially the same ways as do the conditions of work experienced in paid employment. This is not true for men, perhaps because housework is not imperative for men.

Finally, Chapter 11 provides the most far-reaching extension of the interpretive model, from current conditions of work to the intergenerational transmission of values and orientations developed by one's forebears out of their conditions of work in an earlier historical epoch. The analysis shows a consistent relationship between the recency of the abolition of serfdom in the countries from which our respondents' forebears came and their own present-day orientations, even controlling their own occupational conditions. Since the conditions of occupational life under serfdom were characterized by lack of opportunity for occupational self-direction, the analysis suggests the transmission of an historical legacy from those who worked under such conditions to their descendants.

Sample and Methods of Data Collection

The analyses discussed in this Section use the cross-sectional data of the 1964 survey of the entire sample of men, the longitudinal data of the 1964 and 1974 surveys of a subsample of those men, and the cross-sectional data of the 1974 survey of their wives. Because the analyses reported in these chapters were done at different times in the course of the overall research program, the samples used, the methods of analysis employed and, to some degree, the concepts and indices represent the stage of development we had reached at the time of the particular analysis rather than that reached by the time we had completed the longitudinal analyses of Section III. We trust that this will not confuse the reader. We have every reason to believe that, were we to go to the immense effort required to redo all the analyses as we would now do them, the reanalyses would only strengthen our conclusions. As a comparison of Chapter 7 to Chapter 1 shows, reanalyses using longitudinal data and advanced statistical methods strengthen the empirical evidence for our interpretation.

Women and Work: The Psychological Effects of Occupational Conditions*

Joanne Miller,
Carmi Schooler,
Melvin L. Kohn,
and Karen A. Miller

Paid employment is a part of the lives of a large and ever-increasing proportion of women, yet we know little about how women's work conditions affect their psychological functioning and how women's psychological functioning, in turn, affects their conditions of work. The purpose of this chapter is to examine how day-to-day job experiences relate to women's intellectual functioning, self-conceptions, and social orientations. Our hypothesis is that women's job conditions are substantially related to their psychological functioning. In particular, we hypothesize that those job conditions that offer challenge and opportunity for self-direction will be related to favorable self-conceptions, flexible social orientations, and effective intellectual functioning, while those job conditions that subject women to pressure or uncertainty or constrain their opportunities for self-direction will be related to less favorable self-conceptions, more rigid social orientations, and less effective intellectual functioning. Moreover, we hypothesize that the causal ordering is reciprocal, with the conditions and requirements

* This is a revised version of a paper of the same title originally published in the *American Journal of Sociology* (Miller, et al., 1979). We are indebted to Cheryl Keller and Margaret Renfors for their help with statistical analyses and to Carrie Schoenbach for assistance in computer programming and index construction. This paper would not have been possible without Ronald Schoenberg's statistical consultation and inventiveness in modifying the LISREL program to meet our needs.

of jobs both influencing and being influenced by personality throughout adult life.

These hypotheses are derived from earlier research on men (Chapters 3 and 5). In the absence of empirical evidence, however, there are several reasons why we cannot simply assume that conclusions based on research on men are necessarily true for women. On the most general level, women's socialization has been deemed responsible for gender-specific psychological attributes, values, and behavior; Bernard (1981) goes so far as to identify a uniquely female culture that affects women's behavior in all realms of activity, including work. More directly relevant to employment are specific work orientations that have been hypothesized to result from differential socialization by sex. For example, women have been described as having a fear of success (Horner, 1972), as emphasizing peer relationships over work tasks (an argument reviewed by Kanter, 1976), and as not being motivated to work (reviewed by Laws, 1976).

Normative expectations held by both sexes that women's occupational interests will be secondary to family roles may be especially pertinent to the relationship between work and psychological functioning. If housework and child care rather than employment are viewed as a woman's primary responsibilities, an employed woman may experience role conflict and stress that affect her reactions to both roles (Coser and Rokoff, 1971). Even without such role conflict, women who carry dual responsibilities for home and job may become fatigued by the effort needed to fulfill both sets of role requirements. Concern about the maternal role may affect occupational experience also by leading to a belief in the necessity of women interrupting labor force participation during childbearing and pre-school childrearing years. In fact, labor force participation drops sharply for women between the ages of 25 and 30, and increases again for women over 30 (Sweet, 1973). The interruption of employment and potential careers may influence women's reactions to work conditions both before and after the break.

Beyond these attitudinal and behavioral consequences of socialization, there are structural constraints that differentiate women's employment experiences from men's. Many women work in sex-segregated occupations (Gross, 1968; Williams, 1975). Even for women who work in the same occupations as men, sex discrimination in employment and advancement may influence the relationship of work and personality (Kanter, 1976). In particular, the dollar-returns from education and occupational status are lower for women than for men, even when previous work experience and number of hours worked are statistically controlled (Featherman and Hauser, 1976).

Despite all these real or putative sex differences in socialization and occupational opportunity, we hypothesize that the psychological effects of occupational conditions are much the same for adults of both sexes. Granted, women differ from men in the occupational conditions and general life circumstances to which they are exposed. Nevertheless, we believe that the psychological processes of men and women are so similar, and the psychological impact of occupational experience is so powerful, that the effects of particular occupational conditions will not be contingent on the sex of the worker.

Our intent is to focus on those essential job conditions that impinge on the worker most directly, insistently, and demandingly—the structural imperatives of the job.[1] The original analysis of employed men (Chapter 3) found that twelve structural imperatives are significantly related to psychological functioning, independent of education and other occupational conditions. We here consider these same twelve job conditions.[2] We hypothesize that these occupational conditions will be similarly related to women's psychological functioning. We further hypothesize that the magnitudes of the relationships will be similar to those for men.

For women, the great variation in the number of hours worked per week makes this job condition potentially important. We therefore add it to the set of structural imperatives, including it under job pressures.

We begin the description of our analyses by discussing the sample and our means of measuring each respondent's occupational conditions, psychological functioning, and social background. We then examine the relationships between major dimensions of occupational experience and psychological functioning, using increasingly stringent controls to test several alternative interpretations. Next, we explore the possibility that the relationships between occupational conditions and psychological functioning may be conditional on social circumstances or personal preferences. Finally, we develop and assess reciprocal causal models that estimate the degree to which women's psychological functioning both influences and is influenced by their job conditions.

CHARACTERISTICS OF THE SAMPLE

Our sample consists of the employed wives of the men who were interviewed in the 1974 follow-up survey. Interviews were conducted with 555 women,

---

[1] By contrast, most discussions of working women have focused on particular occupations. Illustrative studies of women in particular occupations or occupational groups include research about waitresses (Whyte, 1948), prostitutes (Davis, 1937), executives (Cussler, 1958), nurses (Pearlin, 1962; Davis and Olesen, 1963; Lewin and Damrell, 1978), midwives (Mongeau, et al., 1961), dental students (Linn, 1971), politicians (Constantini and Craik, 1972), service occupations (Howe, 1978), and secretaries and managers (Kanter, 1977)

[2] We use the set of job conditions developed in Chapter 3 rather than the revised set used in Chapter 6 because the analyses reported in this chapter were done before those that led to our modifying the set. There is nothing in the results reported here, or in subsequent analyses, to suggest that the conclusions would be changed in any important respect were we to redo all the analyses using the modified set of job conditions.

90 percent of those eligible. At the time of the interview, 269 of these women were formally employed 10 or more hours per week; these women constitute our sample.

The characteristics of this sample closely approximate those of employed, married women of the appropriate age-range in the general population. In evaluating its usefulness for assessing the interrelationship of women's occupational conditions and psychological functioning, we can say at minimum that this sample is drawn from a large and important segment of the female work force: Married women living with their husbands constitute nearly three-fifths of all employed women. Indeed, the most dramatic increases in labor force participation are occurring among currently married women (U.S. Women's Bureau, 1976; Oppenheimer, 1970).

We nevertheless face two problems of generalizability. First, the sample does not have adequate representation of the youngest and oldest employed women, because it consists of women married to men who were at least 26 years old and no older than 65 at the time of the follow-up survey. It is pertinent to note, though, that within the broad age-range of our sample the relationships between occupational conditions and psychological functioning are not conditional on age. This evidence, while hardly definitive, strengthens our belief that the findings can be generalized to all employed married women.

The second problem of generalizability is whether results based on married women can be extended to the never-married and the previously married. A single or formerly married woman may have greater financial responsibilities for herself and her family (Wolf, 1977), may have more serious career commitments both in terms of subjective investment (Bielby, 1978) and number of hours worked (Hudis, 1976), and may receive higher earnings (Treiman and Terrell, 1975) than a married woman. If the relationships between occupational conditions and psychological functioning differed by marital status because of these or other characteristics, it would be misleading to generalize beyond the currently married. In the course of our analysis, we shall bring pertinent data to bear on this issue. In any case, married women are an appropriate population on which to test our hypothesis that sex-role differences do not alter the effects of occupational conditions on psychological functioning, because employed married women are especially likely to be subject to actual and potential conflicts among occupational, conjugal, and maternal roles.

MEASUREMENT OF VARIABLES

To test our hypotheses about the relationship of women's occupational experience to their psychological functioning, we developed measures of our respondents' occupational conditions, psychological functioning, and social origins. Wherever possible, we used maximum-likelihood confirmatory factor analysis to separate measurement error from concepts (see Joreskog, 1969, 1970).

Structural Imperatives of the Job

Occupational Self-Direction.   The measurement model of occupational self-direction is similar to that developed in Chapter 6 for men, except that it is limited to data for 1974 (see Figure 8.1). We developed a nonorthogonal, three-factor measurement model, allowing correlations between the residuals of some of the indicators, as shown in the Figure. This model has a chi-square of 50.67 with 44 degrees of freedom, for a ratio of 1.15 per degree of freedom, a very good fit of model to data.

Other Structural Imperatives of the Job.   The remaining structural imperatives of the job, which measure several aspects of the individual's place in the organizational structure, job pressures, and job uncertainties, are each indexed by single items. The three aspects of the respondent's place in the organizational structure that we measure are the bureaucratic structure of the firm or organization, ownership/ nonownership, and the number of people over whom she says she has direct or indirect supervisory authority. Of the four job pressures, three are measured by the respondent's appraisals of frequency of time pressure, how dirty she gets in her work, and the number of hours she works in an average week. The fourth, heaviness of work, is our appraisal, based on her description of her work with things. Potentially threatening job uncertainties are measured by the individual's perception of the likelihood of being held responsible for things outside her control, the risk of losing her job or business, and the likelihood of a sudden and dramatic change in income, reputation, or position.

Measures of Psychological Functioning

Intellectual Functioning.   In measuring women's intellectual functioning, we developed models of both their intellectual flexibility and the intellectual level of their leisure-time activities.

Our model of *intellectual flexibility* is meant to reflect women's actual intellectual performance in the interview situation. The measurement model (see Figure 8.2) is similar to that developed for men in Chapter 5, except that it is limited to data for 1974. The chi-square is 17.11 with 12 degrees of freedom, for a ratio of 1.43. As in analyses of men, we focus on the ideational component of intellectual flexibility.

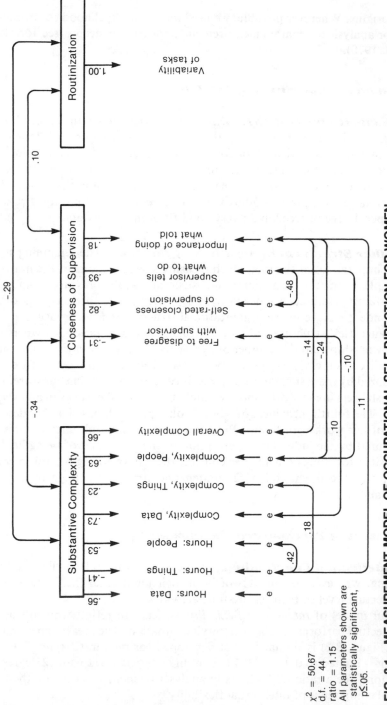

$\chi^2 = 50.67$
d.f. = 44
ratio = 1.15
All parameters shown are
statistically significant,
$p \leq .05$.

FIG. 8.1. MEASUREMENT MODEL OF OCCUPATIONAL SELF-DIRECTION FOR WOMEN

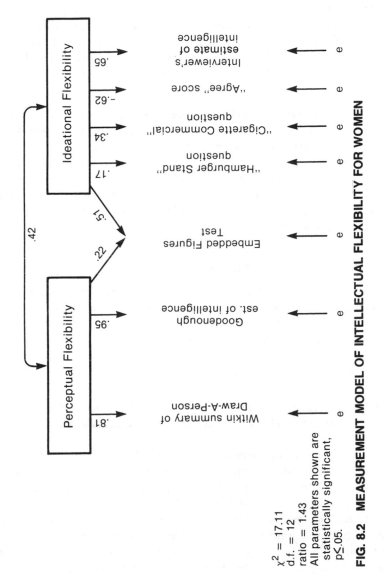

$\chi^2 = 17.11$
d.f. = 12
ratio = 1.43
All parameters shown are
statistically significant,
$p \leq .05$.

FIG. 8.2 MEASUREMENT MODEL OF INTELLECTUAL FLEXIBILITY FOR WOMEN

The measurement model of the *demand people place on their intellectual resources* in their leisure time is based on respondents' reports of their participation in leisure-time activities that require varying levels of intellectual involvement. Included are hours spent watching television, frequency of going to plays, concerts, or museums, number of books read, time spent on hobbies, intellectual level of newspaper reading, and intellectual level of magazine reading. Appendix D summarizes the basic information: the paths from the concept to each of the indicators, the chi-square for the model, and the ratio of chi-square to degrees of freedom.

Social orientations and self-conceptions.   We measure seven dimensions of social orientation and self-conception: authoritarian-conservatism, criteria of morality, receptivity to change, self-confidence, self-deprecation, fatalism, and anxiety. With the exception of self-confidence and self-deprecation, which belong together in one model because they are part of a larger concept, self-esteem, each measurement model consists of one concept and its indicators. All the pertinent information is given in Appendix D.

Measurement of Social Characteristics

The social background characteristics included in our analyses are respondent's age and level of education, her mother's and father's levels of education, her father's occupational status, her racial, national, and religious background, and the urbanness and region of the country of the principal place where she was raised. The indices of social characteristics are the same as those employed in the analysis of men.

RELATIONSHIPS OF STRUCTURAL IMPERATIVES OF THE JOB TO PSYCHOLOGICAL FUNCTIONING

To assess the relationships between occupational conditions and psychological functioning, we do multiple-regression analyses, treating the thirteen structural imperatives of the job as independent variables vis-a-vis each facet of psychological functioning (see "Job" columns in Table 8.1). We find that these occupational conditions, taken all together, have substantial and meaningful relationships with all facets of women's psychological functioning that we have examined. The multiple correlations are impressive, ranging from .38 to .75. Moreover, the multiple-partial correlations for each of the four types of structural imperatives—occupational self-direction, position in the organizational structure, job pressures, and job uncertainties—show that all of them are independently related to at least some aspects of psychological functioning.

Interpreting these relationships requires that we take into account the

Table 8.1. RELATIONSHIPS BETWEEN OCCUPATIONAL CONDITIONS AND PSYCHOLOGICAL FUNCTIONING, CONTROLLING OTHER JOB CONDITIONS AND SOCIAL BACKGROUND (FOR WOMEN)

	Intellectual Functioning				Social Orientations								Self-Conceptions					
	Ideational Flexibility		Intellectual Demand of Leisure Time		Authoritarian Conservatism		Standards of Morality		Receptivity to Change		Self-Confidence		Self-Depreciation		Fatalism		Anxiety	
	Job*	Job+ Social†	Job	Job+ Social	Job	Job+ Social	Job	Job+ Social	Job	Job+ Social	Job	Job+ Social	Job	Job+ Social	Job	Job+ Social	Job	Job+ Social
Occupational Self-Direction																		
Standardized regression coefficients:																		
Substantive complexity	.54	.34	.63	.16	-.38	(-.14)	.33	.20	.28	.18	.21	.18	-.21	(-.12)	...	...	-.25	(-.12)
Closeness of supervision	..‡	...	...	...	.19	.15	-.18	-.18	-.16	-.14	...	...	...	...	.16	.11	...	...
Routinization	-.27	-.21	...	...	.19	.23	.39	.29	.35	.26	...	...	...	...	...	...	...	...
Multiple-partial r	.63	.58	.58	.19	.40	.23	.40	.36	.44	.35	.22	.16	.22	.17	.19	.13	.21	.10
Position in Organizational Structure																		
Standardized regression coefficients:																		
Bureaucratization	.24	.18	.21	(.07)	...	...	...	...	...	...	(-.12)	-.14	...	...	...	...	...	...
Position in hierarchy	...	...	(.10)	.17	(-.06)	-.12	...	...	...	...	.15	.13	...	...	...	...	(-.12)	(-.14)
Ownership	.17	.14	.22	.16	...	...	.16	(.11)	...	...	...	...	...	...	...	...	...	...
Multiple-partial r	.31	.37	.33	.40	(.14)	(.16)	(.16)	(.14)	(.10)	(.05)	.18	.18	(.14)	.18	(.15)	.20	(.15)	(.16)
Job Pressures																		
Standardized regression coefficients:																		
Time pressure	-.22	-.19	-.24	-.20	...	...	...	...	...	...	-.19	-.16	...	...	-.21	-.15	.14	.14
Hours worked	-.12	-.11	...	...	.21	.18	...	...	...	...	-.13	-.14	.13	.16	...	...	(.11)	.13
Heaviness	...	...	(-.04)	-.12	...	...	...	...	...	...	...	...	.17	.15	(.11)	.11	...	...
Dirtiness	...	...	...	...	...	...	...	...	...	...	...	...	...	...	...	...	...	...
Multiple-partial r	.34	.43	.32	.41	.24	.24	(.13)	(.12)	(.14)	(.10)	.26	.24	.24	.25	.23	.23	.21	.24
Job Uncertainties																		
Standardized regression coefficients:																		
Dramatic change	-.10	-.11	...	...	...	...	-.17	(-.11)	...	...	...	...	...	.14	(.10)	...	...	...
Risk of loss of job or business	(-.01)	.06	...	...	...	...	...	...	...	...	...	...	...	...	...	...	...	...
Responsibility for things outside control	-.11	-.10	...	...	...	...	...	...	...	...	...	...	...	...	...	...	.14	...
Multiple-partial r	.23	.32	(.06)	(.12)	(.11)	(.12)	.21	(.15)	(.09)	(.10)	(.11)	(.12)	(.09)	(.06)	(.10)	(.16)	.19	(.16)
Multiple/multiple-partial r for the 13 job conditions	.75	.73	.70	.57	.52	.40	.48	.36	.44	.35	.43	.40	.41	.37	.39	.36	.38	.35

* All 13 job conditions are included in the multiple-regression equations.

† All 13 job conditions together with education; age; racial, national, and religious background; urbanness and region of the country where raised; mother's and father's education; and father's occupational status are included in the equations.

‡ Standardized regression coefficients are not shown when not statistically significant either before or after social background variables are entered into the equation. If significant under one condition but not the other, the nonsignificant coefficient is enclosed in parentheses. All multiple-partial and multiple correlations are shown; if not statistically significant, they are enclosed in parentheses.

N = 269.

processes of socially selective recruitment into and retention in particular occupations. To test whether the relationships between occupational conditions and psychological functioning can be attributed to social characteristics of the workers, we add education, race, age, national background, region of origin, urban origin, religious background, parental education, and father's occupational status to the multiple-regression equations (see the "Job + Social" columns in Table 8.1). The structural imperatives of the job are still highly related to intellectual functioning, social orientations, and self-conceptions. We therefore conclude that the relationships between occupational conditions and psychological functioning cannot be attributed to social selectivity on the basis of education or other social characteristics. Occupational conditions matter in their own right.

Occupational self-direction is most closely associated with intellectual functioning, somewhat less so with social orientations, and only weakly with self-conceptions (see the multiple-partial correlations for occupational self-direction). Specifically, women who do substantively complex and non-routine work tend to be more ideationally flexible, to have more personally responsible moral standards, and to be more receptive to innovation and change. Doing substantively complex work is also related to making intellectually demanding use of leisure time and to having self-confidence; routinization is related to authoritarian-conservatism and to fatalism. Closeness of supervision is not significantly associated with any aspect of psychological functioning. Thus, for women, the components of occupational self-direction that are important for psychological functioning are substantive complexity and routinization, not closeness of supervision.

Position in organizational structure—that is, bureaucratization of the firm or organization in which a woman is employed, hierarchical position, and ownership—is especially pertinent to intellectual functioning but also bears on some aspects of social orientation and self-conception. Specifically, women who are employed in bureaucratic organizations are likely to be ideationally flexible but to lack self-confidence. Those who have high organizational rank are likely to make intellectually demanding use of their leisure time, to be non-authoritarian, to have self-confidence, and not to be anxious. Owners are likely to be ideationally flexible and to make intellectually demanding use of their leisure time.

Job pressures are generally related to ineffective intellectual functioning and adverse self-conceptions. They are associated with less ideational flexibility, less intellectually demanding use of leisure time, less self-confidence, and greater self-deprecation and anxiety. The one exception to the generally adverse effects of job pressures is the inverse relationship between time pressure and fatalism. One reason this may occur is that the activity level engendered by time-pressured work is inconsistent with the passivity inherent in fatalism.

Job uncertainties are important mainly for ideational flexibility. Both the likelihood of a dramatic change in one's job situation and the likelihood of being held responsible for things outside one's control are negatively related to ideational flexibility. On the other hand, risk of loss of job or business is positively related to ideational flexibility—perhaps because the risk of losing one's job motivates an individual to fully utilize her intellectual resources. The other psychological variables to which occupational uncertainties are related are fatalism and anxiety. Women who believe that there may be a dramatic change in their job conditions are more fatalistic than those who do not, and women who are often held responsible for things outside their control are more anxious than those who are not.

In sum, the relationships between job conditions and psychological functioning are psychologically reasonable and, with a few possible and readily explainable exceptions, consistent with our hypotheses. Conditions that facilitate occupational self-direction are associated with more effective intellectual functioning and a generally positive, flexible, and responsible social orientation. Job pressures and uncertainties are in the main, but certainly not without exception, related to ineffective intellectual functioning and negative self-conceptions. These findings buttress our belief that there is a direct connection between everyday job conditions and psychological functioning.

This interpretation must, however, be tested against the alternative hypothesis that the relationships between working conditions and psychological functioning are only a reflection of the extrinsic rewards associated with particular occupations, such as job income and occupational status. To test this possibility, we add income and occupational status to the regression equations and re-examine the relationships between work conditions and psychological functioning. None of the significant coefficients is reduced nor are the effects of income or occupational status themselves significant.

We have found, then, that the relationships between women's actual job conditions and psychological functioning are substantial and real; they cannot be attributed to social background or to extrinsic aspects of the job. The question remains, How do the nature and magnitude of these relationships compare to those for men? To answer this question, we have developed measurement models for men based entirely on the 1974 data and thus directly comparable to those for women, and have done exactly comparable multiple-regression analyses.[3] Table 8.2 compares the magnitudes of the rela-

---

[3] A comparison of men's and women's measurement models for the aspects of psychological functioning that we have studied shows that the relationships of concepts to indicators are much the same. In both populations, every indicator has a statistically significant relationship to the concept it is hypothesized to reflect. In no case does the standardized path from concept to indicator vary by more than .20 between populations; and, in 44 of the 53 pairs, it differs by less than .10. We conclude that the questions used to measure psychological functioning tap similar dimensions for women and men, thus allowing comparisons across populations.

Table 8.2. MULTIPLE-PARTIAL CORRELATIONS BETWEEN OCCUPATIONAL CONDITIONS AND PSYCHOLOGICAL FUNCTIONING, FOR MEN AND WOMEN, CONTROLLING OTHER JOB CONDITIONS AND SOCIAL BACKGROUND

| | Intellectual Functioning | | | | Social Orientations | | | | | | Self-Conceptions | | | | | | | |
| | Ideational Flexibility | | Intellectual Demand of Leisure Time | | Authoritarian Conservatism | | Standards of Morality | | Receptivity to Change | | Self-Confidence | | Self-Deprecation | | Fatalism | | Anxiety | |
	Women	Men	Women	Men	Women	Men	Women	Men	Women	Men	Women	Men	Women	Men	Women	Men	Women	Men
Occupational self-direction	.58*	.52*	.19*	.37*	.23*	.19*	.29*	.32*	.26*	.23*	.16	.06	.17	.29*	.13	.18*	.10	.17*
Position in organizational structure	.37*	.16*	.40*	.10	.16	.07	.14	.12*	.05	.15*	.18*	.06	.18*	.12*	.20*	.16*	.16	.08
Job pressures	.43*	.18*	.41*	.18*	.24*	.13*	.12	.12	.10	.13*	.24*	.13*	.25*	.14*	.23*	.22*	.24*	.13*
Job uncertainties	.32*	.21*	.12	.15*	.12	.16*	.15	.12*	.10	.19*	.12	.05	.06	.12*	.16	.13*	.16	.13*
Total multiple-partial correlation for the 13 job conditions	.73*	.65*	.57*	.50*	.40*	.28*	.36*	.36*	.35*	.38*	.40*	.20*	.37*	.36*	.36*	.33*	.35*	.30*

Note.—Underlined comparison indicates a statistically significant difference between men and women; N = 269 women and 687 men interviewed in 1974.
*Statistically significant correlation, P < .05.

tionships between the structural imperatives of the job and psychological functioning for men and women, using the 1974 data for both. The similarity of these figures is striking. In only two instances can the overall association between occupational conditions and psychological functioning be statistically differentiated by sex. In these two cases—ideational flexibility and self-confidence—the relationship is stronger, not weaker, for women. Women's intellectual functioning, social orientations, and self-conceptions are at least as strongly related to their work experiences as are men's.

The relationships between psychological functioning and the four types of structural imperatives of the job—occupational self-direction, position in the organizational structure, job pressures, and uncertainties—are also generally similar for men and women. The main differences are that position in the organizational structure and job pressures are more highly related to the intellectual functioning of women than of men.[4] Despite these differences, the conclusion we draw is that the relationships between job conditions and psychological functioning are remarkably alike for men and women.[5] There is no evidence that employed women are in any sense psychologically disassociated from their working lives.

CONDITIONAL RELATIONSHIPS

We have found, thus far, that the relationships between occupational conditions and psychological functioning continue to be statistically significant even when subjected to many statistical controls. There is the distinct possibility, however, that these relationships, even though statistically significant for the sample as a whole, may in reality be conditional on women's life circumstances or work preferences. This would be the case, for example, if women who are emotionally committed to their occupations were strongly affected by the substantive complexity of their work while women who are less committed to their occupations were less affected by this job condition.

To test such possibilities, we developed a measurement model of occupational commitment (again see Appendix D). Using this index, we repeated all the multiple-regression analyses, systematically testing whether the rela-

---

[4] Although the general pattern is strikingly similar, there are some differences in the impact of particular occupational conditions; notably, routinization appears to be more generally pertinent for women's psychological functioning and closeness of supervision for men's. (These differences do not result from differences in the variances of routinization and closeness of supervision for the two sexes.)

[5] We should again note, however, that women's job conditions differ from men's. Our data indicate that, compared to men, women are significantly more closely supervised and significantly less likely to be owners, or to occupy a high position in a supervisory hierarchy, or to do complex work with data, things, or people. Women are also less likely to work under time pressure, to work long hours, to do heavy work, to be held responsible for things outside their control, or to expect dramatic changes in their job circumstances.

tionship between a given occupational condition and a given aspect of psychological functioning is conditional on occupational commitment. We do this by including in the regression equation a term representing the linear interaction of that job condition and occupational commitment.[6] For example, a statistically significant interaction between substantive complexity and occupational commitment in the multiple-regression equation for ideational flexibility (all other occupational conditions and pertinent background variables statistically controlled) would indicate that the effect of substantive complexity is conditional on whether or not the women are committed to their occupations. We similarly test the interaction of occupational commitment and every job condition we had found to be significantly related to each of the psychological variables.

Occupational commitment is but one of a multitude of variables that may differentiate women who are more affected by occupational conditions from women who are less affected. Five other circumstances seemed to us to be particularly pertinent: the presence of young children in the home, the number of hours worked per week, preference for being employed or being a housewife, husband's income, and the woman's sense of responsibility for contributing to family income.

We tested all these possibilities. Only a scattered few of the interactions—fewer than would be expected by chance—are statistically significant.[7] Even these few significant interactions seem to be random. There is no evidence that the relationships we have depicted between occupational conditions and psychological functioning are conditional. Rather, these occupational conditions affect women similarly, whatever their life-circumstances or their preferences.

We believe that we have thus far demonstrated that the structural imperatives of women's jobs are strongly related to their psychological functioning. These relationships are not simply a function of education or of other social characteristics that affect the processes by which women are recruited into or retained in their jobs. Furthermore, these relationships are essentially the same for all types of employed women. Our preferred interpretation is that there is a continuing interplay between job and woman, in which job conditions both affect and are affected by a woman's psychological

---

[6] Constructing these multiplicative terms required the creation of factor scores for all of the concepts for which we had developed measurement models. To create these scores, we used Ronald Schoenberg's procedure for deriving factor weights from LISREL, based on Bartlett's method (Lawley and Maxwell, 1971: 109–112).

[7] The original multiple-regression analyses revealed 36 significant relationships between dimensions of occupation and some aspect of psychological functioning (see "Job + Social" columns in Table 8.1). We tested the possibility that each of these 36 relationships is conditional on any of six potentially interactive variables, for a total of 216 tests, less five because hours worked cannot be treated as interactive with itself. Of the 211 interactions tested, ten are statistically significant at $p < .05$—fewer than would be expected by chance.

functioning. But our analyses have not yet established such a causal order-ing. We must construct reasonable causal models that assess the reciprocal effects of job conditions and psychological functioning.

RECIPROCAL CAUSAL MODELS

Ideally, causal models require longitudinal data, which would permit one to assess actual changes in occupational conditions and psychological func-tioning. Our data, unfortunately, are only cross-sectional. We can over-come this limitation to some extent by the use of job-history information. Even though we have no comparable biographical information about the women's psychological functioning at earlier times, the job-history infor-mation does make possible a provisional assessment of the reciprocal effects of current job conditions on current psychological functioning and of cur-rent psychological functioning on current job conditions.[8]

To assess the contemporaneous reciprocal effects of occupational condi-tions and psychological functioning, we again have to make some assump-tions that limit the number of parameters to be estimated (see Chapter 5). Concretely, we posit that those social background characteristics that would not have been evaluated as job credentials by current employers do not directly affect the occupational conditions of the current (1974) job. We also posit that work conditions experienced in the job held immediately before the present job do not have a direct impact on current psychological functioning, but are indirectly linked to the extent that those earlier job conditions determine current job conditions. We have the requisite job-history information for the substantive complexity of work, routinization, closeness of supervision, bureaucratization of the firm or organization, po-sition in the supervisory hierarchy, time-pressure, average hours worked per week, dirtiness, and the probability of being held responsible for things outside one's control.[9]

---

[8] In developing the causal (i.e., linear structural equation) models, we employed the LISREL computer program (Joreskog and van Thillo, 1972), as subsequently modified by Ronald Schoenberg.

[9] These analyses utilize information about the job held immediately before the one the respondent held at the time of the 1974 interview. Information about the immediately previous job is far less precise than current job descriptions. Our assessments of closeness of supervision and routinization are based upon single-item retrospective reports about the overall amount of direction given by the supervisor and the variability of tasks. Substantive complexity is an approximate index based on the *Dictionary of Occupational Titles'* (U.S. Department of La-bor, 1965) ratings of the average level of complexity of work with data, with people, and with things for the occupation described by the respondent, together with the amount of time she reports having spent at each type of activity. (To increase the accuracy of our estimates, we incorporated the measurement model for the occupational self-direction of the current job in an over-time model.) The other occupational conditions of the immediately preceding job are measured by single items.

Ideational Flexibility

As a prototypic analysis, we assess in Figure 8.3 the contemporaneous recip-rocal relationships between ideational flexibility and those job conditions shown by the multiple-regression analysis to bear significantly on this im-portant aspect of psychological functioning. This model shows that sub-stantively complex work, non-routinized work, and a short work week all result in greater ideational flexibility. By contrast, ideational flexibility does not have a statistically significant contemporaneous effect on any of the occupational conditions included in this model.

There is, however, a serious problem in interpreting this model, stem-ming from the lack of longitudinal data about ideational flexibility: The apparent effects of occupational conditions on ideational flexibility may be an artifact of our inability to take account of earlier levels of ideational flexibility. The model is asymmetric: Our assessments of the effects of idea-tional flexibility on occupational conditions necessarily control the condi-tions of the immediately prior job, while our assessments of the effects of occupational conditions on ideational flexibility cannot control ideational flexibility at the time of the earlier job. In that sense, the test of ideational flexibility's effects on occupational conditions is more rigorous than is the test of the effects of occupational conditions on ideational flexibility.[10]

To deal with this problem, we developed a series of causal models in which we introduced earlier ideational flexibility as a hypothetical concept, unmeasured by any indicators. We did this by incorporating into the causal módel hypothetical estimates of the standardized path from earlier to cur-rent ideational flexibility. We tested a range of possibilities in which the stability of ideational flexibility was posited at several plausible levels, from fairly high (.70) to extremely high (.94). The effects of occupational condi-tions on ideational flexibility remain unchanged from the original estimates no matter what the posited stability of ideational flexibility.

We have tried a number of other modifications of Figure 8.3 to test that the causal model is robust; every modification confirms that it is. In partic-ular, the alternative model depicted in Figure 8.4 represents a more accurate portrayal of occupational structure than does the model shown in Figure 8.3. In the earlier model, following the simple logic of multiple regression analysis, we allowed each occupational condition to directly affect idea-tional flexibility, but none of them to affect the others. Figure 8.4 repre-

---

[10] Another problem is that this model provides no way of assessing time-lagged effects. Thus, we could not evaluate the possibility that ideational flexibility might actually affect job conditions over the long run, even if not contemporaneously. Consistent with this possibility is the finding, in a fully longitudinal analysis, that the impact of men's ideational flexibility on the substantive complexity of their work is essentially lagged, rather than contemporaneous (Chapter 5). Similarly, some earlier job conditions may have time-lagged effects on current ideational flexibility. Unfortunately, there is no way to test these possibilities with the data in hand.

sents an attempt, within the rather severe limitations imposed by the cross-sectional nature of our data, to portray occupational structure and its interrelationship with ideational flexibility more accurately. First, we recognize that whenever a woman moves from a more bureaucratic to a less bureaucratic firm or organization, or the reverse, or from a higher to a lower position in the supervisory hierarchy, or the reverse, she necessarily changes jobs. By definition, then, there cannot be contemporaneous direct effects of ideational flexibility (or of other job conditions) on bureaucratization or on hierarchical position. Second, even though hierarchical position did not have a statistically significant effect on ideational flexibility in the multiple regression analysis, and even though bureaucratization did not have a significant direct effect on ideational flexibility in the earlier causal model, we now allow both to have indirect effects through more proximate, directly impinging conditions of work. Hierarchical position might indirectly affect ideational flexibility, for example, by affecting such aspects of the actual work as the complexity of one's dealings with people, a component of sub-

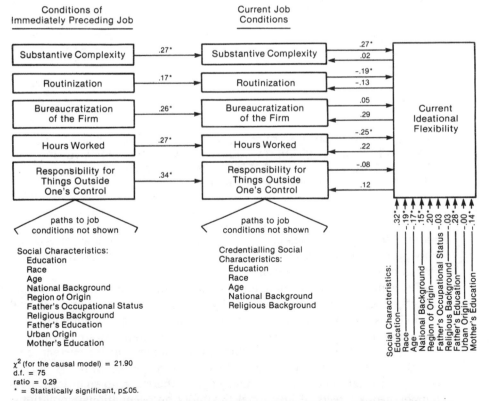

FIG. 8.3. THE RECIPROCAL EFFECTS OF OCCUPATIONAL CONDITIONS AND IDEATIONAL FLEXIBILITY.
(Correlations among residuals not shown.)

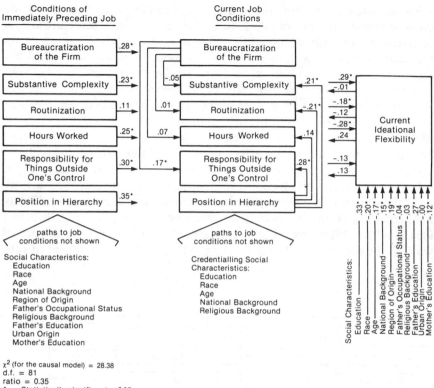

χ² (for the causal model) = 28.38
d.f. = 81
ratio = 0.35
* = Statistically significant, p≤.05

FIG. 8.4. THE RECIPROCAL EFFECTS OF OCCUPATIONAL CONDITIONS AND IDEATIONAL FLEXIBILITY, ALLOWING INDIRECT EFFECTS OF BUREAUCRATIZATION AND POSITION IN HIERARCHY.
(Correlations among residuals not shown.)

stantive complexity. Allowing the possibility of these indirect effects not only portrays a more accurate picture of occupational structure, but also strengthens the identification of the model.

The hypothesis that the individual's place in the organizational structure affects other job conditions and thereby has an indirect effect on ideational flexibility is clearly supported in Figure 8.4. In particular, a high position in the authority structure increases the substantive complexity of work and decreases routinization, both of which in turn directly affect current ideational flexibility. The model also confirms the direct effect of hours worked on current ideational flexibility. Once again, there are no significant contemporaneous effects of ideational flexibility on occupational conditions. Thus, a more realistic model of occupational structure reaffirms the direct importance for ideational flexibility of proximate occupational conditions while pointing to the indirect importance of the organizational structure that defines these proximate job conditions.[11]

Other Facets of Psychological Functioning

Estimating models of the reciprocal relationships between job conditions and leisure-time activities or social orientations or self-conceptions proves to be more difficult than estimating models for ideational flexibility, because our instruments are not nearly as strong. In estimating the paths from occupational conditions to ideational flexibility, we used as instrumentation the strong correlations between earlier job conditions and current ideational flexibility; but the correlations between earlier job conditions and other aspects of current psychological functioning are much weaker. As a result, our models for other psychological variables, comparable to that of Figure 8.4 for ideational flexibility, are only weakly identified and the effects cannot be assessed with statistical confidence. But, if we make an additional restriction on the models—that is, if we do not allow the residuals for either bureaucratization or hierarchical position to correlate with the residual for the particular psychological variable—we are able to achieve sufficient identification to estimate models for the intellectual demandingness of leisure-time activities, authoritarian-conservatism, standards of morality, receptivity to change, and fatalism. These models show that substantively complex work significantly increases the intellectual demandingness of leisure-time activities and that routinization significantly increases authoritarian-conservatism and fatalism and decreases personal responsibility for moral standards.[12] None of the contemporaneous paths from psychological functioning to occupational conditions is statistically significant.

---

[11] If we simplify the model by limiting it to statistically significant paths, the effect on ideational flexibility of the number of hours worked drops from $-.28$ to $-.20$, the effect of substantive complexity drops from .29 to .23, and the effect of routinization increases slightly, from $-.18$ to $-.21$. These changes in magnitude are not so great as to suggest that the models differ in any essential respect.

[12] The multiple-regression analyses indicate that hierarchical position may directly affect authoritarian-conservatism and leisure-time activities. Our reciprocal-effects models allow only indirect effects of hierarchical position on these facets of psychological functioning. We did not allow direct effects because a model that allowed hierarchical position to affect a psychological variable, but did not permit that psychological variable to have either a contemporaneous or a lagged effect on hierarchical position, would not test the direction of effects. If we nevertheless test models that allow hierarchical position to have direct contemporaneous effects, its effect would be significant in both cases, displacing routinization vis-a-vis authoritarian-conservatism and substantive complexity vis-a-vis leisure time. (N.B. In Chapter 9, we develop an alternative model of job conditions and leisure-time intellectuality, which shows both hierarchical position and substantive complexity to significantly affect leisure-time intellectuality.) Hours worked continues to be a significant determinant of both authoritarian-conservatism and leisure-time intellectuality. Although these models portray different pictures of the processes, direct and indirect, by which occupational conditions affect these two facets of psychological functioning, they too show significant contemporaneous effects of job conditions. As in all previous models, neither facet of psychological functioning has a significant contemporaneous effect on any occupational condition.

These results support our belief that women's occupational conditions affect not only their ideational flexibility, but also their psychological functioning in general. In contrast, we have no evidence of any aspect of psychological functioning having a statistically significant contemporaneous effect on occupational conditions.

DISCUSSION

Our findings are based on the employment experiences of a sample of married women currently living with their husbands. Although the majority of female workers is married, we must once again ask whether it is appropriate to generalize our findings to all employed women. We certainly cannot take account of everything that distinguishes married from single, divorced, or separated women; but, in the course of our analyses, we have explored how actual and perceived financial responsibilities, occupational commitment, number of hours worked, and job income might alter the relationship of a woman to her work. Within our sample, the relationships between job conditions and psychological functioning are not conditional on any of these personal preferences or social circumstances. Thus, characteristics commonly cited as distinguishing married from unmarried female workers probably do not limit the generalizability of our conclusions. Nonetheless, without examining a broader sample of the female labor force, we cannot fully determine the consequences of our studying only married women. Similarly, without examining an even broader age-range than that of our sample, we cannot be certain that the very youngest and very oldest employed women do not react differently to their job conditions than do the main body of employed women.

We must, moreover, reiterate the statistical limitations imposed by cross-sectional data. Without information on earlier psychological functioning, we cannot unequivocally estimate the relative magnitudes of contemporaneous reciprocal paths between occupational conditions and psychological functioning. However, the simulated models incorporating a hypothetical measure of earlier ideational flexibility do give strong evidence that our estimates are not spurious. In addition, the similarity between findings based on the women's cross-sectional data and those derived from longitudinal data for men increases our confidence in these results. Although reciprocal models using cross-sectional data must always be examined cautiously, each step in the analysis has reinforced our causal interpretation.

The evidence we have presented indicates that employed women's conditions of work are meaningfully and substantially related to their psychological functioning. We believe that these relationships result not only from the selective processes by which women who enter jobs meet their own and their employers' requirements, but also from the powerful effect of women's work experience on their self-conceptions, social orientations, even intellectual functioning. In support of this interpretation, we have shown that the relationships between occupational conditions and psychological functioning do not simply reflect education or other social characteristics that influence the processes of job recruitment and selection. Nor are these relationships an artifact of such extrinsic aspects of the job as income and status. Moreover, these relationships between occupational conditions and psychological functioning are much the same, whatever the social circumstances or personal preferences of the women. Finally, we have been able to demonstrate, in a series of reciprocal-effects models, that key occupational conditions have causal effects on ideational flexibility. These effects are consistently shown even though rigorous statistical controls are imposed and models making a number of different assumptions are tested. Although we have had to make further assumptions to identify models that assess the relationships between occupational conditions and other aspects of psychological functioning, these models, too, buttress the interpretation that occupational conditions are not only correlated with, but actually affect, psychological functioning.

Our data indicate also that none of the facets of psychological functioning we have examined has a significant contemporaneous effect on occupational conditions. Thus, it would seem that women do not mold their job conditions, at least in the short run, to meet their psychological needs and preferences. In the absence of longitudinal data, however, we cannot draw firm conclusions about longer-term processes.

The findings should also dispel any belief that large segments of the female work force are somehow immune to occupational circumstances—that, for example, mothers of young children, or women who do not think of themselves as having careers, or women who are "only working to supplement the family income" are insensitive to the deleterious effects of routinized work or are unresponsive to the mind-stretching experience of doing substantively complex work. Our data strongly suggest that the major dimensions of occupational experience are similarly related to psychological functioning for all women.

Our findings should also dispel the notion that the relationships between occupational conditions and psychological functioning are not as strong for women as for men. Not only are the overall magnitudes of the relationships we have studied at least as great for women as they are for men but, with interesting variations on the general pattern (see footnote 4), the structural imperatives of the job have effects of roughly similar magnitude for women as for men. No matter what the sex of the worker, job conditions that directly or indirectly encourage occupational self-direction are conducive to effective intellectual functioning and to an open and flexible orientation to others. Job conditions that constrain opportunities for self-direction or subject the worker to any of several types of pressures or uncertainties result in less effective intellectual functioning, unfavorable evaluations of self, and a rigid, intolerant social orientation.

In sum, despite sex-role definitions that have traditionally emphasized maternal and marital responsibilities, work histories that are likely to be interrupted and, for many women, part-time patterns of work, employed women's personality development is directly affected by their current occupational experiences. By focusing on occupational conditions, we do not mean to deny that other aspects of women's lives also influence their psychological functioning; our findings simply show that women are not insulated by other experiences, past or present, from the effects of the structural imperatives of the job. Here, clearly, is evidence that conditions of adult life are important determinants of psychological functioning. For women, as for men, work has a decided psychological impact.

9

The Reciprocal Effects of Job Conditions and the Intellectuality of Leisure-Time Activities*

Karen A. Miller and Melvin L. Kohn

Our intent in this chapter is to examine the relationships between people's job conditions and how they use their discretionary time—time not committed to earning a paycheck or to other activities necessary for meeting the basic physical needs of the family. The reciprocal effects of job conditions and subjective psychological processes have already been documented (Chapters 5-8). We now attempt to assess longitudinally the reciprocal effects of job conditions and one important type of off-the-job behavior—the use of leisure time.[1] We believe that job experiences affect and are affected by what people actually do in their time off the job, just as job experiences affect and are affected by what people feel, believe, and value.

In this analysis, we investigate the mechanisms of transfer between work

* A preliminary version of this chapter was presented at the Japan-U.S. Conference on Social Stratification and Mobility, Hawaii, January, 1980. We are indebted to Margaret Renfors, Cheryl Keller, and Gloria Anderson for their help with statistical analyses. The models in this chapter were estimated by MILS, an advanced version of LISREL (Joreskog and van Thillo, 1972) developed by Ronald Schoenberg.
[1] Chapter 3 made a tentative assessment of the reciprocal relationship between one facet of men's work—its substantive complexity—and their leisure-time intellectuality, using cross-sectional data. Chapter 8 made a tentative assessment of the reciprocal relationships between women's job conditions and the intellectuality of their leisure-time activities, again using cross-sectional data. The present longitudinal analysis builds on, but goes considerably beyond, those earlier analyses.

and nonwork spheres of life. Several recent reviews have summarized a large but inconclusive body of research on this topic (Wilson, 1980; Kabanoff, 1980; Staines, 1980). These reviews discuss two major competing hypotheses about the nature of the relationship between work and nonwork, the so-called spillover hypothesis and the compensation hypothesis (both originally identified by Wilensky, 1960).

The spillover hypothesis implies broadly that there is a basic similarity in the nature of work and nonwork activities. This similarity may be interpreted as the outcome of a direct process of learning-generalization by which the lessons learned in one sphere of life are carried over to other spheres of life. A learning-generalization interpretation is consistent with the theory of Breer and Locke (1965), as well as with our analyses (Chapter 6 and 8) of how job conditions relate to psychological functioning. Alternatively, a similarity between work and leisure activities might result from some underlying personality predisposition affecting both work and nonwork behavior.

The compensation hypothesis, in contrast to the learning-generalization and personality-predisposition hypotheses, implies a negative association between work and nonwork activities, with the causal process usually proposed being that workers seek to compensate in their leisure for what they lack in their work (e.g., people who do dull work might seek stimulation and variety in their leisure-time pursuits).

Two other hypotheses are discussed in the literature. One is that work may facilitate or constrain leisure activities by providing or depleting resources needed for those activities (Staines, 1980). The other, the segmentation hypothesis (Dubin, 1956; Kabanoff, 1980), asserts that work and leisure are psychologically compartmentalized, implying no association between work and nonwork activities.

The research literature does not indicate unequivocal support for any of these hypotheses. We shall test whether direct learning-generalization processes occur; whether there is instead some underlying personality characteristic—specifically, intellectual flexibility—that accounts for people selecting and being selected into jobs and leisure-time pursuits that have similar characteristics; whether people compensate in leisure time for whatever their job conditions do not provide and compensate in work for what they lack in leisure; whether people in their leisure activities use resources their jobs provide and attempt to structure their jobs to maximize resources needed for leisure activities; or whether people compartmentalize their work from their leisure. We shall further consider the possibility that more than one of these processes is involved in the work-leisure relationship. It may well be, for example, that workers learn from some aspects of their work experience, generalizing these lessons to their leisure-time pursuits, but compensate for other aspects of the job in their leisure. It may also be that some job conditions are intrinsically important, while other job conditions affect leisure activities by providing or depleting resources.

This chapter tests these hypotheses with respect to only one, albeit a pivotal, dimension of leisure-time activity—its intellectuality, that is, the extent to which people use their intellectual resources in their leisure time.[2] People may engage their minds in a variety of ways. One way, obviously, is by reading, whether it be newspapers, magazines, or books. People also may use their intellects by looking at works of art, attending dramatic productions, listening to music, or playing a sport that requires thinking or strategy, for example, judo in contrast to jogging. Active pursuit of almost any interest or avocation places at least some demand on one's intellect. On the other hand, there obviously are ways of spending time, such as long hours of watching television, that involve little or no thought.

We examine the intellectuality of leisure-time activities in relation to the same set of job conditions as are examined in the analysis of job conditions and personality in Chapter 6. These conditions identify workers' opportunities for occupational self-direction, their place in the organizational structure, the principal job pressures to which they are subject, and the principal extrinsic risks and rewards built into their jobs. Previous chapters have shown that the ideational component of intellectual flexibility, as measured by performance in the interview situation, is enhanced by work conditions that encourage self-direction and that, conversely, the exercise of self-direction in work is affected by ideational flexibility, at least for men. We here test our preferred hypothesis that there is a similar reciprocal relationship between intellectually challenging job conditions and the extent to which people actually use their intellects in that part of their daily lives most under their control, their leisure-time activities. If so, we should find that intellectually demanding job conditions positively affect leisure-time intellectuality and that intellectually demanding activities performed in leisure time positively affect the intellectual content of work.

Of all job conditions, the substantive complexity of work should be most directly pertinent for intellectual behavior in nonwork realms of life, because substantive complexity is central to the actual content of job tasks and thus to how people must actually behave on the job. Other job conditions should matter less, because they do not characterize the task content itself, but they should nevertheless be pertinent insofar as they set the context within which tasks are performed. Close supervision and routine work should affect leisure-time intellectuality negatively, because these conditions detract from the intellectual challenge of the job. We would expect ownership, bureaucratization of the firm or organization, and hierarchical

---

[2] We attempted to develop a multi-dimensional model of leisure-time activity, but the data were insufficient for measuring dimensions other than intellectuality.

position to affect leisure-time intellectuality positively, insofar as these aspects of a worker's place in the organizational structure facilitate autonomy in decision-making. However, we would expect their effects on leisure-time intellectuality to be primarily indirect, through their affecting more proximate job conditions that, in turn, directly facilitate or restrict the exercise of occupational self-direction.

Since people generally have more discretion in choosing their leisure activities than in selecting or modifying their job conditions, we would expect a stronger effect of job conditions on leisure-time activities than of leisure-time activities on job conditions. Yet, in principle, each can affect the other; the lessons learned in one's off-the-job activities can be applied to the job, just as the lessons of the job can be applied to off-the-job pursuits. Concretely, intellectually stimulating leisure-time activities might lead a worker to maximize his opportunities to exercise initiative and thought in doing his work.

Job conditions that do not themselves increase or decrease the intellectual challenge of the job may nevertheless affect leisure-time intellectuality by providing or depleting time, energy, and money, thereby facilitating or constraining leisure-time activity. We would expect heaviness, dirtiness, time pressure, a high risk of losing one's job and a high probability of being held responsible for things outside one's control to constrain the intellectuality of leisure-time activities by draining physical or psychic energy that could otherwise be used for mental activity in leisure time. Job protections and particularly job income should facilitate the intellectuality of leisure-time activities by providing resources that some of these activities require. Conversely, we expect that people who engage in intellectually demanding leisure activities will attempt to select or to mold their jobs in ways that might facilitate their continuing such pursuits.

INDICES

Intellectuality of Leisure-Time Activity

Our information about people's leisure-time activities is based entirely on interview reports. Because these reports are descriptive, rather than evaluative or interpretive, they can be given considerable credence. Nevertheless, we recognize that only a replication of our analysis based on other types of data could be conclusive.

We asked about diverse activities, each of which could vary in intellectual involvement. From this information we developed the following indices: frequency of attendance at plays, concerts, and museums; number of books read in the preceding six months; time spent working on hobbies; intellectual level of magazine reading; intellectual level of newspaper reading; intellectual level of sports activities; and hours spent watching television.[3] To minimize a social-status or educational bias in our index of leisure-time intellectuality, we deliberately include activities that are performed at all social-stratification levels and at all educational levels— working at hobbies, actively engaging in sports, and watching television. To further insure that we do not mistakenly attribute to a job some effects that really result from a possible socioeconomic or educational bias in our measure of leisure-time activity, we include education and income as independent variables in all our statistical analyses. We also include measures of socioeconomic origins.

We used maximum-likelihood confirmatory factor analysis to develop measurement models of the intellectuality of leisure-time activities. The measurement model for men incorporates both 1964 and 1974 data (see Figure 9.1), while that for women (see Figure 9.2) is necessarily limited to 1974 data.[4] For men, the residuals of all but one of the 1964 measurements are significantly correlated with their 1974 counterparts (the exception being those for the intellectual level of magazine reading). The pattern of the

---

[3] These indices make fuller use of the interview data than do the indices employed in previous chapters. Specifically:

(1) Intellectual level of magazines was coded according to the most intellectually demanding type read: 1—Does not read magazines; 2—Movie or sex; 3—Mass culture; 4—News or self-improvement; 5—Idea, culture, arts-oriented.

(2) Intellectual level of newspaper reading, for which we have data only in 1974, was coded according to the most intellectually demanding section read: 1—Does not read newspapers; 2—Comics or advertisements; 3—Front page only, local news, features, etc.; 4—National/international news, editorial page.

(3) Since only fifty-two percent of the women reported active participation in sports, an index of sports activity could not be incorporated into our measurement model for women. For men, the index of the intellectual level of sports played was based on information about a maximum of three sports. We coded each sport according to a schema that ranks all sports into three intellectual levels: 1—Little or no thinking or strategy required; 2—Some thinking or strategy required; 3—Substantial thinking or strategy required. A weighted average of the intellectual level of sports played by the respondent was then created, with the first sport mentioned given a weight of 3 and the third sport given a weight of 1.

(4) We were unable to code hobbies reliably on an intellectual dimension, and too few respondents read books to make useful a classification of their intellectual level, so we simply use time spent working at hobbies and number of books read as the indicators of intellectuality for these activities.

[4] In developing the measurement model for women, we used data from both employed women and women who are not employed outside the home. We also developed a measurement model for employed women alone and found that model initially to be dominated by three time-linked indicators—frequency of attendance at plays, concerts, and museums, number of books read, and hours spent on hobbies. It appears that we were measuring time available for leisure activities rather than the intellectual content of the activities. To deal with this problem, we allowed the residuals of the time-related indicators to be intercorrelated, thus modelling the availability of time separately from the intellectuality of the activities. The paths from concept to indicators in the resulting model are nearly identical to those in the model for all women; the correlation of factor scores based on the employed-women and all-women measurement models is .99.

If all the men in the sample were married, it would be preferable to have a combined "couples" model, which could include correlations of the residuals of parallel indicators for husband and wife. Since many of the men are not married, such a model is not feasible.

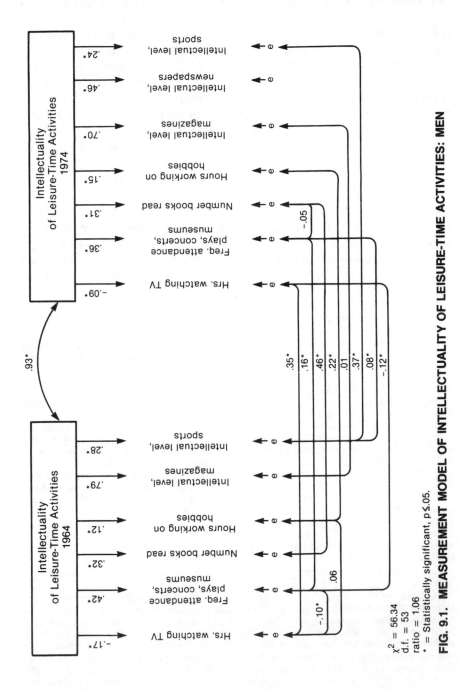

χ² = 56.34
d.f. = 53
ratio = 1.06
* = Statistically significant, p≤.05.

FIG. 9.1. MEASUREMENT MODEL OF INTELLECTUALITY OF LEISURE-TIME ACTIVITIES: MEN

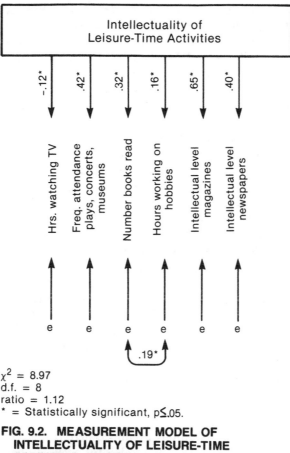

$\chi^2 = 8.97$
d.f. = 8
ratio = 1.12
* = Statistically significant, p≤.05.

**FIG. 9.2. MEASUREMENT MODEL OF
INTELLECTUALITY OF LEISURE-TIME
ACTIVITIES: WOMEN**

other correlations of residuals in the model for men suggests a dimension of outside-the-home versus at-home activity that is distinct from the intellectuality concept.[5] The one correlation of residuals in the model for women (Figure 9.2) is consistent with this pattern. The measurement models fit the data well: The model for men has a chi-square of 56.34 with 53 degrees of freedom, for a ratio of 1.06. The model for women has a chi-square of 8.97 with eight degrees of freedom, for a ratio of 1.12.

In the model for men, the paths from concepts to indicators are of the same rank order and of much the same magnitudes at the two times. The

---

[5] Where both indicators represent either activities that occur outside the home (such as playing sports or attending concerts, plays, or museums) or activities that are generally done at home (such as reading books, engaging in hobbies, or watching television), their residuals are positively correlated. Where one activity occurs outside the home and the other at home, their residuals are negatively correlated.

paths from concept to indicators in the model for women are very similar to those for men, probably in part because husbands and wives tend to share a variety of leisure-time activities. The intellectual level of magazine reading is the dominant positive indicator. Then follow, in approximately the same order for men and for women: the intellectual level of newspaper reading; attendance at plays, concerts, and museums; number of books read in the preceding six months; the intellectual level of sports played (for men); and time spent on hobbies. Hours spent watching television makes a small negative contribution to the overall level of leisure-time intellectuality, probably because many hours of watching television implies a lack of selectivity in what one watches. Admittedly, what we are calling the "intellectuality" of leisure-time activities necessarily involves also an activity/passivity component (intellectually demanding activities cannot be entirely passive) as well as a time component (one cannot engage in intellectually demanding activities without spending time at them). But the relative strengths of the paths from concept to indicators argue that the underlying dimension is neither activity/passivity nor time, but intellectuality.

The ten-year overtime correlation of the intellectuality of leisure-time activities (necessarily estimated only for men) is extremely high—.93. This correlation, of course, is a descriptive statistic. Leisure-time intellectuality could be highly stable because the behavior expresses some consistent facet of individual personality, because of stable environmental conditions, or both. An overtime correlation of .93 does not preclude job conditions from affecting the intellectuality of people's leisure-time activities.

Job Conditions

As noted, the set of job conditions examined here is the revised set developed in Chapter 6. The measurement models for occupational self-direction are those developed in Chapter 6 for men and in Chapter 8 for women. As before, our indices of other job conditions are single-item measures, the same as those employed in Chapter 6 and, as appropriate, Chapter 8.

A PRELIMINARY ASSESSMENT OF THE RELATIONSHIP BETWEEN JOB CONDITIONS AND THE INTELLECTUALITY OF LEISURE-TIME ACTIVITIES

Multiple-regression analysis makes possible tentative assessments, for men and for women, of the relationships between job conditions and the intellectuality of leisure-time activities. Since such assessments assume rather than test causal directionality, they do not tell us whether job conditions affect leisure-time intellectuality, leisure-time intellectuality affects job conditions, or both. But multiple-regression analysis does make it possible to see which job conditions are significantly related to leisure-time intellectuality, with other job conditions and pertinent social characteristics statistically controlled. It thus constitutes a logical first step in the analysis.

We include in the regression equations all social characteristics that we have reason to believe might affect the intellectuality of people's leisure-time activities and for which we have data for both men and women. These are education, age, race, national and religious background, urbanness and region of the country of the principal place where the respondent was raised, mother's and father's education, father's occupational status and the presence or absence of any young children in the current household. It is also desirable to take into account earlier levels of leisure-time intellectuality, lest we attribute to job conditions effects that really result from a pre-existing propensity to engage in activities of greater or lesser intellectuality. Unfortunately, we do not have such information for women, but we can include a measure of the intellectuality of earlier (1964) leisure-time activities in the set of independent variables for men.

We find (see column 1 of Table 9.1) that, even with job conditions and social characteristics included in the equation, the effect of men's earlier leisure-time intellectuality on their later leisure-time intellectuality is very large—a standardized regression coefficient of .78. This indicates that the remarkable stability in the intellectuality of men's leisure-time activities is to a substantial degree independent of their social backgrounds and job conditions. Nonetheless, several job conditions significantly affect leisure-time intellectuality. The most notable is the substantive complexity of work, with a standardized regression coefficient of .29. This substantial positive effect clearly is consistent with the learning-generalization hypothesis and inconsistent with the compensation and compartmentalization hypotheses. So, too, is the small but statistically significant positive effect of ownership. The other statistically significant effects of job conditions, albeit small (their standardized regression coefficients ranging from .03 to .06 in absolute value), are in the main consistent with the facilitator/constraint hypothesis. Thus, job protections and job income enhance leisure-time intellectuality, while time pressure, dirty work, and long hours of work inhibit leisure-time intellectuality. The positive effects on leisure-time intellectuality of closeness of supervision and heaviness of work are possible evidence of compensation, but we must make this interpretation cautiously because both effects may be artifactual.[6] Education appears to have a nega-

---

[6] Both closeness of supervision and heaviness have substantial negative zero-order correlations with the intellectuality of leisure-time activity (for closeness of supervision, $r = -.39$, for heaviness, $r = -.30$). In the case of closeness of supervision, there is some collinearity with substantive complexity ($r = -.61$). With substantive complexity omitted from the equation, closeness of supervision would have a statistically significant effect of $-.05$; with closeness of supervision omitted from the equation, substantive complexity's coefficient would decrease slightly from .29 to .27. Heaviness is correlated rather substantially with dirtiness ($r = .48$), but removing dirtiness from the equation would still leave heaviness with a positive coefficient. It is of course possible that heaviness is multicollinear with a larger set of job conditions. Tentatively, we think that the apparent effect of closeness of supervision on leisure-time intellectuality probably is artifactual but that the effect of heaviness probably is not.

tive effect, albeit small and statistically nonsignificant, but this clearly results from collinearity of education with earlier leisure-time intellectuality. (If earlier leisure-time intellectuality is removed from the equation, the regression coefficient for education becomes +.29.) In sum, despite the very high stability of leisure-time intellectuality, several job conditions appear to affect leisure-time intellectuality. The most important is the substantive complexity of work.

The question necessarily arises: In showing that men's job conditions—particularly substantive complexity—bear on the intellectuality of their

Table 9.1. STANDARDIZED REGRESSION COEFFICIENTS: THE INTELLECTUALITY OF LEISURE-TIME ACTIVITY ON JOB CONDITIONS, SOCIAL CHARACTERISTICS[1], EARLIER LEISURE-TIME INTELLECTUALITY, AND IDEATIONAL FLEXIBILITY

Model that includes:	Men Job Conditions, Social Characteristics & Earlier Leisure-time Intellectuality	Men Job Conditions, Social Characteristics, Earlier Leisure-time Intellectuality, & Ideational Flexibility	Women Job Conditions & Social Characteristics	Men Job Conditions & Social Characteristics
Substantive complexity	.29*	.24*	.14*	.46*
Routinization	−.02	−.02*	.02	.00
Closeness of supervision	.05*	.05*	−.01	.07*
Ownership	.04*	.03	.15*	.10*
Bureaucratization	.03	.03	.03	.05
Position in hierarchy	.00	.00	.13*	−.01
Time pressure	−.04*	−.04*	.04	−.03
Heaviness	.05*	.06*	−.05	.07*
Dirtiness	−.06*	−.06*	−12*	−.11*
Hours of work	−.06*	−.06*	−.20*	−.09*
"Held responsible"	.00	.01	.05	−.01
Risk of loss of job	−.02	−.02	.03	.00
Job protections	.03*	.04*	.03	.01
Income[2]	.04*	.03*	.14*	.04
Education	−.03	−.05*	.44*	.29*
Earlier L.T. intellectuality	.78*	.76*	x	x
Ideational flexibility	x	.10*	x	x
R Squared	.93	.93	.70	.67

[1] Social characteristics are education; age; racial, national, and religious background; urbanness and region of the country of the principal place where raised; mother's and father's education; father's occupational status; and number of children under five years of age in the current household.
[2] For men, job income; for women, family income.
*Significant at the .05 level or better.

leisure-time activities, have we only replicated the analysis of job conditions and ideational flexibility (Chapters 5 and 6), or is leisure-time intellectuality something more than an alternative measure of intellectual functioning? Clearly, ideational flexibility and leisure-time intellectuality have much in common. Both are measures of intellectual performance in off-the-job situations, with leisure-time intellectuality being a measure of cognitive functioning in ordinary non-work realms of life and ideational flexibility measuring cognitive functioning in the rather special but not entirely idiosyncratic circumstances of an intensive interview situation. Moreover, both have extremely high overtime correlations, .93 for each. The two measures are, inevitably, highly correlated with each other: .75 in 1964 and .77 in 1974. Unquestionably, the two concepts have much in common and, from one perspective, the two analyses replicate and thus validate each other.

Yet, ideational flexibility and intellectuality in leisure-time activities are not simply alternative measures of the same thing. They do, after all, measure behavior under quite different circumstances, one the special circumstances of a quasi-test situation, the other the ordinary circumstances of everyday life. More than that, ideational flexibility evaluates how well people perform, while leisure-time intellectuality measures not how well they perform, but whether they organize their lives to have intellectual content. Finally, of crucial importance, we have evidence that job conditions directly affect leisure-time intellectuality, apart from any indirect effect they might have through ideational flexibility. This evidence comes from including current ideational flexibility as an independent variable in the multiple-regression analysis. We find (see column 2 of Table 9.1) that all but one of the job conditions that had significantly affected leisure-time intellectuality still do so, the exception being ownership. Some of the regression coefficients are reduced in magnitude; in particular, that for substantive complexity drops from .29 to .24, suggesting that substantive complexity affects leisure-time intellectuality not only directly, but also indirectly through its effect on ideational flexibility. But, clearly, although the intellectuality of leisure-time activities has much in common with ideational flexibility, the relationships between job conditions and leisure-time intellectuality do not result simply from their joint relationship with ideational flexibility. Admittedly, the relationship between job conditions and leisure-time intellectuality could conceivably result from their joint relationship with some other facet of personality, but ideational flexibility is clearly more pertinent to intellectuality in leisure-time activities than is any other facet of personality.

Comparable analyses cannot be done for women. We lack information about women's earlier leisure-time intellectuality. Moreover, when we attempt to include ideational flexibility in a multiple-regression equation, we encounter serious difficulties of multicollinearity. It is nonetheless instructive that, in comparable regression analyses for men and women that include all fourteen job conditions and pertinent social characteristics (but do not include earlier leisure-time intellectuality or ideational flexibility), most of the job conditions that affect men's leisure-time intellectuality also affect women's leisure-time intellectuality (see columns 3 and 4 of Table 9.1). Thus, to take a pivotal example, the substantive complexity of work has a decided effect on the intellectuality of women's leisure-time activities, just as it has on men's. Still, the effect of substantive complexity on leisure-time intellectuality is not nearly as strong for women as for men (.14 vs. .46). By contrast, some other job conditions—notably, hierarchical position and number of hours worked—appear to be more important for women's intellectual use of leisure time than for men's. Income and education, too, appear to have stronger effects on women's than on men's leisure-time intellectuality, although for women it is family income (as shown in Table 9.1) rather than job income that matters. (An alternate analysis employing women's own job income shows job income to have no effect at all.) For women, we do not find the positive effects of closeness of supervision and heaviness that we find for men; rather, they are negative but statistically nonsignificant.

The multiple-regression analyses assume rather than test a causal ordering from job conditions to leisure-time activities. We do not know whether, for example, the number of hours that people work affects their leisure-time intellectuality or the intellectuality of their leisure-time activities affects how many hours they work. We now proceed to causal models, for both men and women, in which we attempt to assess the reciprocal effects of job conditions and the intellectuality of leisure-time activities.

A CAUSAL MODEL OF MEN'S JOB CONDITIONS AND THE INTELLECTUALITY OF THEIR LEISURE-TIME ACTIVITIES

The causal model for men includes those social characteristics that the research literature and our own earlier analyses give us reason to believe might affect either leisure-time intellectuality or the job placement of men who are at least ten years into their occupational careers. We thus include the respondent's age and his level of education, his race, national background, and religious background, the educational levels of both parents, his father's and grandfathers' occupational levels, the urbanness and the region of the country of the principal place where he was raised, the number of brothers and sisters he had, and the number of children under five years of age in his current household. We also include the respondent's 1964 leisure-time intellectuality and job conditions, as well as the substantive complexity of his "earlier" (pre-1964) jobs.

In estimating models of the reciprocal effects of men's job conditions and the intellectuality of their leisure-time activities, we follow the same procedures as those employed in Chapter 6 for estimating the reciprocal effects of job conditions and personality. The models, thus identified (see Table 9.2), confirm that nearly all of the job conditions that were shown in the multiple-regression analysis to significantly affect the intellectuality of men's leisure-time activities really do have a causal impact. Foremost among these job conditions, once again, is the substantive complexity of work, whose contemporaneous effect on leisure-time intellectuality (a path of .28) surpasses that of any other job condition. This effect is not an artifact of income and education being positively related to both substantive complexity and leisure-time intellectuality. In the model, income directly affects leisure-time intellectuality. Although education does not have a significant direct effect on 1974 leisure-time intellectuality, it is highly correlated with 1964 leisure-time intellectuality, which in turn has a strong carryover to 1974 leisure-time intellectuality. Hence, both income and education are statistically controlled in our appraisal of the effect of substantive complexity on leisure-time intellectuality.

In addition to substantive complexity's strong effect on leisure-time intellectuality, several other job conditions have modest effects. Heaviness, closeness of supervision, and, as we have seen, job income positively affect the intellectuality of leisure-time activities, while long hours of work, dirtiness, and time pressure have negative effects. Routinization, whose effect was not statistically significant in the initial multiple-regression analysis, now has a small but statistically significant negative effect—as we had hypothesized.[7] Over time, ownership and bureaucratization negatively affect leisure-time intellectuality.

As for the effects of leisure-time activities on job conditions: One effect is that intellectuality in men's leisure-time activities increases the substantive complexity of their work.[8] Thus, the learning-generalization process operates not only from job to leisure, but also from leisure to job. Over time, two other job conditions are affected by leisure-time intellectuality. Those who engage in intellectually demanding leisure-time activities are likely to become owners and to work fewer hours. The former we see as possible further evidence of learning-generalization; the latter, as evidence that workers attempt to select or mold their jobs to facilitate their leisure-time activities.

---

[7] We were unable to disentangle statistically the reciprocal contemporaneous effects of job protections and leisure-time intellectuality. (Their zero-order correlation is only − .02.) A test of the lagged reciprocal effects shows that neither is statistically significant.

[8] We are unable to assess simultaneously the contemporaneous and lagged effects of leisure-time intellectuality on substantive complexity. There is an intriguing question, whether leisure-time intellectuality actually affects the substantive complexity of work contemporaneously, as depicted in our model, or whether our inability to assess contemporaneous and lagged effects simultaneously makes a truly lagged effect appear to be contemporaneous. All we can conclude unequivocally is that leisure-time intellectuality sooner or later affects the substantive complexity of work.

Table 9.2. THE RECIPROCAL EFFECTS OF JOB CONDITIONS AND THE INTELLECTUALITY OF LEISURE-TIME ACTIVITIES (MEN)

	Statistically Significant* Effects of:							
	Leisure-time Intellectuality	Substantive Complexity	Routinization	Closeness of Supervision	Ownership	Bureau-cratization	Position in Hierarchy	Time Pressure
On 1974:								
Leisure-time intellectuality	.80(L)[a]	.28(C)	−.03(C)	.05(C)	−.10(L)	−.09(L)	.0[b]	−.04(C)
Substantive complexity	.09(C)	.33(L)	−.11(C)	−.24(C)	.08(C)	.12(C)	.17(C)	.08(C)
Routinization	0	0	.27(L)	0	0	0	−.09(C)	0
Closeness of supervision	0	−.31(L)	0	.08(L)[c]	0	0	−.15(C)	0
Ownership	.10(L)	0	0	0	.54(L)	0	0	0
Bureaucratization	0	0	0	0	−.13(L)	.48(L)	0	0
Position in hierarchy	0	.20(L)	0	0	0	0	.30(L)	.10(L)
Time pressure	0	0	−.12(C)	0	0	−.09(C)	0	.32(L)
Heaviness	0	0	−.11(C)	0	0	0	−.10(C)	0
Dirtiness	0	−.40(C)	0	0	0	0	0	0
Hours of work	−.11(L)	.19(C)	−.08(L)	0	0	−.24(C)	0	0
"Held responsible"	0	.17(C)	0	0	0	0	0	.17(C)
Risk of loss of job	0	0	0	0	.32(C)	0	0	0
Job protections	0	0	.12(L)	0	0	.35(C)	0	0
Job income	0	.16(C)	0	0	.20(C)	.18(C)	.15(C)	0

230

	Heaviness	Dirtiness	Hours of Work	"Held Responsible"	Risk of Loss of Job	Job Protections	Job Income	Education[d]
On 1974:								
Leisure-time intellectuality	.06(C)	−.05(C)	−.06(C)	.0	.0	.0	.07(C)	−.02[e]
Substantive complexity	.0	.0	.0	.0	.0	.07(L)	.0	.08
Routinization	.0	.0	.0	.0	.0	.0	−.10(L)	−.11
Closeness of supervision	−.10(C)	.10(L)	.0	.10(C)	.19(C)	.06(C)	−.12(L)	.0
Ownership	.0	.0	.0	.0	.0	−.10(L)	.0	.0
Bureaucratization	.0	.0	.0	−.05(L)	.0	.0	.0	.0
Position in hierarchy	.0	.0	.0	.0	.0	.0	.0	.0
Time pressure	.0	.0	.0	.0	.0	.0	.19(C)	.0
Heaviness	.21(L)	.27(C)	.09(L)	−.07(C)	.0	.0	.0	−.18
Dirtiness	.0	.39(L)	.15(C)	.0	.0	.0	.0	.0
Hours of work	.0	.13(L)	.16(L)	.0	.0	.0	.25(C)	.0
"Held responsible"	.0	.0	.08(C)	.24(L)	.0	.0	.0	.0
Risk of loss of job	.0	.0	.0	.0	.21(L)	.0	.0	.0
Job protections	.13(C)	.0	.0	.0	.0	.34(L)	.0	−.08
Job income	.0	−.11(C)	.0	.0	.0	.0	.34(L)	.0

* Statistically significant at the .05 level or better unless otherwise indicated.

[a] (L) means a lagged effect (e.g., of 1964 leisure-time intellectuality on 1974 leisure-time intellectuality); (C) means a contemporaneous effect (e.g., of 1974 substantive complexity on 1974 leisure-time intellectuality).

[b] .0 means fixed at .0.

[c] Path from 1964 closeness of supervision to 1974 closeness of supervision, t = 1.95.

[d] Paths from pre-1964 substantive complexity and from social characteristics, with the exception of education, not shown.

[e] Path from education to leisure-time intellectuality, t = 1.27.

There are four possible anomalies in the model, three of which we earlier encountered in the multiple-regression analysis.

One possible anomaly is that closeness of supervision has both a positive direct effect and a negative indirect effect (through substantive complexity) on leisure-time intellectuality. While the sum of the direct and indirect effects is a small, negative total effect ($-.02$), the positive direct effect, though modest (.05), could be interpreted as evidence of compensation. From this perspective, the effect of being closely supervised—taking into account that closely supervised people are likely to work at jobs of little substantive complexity—is to search out leisure-time activities that provide opportunities for exercising one's imagination and one's independent judgment in ways that are not possible at work. In any case, the effect is modest by comparison to that of the direct learning-generalization process exemplified in the effect of substantive complexity on leisure-time intellectuality; but still, there may be a compensatory process occurring.

A second possible anomaly in the model is that heavy work has a positive effect on leisure-time intellectuality, while dirty work—with which it is closely associated—has a negative effect. In contrast to the case for closeness of supervision, though, the indirect effects of heaviness on leisure-time intellectuality are trivial and the total effect is therefore positive, at .06. We are thus inclined to think that heaviness and dirtiness actually do have opposite effects on leisure-time intellectuality, with heaviness being conducive to, and dirtiness being inhibitory of, leisure-time intellectuality. It is pertinent that heaviness is conducive, not to intellectual functioning in general (it has a negative effect on ideational flexibility; see Chapter 6), but specifically to the use of one's intellect in leisure-time activities. Thus, being active on the job—mentally or physically—seems to stimulate being intellectually active off the job.

A third possible anomaly is that the effect of education on the intellectuality of leisure-time activities is negative, albeit small and statistically nonsignificant. This suggests that our model should be respecified—that education should have only an indirect effect on 1974 leisure-time intellectuality, via its strong positive relationship with 1964 leisure-time intellectuality. When we thus modify the model, the anomaly is removed with virtually no change to the rest of the model.

A fourth possible anomaly is that ownership and bureaucratization—which thus far have not been permitted to have direct contemporaneous effects on leisure-time intellectuality—have negative lagged effects. But both have positive indirect contemporaneous effects (at .03 for ownership and .06 for bureaucratization), mainly through their positively affecting substantive complexity and income. Thus, the indirect contemporaneous effects of ownership and bureaucratization seem to be at odds with their direct lagged effects. The issue is clarified by an alternative model that permits position in organizational structure to have both direct lagged effects and direct, unidirectional contemporaneous effects on leisure-time intellectuality. (See the discussion of alternative models in Chapter 6.) Such a model shows the direct contemporaneous effects of ownership and bureaucratization to be positive, the direct lagged effects to be negative, while all other effects remain virtually unchanged. It would thus seem that ownership and bureaucratization may contemporaneously foster intellectuality in men's leisure-time activities, both directly and indirectly through proximate conditions of work, but that over a longer time they inhibit leisure-time intellectuality. We do not know why the long-term effects of ownership and bureaucratization are different from the short-term effects. Hierarchical position, by contrast, poses no anomaly. It does not directly affect leisure-time intellectuality either contemporaneously or over time. Its indirect and hence its total contemporaneous effect is positive, at .06; its total lagged effect also is positive but inconsequential, at .02.

These possible anomalies notwithstanding, the main conclusion of this analysis is that the substantive complexity of work has a strong effect on the intellectuality of leisure-time activities.

A CAUSAL MODEL OF WOMEN'S JOB CONDITIONS AND THE INTELLECTUALITY OF THEIR LEISURE-TIME ACTIVITIES

In the absence of longitudinal data for women, a causal model can provide only a provisional assessment of the relationships between job conditions and leisure-time intellectuality. We do, however, have information about many conditions of the job immediately preceding the one held at the time of the interview—namely, substantive complexity, routinization, closeness of supervision, bureaucratization, hierarchical position, time pressure, dirtiness, hours worked, and the likelihood of being held responsible for things outside one's control. We do not have retrospective information about job income, but since we have a measure of earlier family income, we can include family income, which the multiple-regression analysis showed to be more important than job income for women's leisure-time intellectuality.

We are unable to solve a model that includes all these job conditions and all pertinent social characteristics. If, however, we exclude those job conditions that did not have statistically significant effects in the multiple-regression analysis, we are able to achieve a solution. The reciprocal-effects model, then, includes substantive complexity, hierarchical position, dirtiness, hours of work, family income, and all pertinent social characteristics about which we have information (see Table 9.3).

We deal with the critical limitation of the women's data, the absence of a measure of leisure-time intellectuality at an earlier time, by simulating such a measure. To do so, we make a number of assumptions, all of which follow from the general assumption that the measure of leisure-time intellectuality

Table 9.3. THE RECIPROCAL EFFECTS OF JOB CONDITIONS AND THE INTELLECTUALITY OF LEISURE-TIME ACTIVITIES (WOMEN) (HYPOTHETICAL STABILITY OF LEISURE-TIME INTELLECTUALITY FIXED AT 0.45)

	Statistically Significant* Effects of:						
	Leisure-time Intellectuality	Substantive Complexity	Position in Hierarchy	Dirtiness	Hours of Work	Family Income	Education[c]
On 1974:							
Leisure-time intellectuality	.45(L)[a]	.23(C)	.14(L)	.0[b]	−.18(C)	.10(C)	.14
Substantive complexity	.0	.23(L)	.19(C)	.0	.0	.14(L)	.38
Position in hierarchy	.0	.0	.36(L)	.0	.0	.0	.0
Dirtiness	.0	−.35(C)	.0	.33(L)	.0	.0	.0
Hours of work	.0	.0	.12(C)	.0	.25(L)	.0	.0
Family Income	.33(L)	.0	.10(C)	−.11(L)	.0	.38(L)	.0

[a] (L) means a lagged effect (e.g., of 1964 leisure-time intellectuality on 1974 leisure-time intellectuality; (C) means a contemporaneous effect (e.g., of 1974 substantive complexity on 1974 leisure-time intellectuality).
[b] .0 means fixed at .0.
[c] Paths from social characteristics, with the exception of education, not shown.
*Statistically significant at the .05 level or better.

of women, when they were in the job immediately preceding that held at the time of the interview, would have statistical properties similar to those of the measure of men's leisure-time intellectuality in 1964.[9] We initially fix the stability at a standardized path of .45, making the stability of women's leisure-time intellectuality less than that of men's but greater than that of any job condition, and later do a "sensitivity analysis" in which we increase the hypothetical stability of leisure-time intellectuality over a range of values up to .80, the stability of leisure-time intellectuality in the causal model for men.[10]

---

[9] Specifically, we assume:

(1) That the variance of women's earlier leisure-time intellectuality would be in the same proportion to the variance of women's 1974 leisure-time intellectuality as is the variance of men's 1964 leisure-time intellectuality to the variance of men's 1974 leisure-time intellectuality. This makes the variance of women's earlier leisure-time intellectuality a little smaller than that for 1974.

(2) That the correlations of earlier leisure-time intellectuality with social characteristics would bear the same relationships to the analogous 1974 correlations as do those for men. This makes some of the correlations of earlier leisure-time intellectuality with social characteristics a little larger than those for 1974 leisure-time intellectuality and some a little smaller.

(3) That the correlations between women's earlier leisure-time intellectuality and their earlier job conditions would have similar relationships to the women's analogous 1974 correlations as the correlations between men's 1964 leisure-time intellectuality and 1964 job conditions have to the men's analogous 1974 correlations. We have further multiplied the correlation between women's earlier leisure-time intellectuality and each job condition by the ratio of the women's to the men's overtime correlation for that job condition. Thus, our formula for calculating the correlation between women's earlier leisure-time intellectuality and each job condition is based on the following:

(r, Women's Earlier LT & Earlier Job/r,Women's 1974 LT & 1974 Job) =
(r, Men's 1964 LT & 1964 Job/r, Men's 1974 LT & 1974 Job)
X
(r, Women's Earlier Job & 1974 Job/r, Men's 1964 Job & 1974 Job),

where "LT" means leisure-time intellectuality and "Job" means any particular job condition. We make this correction because most of the overtime correlations of job conditions are smaller for women than for men. This might occur for any or all of the following reasons: because our information about women's earlier jobs is based on retrospective data; because for some job conditions this information is considerably less complete than is comparable information for men; because the jobs held by men in 1964 may have been the same as their current jobs while the information we have for women is always about a different job; and because some women have had interruptions between jobs or other shifts in career that may have made their job conditions actually less stable than men's. Whatever the reasons, the lesser stability of women's job conditions might mean that the ratios of correlations between leisure-time intellectuality and job conditions at two times would be different for women and men.

[10] The path of .45 represents a reasonable baseline estimate of the stability of leisure-time intellectuality because it makes the ratio of that stability to the stability of substantive complexity, the most stable job condition, approximately equal for men and for women. (For this analysis, we use as the stability of women's substantive complexity the value calculated in a preliminary model that does not include a simulated "earlier" leisure-time intellectuality.) A stability of .45 thus assumes that women's leisure-time intellectuality is less stable than is men's, but is more stable than are women's job conditions, just as is the case for men. The assumption that women's leisure-time intellectuality changes more over time than men's is plausible because women's multiple role responsibilities shift over the life course more than do men's, and thus the time and other resources available for leisure also would vary more for women. In any case, we systematically vary the hypothetical stability of leisure-time intellectuality over a range of values, up to that actually found for men.

With the inclusion of a simulated measure of earlier leisure-time intellectuality, the model for women has a structure similar to, but far from identical to, that of the model earlier developed for men. The major differences are that:

1. the prior job we use as a baseline for women is not that of ten years ago but the one held immediately before the 1974 job;
2. fewer job conditions are included;
3. for women, family income rather than job income is included; family income is depicted as affecting, but not being contemporaneously affected by, leisure-time intellectuality.

As does the model for men, the model for women gives priority to the contemporaneous effects of job conditions but allows lagged effects where contemporaneous effects are not statistically significant. Furthermore, employing logic similar to that used in the model for men, we initially allow hierarchical position to have only indirect contemporaneous and direct lagged effects on the intellectuality of leisure-time activities and then, in an alternative model, we allow hierarchical position to have direct contemporaneous effects.

The initial model (Table 9.3) shows that substantively complex work, family income, education, and (over time) a high position in the supervisory hierarchy significantly increase the intellectuality of women's leisure-time activities, while long hours of work decrease the intellectuality of women's leisure-time activities. Leisure-time intellectuality, in turn, has a positive lagged effect on family income. The alternative model, which allows hierarchical position to have a direct contemporaneous effect on leisure-time intellectuality, shows that effect to be statistically significant and positive; this is true whether or not we also allow a lagged effect.[11] The other parameters are not much changed. Thus, whether we depict the effects of hierarchical position as contemporaneous or as lagged, the picture is essentially the same. Substantively complex work markedly increases women's leisure-time intellectuality; in lesser degree, so too do a high position in the supervisory hierarchy, family income, and education; but long hours of work decrease women's leisure-time intellectuality.

Increasing the hypothetical "stability" of leisure-time intellectuality (Table 9.4) reduces the magnitude of education's effect on leisure-time in-

---

[11] The identification is too weak to estimate a direct contemporaneous effect of hierarchical position on leisure-time intellectuality in a reciprocal-effects model that allows all the other job conditions in the model to affect and be affected by leisure-time intellectuality. However, when we modify the model shown in Table 9.3 (in which all the nonsignificant paths have been fixed at zero), by substituting a contemporaneous path from hierarchical position to leisure-time intellectuality for the lagged path in that model, or even when we add the contemporaneous to the lagged path, we are able to test the direct contemporaneous effect of hierarchical position on leisure-time intellectuality.

Table 9.4. RECIPROCAL EFFECTS MODEL (WOMEN)
SENSITIVITY ANALYSIS: HYPOTHETICAL
STABILITY OF LEISURE-TIME
INTELLECTUALITY VARIED

Path to Leisure-time Intellectuality from:	Standardized Stability Fixed at:		
	.45	**.60**	**.80**
Substantive complexity (1974)	.23*	.24*	.25*
Hours worked (1974)	−.18*	−.19*	−.21*
Family income (1974)	.10*	.07	.00
Education	.14*	.06	−.05
Hierarchical position (of immediately preceding job)	.14*	.11*	.08*
Path from Earlier Leisure-time Intellectuality to:			
Family income (1974)	.33*	.31*	.40*

*Statistically significant at .05 level or better.

tellectuality, until it becomes a small, statistically nonsignificant, negative path—just as in the model for men. The effect of family income also is markedly reduced. But, even when we increase the stability of leisure-time intellectuality to .80, making this stability far larger in proportion to that of any job condition for women than it is for men, the effects of substantive complexity and hours of work remain as strong as ever; the effect of hierarchical position, while reduced in magnitude, remains statistically significant. The lagged path from leisure-time intellectuality to family income increases in magnitude. All this holds true whether we model the direct effect of hierarchical position on leisure-time intellectuality as lagged (as in Table 9.4) or as contemporaneous.

The models for men and women are similar, then, in their primary finding—that substantively complex work has a strong positive effect on leisure-time intellectuality. The models are similar, too, in showing that the number of hours worked has a negative effect on leisure-time intellectuality, albeit a stronger effect for women than for men. Greater income also would appear to enhance both men's and women's leisure-time intellectuality, but for women we cannot be certain because the effect disappears at higher hypothetical stabilities of leisure-time intellectuality.

There are also some differences. Dirty work significantly decreases men's leisure-time intellectuality, but has no significant effect for women. A high position in the organizational structure has a direct effect on women's leisure-time intellectuality but only an indirect effect on men's. It would appear, too, that education may directly affect women's leisure-time intellectuality, but not men's; but of this we cannot be certain, because the effect for women disappears in models with a very high hypothetical stability for leisure-time intellectuality. Finally, leisure-time intellectuality increases the substantive complexity of men's work and, in time, increases the probability of their becoming owners and leads to a decrease in number of hours worked. Leisure-time intellectuality does not have these effects for women, but it is conducive, in time, to increased family income.

We are loath to dwell on the differences between the findings for men and women, for the models are not entirely comparable.[12] Thus, for example, we cannot be certain whether our failure to find a significant effect of leisure-time intellectuality on the substantive complexity of women's jobs means that women do not have as much opportunity to mold their jobs as do men or merely that a model with only a simulated measure of earlier leisure-time intellectuality is not powerful enough to detect such an effect. Moreover, the differences are not what is most striking. On the contrary, the most striking finding is the same for both men and women—that substantively complex work markedly increases leisure-time intellectuality. This basic similarity of findings for men and women cannot result entirely from the women being spouses of the men in the sample: Over half the sample of men do not have a working spouse and, of those who do, their job conditions are only moderately correlated with those of their spouses. No matter how we examine the data, every analysis shows the substantive complexity of work to have predominant importance for leisure-time intellectuality, both for men and for women. This is clearly the central finding of all our analyses.

DISCUSSION

Before discussing the import of our findings, we must consider the principal limitations of our data and of our methods of analysis. Some we have already noted: In the absence of first-hand observations, we have had to rely on interview data about job and leisure-time pursuits; we have only single-item measures of several job conditions; our data do not permit the simultaneous assessment of contemporaneous and lagged reciprocal effects; our sample of wives is not ideal for generalizing to all women; we have only

---

[12] To see whether the differences between our findings for men and for women might be artifacts of our methods of modelling—using a much smaller set of job conditions for women and substituting family income for job income—we developed a model for men that is limited to the job conditions in the model for women and contains family income rather than job income. All the parameters in the limited model that were statistically significant in the larger model remain so. (Using family income rather than job income in the model means that the effect of "income" is less than before, but still statistically significant.) We still cannot be certain, though, whether the differences in our findings for men and women—such as they are—represent real gender differences or artifacts of the one remaining discrepancy in the models, i.e., having real information about earlier leisure-time intellectuality for men but having only simulated information for women.

retrospective and somewhat limited information about women's earlier job conditions; we have no information at all about women's earlier leisure-time intellectuality; and, of course, we are dealing with only one dimension of leisure-time activity. We have no way of knowing whether stronger compensatory or personality-predisposition processes might operate between job conditions and other dimensions of leisure-time activity, such as physical-activity level or sociability.

There are other limitations that should also be considered in any assessment of the theoretical implications of our findings:

First, although we have statistically controlled a number of individual characteristics that might affect leisure-time behavior, others have escaped us. We have no information, for example, about health, physical strength, eyesight, or other conditions that could affect people's capacities to engage in various types of leisure-time activities.

Second, although we have included age in our package of statistical controls, this in no way suffices to take account of life-course dynamics. We do not know, for example, whether the extraordinary stability of leisure-time intellectuality that we found for men who are, in the main, well into their occupational careers, would be true also of younger or older men or of women at any age. Nor do we know whether job conditions might affect people just entering their careers differently from people further along in their careers. By the same token, processes of job selection and of job molding might themselves be more amenable to change earlier in the occupational career. On all of this, our linear additive models have nothing to say. Nor is our sample sufficiently large to permit the types of models necessary to assess these possibilities.

Finally, there may be important threshold effects or interaction effects of job and other conditions on leisure-time activities. It may be, for example, that heaviness and dirtiness matter only when they surpass some minimum threshold; or that closeness of supervision affects leisure-time intellectuality only among more- (or among less-) educated people. Testing these possibilities, too, is beyond the capacities of our sample and our mode of analysis.

Still, despite all these limitations, some important conclusions can be drawn from our analyses. Our findings provide strong evidence for the learning-generalization hypothesis, substantial evidence for the facilitator/constraint hypothesis, equivocal evidence—and then only for men—for the compensation hypothesis, substantial evidence against the personality-predisposition hypothesis, and overwhelming evidence against the hypothesis that workers compartmentalize their jobs from their leisure-time activities. Specifically:

The strong, positive effect of the substantive complexity of both men's and women's work on the intellectuality of their leisure-time activities is powerful evidence that people generalize directly from job experience to the activities they perform in their leisure time. The small negative effect of routinization on men's leisure-time intellectuality also is consistent with the learning-generalization hypothesis, as is the positive direct effect (for women) of hierarchical position. The positive effects (for men) of leisure-time intellectuality on substantive complexity and on ownership provide some evidence that direct learning-generalization takes place from leisure-time activities to job conditions as well.

The evidence is generally consistent, too, with the expectation that job conditions that provide time, energy, and money facilitate the intellectuality of leisure-time activity, while conditions that deplete these resources act as constraints. Thus, job income has a modest positive effect, while long hours of work, dirtiness, and time pressure have modest negative effects on men's leisure-time intellectuality. Correspondingly, family income positively affects and long hours of work negatively affect women's leisure-time intellectuality. There is some evidence that leisure-time activities in turn affect these job conditions. Men's earlier leisure-time intellectuality inversely affects the number of hours worked in the current job; and women's earlier leisure-time intellectuality positively affects family income at the current time.

Two of our findings might be interpreted as providing support for the hypothesis that compensation, too, occurs in the relationship between work and leisure, at least for men. (We cannot test in a causal model the same findings for women, but the multiple-regression analyses for women give no evidence of similar phenomena.) Closeness of supervision positively affects men's leisure-time intellectuality. This may be a statistical artifact. If the apparent effect is real, it implies that men who are closely supervised on their jobs compensate by engaging in intellectually challenging leisure-time activities, or that men who are not closely supervised compensate for the intellectual demands of their jobs by engaging in leisure-time activities that do not require thought. We also find that heavy work increases men's leisure-time intellectuality. While this, too, might be a statistical artifact, our analyses lead us to think it is real. If so, it could be interpreted as some sort of compensation between physical and mental activity: Men who do heavy, physically demanding work may compensate off the job by engaging in mentally demanding activities that may not require physical exertion. Correspondingly, men who do sedentary work may compensate by engaging in leisure-time activities requiring heavy physical exertion, activities that may not be very intellectually demanding. There is, however, another and more straightforward possible interpretation—that physical exertion on the job, which we thought might deplete the energy required for intellectually demanding leisure-time activities, actually facilitates intellectual activity off the job, while sedentary work is detrimental to the use of intellect in leisure time. Our original expectation that heaviness would constrain leisure-time intellectuality may have been wrong; heaviness appears, instead, to be facilitative of leisure-time intellectuality.

We find also that the relationships between job conditions and leisure-time intellectuality do not result solely from more intellectually flexible people selecting and being selected into more intellectually demanding jobs and leisure-time pursuits. The evidence is limited to men; our data are inadequate for doing comparable analyses for women. For men, though, the multiple-regression analyses demonstrate that ideational flexibility does not explain the relationships between job conditions and leisure-time intellectuality. Moreover, when we compare the findings of the reciprocal-effects causal model of job conditions and leisure-time intellectuality developed in this analysis with an exactly comparable model job conditions and ideational flexibility (Chapter 5), we see that substantive complexity has twice as great an effect on leisure-time intellectuality as on ideational flexibility. The weight of the evidence thus indicates that the process of learning-generalization between job and leisure time involves more than intellectual flexibility. There is, in addition, a carryover of patterns of behavior from each realm to the other.

Housework As Work[*]

Carmi Schooler,
Melvin L. Kohn,
Karen A. Miller,
and Joanne Miller

In this chapter, we consider whether the conditions of work experienced in paid employment have analogues in unpaid household work and, insofar as they do, whether the psychological concomitants of "job conditions" in housework are similar to those of job conditions in paid employment.[1] Our initial intent had been to focus the housework inquiry on full-time housewives, on the rationale that the conditions they experience in housework are functionally equivalent to the structural imperatives of jobs held by employed women and men; housework might have psychological consequences similar to those of paid employment. As we developed the interview schedule, it became apparent that most questions about housework apply not only to housewives but also to employed women and to many men. We were intrigued by the possibility that housework might affect the psychological functioning of all adults, whether or not they are employed outside the

[*] This chapter was written especially for this book. We are indebted to Carol Richtand for carrying out the statistical analyses.

[1] The close connection between paid employment and unpaid household labor has long been recognized by agricultural and home economists (see Berk, 1980; Walker and Woods, 1976:xvii–xix). Dimensions of paid employment that have been applied to the study of non-market work activity include: wage rates for household labor (Gauger and Walker, 1980); time spent on housework (Manning, 1968; Walker and Woods, 1976; Stafford and Duncan, 1980; Berk and Berk, 1979); and ratings of the social prestige of housewives (Bose, 1973, 1980; Nilson, 1978: and Dworkin, 1981).

home, albeit perhaps not to the same degree. Accordingly, the questions about housework were asked of all adult respondents in the 1974 survey. The present analysis is based on the 555 married couples in the sample.

Our intent has been to focus on the *work* in housework, rather than on social and particularly family roles, as have most sociological studies (e.g., Lopata, 1971). A basic problem in studying housework is to decide precisely what constitutes housework—to differentiate housework from all other activities that occur in the home. To clarify our own thinking, and to guide our respondents, we have defined housework as work that must be done to maintain a household, work that someone would have to be hired to do if family members did not do it themselves.[2] We deliberately differentiate, insofar as it is possible to do so, the interpersonal relationships of the family from household work. The emotional sustenance of spouse and children is not here treated as household work.[3] Thus, talking with members of the family is outside the sphere of "work with people" in housework, unless the discussion pertains directly to housework; we treat talking with members of the family no differently from talking with grocery clerks and with plumbers. We even reluctantly exclude the interpersonal component of child-rearing from the domain we define to be household work, although we certainly do include the cooking, cleaning, and help with schoolwork that are part and parcel of having children in the household. The rationale for this exclusion is that, unless we were to inquire in much more detail than the time constraints of our interview permit, we would have no way to evaluate the complexity of work with people that is involved in the relationship of parent to child. The foci of inquiry, then, are the concrete tasks of running a household, not the interpersonal relationships that constitute a family. Our intention is not a comprehensive analysis of all that takes place in a household but a search for analogues in housework to the structural imperatives of paid employment.

Some of what we have termed the structural imperatives of the job have no direct counterparts in household work. It makes little sense to inquire about the degree of bureaucratization of the organization in which housework is done or about the individual's hierarchical position in a formal supervisory structure. It is even questionable whether the very concept, structural imperatives of the job, applies to housework, for it is not entirely clear what housework *must* be done (e.g., is cleaning under beds necessary?). Nor are the standards at which the various tasks should be per-

---

[2] A similar definition is used by Reid (1934). There remains, however, substantial ambiguity in defining "household tasks" (see the discussions in Berk and Berk, 1979:34–35; Berk, 1980:129–133).

[3] See Gecas's (1976) discussion of the distinction between the roles of parents in socialization and in child care. The differentiation of parenting from housework is considered also in Olson's (1979) exploratory study of mothers' perceptions of the compatibility of these activities.

formed clear: There is more room for people to decide for themselves what they will do and how they will do it in housework than in paid employment. Moreover, there are few external validations such as promotions, profits, or pay raises to serve as signs of a job well done. Even obvious failure, such as the break-up of a household, is far from proof that housework was poorly done. Finally, it is difficult to fix the boundary line between the *work* in housework and the extension of some housework pursuits into leisure-time activities. At what point do cooking, gardening, or furniture repair cease being household work and become hobbies?[4] Housework seems to be more discretionary in character than is paid employment.

Still, there is work to be done in a household and this work does exercise imperatives.[5] Meals need not be of the highest quality, but someone must cook. Someone must clean the house and someone must make repairs. Although the work may be more discretionary than that done in paid employment, it is real. Some conditions of employment outside the home—for example, time pressure, heaviness of work, dirtiness, and substantive complexity—would seem to have quite direct analogues in housework; others, such as closeness of supervision, are more problematic. We here examine the structural imperatives of the job, one by one, to see which can reasonably be thought to have analogues in housework. We then index each of the conditions of household work that seem comparable to job conditions in paid employment and assess its relationships to psychological functioning.

MEASUREMENT OF HOUSEWORK CONDITIONS

Since the questions about housework were asked only in the follow-up study, we have only cross-sectional data. The questions, by deliberate design, parallel those we had asked about paid employment, not only in general content, but even in question wording. This procedure has enabled us to achieve substantial similarity in our indices of analogous conditions encountered in housework and paid employment. As we shall see, the proce-

---

[4] Berk and Berk (1979:229–230) report that their respondents clearly label some household tasks as "work", some as "leisure", and others as both. Child care and meal preparation, for example, represent a mix of work and leisure activity. The degree to which tasks are thought to be pleasant or unpleasant accounts for 80 percent of the variation in whether activities are viewed as work, as leisure, or as both.

[5] Although the discretionary nature of housework must be recognized, we should not exaggerate the degree of discretion actually involved, at any rate for women. Walker and Woods (1976:66) report, for example, only modest correlations between how much a task is liked and the time spent doing that task. The highest correlations are for special clothing care ($r = .17$) and regular house care ($r = .12$). Moreover, Berk and Berk (1979:233) conclude that in the course of a household day as much as one-third of the sequencing of activities is constrained by some sort of necessary order. This is especially true during the morning hours and during meal preparation.

dure has the disadvantage, though, of sometimes providing apparently comparable data that on close inspection turn out not to have the same meaning as data about paid employment, and of sometimes providing less detailed information than might otherwise have been obtained.

It may be that our open-ended questions, more particularly our probes, were insufficiently specific to elicit full descriptions of exactly what respondents do in housework. In our inquiries about housework, we may have lost an advantage from which we had benefited greatly in our job inquiries: When interviewers asked respondents about their jobs, most respondents (particularly male respondents talking with female interviewers) assumed that the interviewer knew little about the specifics of their jobs and, in response to a little adroit probing, gave us rich detail about what they actually do in their work. When interviewers asked respondents about their housework, most respondents (particularly female respondents talking with female interviewers) assumed that the interviewer knew a great deal about the specifics of housework and, unless the probing was particularly skillful, tended to provide few details about what they actually do in their housework. As a result, even with the many suggested probes and the considerable information that we provided interviewers about our intended use of the interview data, these data are not as detailed as are comparable data about paid employment. Were we to begin anew, we would systematically ask specific questions about respondents' work in such key domains of housework as cooking, sewing, and household repairs.

It nonetheless did prove possible to ask questions and to produce indices about several conditions of household work that are comparable to those we use in studying job conditions in paid employment.

Self-direction in Housework

Substantive complexity. Just as in paid employment, by the substantive complexity of housework we mean the degree to which the performance of work requires thought and independent judgment. As we had done in our examination of the substantive complexity of work in paid employment, we inquired in detail about the respondents' household work with data, with things, and with people. To introduce our questions about work with data, we told respondents that this type of work could include such varied tasks as keeping household accounts, balancing a checkbook, reading cookbooks, keeping recipe files, reading books and articles about child care, and helping children with homework. We then asked them to tell us in detail about their own household work involving reading, writing, figuring, or dealing with any kind of written materials. Similarly, in asking about work with things, we told respondents that such work could include cooking, fixing the plumbing, housecleaning, sewing, gardening, operating a washing machine, ironing, bathing and dressing children, driving to the store, and repairing a broken appliance; here, too, we asked for detailed descriptions of what they actually do. In asking about work with people, we emphasized (as we had for paid employment) that we do not mean to include passing the time of day, but only conversations necessary to the work of running a household: for example, talking with children's teachers, discussing finances and household arrangements with one's spouse, dealing with household help or repair people, or dealing with shopkeepers. Again, we asked for detailed information about what respondents actually do in this realm of household work. We also asked, just as we had vis-a-vis paid employment, how much time they spend working with data, with people, and with things. (In the pretests, we had asked respondents to calculate the total amount of time they spend doing housework, but this proved impossible for many people, particularly housewives, to do.)

To appraise the substantive complexity of housework, we developed a measurement model (see Figure 10.1). We use information provided by both husbands and wives, on the rationale that since this is an analysis of married couples, we should depict the substantive complexity of both spouses' housework in the same model.[6] Initially, we used our appraisals of the complexity of each spouse's household work with data, with things, and with people (each coded as comparably as possible to our standard codes for measuring the complexity of work in paid employment); the respondent's estimates of time spent doing each of these three types of household work; and our measures of the complexity of each respondent's work in such key activities as cooking, sewing, repairing, gardening, and reading about matters pertinent to household activities. (The classifications of the complexity of household work are presented in Appendix E.) Including appraisals of the complexity of specific household activities, despite their redundancy with our more general classifications of complexity, takes full advantage of the information about these particular activities. Although all eight measures of complexity shown for wives had initially been included for husbands as well, preliminary analyses revealed that four of them (complexity of work with data, of work with people, of cooking, and of sewing) are not significantly related to the substantive complexity of men's housework.[7] These statistically nonsignificant indicators were dropped from the portion of the model depicting the substantive complexity of men's household

---

[6] We initially tested correlations of the residuals of parallel indicators for husbands and wives, found all to be statistically nonsignificant, and subsequently fixed them at zero.

[7] More detailed accounts of men's household work (Walker and Woods, 1976:58–62; Berk and Berk, 1979:231–232; and Meissner, et al., 1975) show that the task content of husbands' and wives' work in the household differs, that husbands spend far fewer hours on household tasks than do wives, and that the scheduling of husbands' and wives' household activities differs. Gender differences in the nature of household work are assessed in Schooler, K. Miller, and J. Miller (1982).

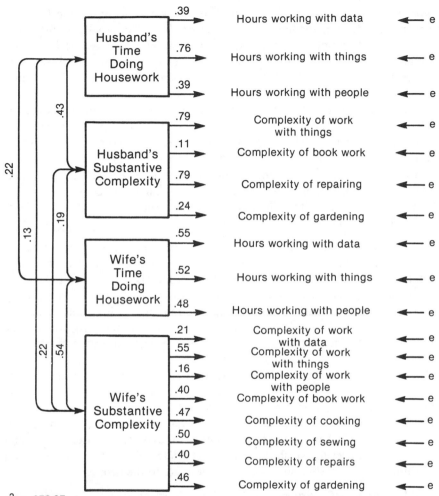

$\chi^2 = 378.97$
d.f. = 129
ratio = 2.94
All parameters shown are statistically significant, p≤.05.

FIG. 10.1. MEASUREMENT MODEL OF COMPLEXITY OF HOUSEWORK FOR HUSBANDS AND WIVES

work. The resultant model fits the data reasonably well, the chi-square being 378.97, with 129 degrees of freedom, for a ratio of 2.94.

This measurement model of the substantive complexity of housework differs from those for the substantive complexity of paid employment in several ways. As we have noted, the housework model of substantive complexity contains information about both spouses. This model also includes appraisals, not only of the complexity of work with data, with things, and with people, but of specific aspects of the work—cooking, sewing, repairing, gardening, reading. The model of the substantive complexity of housework does not, however, include an estimate of overall complexity. Finally, in this model "time" and "complexity" are treated as separate concepts; if they were treated as parts of a single concept, "time" would dominate that concept.[8]

The nature of substantive complexity in housework thus differs considerably from that of the substantive complexity of work in paid employment, particularly for men. The substantive complexity of women's housework, although characterized by complexity in a broad range of activities, is concentrated mainly in the realm of work with things. The substantive complexity of men's housework is even more narrowly characterized by complexity of work with things, particularly in the traditional male role of doing household repairs.

Routinization of housework is, unfortunately, no better measured than is routinization of paid employment: The index is based on a single, relatively subjective question, in which respondents were asked to characterize their household work as involving "doing the same thing in the same way repeatedly, the same kind of thing in a number of different ways, or a number of different kinds of things." It is a serious failing of our inquiry that we did not develop a more comprehensive, less subjective measure of routinization, for we could then have tested the common assertion that housework is exceedingly routine and that this quality of housework has profoundly negative psychological consequences. Because our index is weak, we can test this assertion only partially: If we should find that routinization, as we have measured it, does have the expected psychological effects, we would have prima facie evidence in favor of the assertion's being correct. If, however, we should fail to find such effects, this might mean nothing more than that our index is inadequate to the task.

Closeness of supervision. For this component of occupational self-direction, our inquiry is exploratory. It is equivocal whether an analogy to the phenomenon of close supervision in paid employment applies to housework, where the analogue to the "supervisor" would in most instances be the spouse (at least in this culture).[9] Certainly, the husband-wife

---

[8] Respondents' estimates of time spent working with things, with data, and with people are not mutually exclusive; their intercorrelations are in fact larger than are those among the several measures of complexity. Consistent with this finding is Walker and Woods' (1976:115) finding that nearly all household tasks are sometimes performed simultaneously with other household work activities.

[9] Olsen's (1974) analysis, which we shall discuss more fully in Chapter 12, shows that in three-generation patrilineal households in Taiwan, the mother-in-law may play the role of supervisor.

relationship is far different from the supervisor-supervisee relationship. Not only is each partner in the marriage the "supervisor" vis-a-vis the other's housework, but there is no way to separate their dealings with one another on issues of running the household from their overall marital relationship. We nevertheless thought it worth experimenting, to see whether the questions we had asked about how much latitude the supervisor allows and how supervisory control is exercised would be meaningful when asked about household work. To that end, we translated those questions that might be applicable to housework into the framework of "spouse as supervisor" of household work:

1. When your (wife/husband) wants you to do some household work, does (she/he) usually just insist that you do it, does (she/he) usually ask or suggest that you do it, or does (she/he) leave it up to you?
2. When (she/he) wants you to do some household work, how free do you feel to disagree with (her/him)—completely free, largely but not completely free, moderately, not particularly, or not at all free?
3. How about when you want your (wife/husband) to do some household work—do you usually just insist that (she/he) do it, do you usually ask or suggest that (she/he) do it, or do you leave it up to (her/him)?

Since these questions made sense to the respondents in the pretest surveys, we kept them in the final survey. The resulting data show, however, that the answers reflect a far different reality from that of supervision in the workplace. Few spouses "insist", few are unwilling to disagree. Rather, answers to these questions seem to reflect the difference between having a spouse who shows some interest in one's housework, i.e., who makes requests and suggestions, and having a spouse who shows little interest, i.e., who leaves housework entirely up to the respondent.[10] We failed to tap anything that could reasonably be called closeness of supervision in household work. It is not certain, though, whether there is no such phenomenon or whether our rather mechanical translation of questions designed to be asked about paid employment fails to measure a phenomenon that requires more subtle measurement in this domain. In any event, our analysis of the psychological effects of household work does not include closeness of supervision as one of the conditions of work.

---

[10] It is pertinent that, for both husbands and wives, the measures of "closeness of supervision" correlate positively with the substantive complexity of housework, whereas in paid employment closeness of supervision is negatively related to the substantive complexity of work.

Other Housework Conditions

Because housework is not carried out in a formally structured organization, our usual indices of position in organizational structure (ownership, bureaucratization of the firm or organization, and position in the supervisory hierarchy) have no meaningful parallel in housework. It is possible, though, to measure three job pressures—time pressure, heaviness, and dirtiness. We could not measure the number of hours spent doing housework. (As we have seen, respondents were not able to calculate the total number of hours they spend doing housework. Nor can we use the "time" construct from the measurement model of substantive complexity as a proxy, because it measures, not total time spent in doing housework, but covariation in the amounts of time spent working with data, with people, and with things.) Of the extrinsic risks and rewards characteristic of paid employment, only one has an analogue in household work—being held responsible for things outside one's control. Even for this, we cannot be sure that apparent similarity means real equivalence, since both those holding the worker responsible and the consequences of being held responsible are different in the two contexts. We nevertheless include it in our battery of "job conditions" in household work, to see what its psychological concomitants may be.

ASSESSING THE RELATIONSHIP BETWEEN WOMEN'S HOUSEWORK CONDITIONS AND THEIR PSYCHOLOGICAL FUNCTIONING

As a first step, we examine the hypothesis that women's psychological functioning is related to conditions of housework much as it is to conditions of work in paid employment. To learn which housework conditions are related to psychological functioning independent of social background and of other housework conditions, we use multiple-regression analysis. If housework is meaningfully related to psychological functioning, we can turn to linear structural-equation models to deal with the question of causal directionality.

The independent variables in the multiple-regression equations include the conditions of work experienced in housework and pertinent social background characteristics.[11] Also included (as pertinent statistical controls) are whether the woman is employed outside the home and whether her mother had a full-time job when the respondent was a child. The dependent variables in these equations are ideational flexibility, self-directedness of orienta-

---

[11] The social characteristics included in the multiple-regression analyses are: race, national background, father's occupational status, urbanness of origin, mother's education, father's education, religious background, age of respondent, region of origin, family income, and respondent's education.

tion, and distress. As we have seen in Chapter 6, these three dimensions of psychological functioning provide a partial, but useful, conceptualization of personality.

The analyses (Table 10.1) show that, even with social characteristics statistically controlled, all six of the conditions of household work that we have indexed are significantly related to one or more facets of psychological functioning. Substantive complexity, in particular, is significantly related to all three facets of psychological functioning examined in this analysis.

Five of the six housework conditions are significantly related to ideational flexibility: Substantively complex housework has a rather strong, positive relationship to ideational flexibility, while heavy, dirty, and routinized housework and responsibility for things outside one's control bear negative relationships to ideational flexibility. The relationships between household work and holding a self-directed orientation are similar, albeit weaker and more limited: Substantively complex housework is positively related to having a self-directed orientation; heavy housework is negatively related to having such an orientation. The relationships between housework and distress are, as we should expect, different: Doing substantively complex housework is *negatively* related to distress, while being held responsible for things outside one's control and being time-pressured are positively related to feeling distressed.

In toto, the relationships between women's conditions of housework and their psychological functioning are remarkably similar to those found earlier (Chapter 8) for conditions of work in paid employment. Women whose

Table 10.1. MULTIPLE REGRESSION ANALYSES: WOMEN'S PSYCHOLOGICAL FUNCTIONING ON HOUSEWORK CONDITIONS[a]

	Ideational Flexibility	Self-Directedness	Distress
(Standardized Regression Coefficients)			
Housework Conditions:			
Substantive complexity	.24*	.14*	−.12*
Heaviness of physical labor	−.12*	−.07*	.00
Frequency of being held responsible for things outside one's control	−.06*	−.04	.19*
Routinization	−.06*	−.05	−.01
Dirtiness	−.06*	.00	.05
Frequency of time pressure	.02	.05	.09*

[a] Multiple-regression equations include all social characteristics and conditions of housework as independent variables.
N = 555.
* Statistically significant, .05 level or better. All others are nonsignificant.

housework is substantively complex are more likely to be intellectually flexible and to have a self-directed orientation, while women who experience "job pressures" and "job uncertainties"—i.e., time pressure and the likelihood of being held responsible for things outside one's control—feel distressed.

Do these findings apply both to those women who are employed outside the home and to those who are full-time housewives?[12] For example, housework might affect housewives more than it does women who are exposed, not only to the conditions of housework, but also to the structural imperatives of paid employment.[13] To deal with such issues, we analyze the relationships between psychological functioning and the conditions of work experienced in housework separately for women who are employed outside the home and for women who are not.

These analyses show (see Table 10.2) that the main conclusions we have drawn from the overall analysis apply equally well to both groups of women. In particular, the relationships between the substantive complexity of housework and all three facets of psychological functioning are much the same for women employed outside the home as they are for full-time housewives. Moreover, heavy work is negatively related to ideational flexibility for both groups, while being held responsible for things outside one's control is positively related to distress. Some psychological concomitants of household work do appear, however, to be statistically significant for only one of the two groups. Contrary to what one might expect, though, it is not that housewives' psychological functioning is especially related to housework. Instead, it appears that women who are employed outside the home may react more than do full-time housewives to some conditions of housework: For employed women, but not for housewives, dirty housework is negatively related to ideational flexibility and positively related to distress; heavy housework is negatively related to holding a self-directed orientation; and being held responsible for things outside one's control is negatively related to ideational flexibility. On the other hand, there are two conditions of housework that are significantly related to psychological functioning for

---

[12] The multiple-regression analyses in Table 10.1 do include employment status as an independent variable. (Working outside the home is positively related to ideational flexibility, but is not significantly related to either self-directedness or distress.) These analyses do not, however, test the interaction of employment status with the conditions of housework.

[13] Women employed outside the home presumably spend less time on housework than do women not so employed. However, the difference in time allocated to housework is not as dramatic as one might expect. Walker and Woods' (1976:36) detailed study of time-use indicates that employed wives spend an average of two hours less per day on housework than do housewives. Moreover, although the husbands of employed women are somewhat more likely to participate in housework than are the husbands of full-time housewives, the men's contributions are usually minimal and are generally initiated only when wives are not available. (A review of recent studies on the division of household labor can be found in Miller and Garrison, 1982.)

housewives but not for women who are employed outside the house, only one of which signifies a difference of more than trivial magnitude: Time-pressure is positively related to distress. Thus, the relationship between housework and psychological functioning is at least as pronounced for women who are employed outside the home as it is for full-time housewives.

Causal Models for Women

Although we believe that the multiple-regression findings result in substantial part from housework actually affecting psychological functioning, the direction of causal effects is far from certain. It could be argued that the relationship between housework and psychological functioning results mainly from women's personalities shaping the way they do their housework. For example, women who are ideationally flexible may choose to do substantively complex household tasks. Substantial effects in both directions are also possible, e.g., ideational flexibility may both lead one to do substantively complex housework and result from doing substantively complex housework.

To appraise directions of effects, we turn to linear structural-equation modeling, using the entire sample of women. We do this cautiously, because

Table 10.2. MULTIPLE REGRESSION ANALYSES: WOMEN'S PSYCHOLOGICAL FUNCTIONING ON HOUSEWORK CONDITIONS; SEPARATE ANALYSES FOR WOMEN WHO ARE AND WHO ARE NOT EMPLOYED OUTSIDE THE HOME[a]

	Ideational Flexibility		Self-directedness		Distress	
	Employed	Not Employed	Employed	Not Employed	Employed	Not Employed
(Standardized Regression Coefficients)						
Housework Conditions:						
Substantive complexity	.23*	.25*	.17*	.10*	−.11	−.13*
Heaviness of physical labor	−.09*	−.11*	−.16*	.01	.03	−.05
Frequency of being held responsible for things outside one's control	−.09*	−.03	−.07	−.02	.16*	.21*
Routinization	−.05	−.05	−.07	−.05	.01	−.03
Dirtiness	−.12*	.00	.00	.02	.13*	−.02
Frequency of time pressure	.07	−.05	.09	.00	.04	.16*

[a] Multiple-regression equations include all social characteristics and conditions of housework as independent variables.
Number of women employed outside the home = 269.
Number of women not employed outside the home = 286.
* Statistically significant, .05 level or better. All others are nonsignificant.

we have only cross-sectional information. Our causal estimates cannot take account of "earlier" psychological functioning or pre-existing patterns of household work. Furthermore, the lack of longitudinal data makes identification of the structural-equation models difficult. Nevertheless, if we make several rather strong assumptions, it is possible to estimate some limited but instructive models of the reciprocal effects of household work and the principal facets of psychological functioning.

Part of the necessary instrumentation is provided by postulating that certain external conditions affect housework directly but affect psychological functioning only indirectly. The pertinent conditions, which may affect the amount and difficulty of housework, are the distances from home to public transportation and to shopping; the number of people in the household *other than* the respondent, her husband, and her children; the age of the youngest child; and the number of hours per week her husband is employed. These provide instrumentation—albeit not very strong instrumentation—for the paths from housework to psychological functioning. Unfortunately, we have no instruments for the reciprocal paths from psychological functioning to housework. To identify those paths, we use a technically correct but weak alternative procedure, that is, fixing at zero the correlations between the residuals of conditions of household work and the residual of whichever facet of psychological functioning is examined in the model (see Heise, 1975:181). These restrictions alone do not provide sufficiently strong identification to create statistically sensible models. We therefore make the further restriction of limiting which social characteristics are permitted to affect each of the conditions of housework.[14] Even then, we are not able to achieve meaningful models that contain all six conditions of household work or even all those conditions that are statistically significant in the multiple-regression analyses. It is possible, though, to estimate models for ideational flexibility and for self-directedness of orientation that include two conditions of household work that were of central importance in the multiple-regression equations—substantive complexity and heaviness.[15]

The principal findings of these models (see Table 10.3) are that doing substantively complex housework increases women's ideational flexibility

---

[14] To choose which social characteristics would be permitted to affect each housework condition, we performed multiple-regression analyses of the housework conditions on the social characteristics. Those social characteristics that have statistically significant regression coefficients in the multiple-regression analyses are permitted to affect the particular conditions of housework in the causal models.

[15] Since heaviness does not significantly affect distress in the multiple-regression analysis, a causal model for distress should be based on different conditions of household work. The most appropriate is a model using substantive complexity and the likelihood of being held responsible for things outside one's control. Such a model shows no statistically significant effects of housework conditions on distress or of distress on housework conditions. The tendency, though, is for substantive complexity to affect and be affected by distress negatively and for "held responsible" to affect and be affected by distress positively.

Table 10.3. CAUSAL MODELS FOR WOMEN

	Ideational Flexibility	Self-directedness
(Standardized Coefficients)		
Housework to Personality:		
Substantive complexity to:	.24*	.23*
Heaviness of physical labor to:	−.13*	−.11*
Personality to Housework:		
To substantive complexity:	.01	−.12
To heaviness of physical labor:	.03	.05
Chi-square	123.21	91.54
Degrees of Freedom (for the causal model)	53	53

Note: All paths shown to be statistically significant remain so if nonsignificant paths are fixed at 0.
N = 555.
*Statistically significant, .05 level or better. All others are nonsignificant.

and self-directedness, while doing heavy household work decreases both. To our surprise, neither facet of psychological functioning significantly affects either the substantive complexity or the heaviness of housework. This finding can hardly be regarded as definitive, though, because we had no instruments to identify the causal paths from psychological functioning to housework and relied solely on the weak alternative of fixing the correlated residuals at zero.

These models, limited though they be, supplement the multiple-regression findings by providing evidence that two focal aspects of housework affect, rather than merely reflect, women's psychological functioning. In particular, these findings strengthen the supposition that doing substantively complex housework increases ideational flexibility and self-directedness, just as does substantively complex work in paid employment. Thus, bearing in mind the many assumptions we have had to make, these causal analyses provide at least modest evidence that a central finding of our occupational studies—the pronounced effects of the substantive complexity of work on ideational flexibility and on holding a self-directed orientation—applies not only to women's paid employment but also to their housework.

ASSESSING THE RELATIONSHIP BETWEEN MEN'S HOUSEWORK CONDITIONS AND THEIR PSYCHOLOGICAL FUNCTIONING

In exploring the relationships between men's housework and their psychological functioning, we use parallel procedures to those used for women, except that we are able to include as independent variables measures of the men's earlier psychological functioning. (The conclusions discussed below would be the same if earlier psychological functioning were excluded from the analyses.)

Multiple-regression analyses (see Table 10.4) indicate that the substantive complexity of men's housework is not significantly related to any facet of psychological functioning included in this analysis—a decidedly different picture from what we have found for women and for the substantive complexity of men's work in their paid employment. There are, however, some statistically significant relationships between other aspects of men's housework and their psychological functioning. The core findings revolve around heavy and time-pressured work. Doing heavy housework is positively related to ideational flexibility and self-directedness of orientation and is negatively related to distress. Time-pressure, in sharp contrast, is negatively related to ideational flexibility and self-directedness and is positively related to distress.

What is particularly striking about these findings is that, for men, heavy household work has psychological concomitants similar to those of substantively complex work in paid employment. When interpreting this phenomenon, we must remember that for men "substantive complexity" is dramatically different in the two realms of work: In household work, doing substantively complex work means doing complex work with things, principally work related to repair of household equipment and upkeep of the home. In paid employment, on the other hand, doing substantively complex work means, most of all, doing complex work with data and with people, rather than with things. It is not surprising, then, that in household work

Table 10.4. MULTIPLE REGRESSION ANALYSES: MEN'S PSYCHOLOGICAL FUNCTIONING ON HOUSEWORK CONDITIONS[a]

	Ideational Flexibility	Self-directedness	Distress
(Standardized Regression Coefficients)			
Housework Conditions:			
Substantive complexity	.00	.00	−.04
Heaviness of physical labor	.05*	.13*	−.08*
Frequency of being held responsible for things outside one's control	.06*	−.03	.07
Routinization	−.01	.06*	.01
Dirtiness	.01	.01	.08*
Frequency of time pressure	−.09*	−.09*	.10*

[a] Multiple-regression equations include all social characteristics and conditions of housework as independent variables.
N = 555.
* Statistically significant, .05 level or better. All others are nonsignificant.

the correlation between heaviness and substantive complexity of the work is both positive and strong (+ .56), nearly twice as strong as the corresponding correlation for women (which is + .30) and opposite in sign to the correlation between the substantive complexity and the heaviness of men's work in paid employment (− .37). The zero-order correlations of substantive complexity of household work with ideational flexibility, self-directedness, and distress are actually of the same sign and of similar magnitudes to those for heaviness; but, in the multiple-regression equations, where each condition of work is statistically controlled on the other, it is heaviness that prevails.[16]

CAUSAL MODELS FOR MEN

Just as we did in the analysis of women, we turn to linear structural-equation modeling to estimate the reciprocal effects between the conditions men experience in housework and their psychological functioning. The general structure of the causal models is the same as that of the models for women, with two exceptions, both of which involve the use of data from the men's baseline interviews. The stability of psychological functioning is taken into account by allowing psychological functioning in 1964 to affect 1974 psychological functioning. (This, of course, strengthens the identification of the model.) The respondent's very general estimate in the earlier interview of the amount of time he spends "working around the house" is allowed to affect all current conditions of housework. (This, too, strengthens the identification of the model, albeit modestly.)

As was true for women, we cannot produce statistically sensible models for men that include all the conditions of housework. We have therefore tested several limited models. The models that are most crucial to our interpretation include substantive complexity, which in the multiple-regression equations failed to have the psychological effects we have come to expect of it, and heaviness, which showed the pattern expected for substantive complexity. These models (see Table 10.5, part A) entirely support the conclusions drawn from the multiple-regression analyses. Heaviness significantly affects ideational flexibility, self-directedness, and distress; substantive complexity does not significantly affect any of them.

None of the three facets of psychological functioning significantly af-

---

[16] It is possible that housework might have psychological concomitants more like those of paid employment for those men who participate actively in housework than for men whose participation in household work is minimal. We have tried several approaches to isolating some sub-population of men who engage more fully in household work, e.g., by focusing on those men whose wives are employed outside the home. Neither this approach, nor any other that we have tried, isolates a group of men whose psychological reactions to the conditions of work experienced in housework are similar to what we have found for men's psychological reactions to the conditions of work experienced in paid employment.

Table 10.5. CAUSAL MODELS FOR MEN

	Ideational Flexibility	Self-directedness	Distress
(Standardized Coefficients)			
A.			
Housework to Personality:			
Substantive complexity to:	.00	−.03	.09
Heaviness of physical labor to:	.04*	.10*	−.13*
Personality to Housework:			
To substantive complexity:	.07	.04	−.09
To heaviness of physical labor:	.05	.06	.03
Chi-square	178.72	146.64	145.26
Degrees of Freedom	62	62	62
(for the causal model)			
B.			
Housework to Personality:			
Heaviness of physical labor to:	.05*	.11*	−.12*
Time pressure to:	−.08*	−.11*	.11*
Personality to Housework:			
To heaviness of physical labor:	.03	.04	.06
To time pressure:	.11*	.07	.04
Chi-square	186.68	151.48	153.95
Degrees of Freedom	65	65	65
(for the causal model)			

Note: All paths shown to be statistically significant remain so if nonsignificant paths are fixed at .0
N = 555.
*Statistically significant, .05 level or better. All others are nonsignificant.

fects either the heaviness or the substantive complexity of the housework that men do. This is of course consonant with the findings for women. It is even more surprising for men, because the models are better identified and because housework is often discretionary for men. We had expected that personality might decidedly affect the tasks men do in housework; the data suggest otherwise.

Models that include the two housework conditions that were of central importance in the multiple-regression analyses, heaviness and time-pressure, are also instructive (see Table 10.5, part B). Heaviness again significantly affects all three facets of psychological functioning and is not significantly affected by any of them. Time-pressure significantly affects self-directedness and distress and is not significantly affected by either of them. The model for ideational flexibility, though, contains what may be a statistical anomaly: Time-pressure affects ideational flexibility significantly and negatively; ideational flexibility affects time-pressure significantly and positively. We do not think the identification of this model strong enough to preclude the possibility that either or both of these reciprocal effects are artifactual. The entire set of men's models does, however, confirm the general findings about the psychological effects of heaviness and suggests that time-pressure, too, has a causal impact on orientation, even if not necessarily on ideational flexibility.

DISCUSSION

The study of housework is the most enigmatic of our investigations. Problems abound, some anticipated, others not. There remains some question about the applicability to housework of a frame of reference developed for paid employment. Also in question are the adequacy of the indices of household work. The conclusions we can draw from these analyses are further limited by shortcomings in our data. Since we did not interview women in the 1964 survey, we have no measures of women's earlier psychological functioning or of the housework they did at that time. Moreover, because in the earlier survey we asked only a single sketchy question about time spent in "work around the house", we have little information about the nature of men's housework at that time. These limitations make our assessments of causal relationships much more tentative than would be the case if we had longitudinal data.

Nevertheless, our findings do provide evidence that women's psychological functioning is related to the housework they do. Ideational flexibility is positively related to doing substantively complex housework and negatively related to doing housework that is heavy, dirty, routinized, or in which the woman believes she is likely to be held responsible for things outside her control. Self-directedness of orientation is positively related to doing substantively complex housework and negatively related to doing dirty housework. Distress is related to doing housework under felt pressure of time or under circumstances where a woman believes she may be held responsible for things outside her control. All these findings are consonant with earlier analyses of the effects of paid work on psychological functioning. Furthermore, our causal analyses—even though limited by the absence of longitudinal data—do support the belief that, for women, doing substantively complex housework results in increased ideational flexibility and a more self-directed orientation. Doing heavy housework results in a diminution of both.

The analyses of the relationship between men's housework and their psychological functioning indicate that, for men, it is not the substantive complexity but the heaviness of housework that is of central importance. The psychological effects of heavy housework are more similar to those of substantive complexity in paid employment than to those of heavy work in paid employment. As we have seen, heaviness and substantive complexity of housework are positively and substantially related, which is inconsistent with what we find in paid employment. This raises questions about the dis-aggregation of heaviness and substantive complexity: Our analyses may exaggerate the importance of heaviness and underestimate that of substantive complexity. We nevertheless believe that in the realm of housework heaviness does have a real psychological impact and is not merely indicative of involvement in housework. Why doing heavy housework should have such a psychological effect is, however, unclear. One possibility is that physical exertion in an off-the-job context facilitates both intellectuality and a sense of efficacy, while sedentariness is detrimental to both. It may be that doing heavy work, particularly in the relatively discretionary realm of the household, fulfills men's self-image of competence and effectiveness. Another possibility is that, for men, heavy household work not only tends to be substantively complex, but may also have other positive qualities that our analysis has failed to identify.

Equally puzzling is why the substantive complexity of men's household work ceases to be significantly related to their psychological functioning when other housework conditions are statistically controlled. The limitations of our analysis are such that we cannot accept as certain the null hypothesis that no such relationships exist. Still, we think the findings real: the substantive complexity of men's housework fails to have the same psychological impact as does the substantive complexity of paid employment.

Perhaps it is simply that men's housework is concentrated on working with things, particularly doing repairs, while women's housework—though focused on work with things—is nevertheless broader in scope. For example, complexity of "bookwork" is a major component of the substantive complexity of women's housework but is not even a significant indicator of men's housework. Perhaps substantive complexity affects ideational flexibility and self-directedness only when the work involves some substantial component of work with data or with people.

Another possible—and we think more persuasive—explanation lies in the differential meaning of housework for men and for women. For many women, household work has much the same demand characteristics as does the work required in paid employment; thus, housework is a structural imperative whose psychological effects are similar to those of the structural imperatives of paid employment. For most men, in contrast, housework exerts no such imperative and thus does not have psychological effects similar to those of paid employment. If this interpretation is correct, the absence of significant relationships between the substantive complexity of men's housework and their psychological functioning, even though unanticipated, can be seen as consistent with our general interpretation. It may only be when it is imperative that work demands be met that the conditions of work have their usual psychological effects.

Serfdom's Legacy: An Ethnic Continuum*

Carmi Schooler

In this chapter, we evaluate the effects of ethnicity on the values and orientations of the representative sample of U.S. men interviewed in the 1964 cross-sectional survey.[1] The basic question posed is whether ethnic groups can be conceptualized as existing along a meaningful continuum that reflects social-structural conditions known to affect individual psychological functioning. In the course of answering this question, we deal with more general questions: Does ethnicity have psychological effects independent of those of other social characteristics? If so, which facets of values and orientation are affected?

The problem of the independence of ethnic effects is as central to the study of ethnicity in America as it is to cross-national research. Cross-cultural investigators have long debated whether cross-national variations in behavior are the results of differences in socioeconomically determined

* This is a revised version of a paper of the same title originally published in the *American Journal of Sociology* (Schooler, 1976). I would like to thank Mimi Silberman for her help in performing the statistical analyses and Pearl Slafkes for her editorial help.

[1] This analysis was done before the longitudinal data of the follow-up study were available. It utilizes the methods of analysis and the indices then available. There is no reason to believe that the conclusions would be changed in any important respect if a reanalysis were done, using the data of the follow-up study and the indices subsequently developed on the basis of confirmatory factor analysis.

social structures or of differences in historically determined cultural patterns. Viewing this problem, the anthropologist Caudill wrote:

> Middle-class managerial personnel in England and France may have more in common than either group has with working-class machine operators in their own country. At the same time, however, I do not think that anyone would say that such Englishmen and Frenchmen are indistinguishable in their approach to work, politics, family life, or sexual activity. They are different in those historically derived and culturally patterned ways of thinking, feeling, and behaving that are passed on, often unknowingly, from one generation to the next . . . . I believe that each of these dimensions—position in modern social structure, and continuity of historical culture—exerts a relatively independent influence on human behavior, and that both dimensions need to be considered simultaneously in the investigation of the psychological characteristics of a people. [1973:241]

We postulate an interdependent relationship between culture and socioeconomic structure, envisioning that their interaction over time affects both an individual's functioning and his values, Under such a model, historical circumstances affect a society's social structure, which in turn changes its cultural values. The resultant values, however, may continue to be transmitted long after the original historical and social circumstances have ceased to exist.

The general hypothesis is that Americans belonging to ethnic groups that originated in European countries whose mores have been influenced by a relatively recent history of feudal subjugation differ in their intellectual functioning, orientation to authority, and moral value systems from Americans belonging to ethnic groups coming from European countries where the institutions of feudal serfdom were never fully established or ceased to exist in the more distant past.

In line with this hypothesis, the major European ethnic groups can be thought of as falling along a continuum that reflects the time of the release of the peasantry from serfdom in the ethnic homeland (see Table 11.1). Such an ordering of ethnic groups can be seen as operating on two levels. On the level of index construction, it ranks countries objectively by a procedure that does not capitalize on chance. On a more substantive level, there is, as we shall see, considerable evidence that such an index ranks countries according to the degree of occupational self-direction and the number of behavioral options that were available to the agricultural sector of the population, the very segment from which most immigrants to America came (Handlin, 1951; Kennedy, 1964).

Although the ethnic continuum is ordered according to the time serfdom ended, it actually reflects both the degree and recency of a set of parallel and interrelated legal, economic, and occupational constraints on the lives of the mass of preindustrial agricultural workers. Of course, since this complex web of interrelated constraints on the individual's independence oc-

Table 11.1.   ETHNIC CONTINUUM

| Area of Origin | End of Serfdom | |
	Date	Circumstances
Scandinavia	. . .	Never established in Sweden and Norway (*Encyclopedia Britannica;* Gwatkin and Whitney *1957*).
England	1603-25	In the reign of James I: "With the Tudors, serfdom disappeared in England" (Smith 1922, p. 7660).
Ireland	. . .	Because of the hypothesized importance of a tradition of autonomy and personal responsibility, Ireland, which had been a dependency under the tight control of England, is given a place in the continuum directly below England.
German states	1807-33	Changes that abolished serfdom were initiated before 1815 (Crawley 1965, p. 52), the Emancipation Edict of October 9, 1807, being of central importance. The last principality abolished serfdom in 1833 (Smith 1922, p. 7661).
South and central Italy	1848	As part of the abolition of serfdom in the Austro-Hungarian Empire (Bury 1964, pp. 413—414).
Eastern Europe (greater Russia, Poland, etc.)	1861	Alexander II abolished serfdom by imperial ukase (Bury 1964, p. 372).

curred in the diverse contexts of unique national histories, the present ranking—based as it is on the times of the ending of legal serfdom—does not reflect perfectly the exact chronology and severity of the other components of this web of constraints. However, such a ranking does seem to provide a reasonable and nonarbitrary way of ordering European countries according to the general magnitude and recency of constraints placed upon the autonomy of the individual peasant.

It is, of course, impossible to confirm each link in the causal chain leading from an ethnic group's past historical circumstances to the present psychological functioning of its descendants. However, we shall try to demonstrate that such a model, emphasizing as it does the effects on American ethnic groups' cultural values of historical conditions that restricted individual autonomy, represents a parsimonious and compelling explanation of present ethnic differences.

Of all the restrictions on personal autonomy reflected by the continuum, most straightforward are the legal constraints of serfdom. Despite the local variations,

> There was . . . one feature common to European serfdom wherever it existed. A peasant was recognized as unfree if he was bound to the will of his lord by ties that were degrading and socially incapacitating and that were

recognized as a fundamental part of the legal and social structure of the land rather than the result of an agreement or contract between lord and peasant. In practice this meant that the lord had legal jurisdiction over his peasant to the complete or nearly complete exclusion of the state, so that to all intents and purposes the only rights the peasants had were those the lord was willing to allow him. [Blum, 1960:12]

Thus, for instance, according to a medieval English canon lawyer, "If they be serfs, I say that they are bound to pay the tallages [a form of tax the lord could arbitrarily impose on his serfs] newly imposed on them, even those that tend to profit their lords alone, for serfs and their possessions are the property of their lords" (Bennett, 1938:138). In fact, " . . . This lack of protection from the arbitrary power of the lord was seen as part of the definition of serfdom. Hence Bracton's famous definition: 'For that is an absolute villainage, from which an uncertain and indeterminate service is rendered, where it cannot be known in the evening what service is to be rendered in the morning" (p. 99). Even such a paucity of legal rights as described by these English examples of the legal defenselessness of serfs against the power and arbitrariness of their lords pales before the conditions of serfdom in Russia. "The only essential differences between the Russian serf and the American Negro slave that a contemporary apologist for serfdom could think of were that the serf had the privilege of taking the oath of allegiance to the Tsar, paying a personal tax, and serving in the army" (Blum, 1961:468–469).[2]

The rankings of the ethnic continuum seem also to mirror the degree of economic independence of the peasantry. Those countries without a recent history of serfdom seem to have been characterized by a low proportion of large estates and a high proportion of moderate- and small-scale farmers who owned or controlled farms large enough to give them some measure of economic independence (Blum, 1960).[3] There is some indication that the rankings also parallel the relative availability of commercial shipping and fishing industries as alternate sources of livelihood in the preindustrial period (Lewis, 1958; Slicher Van Bath, 1963). Such ready availability of an alternative to serfdom would also loosen the peasants' bonds to the land.

---

[2] There is some evidence that the continuum reflects not only the legal but also the political rights of the peasantry. "No matter what the form of the government . . . , most peasants had no formal organized way of expressing their political, social, and economic demands or of influencing the decision of their rulers at the national or provincial level . . . Exceptions to this general rule were Norway, Sweden . . . and to a much lesser extent . . . England . . . ." (Blum, 1960:119).

[3] Similarly, Wallerstein (1974) comments, "The yeoman farmers were drawn . . . even more narrowly, principally from northwest Europe" (p. 87). A more extensive discussion of the relatively high prevalence of small independent farmers in England and the Dutch republic can be found on pp. 239–250, and the relatively greater power of the English yeoman than that of his German counterpart is noted on p. 177.

Historical evidence suggests further that, in those countries where serfdom was more remote in time, there may have been a tendency toward a greater degree of livestock farming, a form of farming in which the individual had a relatively high degree of independence and decision-making (Wallerstein, 1974). "Livestock farming is capital-intensive and labour-extensive; it forms, in this respect, a striking contrast to the business of arable farming. The stock-farmer has to think continually in terms of money and to have money at his disposal. Livestock breeding and trading require a good head for cost and sale prices, for which a strong business sense is essential" (Slicher Van Bath, 1963:130).

The continuum also reflects other differences in the nature of the work performed by agricultural workers in the various countries. Thus, historical evidence indicates that the ethnic ranking generally follows the chronology of the introduction of the "new agronomy." This system, customarily viewed as the start of modern agriculture, involved the introduction of a four-course crop rotation system, an emphasis on fodder crops, the disappearance of fallow years, and the consolidation of the individual farmer's fields. Once accepted, it affected both the motivation of the farmer and the technical complexity of his work. This new system permitted him to take advantage of technologically more complex farming techniques, decreased his interdependence with his fellows, and, by increasing his control over his own land, served to raise his feelings of individualism (Slicher Van Bath, 1963; Blum, 1960; Heckscher, 1954; Bloch, 1967).

Little freedom of action was left to the individual in the traditional three-course, strip-plot, fallow rotation system that had predominated prior to the new agronomy, particularly where serfdom was prevalent. Under that system, each farmer's land consisted of a number of noncontiguous strips interspersed with those of his lord and his fellow villagers.

> The strip system required them [the serfs] to do all of their field work communally. That is, they all had to perform the same agricultural operations at the same time. To mention just two difficulties that . . . individualistic practices would have occasioned—crops would have matured at different times, and in getting in and out to tend one strip damage would have been done to the still unripe crops in the neighboring strips. Secondly, after the crops were in, the field was often used as a pasture for villagers' livestock. This could not have been done if the crops in the field had different harvesting times. Communal farming was the only practicable method. This necessitated constant agreement and close cooperation among all the peasants and some form of central control . . . [Blum, 1960:15]

> On the common fields, the whole community acted in common. The animals . . . were driven away on a certain day . . . determined by immemorial custom, then there followed the ploughing and sowing of the crop for the year . . . and in all this there was but little room for individual choice. The

peasant was chained down to a routine that was, seemingly, unbreakable [Bennett, 1938:51.]

Nor was the serf's economic relationship with his master one that would encourage him to exercise his innovativeness and ingenuity in an effort to increase his yield (Slicher Van Bath, 1963; Bloch, 1967; Blum, 1960). When working on his lord's fields, the serf had even less freedom, being constantly under the supervision of the lord's overseers. The medieval agricultural manual of Walter of Henley warns: "Let the bailiff . . . be all the time with the ploughmen, to see that they do their work well and thoroughly and at the end of the day see how much they have done . . . to guard against their fraud" (Bennett, 1938:113). And even non-field-related work required little or no skill. Here too the serf provided only physical labor, carrying out his assigned tasks under the close supervision of master craftsmen (Bennett, 1938). Finally, even "when the peasant had performed all the ploughings . . . demanded of him he was still under many obligations—his lack of freedom showed itself in many ways—he could neither brew nor bake where he would . . . grind his own corn, sell his beasts, give his daughter in marriage, nor do many other things without the lord's permission . . . the lord's power was about him on all sides . . . "(Bennett, 1938:129). In sum, there is ample reason to believe that, in terms of legal rights, economic freedom, and occupational conditions, the ethnic continuum reflects both the opportunity for autonomy and the complexity of decision-making open to the peasantry.

This description of the interrelated legal, economic, and occupational correlates of the ethnic continuum is in almost complete accord with Wallerstein's account of the geographical division of agricultural labor that took place in Europe between 1450 and 1640, the period of the development of capitalistic agriculture. According to Wallerstein (1974), this division of labor is best understood in terms of three geographical areas: the core (centered in northwestern Europe and Germany west of the Elbe River), the semiperiphery (southern Europe), and the periphery (Europe east of the Elbe).

During this period the core areas were " . . . in the process of dividing the use of . . . land for pastoral and arable products. This was only possible as the widening market created an ever larger market for the pastoral products, and as the periphery of the world-economy provided cereal supplements for the core areas. The semiperiphery was turning away from industry . . . and toward relative self-sufficiency in agriculture" (p. 116). The "world-economy was based precisely on the assumption that there were in fact these three zones and that they did, in fact, have different modes of labor control." These modes can be seen as related to "product and productivity . . . Slaves [used at that time for sugar cultivation] . . . are not useful in large-scale enterprises whenever skill is required. Slaves cannot be expected to do more than what they are forced to do. Once skill is involved, it is more economical to find alternative methods of labor control . . . . This resulted in a form of serfdom wherein the peasants are required by some legal processes enforced by the state to labor . . . on a large domain producing some product for sale on the world market" (pp. 87-91). ". . . The semiperiphery represents a midway point on a continuum running from the core to the periphery . . . in labor control [it exhibits] an in-between form, share-cropping" (pp. 102-103). " . . . In the core, the situation was different in a number of respects . . . Agriculture was more intensive . . . More intensive agriculture requires better terms for the peasant. In addition, part of the land was shifted from arable to pastoral use. The result was less coercion . . . The coercion was to be more indirect via marketing mechanisms." Therefore, "The occupational range of tasks in the core areas was a very complex one; the trend in the core was towards variety and specialization" (pp. 100-102).

The application of Wallerstein's categorization results in essentially the same ranking of countries as that of the ethnic continuum (Table 11.1). Thus, according to Wallerstein, Sweden—though economically not highly developed—followed the model of the core countries, not only because the weather was not conducive to specialization in the growth of cereal grains, but also because of "a peasantry that was strong and well organized" (p. 312). Ireland, though in a semicolonial relationship to England, "became integrated into the British division of labor" (p. 281), a fair amount of her land being devoted to the raising of sheep for wool production. However poor the condition of the Irish peasantry, their subjugation to their masters rarely reached the level found in Europe east of the Elbe River. From this perspective, present-day Germany has two quite different parts: a core area west of the Elbe and a peripheral one east of it, so that taken as a whole it ranks below Ireland in terms of the degree of autonomy and level of skill of its agricultural workers. Italy, being in the semiperiphery, ranks below Germany, while what is now Poland and Russia, in the periphery, lie at the bottom of the scale.

Thus, Wallerstein's historiographic analysis of the geographic distribution on the European continent of various forms of agricultural production and their concomitant methods of labor control strongly supports the historical accuracy of the hypothesis that the ethnic continuum does rank countries according to the complexity of occupational tasks and the degree of self-direction characterizing the agricultural sectors of the population.

The social conditions reflected by the continuum can be hypothesized as having affected the peasant cultures of ethnic homelands in ways that would act upon intellectual functioning, stance toward authority, and standards of morality. In terms of intellectual functioning, earlier research indicates that intellectual performance is improved by exposure to relatively complex environments in which the individual is called upon to make decisions on the basis of a wide variety of factors (Schooler, 1972) and that occupations characterized by close supervision, routinization, or substantively simple tasks decrease their incumbents' intellectual flexibility and the intellectual demandingness of their leisure activities (Chapters 1 and 3). Since, as we have seen, the work done by serfs was generally highly routinized, closely supervised, and substantively simple and the number of options available to them in the other areas of their existence were severely limited, it seems likely that cultures developed under such social and occupational conditions would not emphasize the development of intellectual capacities and interests.

Similarly, persons living and working under such restrictive conditions seem to develop an essentially authoritarian-conservative, conformist stance toward authority (Chapters 1 and 3; Schooler, 1972). Accordingly, it can be expected that individuals belonging to ethnic groups from cultures more recently and more strongly affected by the institutions of serfdom would hold conformist values and orientations.

Finally, ethnic groups from countries where interpersonal relationships have most recently and pervasively been regulated by the formal rules of feudal serfdom may view moral autonomy as less important than do ethnic groups from countries where such relationships were relatively free and unstructured. As used here, "moral autonomy" means that the individual holds an internalized set of moral standards, accepts responsibility for his fate, and readily acts as his own critic. Taken together, the foregoing hypotheses suggest that the differences found among European ethnic groups in present-day America result from cultural values that are the residue of historical processes that occurred on another continent and in other centuries.

INDICES AND METHOD OF ANALYSIS

The data used in this analysis come from the 1964 cross-sectional survey of U.S. men employed in civilian occupations. The analysis excludes Jews and is further limited to whites who either were born in Europe or had a parent or grandparent born there. Such a nationality-based definition of ethnicity is somewhat more stringent than many of those frequently used, in that it attempts to differentiate the effects of national origin from those of race and religion.

Of the many facets of psychological functioning indexed in Chapters 1–3, seven were chosen for the analyses reported here.

Two are directly related to intellectual functioning:

1. *Intellectual flexibility,* as evidenced by performance in handling cognitive and perceptual problems.[4]
2. *Intellectually demanding use of leisure time.*

Two others can be seen as measuring orientation to authority:

3. *Authoritarian conservatism:* rigid conformance to the dictates of authority and intolerance of nonconformity, as opposed to open-mindedness.
4. *Self-direction,* in contrast to conformity to external authority, as a parental value.

Three can be seen as related to moral autonomy:

5. *Personally responsible standards of morality,* the most central of the three, measuring a continuum of moral positions from defining, maintaining, and holding oneself responsible for one's own moral standards, to believing that morality consists of strict adherence to the letter of the law and keeping out of trouble.
6. *Attribution of responsibility to self for control over one's own fate,* instead of believing that one is controlled by outside forces.
7. *Self-deprecation,* the self-critical part of self-esteem: the degree to which men criticize themselves for not living up to their own standards.

Earlier analyses of the present body of data (Schooler, 1972) suggest that in the United States growing up in a relatively complex and multifaceted environment—being young, having a well-educated father, being reared in a nonfundamentalist religion, and being raised in an urban environment or in an area far from the South—results in a relatively high level of intellectual functioning, a rejection of external constraints, and a belief that what takes place within oneself is of great importance. Since these effects are similar to the hypothesized effects of ethnicity, the pertinent social characteristics should be statistically controlled. The basic form of analysis employed is multiple regression, in which the linearized ethnic variable is used as an independent variable in multiple-regression equations vis-a-vis the several facets of psychological functioning, treated here as dependent variables. The relevant social characteristics are statistically controlled by including them as independent variables in the multiple-regression equations.

---

[4] The overall measure of intellectual flexibility used in this chapter is the summation of the ideational and perceptual flexibility factor scores (see Chapter 2). Findings based on analyses done with each of the two measures separately, although not so clearcut, are generally in accord with the findings presented here.

PSYCHOLOGICAL EFFECTS OF ETHNICITY

We begin with analyses that directly test the hypotheses about the effects of the ethnic continuum on intellectual functioning, orientation to authority, and moral-value systems. Later, in examining alternate explanations of the findings, we address the more general questions about the independence, power, scope, and linearity of the hypothesized ethnic variable.

Even when age, father's education, religion, rurality, and region of the country in which the individual was reared are statistically controlled, all the hypotheses about the effects of ethnicity are confirmed (Table 11.2). Individuals from ethnic groups that originated in countries with a longer history of freedom from serfdom show a higher level of intellectual functioning (Table 11.2, columns 1, 2). The regression coefficient for ethnicity vis-a-vis intellectual flexibility is both significant and in the appropriate direction. The regression coefficient for ethnicity vis-a-vis intellectually de-

Table 11.2. EFFECTS OF ETHNIC CONTINUUM, CONTROLLING FIVE ANTECEDENT VARIABLES, SOCIAL STRATIFICATION, AND OCCUPATIONAL SELF-DIRECTION (N = 930)

Psychological Characteristics	Controlling Antecedent Variables		Controlling Antecedent Variables and Social Stratification		Controlling Antecedent Variables and Occupational Self-direction	
	β (1)	P (2)	β (3)	P (4)	β (5)	P (6)
Intellectual flexibility	.146	.001	.123	.001	.116	.001
Intellectually demanding use of leisure time	.053	N.S.*	.030	N.S.*	.023	N.S.*
Authoritarian conservatism	−.172	.001	−.152	.001	−.149	.001
Self-directed parental values[a]	.134	.005	.113	.015	.109	.02
Personally responsible morality	.172	.001	.162	.001	.159	.001
Sense of control over one's fate	.091	.01	.085	.025	.086	.02
Self-deprecation	.098	.005	.102	.005	.105	.005

Note.—Antecedent variables are: age, father's education, rurality, religion, and region of the country in which reared. The weightings for these variables can be found in Schooler (1972).
[a] This question was asked only of parents of children aged three to 15 years (N = 489).
*When linear analysis of covariance is used, the relationship between ethnicity and intellectually demanding use of leisure time is significant (F = 7.70, P < .006). The difference between the significant finding and the nonsignificant one seems to lie primarily in the exact population used, the significant finding occurring in that segment of the population for which data are available on all relevant social characteristics.

manding use of leisure time is also in the predicted direction, although its significance is somewhat equivocal (see notes to Table 11.2). The predictions about stance toward authority also prove to be correct. Members of ethnic groups from countries relatively remote from serfdom are less authoritarian and are more likely to value self-direction, rather than conformity, for children (columns 1, 2). Evidence for the hypothesis that persons from ethnic groups long free from serfdom place a greater value on moral autonomy is found in their tendency to have more personally responsible moral standards, to believe themselves responsible for their own fates, and to be more self-critical than are members of ethnic groups more recently emerged from feudalism (columns 1,2).

Further evidence that the ethnic experience is an important determinant of these differences can be found in the increased strength of the relationships of ethnicity to the pertinent facets of psychological functioning among respondents who report that their ethnic membership has had a strong or moderate influence on their lives. The regression coefficients of six of the seven facets of psychological functioning on ethnicity are higher among respondents who see their ethnic membership as important, as compared to those who see their ethnicity as having had little or no influence (see Table 11.3).

All these findings support the hypotheses about the effects of serfdom. As predicted, compared to members of ethnic groups from countries where serfdom continued until relatively recently, Americans from ethnic groups originating in countries where the institutions of serfdom were abolished in the more remote past show more effective intellectual functioning, a non-

Table 11.3. EFFECTS OF ETHNIC EXPERIENCE, CONTROLLING AGE, FATHER'S EDUCATION, RURALITY, RELIGION, AND REGION OF THE COUNTRY IN WHICH REARED

Psychological Characteristics	Great or Moderate (N = 325) β	Not Much or Not At All (N = 563) β
Intellectual flexibility	.173	.119
Intellectually demanding use of leisure time	.053	.028
Authoritarian conservatism	−.239	−.112
Self-directed parental values	.027	.103
Personally responsible morality	.280	.124
Sense of control over one's fate	.027	.103
Self-deprecation	.163	.065

Note.—The question on self-directed parental values was asked only of parents of children aged three to 15 years (great or moderate, N = 150; not much or not at all, N = 310).

conformist orientation, and a concern for moral autonomy.[5] The differences are even more pronounced among those who see their ethnic experience as having affected them.

ALTERNATE EXPLANATIONS

Although the predicted relationships have been found, many explanations other than these hypotheses are conceivable. The most plausible alternate explanation is that ethnicity is not distinct from social stratification. This possibility can be assessed by adding the respondent's present social-stratification position, as measured by the Hollingshead Index of Social Position, to the five social characteristics used, along with ethnicity, as independent variables in the multiple-regression equations. Doing so leaves virtually unchanged the effects of ethnicity on intellectual functioning, orientation to authority, and moral autonomy (see Table 11.2, columns 3, 4). It is reasonable, therefore, to conclude that ethnicity does have an effect distinct from that of adult social-stratification position and antecedent social characteristics.

Although these findings further substantiate the hypotheses, it could still be argued that the imposition of a linear continuum is artificial and arbitrary and distorts the true nature of ethnic differences. Fortunately, it is possible to assess directly the degree to which the linearization of an independent variable accounts for the total variance in a dependent variable "explained by" that independent variable. This can be done by using analysis of variance to compare the proportion of the variance accounted for by the linear trends (i.e., by the rankings and equality of intervals assumed by our dimensionalization) to that accounted for by nonlinear trends (i.e., the variance in the dependent variable accounted for by aspects of ethnicity other than the linear variable we have constructed). Only two significant nonlinear trends were found—both in the presence of even more powerful

---

[5] Suggestive evidence in support of our hypothesis is obtained by examining the response patterns of segments of the population not included in the subsample of European ethnic groups. As might be predicted from a simple extension of the hypothesis, blacks, who have the most recent history of legal servitude among all American groups, show most strongly the pattern of response typical of ethnic groups with a relatively recent history of serfdom. Non-Jewish Caucasians, all of whose grandparents were born in the United States, are in the same general range as the Irish. (This position might well have been predicted on the basis of our rules for ranking ethnic groups, since the United States, too, was once an English colony.) Finally, although individuals belonging to the diverse ethnic groups making up the Austro-Hungarian Empire were not included in the overall analysis because of the limited number of respondents from each of the cultural and linguistic groups, it is worthy of note that, in accord with the general hypothesis, their aggregate scores on the various psychological characteristics tend to fall in the same range as do those of the Germans and the Italians.

linear trends (respondents of English and Italian origins have somewhat more opportunistic moral standards and a lower level of intellectual flexibility than would be predicted by their position on the ethnic continuum).[6]

Another possible objection to the continuum might be to the potential overlap of ethnicity with religion. Although the exclusion of Jews from the analyses limits some of the potential effects of religion and although differences in liberality among Christian denominations and sects are statistically controlled, religion is obviously closely intertwined with ethnicity. To demonstrate that the effect of ethnicity is independent of that of religion, two additional analyses were performed. In one, an analysis of variance was carried out, with religion and ethnicity as the categorical variables and their interactions tested. There are no significant interactions for any of the facets of psychological functioning with which we are concerned.[7]

We make an even more stringent test of whether ethnicity has psychological effects independent of those of religion by examining Catholics and Protestants separately (see Table 11.4). In six of the seven multiple-regression equations, the regression coefficients for ethnicity remain roughly the same as those based on the entire sample. For Catholics, the only regression coefficient noticeably reduced is that for attribution of responsibility for one's fate; for Protestants, the only one substantially reduced is standards of morality. In both cases, although the strength of relationships is very much reduced, the direction of effect is unchanged—a trend consonant with the absence of significant interactions between religion and ethnicity. Moreover, in the case of moral responsibility, within the predominantly Protestant ethnic groups and their major religious subdivisions, ethnicity does tend to have its predicted independent linear effect (see Table 11.5).

The foregoing alternate explanations are predicated on the possibility that the ethnic effects are spurious or artifactual. One might, instead, ac-

---

[6] A slightly altered ranking of the ethnic continuum might be made on the basis of the suggestions of some authors that in the mid-20th century peasants in southern Italy and in Sicily remained as subservient to large landlords as their serf ancestors had been (Muraskin, 1974; Galtung, 1971). If so, Italy might well be ranked behind, rather than ahead of, eastern Europe. For some of the psychological characteristics, such a change in the ordering of the ethnic groups both decreases the nonlinear and increases the linear effects of ethnicity slightly. It is, however, probably just as well to avoid the possibility of capitalizing on chance by following the statistically somewhat more conservative course of adhering to the hypothesized rankings.

[7] This lack of significant interactions between religion and ethnicity persisted throughout the testing of an extended series of interaction models in which: (1) neither the ethnic groups nor the different religious denominations are treated linearly; (2) both religion and ethnicity are linearized; (3) ethnicity is linearized and religion not linearized; (4) religious groups are combined into only two categories—Protestant and Catholic—and ethnicity is linearized; (5) religious groups are combined into two categories and ethnicity is not linearized.

Table 11.4. ETHNIC EFFECTS: PROTESTANTS AND CATHOLICS
ANALYZED SEPARATELY

Psychological Characteristics	Catholics (N = 416) β	Protestants (N = 450) β	Total Population* (N = 930) β
Intellectual flexibility	.174	.076	.146
Intellectually demanding use of leisure time	.038	.044	.053
Authoritarian conservatism	−.196	−.112	−.172
Self-directed parental values‡	.099	.141	.134
Personally responsible morality	.228	.032	.172
Sense of control over one's fate	.014	.102	.091
Self-deprecation	.076	.089	.098

Note.—For Protestants, all five antecedent variables were controlled. For Catholics, inclusion of religious liberality would have been meaningless, so only age, father's education, rurality, and region of the country in which reared were included.
*Table 11.2, cols. 1, 2.
‡This question was asked only of parents of children aged three to 15 years (Catholics, N = 213; Protestants, N = 230).

cept the reality of the relationships between ethnicity and intellectual functioning, orientation to authority, and moral autonomy but see these relationships as resulting from processes other than direct cultural transmission. In particular, it may be that members of diverse ethnic groups have different occupational histories because of either voluntary choice or discrimination. Perhaps members of ethnic groups whose cultures have been influenced by relatively recent histories of serfdom are less prone to choose self-directed occupations than are those from ethnic groups more remote

Table 11.5. ETHNICITY AND PERSONALLY RESPONSIBLE
STANDARDS OF MORALITY AMONG MAJOR
RELIGIOUS SUBDIVISIONS OF PREDOMINANTLY
PROTESTANT ETHNIC GROUPS

Areas	Old Established (Episcopal, Congregational, Presbyterian) X̄	N	Lutheran X̄	N	Methodist X̄	N	Baptist, Fundamentalist, Transitional Sects X̄	N
Scandinavia	53.6	11	53.5	12	52.9	12	56.1	5
England	51.7	21	. . .	. . .†	50.6	21	52.9	23
Germany	49.6	23	51.9	74	51.0	23	53.7	26

Note.—Controlling for age, region, rurality, and father's education. Analysis of covariance, $F_{(1,276)}$: ethnic linear, $F = 2.19$, $P = .14$; ethnic nonlinear, $F = 1.10$, $P < .30$; linear (ethnic X religion), $F = .42$, $P = .52$.
†N < 5

from serfdom. If that were the case, rather than resulting from direct cultural transmission, the ethnic differences in psychological functioning might result from ethnic differences in occupational experiences, which in turn affect those very psychological characteristics. Furthermore, those from ethnic groups more recently emerged from serfdom may be at a disadvantage in obtaining self-directed jobs, even if they should want them; the ethnic continuum is correlated with the level of esteem in which ethnic groups are held and hence quite possibly with the degree of discrimination individuals face in seeking generally high-status, self-directed jobs (Bogardus, 1928; Spoerl, 1951).

Whether because of voluntary choice or because of discrimination, occupational selection among ethnic groups has occurred: The regression coefficient of occupational self-direction on ethnicity is significant and in the predicted direction (.084, P < .015).[8] However, ethnic differences in occupational self-direction do not explain the differences in psychological functioning; including occupational self-direction as an independent variable in the multiple-regression equations leaves the effects of ethnicity virtually unchanged (see Table 11.2, columns 5, 6). Thus, ethnic differences in psychological functioning are transmitted in some way other than through the effects of occupational selection on occupational self-direction.

DISCUSSION

We began this chapter with a series of questions about the nature and psychological effects of ethnicity in America. The analyses provide substantial evidence that ethnicity does have psychological effects and that these effects are generally independent of adult social-stratification position and of social characteristics indicative of the complexity of childhood environment. Furthermore, the effects of ethnicity appear to be stronger among respondents who report their ethnic experience to be important.

The findings also indicate that the psychological effects of ethnicity are congruent with the hypothesis of a historically determined continuum reflecting the social, legal, economic, and occupational conditions of the European countries from which American ethnic groups emigrated. Furthermore, the apparent effects of those conditions on the cultures of the ethnic groups are remarkably similar to the effects that analogous social and occupational conditions have on the individual in present-day America. Such a similarity raises the possibility that social and occupational conditions prevailing within a society may affect its culture in a manner analogous to the way that an individual's occupational experiences affect his

---

[8] To create an overall index of occupational self-direction, we used the factor loadings for the first unrotated factor of the entire set of items indicative of the use of initiative, thought, and independent judgment in work.

psychological functioning. Serfdom and its correlates involved living and working under someone else's control in situations that offered few options. Ethnic groups with a recent and pervasive history of serfdom show the intellectual inflexibility, authoritarian conservatism, and legalistic morality typical of men working under such circumstances.

On the other hand, belonging to an ethnic group that has long been free from serfdom has the same general relationship with intellectual functioning, orientation to authority, and moral autonomy as does working in a self-directed job. Both characteristics seem to produce persons who are intellectually more effective, who believe that they have some control over their lives, and who feel that the ultimate locus of ethical responsibility is within themselves, rather than in authorities, the law, or other external enforcers of conformity. The internalization of ethical responsibility by those from such ethnic groups also seems to decrease the likelihood of their shifting the burden of ethical responsibility onto others, tending to make them more self-critical.

Underlying the tentative tone of these conclusions are two lingering doubts. Is ethnicity the actual and nonspurious cause of the psychological differences? If so, is it the interrelated legal, economic and occupational correlates of serfdom that are centrally involved in the causal processes?

The answer to the first question—Have we found true ethnic differences?—is very probably yes. The statistical controls used in these analyses seem to rule out the possibility that the results are artifacts of rurality, region, age, religion, father's education, present social-stratification position (as measured by education and occupational status), and substantive complexity of present occupation. The ethnic differences in psychological functioning consistently remain when these characteristics are controlled. If the ethnic differences were spurious, they would have had to result from something outside this wide range of variables.

Our conclusions about the centrality of serfdom to the causal process resulting in ethnic group differences in psychological functioning must remain somewhat tentative. Here, too, certain alternate hypotheses may be ruled out. The ethnic continuum reflects the time of the end of serfdom and its severity, not climate, time of industrialization or urbanization of the homeland, time of major immigration to the United States, or social-stratification position and motivation of the immigrants.[9] Since these char-

---

[9] Some of the more notable discrepancies between the ethnic groups' rankings on these variables and their rank order on the continuum are the following: England and Germany were industrialized and urbanized before the Scandinavian countries (Crawley, 1965); Russia and Italy, at the same end of the continuum, have distinctly different climates; and the peak of Irish immigration was 40 years earlier than that from Scandinavia (Kennedy, 1964). Finally, among the ethnic groups under consideration, the German group was the only one with a noticeably large middle-class and urban minority, and the only one whose motives for migration included political as well as economic elements (Kennedy, 1964).

acteristics do not parallel the ethnic continuum, they may be added to the list of those that are not primary causes of the psychological differences. Such an augmented list seems to suggest that the ethnic continuum is not the result of differential immigration patterns or of social patterns unrelated to ethnicity. It seems likely that we are in fact dealing with the remnants of cultural patterns originating in the agricultural sectors of the homeland, brought over by the immigrants and continued to some extent by their descendants.

It is, of course, still possible that the psychological differences found among ethnic groups result from conditions unrelated to the processes described above. Although such alternate possibilities cannot be excluded, the causal processes they postulate would have to operate independently of any intervening mechanisms represented by the variables that have been statistically controlled. An interpretation that emphasizes the effects on ethnic groups' cultural values of historical conditions in Europe that restricted the individual's autonomy does seem to represent a parsimonious and compelling explanation of certain ethnic differences in present-day America.

The ethnic differences we have found in psychological functioning are admittedly modest and circumscribed. Possibly, if this analysis were not limited to dealing with structured survey data, differences in the characteristic flavor of the various ethnic groups might emerge more clearly. One would not readily try to linearize the difference between a smorgasbord and an antipasto. On the other hand, the hypotheses underlying the ethnic continuum are based on previous findings of how occupational conditions affect individual functioning. To the extent that the ethnic continuum's explanatory power is based on historical differences in occupational conditions, it not only gives meaning to the present findings, but also extends the likely range of occupational effects, from the individual to the culture of which he is a part. In addition, as we have seen, the differences in occupational self-direction reflected by the ethnic continuum seem to have been paralleled by legal, economic, and social constraints on the individual's freedom. The interpretation suggests that a considerable range of historical circumstances may have combined to determine, at least partially, the differences among American ethnic groups in intellectual functioning, orientation to authority, and moral autonomy. Thus, although no longer serfs, Americans from ethnic groups with a recent history of serfdom appear to be heirs to cultural traditions whose values were molded by the oppressed lives of their ancestors.

SECTION V

Reassessment

The Cross-National
Universality of the
Interpretive Model*

Melvin L. Kohn
and Carmi Schooler

In the preceding Section of this book, we considered the *generalizability* of our interpretation, particularly that part of the interpretation concerning the relationship between job conditions and psychological functioning. We found that our model of the relationships between job conditions and psychological functioning applies to women (not just to men), to leisure-time behavior (not just to intrapsychic functioning), to housework (not just to the conditions of work encountered in paid employment), and to the intergenerational transmission of values and orientations (not just to the psychological effects of currently experienced job conditions). Now we consider another type of generalizability, the cross-national *universality* of our interpretive model.

The evidence presented thus far in this book is based mainly on research

* This chapter, although prepared especially for this book, has had a long evolution. Its origins go back to an essay, "Reassessment, 1977" (Kohn, 1977), written for the second edition of *Class and Conformity,* which reviewed the thesis of that book in the light of research done in the eight years since the first edition was published. The essay was considerably revised and retitled "Personlichkeit, Beruf, und soziale Schichtung: Ein Bezugsrahmen" (Kohn, 1981a) for a German-language volume that included several of the chapters in the present volume. With slight modification, that version of the essay was published also in English as "Personality, Occupation, and Social Stratification: A Frame of Reference" (Kohn, 1981b). The essay was again revised, part of it in collaboration with Bogdan Mach, for publication in Polish by the Polish Scientific Publishers in a volume whose contents will overlap considerably with those of the present volume. This chapter borrows, also, from Slomczynski, Miller, and Kohn (1981).

we have conducted in the United States, using one representative sample of employed men and the wives of a subsample of those men. Can our findings and interpretations be generalized more broadly? Fortunately, there have been studies conducted in the United States and in several other countries that test important parts of our thesis. Of particular importance are two studies, one conducted in Poland, the other in Japan, whose methods closely parallel those of our U.S. study. The Polish study was conducted in 1978 by Kazimierz M. Slomczynski, Krystyna Janicka, and Jadwiga Koralewicz-Zebik; the main analyses on which we draw are presented in Slomczynski, Miller, and Kohn (1981). The Japanese study was conducted in 1979 by Atsushi Naoi and Ken'ichi Tominaga; the main analyses on which we draw are presented in Naoi and Schooler (1981). In discussing both the Polish and the Japanese studies, we make use also of as-yet unpublished findings from ongoing analyses of these data.

We consider, in logical sequence, the evidence vis-a-vis each of the three major elements of our thesis: the relationship of social stratification to psychological functioning; the reciprocal effects of occupational self-direction and psychological functioning; and the role of occupational self-direction in explaining the relationship of social stratification to psychological functioning. This means that we shall discuss the Polish and Japanese studies repeatedly, because their findings are repeatedly pertinent.

THE RELATIONSHIP OF SOCIAL STRATIFICATION TO PSYCHOLOGICAL FUNCTIONING

The first element in our thesis is that social stratification is consistently related to values, orientations, and cognitive functioning, with people of higher social-stratification position being more self-directed in their values, having orientations to self and to society consonant with such values, and being more effective in their intellectual functioning than are people of lower social-stratification position. Can these findings be generalized and our interpretation applied beyond the particular U.S. sample we studied? Do the findings and interpretation apply as well to other countries? We consider the evidence, in turn, for valuation of self-direction, orientations to self and society, and intellectual flexibility.

The Relationship of Social Stratification to Values

Research on values has been limited almost entirely to *parental* values. That there have been many studies of parental values and a near-absence of studies of values-for-self undoubtedly reflects the strong theoretical interest of social scientists in parent-child relationships. In part, too, the failure of other investigators to utilize our index of values-for-self reflects the obvious deficiencies of our original index; the one investigation that does include a measure of values-for-self, the Japanese replication, is a recent inquiry that employs, not the original index, but the revision developed for the follow-up study. Thus, although we would like to examine the relationship of social stratification to both parental values and values-for-self, we have in fact examined the issue only for parental values.

Self-direction versus conformity as a universal dimension of values. If our interpretation of the relationship between social stratification and values is correct, then self-direction versus conformity to external authority should be a fundamental dimension of values, not only in the United States, but wherever social stratification is closely linked to occupational self-direction—as seems to be generally the case, certainly in industrialized societies.

To test the hypothesis that self-direction versus conformity to external authority is a universal dimension of parental values, Kohn and Schoenbach (1980) did exploratory factor analyses of data on parental values that had been collected in studies done in several countries. Every body of data that they considered contains a strong self-direction/conformity factor. This includes the data of several U.S. studies, not only studies of particular cities (Washington, D.C.; Louisville, Kentucky; Detroit, Michigan), but also the 1973, 1975, and 1976 National Opinion Research Center (N.O.R.C.) General Social Surveys, whose samples are representative of the entire adult population of the United States. They also found a strong self-direction/conformity factor in several bodies of data supplied by colleagues who had conducted studies in other countries—Pearlin (1971) in Turin, Italy; Stephen Olsen (1971) in Taipei, Taiwan; Bertram (1976a) in Duesseldorf, Federal Republic of Germany; Hynes (unpublished) in Dublin, Ireland; Sokolowska and Firkowska-Mankiewicz in Warsaw, Poland (see Sokolowska, et al., 1978 or Firkowska, et al., 1978); Barnas (unpublished) in Tokyo, Japan; and Schooler and Smith in Kobe, Japan (see Smith and Schooler, 1978 or Schooler and Smith, 1978). In sum, there is a self-direction/conformity dimension to parental values in all industrialized countries that have to our knowledge been studied and even in one society (Taiwan) that was, at the time of inquiry, less industrialized.

Confirmatory factor-analytic models of parental values based on the data of the Polish and the Japanese replications provide even stronger evidence for the universality of a self-direction/conformity dimension. Both models use cross-sectional data, but in all other respects they are strikingly similar to our model for the United States (see Appendix C). Both are two-factor models, the first factor being valuation of self-direction versus conformity to external authority, the second being valuation of striving for success. These models provide unequivocal evidence that self-direction versus conformity to external authority is an underlying dimension of parental values not only in the United States, but also in (at least one) non-capitalist and (at least one) non-Western society.

We conclude that self-direction versus conformity to external authority truly is a universal dimension of parental values.

Social stratification and parental valuation of self-direction. There have been many studies testing the relationship of social stratification to parental valuation of self-direction. Although few of these studies are precise replications of ours, they nevertheless test our conclusion that the higher parents' social-stratification positions, the more likely they are to value self-direction for their children; the lower parents' social-stratification positions, the more likely they are to value conformity to external authority.

The finding has been confirmed in the United States by Franklin and Scott (1970), by Clausen (1974), by Campbell (1978), and by Morgan, Alwin, and Griffin (1979).[1] Data for the most extensive U.S. tests of the relationship between social stratification and parental valuation of self-direction have been provided by the N.O.R.C. General Social Surveys, beginning with that of 1973. Several of these surveys include a modified version of our parental-values questions, as well as a standard battery of questions about the respondents' social characteristics. Wright and Wright (1976), in an analysis of the 1973 survey, and Kohn (1976b), in a reanalysis of the same data, found the relationship between social stratification and fathers' valuation of self-direction/conformity to be essentially the same as we had found it to be in the analysis of our 1964 cross-sectional data (Chapter 1). Moreover, in an extension that goes beyond what our own data permitted, the analyses of the N.O.R.C. data found social stratification to be substantially correlated with mothers' valuation of self-direction. This conclusion holds whether women's own educational and occupational positions or their husbands' educational and occupational positions are used to index mothers' social-stratification positions. Kohn repeated all these analyses, with the same results, using the 1975 N.O.R.C. survey. Moreover, Kohn's analyses of both the 1973 and the 1975 N.O.R.C. data show that the correlation between social-stratification position and parental valuation of self-direction remains strong even when all other major lines of social demarcation are statistically controlled.

There have also been several confirmations of the relationship between social-stratification position and parental valuation of self-direction in studies conducted in other countries: in Turin, Italy, by Pearlin (Pearlin and Kohn, 1966; Kohn, 1969, Chapter 3), in Taiwan, by Stephen Olsen (1971);

---

[1] There have also been several intensive studies of working-class life, using methods quite different from our own formal, structured techniques, that confirm our picture of working-class parental values (see, in particular, Sennett and Cobb, 1973; LeMasters, 1975; and Rubin, 1976).

in France, by Perron (1971); in Great Britain, by Platt (unpublished); in Ireland, by Hynes (unpublished); in the Federal Republic of Germany, by Bertram (unpublished; for a description of the overall study, see Bertram 1976a,b) and by Hoff and Gruneisen (1978); and in Poland, by Sokolowska and Firkowska-Mankiewicz (see Sokolowska, et al., 1978 or Firkowska, et al., 1978).

The strongest evidence comes from the Polish replication study, for, as we have seen, that study uses a confirmatory factor-analytic measurement model of parental values. Moreover, it is based on a national sample of urban Poland. In that study, the correlation between fathers' social-stratification positions and their valuation of self-direction for children is .46, precisely the same figure as obtains in a cross-sectional analysis of our 1964 U.S. data.

We conclude that the universality of the relationship between social stratification and parental valuation of self-direction versus conformity to external authority has been convincingly substantiated.

The Relationship of Social Stratification to Self-conceptions and Social Orientations

There has been so much research on the relationships of social stratification to self-conceptions and social orientations that it is impossible to review it here. With the possible exception of Simpson's (1972) finding that the relationship between education and authoritarianism may not obtain in all countries, none of the studies of which we know presents findings that are in any important way inconsistent with ours.[2] These many studies provide supportive, even if not definitive, evidence of the universality of the relationship between social stratification and orientations to self and others.

The most precisely comparable evidence comes from the Polish and Japanese replications. The Polish study finds relationships between social-

---

[2] In addition to evidence further confirming the long-recognized relationship between social stratification and authoritarianism, there have been new conceptualizations of authoritarianism. Even before the publication of the first of our studies, Kelman and Barclay (1963) had argued that authoritarianism can best be interpreted as measuring narrowness of perspective. Their argument is certainly consistent with our treatment of authoritarian conservatism as implying a lack of open-mindedness. But, although we said that tolerance of nonconformity requires breadth of perspective, we did not develop the implications of this idea. Picking up where we left off, Gabennesch (1972) has suggested that what is centrally at issue is a process of reification: "We may infer from Kohn's findings that individuals with narrow perspectives seem more likely to view the social world in fixed, absolute terms. Such people appear to conceive of social reality as encompassing a superordinate normative dimension, an external locus where events are determined, where moral authority resides, and to which men must adapt themselves." (pp. 862–863; see also Roof, 1974). Gabennesch draws a parallel between this conception of authoritarianism and Piaget's conception of moral realism. An equally important connection to which Gabennesch's analysis draws attention is that between authoritarian conservatism—seen as reflecting narrowness of perspective and reification—and intellectual flexibility.

stratification position and the three facets of social orientation measured in that study—authoritarian conservatism, standards of morality, and trustfulness—that are markedly similar to those found in our U.S. research. The correlations, in fact, are nearly identical to those obtained in cross-sectional analyses of the 1964 U.S. data.

The relationships between social-stratification position and self-conceptions, however, are decidedly different in the two countries. In the United States, the correlations between social-stratification position and self-conceptions, although smaller than those between stratification position and social orientations, are consistent: Men of higher position are more likely to have favorable self-conceptions, just as they are more likely to have favorable orientations to the larger society. In Poland, not only are the magnitudes of the correlations small but, unlike the United States, higher position is not uniformly associated with more favorable self-conceptions. The most notable cross-national difference is in the relationship between social-stratification position and self-confidence. In the United States, higher position is associated with more self-confidence, but in Poland the opposite is true. Similarly, albeit less strikingly, for anxiety: In the United States, higher position is associated with somewhat less anxiety, but in Poland higher social position is associated with slightly greater anxiety. The difference between the two countries is less pronounced for self-deprecation, higher position being associated with less self-deprecation in both countries. Still, the relationship is stronger in the United States than in Poland. There is essentially no difference between the United States and Poland with respect to idea-conformity: In both countries, higher position is associated, to a modest but significant degree, with greater independence in one's ideas.

It is not altogether clear why social stratification does not bear the same positive relationship to favorable self-conceptions in Poland as in the United States. We shall soon consider the possibility that occupational self-direction fails to enhance self-conceptions in Poland, hence does not result in men of higher social-stratification position developing more favorable self-conceptions. Still, even if occupational self-direction does not enhance self-conceptions in Poland, one might nevertheless expect higher social-stratification position to result in favorable self-conceptions.[3] Why does it not? One possible explanation is that, in the aftermath of World War II and with the rapid reindustrialization of Poland, many people of working-class and peasant backgrounds who might not otherwise have had the opportunity for higher education and responsible jobs did get these opportunities.

---

[3] Rosenberg and Pearlin (1978), while accepting our interpretation of the role of occupational self-direction in explaining the relationship between social stratification and self-esteem, speculate that there may be other intervening mechanisms as well. In particular, they suggest that such processes as social comparison and reflected appraisals might contribute to higher stratification position leading to greater self-esteem.

This resulted from several historical processes: the Nazis'. systematic massacre of the Polish intelligentsia, the rapid increase from pre-war levels in industrialization and bureaucratization, and the deliberate policy of socialist governments to make educational opportunities available to the children of workers and peasants. It is possible that rapid social mobility created feelings of self-doubt among some people who came to occupy higher positions. Alternatively, during the transitional stages to a new economic and political system, higher positions may be more precarious than lower positions. As a consequence, people in higher positions may wonder whether they really are able, and will be allowed, to carry out the responsibilities of their jobs. Another possible explanation focuses on the widespread belief, in part a derivative of the aristocratic culture of pre-war Poland, that status is not so much a result of superior job performance as of fate or the intervention of well-placed friends. Hence, finding oneself in a high position would provide little assurance of one's ability to meet the demands of the position.

These explanations focus on the reasons why Polish men of higher educational and occupational position may have less favorable self-conceptions than one might have expected. It is at least as pertinent to ask why Polish men of lower educational and occupational position may be more self-confident and less anxious than might have been expected. Although, as individuals, these men may not have experienced much social mobility, certainly the segment of the society to which they belong—the working class—benefitted from post-war changes in socialist Poland. At the time of the interviews in 1978, their economic situation had improved and they were held in higher social regard; there was every reason for them to feel more confident. Post-war changes in Polish social structure had enhanced the circumstances of the working class to a much greater extent than those of white-collar workers and professionals.

Whatever the explanation, the relationships between social stratification and self-conceptions in Poland clearly are different from what we find them to be in the United States.

Thus far, only preliminary analyses of the relationships of social stratification to self-conceptions and social orientations have been done for Japan. (These analyses have not progressed to the point of developing a measurement model of social-stratification position; *pro temp,* we use the two-factor Hollingshead index as an approximate index of social-stratification position.) In general, these preliminary analyses confirm that the relationships of social stratification with social orientations are similar in sign to, albeit perhaps smaller in magnitude than, those found in cross-sectional analyses of data from the United States and Poland.

The relationships of social stratification with self-conceptions are not quite the same as those that obtain either in the United States or in Poland. Those for self-confidence, self-deprecation, idea-conformity, and fatalism are similar to what we have found for the United States: Men of higher social-stratification position are more self-confident and less self-deprecatory, less likely to be conformist in their ideas, and less fatalistic in their beliefs than are men of lower stratification position. For anxiety, though, there is little if any relationship; it may even be that Japanese men of higher social-stratification position are *more* anxious than are Japanese men of lower position. Although more like the U.S. findings than those of Poland, the Japanese findings again belie the universality of the relationships found in the U.S. between social stratification and self-conceptions.

Overall, then, there is considerable cross-national confirmation of our U.S. findings that substantial relationships exist between social stratification and social orientations. On the other hand, the relationships between social stratification and self-conceptions—which are weaker in magnitude than are those for social orientations even in the United States—certainly are not universal.

The Relationship of Social Stratification to Ideational Flexibility

There is, as is well known, a sizeable research literature demonstrating a positive relationship between social stratification and standard measures of cognitive functioning. If we treat these measures of cognitive functioning as reflecting intellectual performance in a test situation (eschewing dubious inferences about these tests being measures of innate capacity; see Gould, 1981), then certainly this considerable body of research supports our interpretation that social-stratification position is positively related to effective intellectual functioning. Our own index of intellectual flexibility has been employed in only two studies—the Polish and Japanese replications. Both studies develop confirmatory factor-analytic models of intellectual flexibility very similar to our own, except for their being based on cross-sectional data. Both studies confirm a strong positive relationship between social stratification and ideational flexibility.

THE RECIPROCAL EFFECTS OF OCCUPATIONAL SELF-DIRECTION AND PSYCHOLOGICAL FUNCTIONING

In reviewing the evidence about the relationships between job conditions and psychological functioning, we focus on those studies that deal with conditions that facilitate or restrict the exercise of occupational self-direction. Were we to attempt to review the many studies of bureaucratization, of ownership and hierarchical position, or of job pressures, uncertainties, and other allegedly stressful job conditions, a brief essay intended only to assess the universality of our interpretive model would itself become a book.[4] The heart of our thesis is the importance of occupational self-direction for psychological functioning. What evidence is there from other U.S. studies to confirm or refute our findings about the relationship between occupational self-direction and psychological functioning? What evidence is there to tell us whether this relationship obtains in other countries as well?

There have been several studies that have examined the relationship between occupational self-direction—or, what is more usually the case, some analogue to or approximate measure of occupational self-direction—and one or more aspects of psychological functioning.[5] Particularly pertinent are two studies that confirm the importance of occupational self-direction for values. The first, by Hoff and Gruneisen (1978; Gruneisen and Hoff, 1977), in the Federal Republic of Germany, used occupational indices similar to our measures of occupational self-direction and found them to be substantially related to parental values, especially as these values guide parents' behavior in critical situations. The second, by Mortimer and Lorence (1979a) in the United States, is a longitudinal analysis of "work autonomy" (which they see as an approximation to our occupational self-direction) and occupational values in a sample of University of Michigan graduates. Using reciprocal-effects models similar to those we have employed, they found clearcut evidence that work autonomy results in greater emphasis on both intrinsic and people-oriented, as distinct from extrinsic, work values. The

---

[4] We must take note, though, of criticisms that our treatment of ownership (particularly but not only in Chapter 4) does not take proper account that a representative sample of employed men includes only a small proportion of owners, virtually none of them owners of sizeable amounts of capital (see Gordon, 1978–1979; Aldrich and Weiss, 1981; Archibald, et al., 1981; Schweitzer, 1981). Chapter 7 attempts to take cognizance of these criticisms.

[5] Few studies have had the requisite detailed descriptive data for an index of substantive complexity similar to ours. To fill the gap, several approximate measures of substantive complexity have been developed, beginning with our index of the substantive complexity of past jobs in Chapter 3; including also Temme's (1975), now used by N.O.R.C. in the codes it provides for its General Social Surveys; Spenner's (1977, 1980); and Cain and Treiman's (1981). All of these indices extrapolate from *Dictionary of Occupational Titles'* classifications of the average level of complexity of work with data, with things, and with people for an entire occupation to the substantive complexity (or even to the occupational self-direction) of a particular job. Used cautiously, such indices do provide serviceable approximations for use in studies that lack precise data about the substantive complexity of particular jobs. It must be kept in mind, though, that such approximate indices seriously underestimate the magnitudes of the relationships of substantive complexity with other variables.

In an effort to create an approximate measure of "authority" (akin to our closeness of supervision), Spaeth (1979) uses the *Dictionary of Occupational Titles'* classifications, including the complexity of work with people, in a larger measurement model of "vertical differentiation among occupations". It does not seem to us, though, that the *Dictionary's* classification of complexity of work with people (see Appendix B) provides a reliable basis for indexing authority relations; moreover, this usage of complexity of work with people ignores the close empirical and theoretical relationship between complexity of work with people and complexity of work with data. Spenner's (1980) alternative approach, using the *Dictionary's* ratings of the qualities a worker needs to do the job as a basis for producing ratings of closeness of supervision, seems to us to be a better justified approximation.

same authors (1979b), in a further analysis of these data, demonstrated that work autonomy has pronounced effects on self-confidence. Even among that portion of the workforce that has the greatest opportunity for occupational self-direction, and even taking their pre-employment values and self-concept into account, occupational self-direction has notable effects on pertinent aspects of values and self-conception.

Several studies have focused on closeness of supervision. In a Canadian study, Coburn and Edwards (1976) found that closeness of supervision is negatively related to fathers' valuation of self-direction. (They employed a concept, "job control", which they see as approximating our concept, occupational self-direction, but which we see as roughly equivalent to our concept, closeness of supervision.) In another Canadian study, Grabb (1981a) showed that job control (somewhat differently measured) is related to men's feelings of political powerlessness. In a Norwegian study, Dalgard (1981) employed our index of closeness of supervision, which he found to be related to psychiatric problems, even with such social characteristics as age, education, income, type of work, and type of neighborhood statistically controlled.

In an imaginative, yet rigorous, extrapolation from our research, Nancy Olsen (1974) reasoned that there is a parallel between the situation of closely supervised employed men and that of daughters-in-law in patrilineal extended families, where young women are subject to the authority and direction of their mothers-in-law. Daughters-in-law in three-generation households should therefore resemble working-class men in placing a high value upon their children's conformity, while those in nuclear families should place more emphasis on self-direction. To test this hypothesis, Olsen carried out a comparative study of two- and three-generation families in Taiwan. She used an ingenious research design, which permitted her to control statistically for urbanness, social stratification, size of family, sex of the child, and ordinal position of the child. Her analysis clearly showed that living in a three-generation household affects women's values in much the same way that close supervision on the job affects men's values. She also convincingly argued that this finding does not result from women who value conformity being more likely to marry into households that include mothers-in-law. She was even able to demonstrate empirically that her findings do not result from higher valuation of the traditional Chinese ethic by women who live in extended households.

An even bolder (but, unfortunately, not nearly as rigorous) extrapolation from our closeness-of-supervision concept was employed in a study by Ellis, Lee, and Petersen (1978; see also Petersen, Lee, and Ellis, 1982). They hypothesized that people who live in cultures that emphasize close supervision of individual behavior in spheres of life ranging from economic and political organization to family structure and conceptions of the supernatural will value children's conformity to external authority. Their analysis of a large sample of mainly nonindustrialized cultures yielded results thoroughly consistent with their expectations. Such an inquiry, of course, is open to alternative interpretations; all that one can conclude with confidence is that there is a general congruence between a societal emphasis on supervision and a culturally shared belief that it is desirable for children to conform to adult authority.

The closest approximations to the methods and objectives of our own research are provided, once again, by the Polish and Japanese replications.

The Polish study examines the reciprocal relationships of occupational self-direction (a second-order concept, indexed by substantive complexity, closeness of supervision, and routinization) with ideational flexibility, parental valuation of self-direction, and several facets of self-conception and social orientation. Since the data are cross-sectional, two types of models are tested: models that do not include a measure of "earlier" psychological functioning; and models that simulate such a measure by fixing a path from a hypothetical earlier level of psychological functioning to an actual current level, much as was done in our analyses of the cross-sectional data for women in Chapters 8 and 9. The magnitudes and statistical significance of the effects of occupational self-direction on ideational flexibility, parental valuation of self-direction, and social orientations vary considerably, depending on whether or not such a hypothetical path is allowed and, if it is allowed, the magnitude at which it is fixed. The results nevertheless consistently suggest that occupational self-direction does have a causal impact on all these facets of psychological functioning.

Occupational self-direction does not, however, appear to affect self-conceptions in Poland—which undoubtedly is the most important reason why social-stratification position is not related to self-conceptions in Poland as it is in the United States. Somehow, in the United States, the learning-generalization process by which the lessons of the job are carried over to one's values and social orientations occurs also (albeit, not as strongly) for one's orientations to self. In Poland, either occupational self-direction does not enhance self-conception or something interferes with such enhanced self-conception being carried over to nonoccupational spheres of life.

The Japanese study examines the relationships between psychological functioning and occupational self-direction (here, too, a second-order concept) in models that contain also time-pressure, hierarchical position, ownership, and bureaucratization. As in the analyses of the Polish study, the lack of longitudinal data about psychological functioning is addressed by fixing at reasonable values paths from hypothetical earlier psychological functioning to actual later psychological functioning. As in the analyses of job structure and psychological functioning in Chapter 6, ownership, hierarchical position, and bureaucratization are depicted as affecting psychological functioning in two alternative ways: directly, as having unidirectional effects on psychological functioning, and indirectly, via more proximate job conditions. In both types of models, occupational self-direction is found to have statistically significant positive effects on ideational flexibility, personally responsible standards of morality, and trust, and to have significant negative effects on authoritarian conservatism, idea conformity, fatalism, and self-deprecation. In models that do not allow position in the organizational structure to directly affect psychological functioning, occupational self-direction also has a significant positive effect on self-confidence and a significant negative effect on anxiety.

In summary, the findings from studies done both in the United States and in other countries are strongly supportive of the conclusions we have reached in our own research about the effects of occupational self-direction on cognitive functioning, values, and social orientations.[6] The Japanese data lend support even to our conclusions about the relationship of occupational self-direction with self-conceptions. The Polish data, however, show that occupational self-direction does not have consonant effects on self-conceptions in that country. We take it as a universal that occupational self-direction is conducive to effective cognitive functioning, valuing self-direction, and having social orientations consonant with such a value. The universality of the relationships between occupational self-direction and self-conceptions—relationships that never appeared to be strong even in our U.S. data—must now be considered problematic.

THE ROLE OF OCCUPATIONAL SELF-DIRECTION IN EXPLAINING THE RELATIONSHIP OF SOCIAL STRATIFICATION TO PSYCHOLOGICAL FUNCTIONING

There have been attempts in several countries to test the universality of the central element of our thesis, that occupational self-direction plays a crucial role in explaining the relationships of social stratification to values, orientations to self and society, and cognitive functioning.[7] Some of these studies fall far short of being exact replications, yet all are instructive.

---

[6] Many other investigators have adopted the concepts, occupational self-direction, substantive complexity, and closeness of supervision, using them for such diverse purposes as reinterpreting the status-attainment model (Spaeth, 1976), proposing a new method of classifying the occupational structure of the U.S. economy (Temme, 1975), studying the relationship between "autonomy" in parents' job conditions and the moral development of their children (Bertram, 1976a), reassessing the psychological impact of complex role-sets (Coser, 1975), proposing a theory of vertical occupational differentiation (Spaeth, 1979), interpreting the effects of fathers' occupational experiences on their sons' occupational choices (Mortimer, 1974 and 1976), and reconceptualizing the relationship between social stratification and ego development (Kusatzu, 1977).

[7] With the exception of the Polish replication, all the studies to be discussed use partial-correlational techniques for assessing the degree to which occupational self-direction explains the psychological effects of social stratification. The Polish replication, like our analysis in Chapter 7, assesses the proportion of the total *effect* of social stratification on a particular facet of psychological functioning that is indirect, via occupational self-direction.

The first study, by Pearlin (Pearlin and Kohn, 1966; Kohn, 1969, Chapter 9) in Turin, Italy, was actually carried out before our 1964 baseline survey in the United States, but was conceived as a cross-national replication of the U.S. study. Since fieldwork for the Turin study was conducted before planning for the U.S. study had been completed, its indices, particularly of occupational self-direction, are only approximate versions, not fully developed, of those used in the U.S. study. Still, the Turin study gave the first evidence that the relationship between social stratification and fathers' valuation of self-direction for children is substantially attributable to occupational self-direction. The Turin study even provided evidence (Kohn, 1969:149–151) that the relationship between men's social-stratification positions and their wives' values is, to a lesser but still substantial degree, attributable to the men's job conditions. Thus, Turin provided grounds for concluding that social stratification exerts its impact on parental values, at least in industrialized, capitalist, Western societies, in substantial part because of the association between stratification position and the exercise of occupational self-direction.

A second study, by Stephen Olsen (1971), confirmed in Taiwan the correlation between social stratification and parental valuation of self-direction versus conformity to external authority, both for fathers and for mothers. But when Olsen statistically controlled his measures of occupational self-direction, he found that the correlations between stratification and values were not appreciably reduced. Four possible interpretations are: Olsen's very approximate indices of the pertinent occupational conditions may be insufficient; or, in the decidedly different occupational structure of (then) partially industrialized Taiwan, dimensions of occupation other than closeness of supervision and substantive complexity may be more important for explaining the relationship between stratification and values; or, in Taiwan, perhaps economic, political, or other nonoccupational life-conditions are the bridge between stratification and values; or, finally, middle-class Taiwanese may have adopted Western values while working-class Taiwanese may still hold traditional, Confucian values. Olsen's data do not permit us to choose among these alternatives with any degree of confidence.

A third study, conducted in Peru by Scurrah and Montalvo (1975), found correlations similar to those we had found between social stratification and such aspects of orientation as fatalism, trust, and anxiety. They asked whether these relationships could be explained by stratification-related differences in occupational self-direction. To some degree they could: Statistically controlling indices of substantive complexity and closeness of supervision reduced the correlations by from nineteen to twenty-eight percent. These reductions, however, are smaller than those we had obtained. Perhaps Scurrah and Montalvo's weak findings reflect the disadvantages of relying on approximate indices. Or perhaps it is just that their sample is limited to workers employed in retail stores. The data do not permit us to judge. Nevertheless, the study raises further doubts about whether occupational self-direction is as important for explaining the relationships of social stratification with self-conceptions and social orientations in partially industrialized as in more fully industrialized societies.

Stronger evidence is produced by studies conducted in more industrialized societies.

A Canadian study, by Grabb (1981b), confirms that the relationships of both occupational status and education to "self-actualization values" (i.e., valuing life goals that emphasize self-development, personal accomplishment, activity, and control over one's life) are substantially attributable to "intrinsic job qualities". ("Intrinsic job qualities" are as close an approximation to occupational self-direction as Grabb was able to achieve in a secondary analysis.)

Using indices of occupational self-direction that are much closer to those we employed, Eugene Hynes, in an as-yet unpublished study of Dublin, Ireland, focused on the core issue of whether the relationship between social stratification and fathers' valuation of self-direction versus conformity to external authority can be attributed to occupational self-direction. His analyses provide evidence that it can. He finds the correlation between fathers' occupational status and their valuation of self-direction to be .21; this correlation is reduced by 81 percent when the substantive complexity of work, routinization, and closeness of supervision are statistically controlled. He also finds a correlation of .26 between fathers' educational levels and their valuation of self-direction; this correlation is reduced by 46 percent when occupational self-direction is statistically controlled. These findings clearly are consistent with what we have found for the United States.

The Polish and Japanese studies once again provide the most precise replications of all. As we have seen, the Polish study confirms strong relationships of social-stratification position with ideational flexibility, parental valuation of self-direction, and social orientations, albeit not with self-conceptions. The study further finds the same strong reciprocal relationship between occupational position and occupational self-direction as obtains in the United States. It is no surprise, then, that analyses much like those of Chapter 7 show the relationships of social-stratification position to ideational flexibility, parental values, and social orientations to be very substantially attributable to occupational self-direction. (Occupational self-direction appears to explain even more of the effect of education on values and social orientations in Poland than in the United States.) As we have seen, though, occupational self-direction does not enhance self-conception in Poland, which at least partly explains why there is not a positive relationship between social stratification and self-conception in that country.

The Japanese analyses are still in process; our conclusions must therefore be provisional. Nevertheless, the data do seem to show that the relationships of social stratification with ideational flexibility and with social orientations are largely attributable to occupational self-direction. The situation is somewhat more complex for the relationships between social stratification and self-conceptions. Although there is evidence that occupational self-direction may have a negative effect on anxiety, there is little relationship between social stratification and anxiety in Japan, hence little to explain. As we have seen, though, self-confidence, self-deprecation, idea-conformity, and fatalism are all related to social stratification. In large part, this is because of their relationship to occupational self-direction. In sum, occupational self-direction appears (at this stage of the analysis) to explain, in substantial part, the relationship of social stratification to ideational flexibility, to social orientations, and to the four aspects of self-conception that are related to social stratification in Japan.

Overall, then, there is now considerable cross-national evidence in support of our interpretation that occupational self-direction plays an important role in explaining the relationships of social stratification with ideational flexibility, parental values, and social orientations. The picture is less clear for self-conceptions. It would appear that the relationships of social stratification and occupational self-direction to self-conceptions are contingent on the cultural, social-structural, and historical circumstances of the countries studied. By contrast, the relationships of social stratification and of occupational self-direction to values, to social orientations, and to cognitive functioning are stronger and seem to be essentially universal, at least in industrialized societies.

CONCLUSION

The many studies testing our interpretive model—particularly the two most exact and most comprehensive replications, conducted in Poland and Japan—provide strong evidence for the universality of the main elements of our thesis. Poland and Japan provide crucial tests of the applicability of the model to societies quite different from that of the United States: Poland, a socialist society; Japan, a non-Western society with an especially pronounced division of the economy into primary and secondary sectors. That the Polish and the Japanese findings are so strongly supportive of every element of the interpretive thesis save one (the exception, of course, being the relationships of social stratification and occupational self-direction to self-conceptions) provides powerful evidence that our interpretation extends far beyond our own data and far beyond the single capitalist, Western society that is the United States. The systematic comparative evidence from Poland and Japan, together with the more limited evidence provided by the many other studies reviewed in this chapter, strongly suggests that our interpretation applies to industrialized societies generally. There is also considerable evidence that, social stratification aside, occupational self-direction and its components have important effects on values, orientations, cognitive functioning, and other facets of psychological functioning.

13 | Unresolved Interpretive Issues*

Melvin L. Kohn

In this book, we have developed and established strong empirical support for an interpretation of the interrelationship of social stratification, job conditions, and psychological functioning. We have found this interpretation to be applicable far beyond the one Western, capitalist society that is the United States. We have also found that the heart of the model, depicting the reciprocal relationships between job conditions and psychological functioning, applies considerably beyond *men's* job conditions and *intrapsychic* functioning. This evidence clearly attests to the general validity of the model. Still, there are many unresolved issues. Although the model is fairly comprehensive, important parts are incomplete. Moreover, although the empirical evidence in favor of our interpretation is formidable, alternative interpretations of important components certainly are possible.

In this chapter, we examine some of the principal issues that remain unresolved.[1] We begin by reconsidering the heart of the model, the relation-

---

* This chapter was prepared especially for this book, but it borrows from several earlier essays, namely, "Occupational Structure and Alienation" (Kohn, 1976a), "Reassessment, 1977" (Kohn, 1977), "Job Complexity and Adult Personality" (Kohn, 1980), and "On the Transmission of Values in the Family: A Preliminary Formulation" (Kohn, in press).

[1] Our concern here is not with the many technical problems discussed at several points in the book, but with broader theoretical issues. The distinction, of course, is rather arbitrary: for example, we have treated the desirability of having measurements at three times and at closer intervals than ten years as a technical issue, but the issue clearly has theoretical import. It bears

ship between job conditions and personality, asking whether alternative formulations are possible. Then we discuss the effects of education on personality development—a portion of the interpretation not nearly as well developed as is that concerning job and personality. In this context, we describe our current efforts to deal more fundamentally with the processes by which and the extent to which educational experience affects psychological functioning. Next, we consider a logical extension of the interpretive model, the interpersonal processes by which the values and orientations that have been influenced by job and stratification are transmitted from the jobholder to other family members. Finally, there is the critical question of the utility of our findings for social policy. Can our findings be utilized for purposive social change? Can job conditions be modified to increase opportunities for occupational self-direction? To anticipate: perhaps, and we hope so, but not readily.

THE PROCESSES BY WHICH JOB AFFECTS PERSONALITY

Our interpretation is straightforward: The structural imperatives of the job—particularly those conditions that facilitate or restrict the exercise of self-direction in work—affect workers' values, orientations to self and society, and cognitive functioning primarily through a direct process of learning from the job and generalizing what has been learned to other realms of life. Although other processes may also be involved (see Chapter 9), learning-generalization does seem to be predominant.

We readily acknowledge that job conditions are not the only social-structural conditions that affect psychological functioning. We have shown, for example, that housework affects psychological functioning, and there is ample evidence (Kohn, 1969, Chapters 4 and 5; Schooler, 1972 and Chapter 11 of this book) that other lines of social demarcation—race, national and religious background, urbanness, and region of the country, among others—also are related to psychological functioning. Our evidence demonstrates, though, that job conditions have a decided psychological impact.

Each element of our interpretation of the job-personality relationship can be questioned. We therefore reconsider, in turn, our characterization of

---

on the question, whether the effects of psychological functioning on job conditions occur principally through processes of occupational selection or through processes of job molding. Some of the other principal technical issues are problems of identification in causal modelling (pertinent here is Kessler and Greenberg, 1981); the desirability of developing multi-indicator measurement models, based on objective information—as we have done for substantive complexity—for other job conditions; the desirability of confirming our interview-based information with observational data; and the limitations of basing our analyses on data provided by a random sample of the employed population, data that provide scant information on the organizational, interpersonal, and technological contexts of work.

the pertinent job conditions, our treatment of the learning-generalization process, and our conceptualization of personality.

Characterization of Job Conditions

Objective job conditions and subjective appraisals of the job.   Our approach deliberately focuses on objective conditions of work—what a worker does, who determines how he does it, in what physical and social circumstances he works, to what risks and rewards he is subject—rather than on his subjective appraisals of those job conditions. Granted, we have not always succeeded: Our measures are based on interview reports, not on observations by trained analysts; moreover, even for indices based on interview reports, some are more subjective than need be. Still, our *intent* has consistently been to measure job conditions as objectively as possible. An alternative approach employed by many investigators deliberately begins with subjective indices of job conditions, rather than with job conditions as an outside observer might appraise them, on the rationale that job conditions become important for psychological functioning only when they enter into the perceptions of workers. Investigators using this approach measure boredom rather than routinization, interest in the work rather than its substantive complexity, and "alienation in work" rather than actual working conditions. Such an approach ignores the possibility that there may be a gap between the conditions to which a worker is subject and his awareness of those conditions. The presence or absence of such a gap is itself problematic and may be structurally determined. Moreover, conditions felt by a worker to be benign may have deleterious consequences, while conditions felt to be onerous may have beneficial consequences.

Obviously, the ideal research design would include measures both of objective working conditions and of workers' subjective appraisals of those conditions. It would then be possible to assess empirically how objective conditions become transformed into subjective experience and how objective conditions and subjective perceptions of those conditions together affect off-the-job psychological functioning and behavior. Such an assessment would not be simple to carry out, but it would be feasible.

Interpersonal context and interpersonal relations.   In our emphasis on the structural imperatives of the job, we may have underestimated the importance of the interpersonal contexts of work and of interpersonal relationships on the job; a random-sample survey of the employed population is not optimal for studying such phenomena. We may also have given short shrift to the possibility of interactions between job conditions and interpersonal processes. House (1980), for example, finds that workers who have positive, supportive relations with their coworkers and supervisors are less affected by stressful job conditions than are workers who do not perceive their coworkers and supervisors to be supportive. While House's evidence is less than fully convincing, the hypothesis is certainly tenable.

It is also possible that our central concept, the substantive complexity of work, underestimates the importance of interpersonal relatedness by combining complexity of work with people with complexity of work with data and with things into a single overarching concept, rather than treating work with people as a separate domain. We see the complexity of work with people as no more important than complexity of work with data or with things: Of primary importance is complexity; of only secondary importance is whether complex work is done with people, with data, or with things. An alternative approach (exemplified by Coser, 1975) sees complexity of work with people—more precisely, complexity of role-sets—as having pivotal importance, with other aspects of complexity being only ancillary. From that point of view, our index of substantive complexity is a proxy for what is really important about work—the complexity of one's role relationships. In the absence of a precise measure of complexity of role-sets, it is not possible to assess that assertion empirically.

Equivalents to occupational self-direction. It is possible that other conditions of life may serve as "equivalents" to occupational self-direction, providing opportunities for self-direction either in job-related activities or in nonoccupational spheres of life. House has speculated (1981:552), for example, that "[w]orkers may also have other occupational experiences that modify or compensate for the degree of self-direction in their particular job. Workers in non-self-directed jobs may . . . participate in union activities or organizational decision making in ways not captured in Kohn's measures." Perhaps so, but our (admittedly incomplete) analyses of Chapter 3 give little indication that other occupational involvements can compensate for lack of opportunity to be self-directed in one's work.

We do think, though, that there may be *non*occupational equivalents to occupational self-direction. As we have observed, housework may be equivalent to paid employment in its effects on women's psychological functioning. We had hoped to examine volunteer activities as another possible source of nonoccupational self-direction. Unfortunately, our data proved to be insufficient—mainly because few respondents reported such activities. We searched, too, for nonoccupational equivalents to occupational self-direction in the lives of those men in the follow-up study who had retired, but (as a result of our deliberately limiting the follow-up study to men less than 65 years of age) there were too few retired men to make such an analysis worthwhile. That we have thus far succeeded in finding equivalents to occupational self-direction only in housework (and, as will shortly be seen, in formal education) may mean only that our data are inadequate for studying equivalence in other realms of life. The issue is certainly worth pursuing.

The Learning-Generalization Process

As noted above, our findings have consistently suggested that the predominant process by which the lessons of work are generalized to other realms of life is learning-generalization—a straightforward translation of the lessons of the job to outside-the-job realities. Thus, people who do complex work come to exercise their intellectual prowess not only on the job, but also in their nonoccupational lives. They become more open to new experience. They come to value self-direction more highly. They even come to engage in more intellectually demanding leisure-time activities. In short, the lessons of work are directly carried over to nonoccupational realms. Admittedly, we stretch the term "learning" when we apply the concept "learning-generalization" to the processes by which job pressures and uncertainties lead to distress; but even here the crux of the matter is that job experiences have straightforward psychological effects. In any case, it certainly does not stretch the meaning of "learning" to speak of learning from the experience of occupational self-direction and applying these lessons to nonoccupational realities.

We do not know why occupational self-direction has greater effects on cognitive functioning and on social orientations than on self-conceptions (see Chapter 12). Even for self-conceptions, though, the predominant *process* by which job affects person seems to be learning-generalization.

Several questions about the learning-generalization process remain unresolved: the timing of effects; the possibility that job conditions may affect personality only when they surpass some threshold; the question, whether job conditions affect all workers similarly; and the possibility that job conditions might affect off-the-job psychological functioning through workers' subjective feelings about the job. All these possibilities are worth examining.

The timing of effects. Our longitudinal analyses tell us little about the timing of the effects of job on personality, because these analyses are locked into the confines of a research design that measures change only once, ten years after the baseline measurements of job conditions and of psychological functioning. From such information, we can properly infer that job conditions do affect psychological functioning, but we cannot say when such processes begin, whether they are continuous or discontinuous, or whether they taper off after some time or cumulate indefinitely. It may be that some effects of job on person occur even before the individual actually experiences the new working conditions, in anticipation of the conditions that will be encountered or of what the new job will signify. For example, a promotion that entails an increase in status might lead to an increase in self-esteem even before—or, perhaps, especially before—the individual actually begins a new job. Other job conditions might have their impact early on, tapering off as the individual grows accustomed to the conditions of work. It is possible, for example, that tasks that seem at first to be challenging will in time become old hat. The opposite might also happen; for example, some job conditions—one thinks of noise and of time-pressure—might become more onerous as one endures them longer. There are other obvious possibilities, all of them requiring that we regard our findings as representing the net outcome of many processes, some of which may have run their course long before the ten-year follow-up interview, some of which may after ten years still be ongoing, and some of which may barely have gotten underway. Description and analysis of the many strands of the actual process require a much more fine-grained analysis than we have done, using data collected at closer intervals.

Threshold effects. There is a distinct possibility that the effects of (at least some) job conditions on (at least some) facets of psychological functioning might depend on the particular condition exceeding some critical threshold. Closeness of supervision, for example, might increase idea-conformity only when the degree of supervisory control reaches a particular level. Our analyses have not dealt with this possibility; the nature of our data and of our research design would make it difficult to do so. We must acknowledge the possibility, though, that job conditions may affect psychological functioning only when some threshold level is reached.

Subgroup variations in the effects of job on person. At many points in this book, we have considered whether the observed relationships between job conditions and psychological functioning hold, not only "on the average" for the entire population of employed people, but specifically for particular subgroups of the population: e.g., for both men and women, for both manual and nonmanual workers, for people employed in profit-making firms and for those employed in nonprofit organizations, and (when examining housework) for women who are employed outside the home and for full-time housewives.

Although we have repeatedly done analyses of strategic subgroups of the population, we have done many fewer such analyses than we should have liked.[2] Take, for example, an often-mentioned challenge to the interpreta-

---

[2] Separate analyses of subgroups are difficult to do when using linear structural-equation procedures, not only because such analyses require substantial numbers of cases in each of the pertinent subgroups, but also because of technical difficulties in the application of linear structural-equation modelling to such analysis. Each analysis requires redoing the measurement models for that particular subgroup, recalculating the correlations among concepts, adjusting these correlations for unreliability due to measurement error, and re-estimating the causal models—a formidable undertaking. An alternative procedure, often employed in multiple-regression analysis, of using interaction terms as independent variables in the equations has not yet been fully developed for structural-equation analysis involving reciprocal effects.

tion that job conditions affect all workers similarly—the "fit" hypothesis, which holds that job conditions have differential effects, depending on how the demands of the job fit the needs, values, and capacities of the individual worker (see Locke, 1976; but see also Mortimer, 1979). Substantively complex work, for example, might be stimulating to most workers, yet be more burden than challenge to those workers who value extrinsic over intrinsic qualities of work. Our analyses of the interaction of occupational values and job conditions (in Chapters 3 and 4) cast doubt on the fit hypothesis. They suggest that occupational self-direction is related to such basic needs and values as to be important to all workers, at least under the conditions of working life generally experienced in the United States. These analyses, however, have been far from definitive. Analysis of (linear) interactions does not exhaust the possibilities of subgroup variations. Moreover and more important, these analyses have been only cross-sectional; we have not yet attempted longitudinal analysis of how job conditions affect and, in turn, are affected by occupational values. Nor have we considered many other aspects of fit—e.g., the relationship between aspirations and job conditions or between physical stamina and job conditions. Fit may yet be shown to play a part in the process, if not as the main theme, at least as a secondary theme. Fit must also be kept in mind in evaluating any proposal to modify job conditions, for job-modification plans might either increase or decrease the disparities between job requirements and workers' needs, values, or abilities, with consequences that are difficult to predict.

Even more complex—and not yet attempted—would be an analysis that took account of the many important events unrelated to job that have occurred in people's lives in the ten-year interval between our baseline and follow-up surveys—marriages and divorces, illnesses, happy and unhappy experiences of many sorts. We do have pertinent data for the subsample of men in the follow-up study, but we may not have the requisite size of sample to carry out a thoroughgoing analysis. For now, we can only note the possibility that job conditions may affect people differentially, depending on other major events occurring in their lives.

Finally—and from a sociological perspective, most important—is the possibility that reactions to job conditions may differ, not because of individual variations in needs, values, or abilities, but because of socially patterned differences in how job conditions intersect with other aspects of people's lives. Two questions of considerable theoretical importance are pertinent here: Do job conditions affect workers similarly at different stages of the life course? (See Elder, 1974; Elder and Rockwell, 1979; Baltes, 1982; Riley, 1979.) For example, might job conditions have a more (or less) pronounced effect on young, unmarried workers than on new parents or on people whose children are grown and out of the home? Furthermore, do job conditions affect workers similarly at different stages of career? (See Wilensky, 1961; Ladinsky, 1976.) For example, might job conditions have a more (or less) pronounced effect on people in their initial jobs than on people who have settled into jobs that appear to offer no further prospect of change?[3]

To state the issue most generally: Many conditions of life may possibly enhance or diminish (perhaps accelerate or slow down) the effects of job on personality. Some of these conditions are tied to life course or career; others, to ethnicity or region of the country or urbanness; still others, to involvement in nonoccupational roles—leisure-time activities, family roles, housework. Whatever gives rise to these conditions, the possibility that they may enhance or diminish the effects of job on personality is worthy of analysis.[4]

Subjective feelings about the job as mediators.   It may be that the effects of job conditions on off-the-job psychological functioning are mediated by workers' subjective feelings about the job. Two such subjective reactions—job satisfaction and stress—are particularly worth considering, because they have been the subject of extensive research.

In many studies, job satisfaction is treated as if it were the only psychological consequence of work. Our findings clearly refute this assumption. There is, however, another possibility: Job satisfaction may be an intervening link between job conditions and off-the-job psychological functioning. The rationale is that people who are satisfied with their jobs are likely to transfer such favorable orientations to their appraisals of self and of the larger world. Our data, though, offer no evidence of a close connection between job satisfaction and orientations to self or to nonoccupational social reality. The correlations between job satisfaction and the several facets of values and orientations that we have measured are neither strong nor consistent (see Kohn, 1969:178–180). Moreover, for job satisfaction to play an important intervening role in the relationship of job conditions to off-the-job psychological functioning would require job satisfaction to have a considerably stronger relationship to job conditions than it has (see Chapter 3; see also J. Miller, 1980; Kahn, 1972). There is no reason to accord to job satisfaction the role of intermediary; job satisfaction (or dissatisfaction) is simply one of many psychological consequences of work.

Another candidate for the role of intervening link in the processes by which job affects psychological functioning is stress. The hypothesis is that

---

[3] We are now doing a life-course analysis of education, occupational self-direction, and ideational flexibility for Polish and U.S. men (J. Miller, Slomczynski, and Kohn, 1982). We would like to do many more such analyses, but, realistically, it will require a major improvement in ease of doing subgroup analyses before we can do all that would be desirable.

[4] It is pertinent, though, that in an extensive series of tests of interactions between job conditions and nonoccupational (particularly family) roles, Mortimer, Lorence, and Kumka (in preparation) have found few statistically significant interactions.

job conditions affect psychological functioning, in whole or in part, because they induce feelings of stress, which in turn have longer-term psychological consequences, such as anxiety and distress. We know of no research, with the partial exception of House's (1980), that tests this interpretation, for no study includes measures of all the necessary elements: objective job conditions, felt job stress, and pertinent aspects of psychological functioning. Most studies addressed to the stress hypothesis fail to measure actual job conditions. Studies that do measure job conditions typically do not measure whether these job conditions are felt to be stressful, hence can only *infer* that stress plays the role of intervening link between job and off-the-job psychological functioning. Since our study is of the latter type, it cannot provide direct evidence about the validity of the stress hypothesis. Our findings of Chapter 6 do, however, cast some doubt on stress interpretations, for they indicate that purportedly stress-inducing job conditions do not have uniformly deleterious psychological consequences—as would be implied by many stress interpretations (but see LaRocco, House, and French, 1980). In any case, our findings suggest that although job conditions generally believed to produce stress may affect distress, they are not of any great importance for ideational flexibility or for self-directedness of orientation.

We conclude that what people do in their work directly affects their cognitive functioning, their values, their conceptions of self, and their orientations to the world around them. Hence, doing substantively complex work tends to increase one's respect for one's own capacities, one's valuation of self-direction, one's intellectuality (even in leisure-time pursuits), and one's sense that the problems one encounters are manageable. We see no need to posit that subjective feelings about the job necessarily play an intermediary role in this process; the structural imperatives of the job can directly affect all aspects of people's thinking and feeling. But, since our research does not rule out alternative interpretations of psychological process, our evidence is not definitive.

The Structure of Personality

When one considers how broad a range of orientations is encompassed in our measurement model of self-directedness and distress (Chapter 6), it is clear that these two underlying dimensions of orientation summarize a great amount of information about personality.[5] By adding ideational flexibility,

---

[5] In discussing the several facets of orientation, we have also divided them into two clusters, "self-conceptions" and "social orientations". We do not think of self-conceptions and social orientations as well-defined concepts. They are not dimensions that underlie the several facets of orientation but merely a division of those facets into two clusters. Moreover, the dividing line between the two is unclear (idea-conformity, for example, partaking of both). They are useful descriptive terms, rubrics that provide a convenient way of summarizing findings. Self-directedness and distress, by contrast, are fundamental dimensions of orientation, dimensions that underlie the many, more specific, facets of orientation that we have measured.

we increase the scope of our model of personality even further, thereby encompassing in three dimensions a parsimonious depiction of many important facets of personality.

The analyses of Chapters 6 and 7 attempt to portray the *structure* of the interrelationships of ideational flexibility, self-directedness of orientation, and distress. To some extent, these analyses succeed; certainly, they establish the centrality of self-directedness to this three-dimensional depiction of personality. Yet, the issue of whether ideational flexibility significantly affects self-directedness is left in doubt. Unquestionably, the model must be treated as provisional, pending replications. We also recognize that this conceptualization of personality is partial.[6] Our claim is simply that thinking of personality in terms of the interrelationship of these three dimensions has proved useful for our analyses of social stratification, job, and personality. Even though our conceptualization of personality was developed for this particular theoretical purpose, it may have utility for other analytic purposes as well.

In this depiction of personality, self-directedness is clearly of central theoretical—and, as it turns out, empirical—importance.[7] Ideational flexibility follows close behind. Distress has been of less interest, mainly because distress is only modestly related to social-stratification position (a point confirmed in an as-yet unpublished analysis of several bodies of data by Ronald Kessler; see also Kessler and Cleary, 1980).[8] Still, distress does affect self-directedness, even if only modestly. Moreover, although tangential to the main thrust of our interpretation, the findings (Chapter 6) that op-

---

[6] In particular, our model makes no attempt to portray the relationship between *values* and *orientations,* treating self-directedness of orientation as a proxy also for self-directed values. As a first approximation, this is not unreasonable, since (as we have seen in Chapter 7) self-directed values and self-directedness of orientation are mutually reinforcing. A more refined model, though, should clearly establish the place of values in an overall depiction of personality.

[7] "Self-directedness of orientation" is a cumbersome expression, but we have been unable to find a simpler term that does full justice to the range of phenomena encompassed. Antonovsky's (1979) term, "sense of coherence," is a possible alternative, but it does imply a somewhat different emphasis. Another possible alternative, widely employed in the psychological research literature, is "locus of control," i.e., feeling in control over one's life versus feeling subject to external control (see Rotter, 1966). This concept may have a narrower focus than ours. In any case, the "locus of control" concept has been employed in some studies of job conditions and psychological functioning (see Andrisani and Nestel, 1976; Andrisani and Abeles, 1976; Spector, 1982), with findings altogether consonant with ours. There are also characterizations of personality development that, although not entirely equivalent to our conceptualization, are in important respects analogous. The stage-theories of moral development of Piaget (N.D.), Kohlberg (1976; Kohlberg and Gilligan, 1972), and Habermas (1979) certainly have much in common with what we mean by conformity to external authority versus self-directedness, even though ours is decidedly not a stage-theory. Pertinent, too, is Bernstein's (1971, 1973) sociolinguistic distinction between the "restricted code" of the working class and the "elaborated code" of the middle class.

[8] Parenthetically, we do not see distress as necessarily more pertinent to mental disorder than is self-directedness. On the contrary, we think that a conformist orientation may be of crucial importance in the etiology of one major type of mental disorder—schizophrenia (on this, see Kohn, 1972, 1973, 1976c).

pressive job conditions lead to distress and that, more generally, conditions of work characteristic of employment in the secondary labor market are productive of distress, are certainly in accord with our general interpretation.

THE EFFECTS OF EDUCATION ON PSYCHOLOGICAL FUNCTIONING

There are two distinct questions involved in appraising the effects of education on psychological functioning: To what extent (and how) does the effect of education on psychological functioning result from the role that education plays in job placement? To what extent (and how) does the educational experience itself affect psychological functioning?

Education's Role in Job Placement

It has become increasingly evident in the course of our research that some substantial portion of education's effects on ideational flexibility, values, and orientations is indirect, through education's role in job placement and hence as a determinant of job conditions. The very reason we had initially looked to such job conditions as substantive complexity, closeness of supervision, and routinization as possible keys to understanding the relationship of stratification to values and orientations is that "few other conditions of life are so closely bound up with education and with occupational position." In particular, education is a prime determinant of the substantive complexity of work; and substantive complexity, in turn, has an appreciable effect on psychological functioning. Education is crucial for the very job conditions that most strongly affect ideational functioning, values, and orientations; these indirect effects add greatly to whatever direct effects education may have.

Although our analyses clearly indicate that education is an important determinant of job conditions, they do not enable us to distinguish between education as job prerequisite in the sense of providing necessary intellectual skills and training, education as providing credentials for the job, and education as teaching values and forms of behavior appropriate to the job (see Meyer, 1977). That education has important indirect effects, through job placement, on ideational flexibility, values, and orientations seems reasonably certain; how education exercises these effects remains to be explained.

Nonoccupational Effects of Education

Since our analyses begin after adult respondents have completed their formal educations, we have had no way of assessing the effects of personality on educational attainment. We have therefore treated education as exercising unidirectional effects on psychological functioning. This specification undoubtedly exaggerates the magnitudes of these effects. Still, it is altogether implausible that what appear in these analyses to be the effects of education on psychological functioning could actually result entirely from personality affecting educational attainment; education must have *some* direct effect on personality. Admittedly, though, this is an a priori argument; our analyses have been inconclusive as to the magnitudes of the direct effects of education on personality.

Even though our analyses of adults offer no trustworthy guide to assessing the magnitudes of effects, they do tell us something about the processes by which education affects personality. In particular, the analyses of Chapter 7 refute our earlier hypothesis that education's effects on values and orientations result in substantial part from education's affecting intellectual flexibility, which in turn affects values and orientations. We find, instead, that education directly affects values and orientations and that, furthermore, some of education's effect on ideational flexibility is via education leading to a more self-directed orientation. Insofar as these analyses lead to our rejecting a faulty hypothesis, they clarify the process. The question remains, though, what is there about the educational experience that affects values and orientations? Analyses of adults, who have completed their formal educations, shed little light on this question. To learn whether and how education affects personality development, one must turn to students—as we are now doing. Even in studying students, we are not able to account for personality development before formal schooling began. Still, it is possible to assess the effects of education on the further development of personality.

Our analyses of adults have necessarily focused on educational attainment—number of years of formal schooling. In moving from adults who have completed their formal educations to children and young adults who are in process of being educated, we shift the focus from past educational attainment to the ongoing educational experience. There is a definite link between educational level and the nature of educational experience: As children and young adults move through the school system, they have increasing opportunity to be self-directed in their schoolwork (Bowles and Gintis, 1976). We hypothesize that the experience of "educational self-direction" leads to greater ideational flexibility, increased valuation of self-direction, and a self-directed orientation to self and society. In a sense, our learning-generalization model of how job affects personality has treated "work" as a socializing experience. Now we turn the tables, applying the same interpretive model to education that we have heretofore applied to occupation.[9] Ours is a socialization model of education, albeit one in which

---

[9] Two important studies, by Rosenbaum (1976) and by Bowles and Gintis (1976), adopt a similar interpretive strategy. Both investigations imaginatively extrapolate from our analyses of the processes by which occupational conditions affect values and orientations, applying the same analytic logic to the educational sphere.

the main vehicle of socialization is the experience of learning rather than the content of what is taught. The underlying assumption is that self-direction is as important in young people's school experiences as in older people's job experiences.

In our ongoing research, Karen A. Miller, Kohn, and Schooler (1982) are testing the hypothesis that educational self-direction affects personality development. The data are provided by interviews with children of the men in our follow-up subsample. The men had been asked in the baseline survey about values vis-a-vis children in the age-range, three to fifteen years, who by the time of the follow-up survey were thirteen to twenty-five years old—many of them junior high, high school, or college students. In our interviews, we asked the students a series of questions about their current educational experiences, questions that provide the basis for an index of "educational self-direction". We think of educational self-direction as a direct analogue to occupational self-direction, defining it to mean the use of initiative, thought, and independent judgment in schoolwork. The analogy extends even further, for we think of two major conditions as facilitative of educational self-direction: substantively complex schoolwork and freedom from close supervision (by teachers, whom we treat as the equivalent of supervisors in paid employment). The analogy works well. It proves possible to develop a thoroughly satisfactory measurement model of educational self-direction, one that is applicable to both high school and college students.

In doing causal analyses of children's educational self-direction and psychological functioning, we face the same problem we faced earlier, in analyses of women—the lack of longitudinal data. Here, however, we have one tremendous advantage: We have information about the psychological functioning of the students' parents. This means that, in examining the relationship between educational self-direction and any facet of psychological functioning, we are able to statistically control both mothers' and fathers' levels of functioning. We have thus far developed one provisional model—a model of the reciprocal effects of educational self-direction and ideational flexibility, taking into account parents' ideational flexibility, age and school grade of the child, the extent to which the child's school courses are compulsory or elective, and pertinent social characteristics of the child and the family. The model shows educational self-direction—in particular, the substantive complexity of schoolwork—to have a sizeable effect on ideational flexibility.

These initial results provide encouraging support for the belief that our interpretation of job and personality can be applied to school and personality. Much more remains to be done in this analysis, though, particularly in extending the model to values and orientations.

THE INTERGENERATIONAL TRANSMISSION OF VALUES

Our emphasis throughout has been on the processes by which people's conditions of life—job conditions in particular—affect their values, conceptions of reality, and cognitive functioning. It is a logical extrapolation from our thesis to hypothesize that the psychological effects of job conditions extend not only to people immediately affected by those conditions but also, by processes of value-transmission, to others, particularly to family members.[10]

A primary focus of many analyses in this book has been the effects of social stratification and job conditions on parents' values. Although we have elsewhere considered also the relationship of parental values to child-rearing practices (see Kohn, 1969: Chapters 6 and 7; Kohn, 1977 and 1981b), in this book we have not looked beyond parental values, as if the very fact of parents' valuing self-direction or conformity to external authority necessarily implied that parents would behave appropriately to their values and even that parents' values would be successfully transmitted to their children. We do not so believe.[11]

We see parent-to-child value transmission as embedded in a larger social context, a context that is to some extent deliberately designed by parents but is to some extent beyond parental control, often beyond parental knowledge. Moreover, while it is true that parents and children experience largely similar social environments, it is also true that their environments diverge in significant ways. Not only do parents and children spend much of their time doing different things in different social institutions, but, as Rosenberg (1979) showed, the same social-structural conditions may impinge on adults and children in decidedly different ways. It is necessary to see how parent-

---

[10] Our focal interest in this discussion is parent-child value-transmission. Also pertinent is husband-wife value-transmission. It is an open question whether (and if so, how) men's job conditions affect their wives' values and orientations, and whether (and if so, how) women's job conditions affect their husbands' values and orientations. An analysis of data from Turin, Italy (Kohn, 1969:149-151) found that men's job conditions are meaningfully related to their wives' values for children. But that study gave no information about the processes involved, nor could it examine the corresponding effects of women's job experiences on their husbands' values. The parallel interviews with husbands and wives in the follow-up study may enable us to do both. It is not certain, though, whether such an analysis is feasible without longitudinal data for both husbands and wives.

[11] There is, in fact, precious little evidence that parents and children do have similar values (Furstenberg, 1971; Bengtson, 1975; Troll and Bengtson, 1979). What positive evidence there is concerns mainly political orientations, religious beliefs, and "life styles", not values as such or even general orientations to social reality. Studies of values have consistently found rather modest levels of agreement—correlations of no more than .15 to .25—between parents and children (Clausen, 1974; Bengtson, 1975; Skvoretz and Kheoruenromne, 1979; Gecas, 1980; Nowak, 1981). Since these studies do not take unreliability of measurement into account, it would be unwise to place great reliance on the precise magnitudes of the correlations found. In any case, the evidence, though far from definitive, certainly raises doubts about the extent of parent-to-child value transmission.

to-child value transmission fits into a much more general process whereby a child's conditions of life, both those that are intentionally and those that are inadvertently imposed by parents, affect that child's values (Kerckhoff, 1976). Rather than assuming a high correspondence between parents' and children's values, we should treat the degree of correspondence as problematic, in part a function of social-structural conditions.

The transmission of values in the family is a much more complex process than has generally been realized. Even calling the problem one of "transmitting" values may be so great an oversimplification as to be a misnomer. The transmission of values in the family is but one part, albeit a crucial part, of a much more general process by which children's conditions of life at home and in school, as well as their direct and vicarious experiences of the larger social world, come to shape their values. (For a provisional model of this process, see Kohn, in press.) In our further research, we intend to examine this process in some detail.[12] The data collected in the interviews with respondents' children in the follow-up study should provide the materials with which to refine and, to some degree, test a general model of the intergenerational value-transmission process.

THE MODIFICATION OF JOB CONDITIONS

Our analyses have dealt with job conditions as they are experienced by a representative sample of the civilian work force. We have neither examined the historical processes that led to those conditions nor have we tried to change job conditions through experimental manipulation. Our data bear on these issues only insofar as they suggest that the effects of psychological functioning on job conditions are predominantly lagged rather than contemporaneous—implying that job conditions are not readily modified. Workers change their conditions of work either by changing jobs or by a gradual process of modifying the conditions under which they work. This, of course, says nothing about the ease or difficulty of institutional changes in job conditions. That issue cannot be addressed with our data. Yet, it is incumbent on us to comment on it, if only to prevent others from too quickly extrapolating from our findings to prescriptions for social change.

The Historical Process

In one sense, the historical processes by which the job structure of the present United States economy developed are irrelevant to whether it is pos-

---

[12] In the course of that analysis, we intend also to fill an obviously important gap in the empirical analyses reported in this book—an examination of the relationships of working mothers' social-stratification positions and job conditions to their values for children. (Pertinent to the measurement of working mothers' stratification positions is Schoenbach, 1982.)

sible to change conditions of work by deliberate design. Yet, knowledge of the historical processes might provide insight into what forces would facilitate and what forces would impede attempts to change job conditions. Unfortunately, the historical record is not at all clear. It has been argued that the main trend of the past 50 years has been ever-increasing complexity of work, a result of ever-increasing technological requirements (see Blauner, 1964; see also Kohn, 1969:193-194). This reading of history sees the economy as having required an increasingly educated work force and as having had less and less need for semi-skilled and unskilled workers capable of doing only routinized tasks. Another reading of the same evidence is that there has been a relentless process of breaking jobs down into simple components, not because this necessarily made for a more efficient productive process, but because it enabled management to gain control over workers (see Braverman, 1974; Goldman and Van Houten, 1980a,b; Carchedi, 1975a,b).

Our own data are, of course, irrelevant to this discussion; even our finding that bureaucratized firms and organizations offer their employees substantively more complex work than do less bureaucratized firms and organizations says nothing about whether or not bureaucratized firms and organizations would offer even more complex work if those in control were not motivated to keep the work as simple as technology permits. Undoubtedly, contradictory processes have operated and continue to operate (see Wallace and Kalleberg, 1982); we are not here able to assess the partial and conflicting evidence as to which process has predominated. For our immediate purposes, it is sufficient to note that any effort to change job structure may require contending not only with the technological requirements of the work, but also with political and economic constraints.

Modifying Job Conditions

It seems a reasonable extrapolation from our findings, that deliberately instituted change in pivotal occupational conditions would actually affect people's values, orientations, and intellectual functioning. But would it? Would alienation, for example, be alleviated by occupational rearrangements, by worker participation in "management" decisions, or by the organization of work teams? We should not necessarily expect dramatic changes in job conditions to bring about dramatic changes in personality. On the other hand, our findings suggest that even small changes in job conditions may have small but enduring—and therefore, in the long run, important—psychological consequences.

Although experiments in the restructuring of work are being conducted in several countries, we know of none that adequately assesses the consequences of changes in job conditions for the psychological functioning of affected workers (see Berg, et al., 1978). Some experiments seem not even to recognize that the most important work conditions are embedded in larger social and economic structures. Other experiments—perhaps most—deal only with job conditions that we see as having secondary or even trivial importance for psychological functioning. Our findings imply that unless experiments give workers meaningful opportunities to exercise occupational self-direction, the experiments will have little effect on workers' off-the-job psychological functioning, least of all on their ideational flexibility and self-directedness of orientation. On the other hand, we would expect experiments that do increase workers' control over central conditions of work to have a substantial psychological impact (see Kahn, 1975). One important question is how large a measure of individual control, as against a share in group decision-making, is required for a worker to have sufficient command over his essential occupational conditions that it really matter.

An even more critical issue may be whether job conditions can be substantially modified, not just as an experiment but as a regular practice, in such a way as to increase workers' opportunities for occupational self-direction (see Berg, et al., 1978; Cole, 1979). If so, can this be done within the structure of a capitalist enterprise or does it require worker ownership of the firm or even worker control over the means of production generally? For that matter, is substantial modification of job conditions possible even under conditions of worker ownership? Despite considerable research and much discussion of the issues, the answers to these questions are largely unknown. The evidence about worker-owned companies within a capitalist economy is equivocal (see Stern and Whyte, 1981), the general finding being that no real effort has been made in most such firms to change job structure. Nor is the evidence from socialist countries at all clear. The efforts to change job structure in Yugoslavia (see Denitch, 1976) are well known, but it is far from certain how much change has actually occurred in job conditions, per se. As for the socialist countries of Eastern Europe, their modal form of industrial organization seems to be as hierarchical as is that of most firms and organizations in the United States.

In short, we know of no answers to the questions, whether and, if so, how it is possible to modify the structural imperatives of the job. That it is desirable to do so seems unequivocal: It would be difficult to deny that increasing workers' opportunities for occupational self-direction would have beneficial consequences. Translating this eminently desirable goal into a plan for social change seems to us, though, to be an immensely difficult task.

Appendices

A

Methods of the 1964 Cross-Sectional Survey and of the 1974 Follow-Up Survey

THE 1964 CROSS-SECTIONAL SURVEY

Sample Selection

The sample employed in the 1964 survey is an area probability sample of 3101 men. (For information about the sampling method used, see Sudman and Feldman, 1965.) These men are representative of all men in the United States, 16 years of age or older, who were at that time employed in civilian occupations at least 25 hours a week. Because our focus of inquiry is job conditions, and because the experiences of unemployment might overshadow the experiences of past employment (see Bakke, 1940), we excluded men not currently employed. We also excluded men in the military, since the problems both of sampling and of inquiry seemed too formidable to make their inclusion worthwhile. We excluded women, because their inclusion would have required a much larger sample. We did not exclude any men on grounds of race, language (a few men were interviewed in languages other than English), or any other basis.

In interviewing fathers, we wanted to direct the questions about values and parent-child relationships to one specific child, so chosen as to insure an unbiased selection and an even distribution of ages. The mechanism for doing this was to require the interviewer to list all children aged 3 through

15 who were living at home, and then to focus all questions about parent-child relationships on one particular child, selecting that child through a random-sampling procedure.

Development of the Interview Schedule and Administration of the Survey

If ever investigators had the opportunity for unhurried planning, we did. We spent many months drawing up and refining lists of dimensions of occupation and of psychological functioning; reading all sorts of relevant, tangential, and barely relevant materials; doing informal, unstructured interviews; and preparing long lists of questions to try out on respondents. The intent was to begin with a comprehensive, even if horrendously long, interview schedule and then to pare it down ruthlessly.

We carried out the early rounds of unstructured and, later, structured pretest interviews in the Washington-Baltimore area. The final pretests were conducted by the National Opinion Research Center (NORC), which carried out 100 interviews—six in each of ten widely separated places, with an emphasis on small town and rural areas, plus twenty in Chicago and twenty in New York City, with an emphasis in these cities on less educated respondents. (The intent in concentrating on small town, rural, and less educated urban respondents was to subject the interview schedule to the most demanding tests.) We received detailed reports about all the interviews and met with the interviewers from Chicago and New York to discuss each question in the interview schedule. The batteries of items designed to measure the several aspects of self-conception and social orientation were tested for their scale characteristics, other items for their clarity of meaning and distributional characteristics. The schedule was revised and shortened once again, and then it was ready for use in the survey proper.

The survey was carried out by the field staff of NORC during the spring and summer of 1964. The completed interview schedules were then turned over to us for coding and analysis.

Rather than include the entire questionnaire in this Appendix, we have included the pertinent questions in the text (or in footnotes) at the places where indices of major concepts are developed. For the entire questionnaire, see Kohn, 1969, Appendix C.

Nonrespondents

Overall, 76 percent of the men selected for the sample gave reasonably complete interviews. Considering that it is more difficult to get employed men than most other people to participate in a survey, and that the interviewers were asking them to undertake an especially long interview (the median interview took two and a half hours), we think this rate is acceptable. But from the point of view of generalizing to the population at large, it is important to examine the characteristics of the nonrespondents.

First, a general classification of the reasons for the losses (Table A.1): Two-thirds of the nonrespondents simply refused to be interviewed; most of the others were not available for one reason or another—in some cases because of illness or other incapacity, in others because the interviewer could not find them at home at a time convenient for an interview. In only a minute proportion of cases was an interview broken off, once begun.

Loss of respondents assumes particular importance if it occurs disproportionately in delimited segments of the population. For our research, it is especially important that nonrespondents not be concentrated in a particular social stratum. A complete analysis of this issue is not possible here, for we lack data on the socioeconomic status of many of the nonrespondents. One important source of information, however, is available to us: Most medium-sized cities have had city directories that contain tolerably accurate occupational data. For those cities, it was possible to determine whether or not the nonrespondents differ in occupational level from the men who granted interviews.

We find little difference overall (Table A.2). The one exception is that the nonresponse rate for small business owners is somewhat higher than that for other men, but this difference is probably an artifact of city directories having more complete coverage of such men. We conclude that, for cities where data are available, nonresponse rates do not seem to vary appreciably by occupational level. Furthermore, for those cases where data about occupational level are available, there is no relationship between the occupational levels of nonrespondents and their reasons for not granting an interview. Nor is there any relationship between nonrespondents' occupational levels and the interviewers' characterizations of their apparent atti-

Table A.1. TYPES OF NONRESPONSE

	Number	Proportion of Original Sample
Completed interviews	3101	.76
Incomplete or lost interviews:		
Refusals	650	.16
Breakoff	46	.01
Temporarily unavailable (ill, hospitalized, etc.)	97	.02
Never at home, on repeated visits	118	.03
Interviewer made contact, but respondent not at home on subsequent visits	41	.01
Other (or inadequate data)	52	.01
Total	4105	1.00

The refusals through other (or inadequate data) rows are bracketed together as .24.

Table A.2. RATES OF NONRESPONSE, BY OCCUPATION LEVEL
(FOR CITIES HAVING CITY DIRECTORIES)

Hollingshead Occupational Rating	Original Sample Size	Number of Non-respondents	Rate of Non-response
Higher executives, professionals, etc.	68	12	.18
Business managers in large concerns, proprietors of medium-size businesses, etc.	60	9	.15
Small business owners, semi-professionals, etc.	196	61	.31
Clerical and sales workers, technicians, owners of little businesses, etc.	136	18	.13
Skilled workers	231	56	.24
Semiskilled workers	198	38	.19
Unskilled workers	77	9	.12
Total for these cities	966	203	.21

tudes. Rates and types of nonresponse do not seem to be appreciably related to social-stratification position.

There is, however, one social characteristic that made a notable difference in the rate of nonresponse—the size of the community in which men live. These rates are directly proportional to size of community (Table A.3). Nothing in the data explains this phenomenon. The simple fact is that the larger the community, the more difficult it was to get employed men to grant long interviews.

These analyses suggest that our final sample is reasonably representative of the population to which we generalize, except insofar as it underrepresents larger cities and overrepresents smaller communities. Further comparisons of the characteristics of the 3101 men interviewed in the 1964 survey with the characteristics of employed males enumerated in the 1960 decennial Census indicate that the sample is, in fact, closely comparable to the population of employed men. There are only two types of discrepancy between the characteristics of the sample and those of employed males generally: (1) As was shown by the analysis of nonrespondents, the sample underrepresents men in the largest metropolitan areas. (2) Our selection criteria imposed certain limitations, i.e., that the respondents be at least sixteen years old, be currently employed, and be employed at least twenty-five hours per week. Differences between these criteria and the Census definition of "employed males" are reflected in the findings that our sample is somewhat older and better educated than are employed males generally, with a larger proportion married and a smaller proportion at the very bottom of the income range. Aside from differences in criteria and the sample bias against metropolitan areas, though, the sample matches the Census data quite closely. The sample can thus be taken to be adequately representative of the population to which we generalize.

Table A.3. RATES OF NONRESPONSE, BY SIZE OF COMMUNITY

	Original Sample Size	Number of Non-respondents	Rate of Non-response
Metropolitan areas of 2 million population or more	1055	354	.34
Other metropolitan areas	1672	418	.25
Nonmetropolitan counties containing a city of at least 10,000 people	599	115	.19
Nonmetropolitan counties with no city of at least 10,000 people	771	109	.14
(Not classifiable)	8	8	
Total	4105	1004	

THE 1974 FOLLOW-UP STUDY

The men chosen for the follow-up study were a representative subsample of the 2553 men in the original sample who were less than 55 years old at the time of the initial study and thus would be less than 65 years old when reinterviewed. The primary reason for the age-restriction was that a large proportion of the older men would be retired, making them inappropriate for the main thrust of the inquiry—assessing the reciprocal effects of ongoing occupational experience and psychological functioning. Excluding the older men also has the desirable consequence of increasing the proportion of men who had children about whom we inquired in the original study.

Wherever a selected man was married at the time of the follow-up interview, we attempted to interview his wife. We also attempted to interview one child in each family, the one about whom questions about parental values and child-rearing practices had been asked in the 1964 survey. Since the children were three to fifteen years old in 1964, their age range, ten years later, was thirteen through twenty-five. Our intent was to try to interview these children wherever they lived, wherever they were in their educational, occupational, and family careers.

Generalizability of the Subsample

NORC succeeded in interviewing 78 percent of the men who had been randomly selected for the follow-up study, 687 men in all. We assess the generalizability of this subsample by two types of analysis.

The first type of analysis involves systematic comparison of the social and psychological characteristics of the men who were reinterviewed to the characteristics of the men who were randomly excepted from the follow-up study, who constitute a representative subsample of the overall sample and thus are an appropriate comparison group. The differences between the two subsamples are few and small in magnitude: The men who were reinterviewed were, as of the time of the original interviews, a little more intellectually flexible, somewhat more trustful, slightly lower in self-confidence, and somewhat more "liberal" in their religious backgrounds than were those in the comparison group. But the two groups do not differ significantly in most of the characteristics important to our analyses—e.g., education, social-stratification position, major occupational characteristics, age, and even urbanness.

Our second method of assessing the representativeness of the follow-up sample is to repeat the major substantive analyses of Chapters 1–4, particularly those of Chapters 1 and 3, again using the 1964 data, but this time limiting the analyses to those men whom we succeeded in reinterviewing in 1974. We have repeated all the principal analyses of the relationships among social stratification, occupational conditions, and psychological functioning. The smaller size of the subsample means that several secondary avenues cannot be explored and that some findings are no longer statistically significant. But the main findings hold up uniformly well. Thus, we can proceed to analyze the longitudinal data with confidence that whatever we find can be generalized to the larger population of employed men in the United States.

Classifications of the
Complexity of Work

The classifications of the complexity of men's work with data, with people, and with things are based on those of the *Dictionary of Occupational Titles* (United States Dept. of Labor, 3rd edition, 1965, Vol. 2: 649–650).[1] The classification of the overall complexity of the job is new.

COMPLEXITY OF WORK WITH DATA

Data are defined as information, knowledge, and conceptions obtained by observation, investigation, interpretation, visualization, mental creation.

---

[1] Aside from elaborating on the *Dictionary's* code for the complexity of work with data (by adding a category for "reading instructions"), we have adopted its classificatory system virtually intact. There are some differences, however, in how we use the system, principally in that: (1) We assess supervision more attentively (the *Dictionary* sometimes classifies supervisors on the basis of what their subordinates do). (2) We have greater flexibility in our ratings of multiple job-functions, whereas the *Dictionary* sometimes has to limit its ratings to one function. (3) Our judgments of the degree of complexity in men's work with data are more stringent than are some of those used in the *Dictionary*. (4) We assign a rating to things in many instances where the *Dictionary* describes dealings with things but evaluates them as "nonsignificant." (5) We emphasize a relationship to people in the case of consultants and teachers, where the *Dictionary* sometimes rates them solely on the basis of their consultation or teaching. These differences are relatively minor; they result mainly from the difference between our research purposes and the employment counseling purposes for which the *Dictionary* is designed.

Although the third edition of the *Dictionary* appeared long after our survey was undertaken, our plans were based on it, thanks to the foreknowledge and advice provided by Sidney Fine, the originator of this important classificatory system.

Written data take the form of numbers, words, symbols; other data are ideas, concepts, oral verbalization.

1. *No Significant Relationship.*
2. *Reading Instructions:* Following written instructions, generally of a simple and highly specific nature.
3. *Comparing:* Judging the readily observable functional, structural, or compositional characteristics (whether similar to or divergent from obvious standards) of data, people, or things.
4. *Copying:* Transcribing, entering, or posting data.
5. *Computing:* Performing arithmetic operations and reporting on and/or carrying out a prescribed action in relation to them. Does not include counting.
6. *Compiling:* Gathering, collating, or classifying information about data, people, or things. Reporting and/or carrying out a prescribed action in relation to the information is frequently involved. Applying routine standard tests to determine conformance to specifications. Reporting and/or carrying out prescribed actions to attain specifications called for by tests may also be involved. Examples are routine testing, checkout, and troubleshooting of circuits, mechanical units, and subsystems; drafting plans and blueprints from sketches; fabrication from blueprints; and scheduling events within known conditions. Does not involve fundamental changes of input and output.
7. *Analyzing:* Examining and evaluating data. Presenting alternative actions in relation to the evaluation is frequently involved. Examples are: evaluating items for purchase; exploring modifications and adaptations of existing designs and testing them; carrying out feasibility studies of revised inputs, including developing new tests or extending range of old ones.
8. *Coordinating:* Determining time, place, and sequence of operations or action to be taken on the basis of analysis of data; executing determinations and/or reporting on events. Deciding whether emerging performance and/or problems call for new goals, policies, or procedures.
9. *Synthesizing:* Integrating analyses of data to discover facts and/or develop knowledge, concepts, or interpretations. Conceiving new approaches to problems, including their restatement; discovering new facts and relationships; inventing new devices; creating original works of art; or reinterpreting existing information and ideas.

COMPLEXITY OF WORK WITH THINGS

Things are defined as inanimate objects as distinguished from human beings; substances or materials; machines, tools, equipment; products. A thing is tangible and has shape, form, and other physical characteristics.

1. *No Significant Relationship.*
2. *Handling:* Using body members, hand tools, and/or special devices to work, move, or carry objects or materials. Involves little or no latitude for judgment with regard to attainment of standards or in selecting appropriate tool, object, or material. Examples include situations that involve a small number of special tools obvious as to purpose, such as a broom, a special purpose end wrench, a grass shears, go/no-go gauges. Dimensional precision can vary from rough to fine, being built into the structure of the task(s).
3. *Feeding-Offbearing:* Inserting, throwing, dumping, or placing materials in or removing them from machines or equipment which are automatic or tended or operated by other workers. Repetitive, short duration work actions are usually paced by the machine. The standards depend on the existence of appropriate controls in the machine.
4. *Tending:* Starting, stopping, and observing the functioning of machines and equipment. Involves adjusting materials or controls of the machine, such as changing guides, adjusting timers and temperature gauges, turning valves to allow flow of materials, and flipping switches in response to lights. Little judgment is involved in making these adjustments.
5. *Manipulating:* Using body members, tools, or special devices to work, move, guide, or place objects or materials. Involves some latitude for judgment with regard to precision attained and selecting appropriate tool, object, or material, although this is readily manifest.
6. *Driving-Operating:* Starting, stopping, and controlling the actions of machines or equipment for which a course must be steered, or which must be guided, in order to fabricate, process, and/or move things or people. Involves such activities as observing gauges and dials; estimating distances and determining speed and direction of other objects; turning cranks and wheels; pushing clutches or brakes; and pushing or pulling gear lifts or levers. Includes such machines as cranes, conveyor systems, tractors, furnace charging machines, paving machines, and hoisting machines. Excludes manually powered machines such as handtrucks and dollies, and power assisted machines such as electric wheelbarrows and handtrucks.
7. *Operating-Controlling:* Starting, stopping, controlling, and adjusting the progress of machines or equipment designed to fabricate and/or process objects or materials. Operating machines involves setting up the machine and adjusting the machine or material as the work progresses. Controlling equipment involves observing gauges, dials, etc., and turning valves and other devices to control such factors as temperature, pressure, flow of liquids, speed of pumps, and reactions of materials. Several variables are involved and adjustment is more frequent than in tending.

8. *Precision Working:* Using body members and/or tools or work aids to work, move, guide, or place objects or materials in situations where ultimate responsibility for the attainment of standards occurs and selection of appropriate tools, objects, or materials, and the adjustment of the tool to the task require exercise of considerable judgment.

9. *Setting Up:* Adjusting machines or equipment by replacing or altering tools, jigs, fixtures, and attachments to prepare them to perform their functions, change their performance, or restore their proper functioning if they break down. Workers who set up one or a number of machines for other workers or who set up and personally operate a variety of machines are included here.

COMPLEXITY OF WORK WITH PEOPLE

People are defined as human beings; also animals dealt with on an individual basis as if they were human.

1. *No Significant Relationship.*

2. *Serving:* Attending to the needs or request of people or animals or the expressed or implicit wishes of people. Immediate response is involved.

3. *Receiving Instructions-Helping:* Attending to the work assignment instructions or orders of supervisors. (No immediate response required unless clarification of instruction or order is needed.)

4. *Speaking-Signaling:* Talking with and/or signaling people to convey or exchange information. Includes giving assignments and/or directions to helpers or assistants.

5. *Persuading:* Influencing others in favor of a product, service, or point of view.

6. *Diverting:* Amusing others.

7. *Supervising:* Determining or interpreting work procedures for a group of workers, assigning specific duties to them, maintaining harmonious relations among them, and promoting efficiency.

8. *Instructing:* Teaching subject matter to others, or training others (including animals) through explanation, demonstration, and supervised practice; or making recommendations on the basis of technical disciplines.

9. *Negotiating:* Exchanging ideas, information, and opinions with others to formulate policies and programs and/or arrive jointly at decisions, conclusions, or solutions.

10. *Mentoring:* Dealing with individuals in terms of their total personality in order to advise, counsel, and/or guide them with regard to

problems that may be resolved by legal, scientific, clinical, spiritual, and/or other professional principles.

OVERALL COMPLEXITY OF THE JOB

1. Not at all complex. Altogether routine and takes no thought —individual can daydream and still perform his work satisfactorily.
2. Minimal thought. A certain degree of attention is required; for example, to keep from getting hands caught in machinery, to be certain to pick up the right pieces, to remember where something was put. But no planning, scheduling, calculating, or prolonged thought is required.
3. Simple measurements, scheduling of activities, or rudimentary planning may be required, but most or all considerations are readily apparent and predictable and not very many considerations are needed for any decision.
4. Problem-solving, involving relatively simple remedies for unforeseen circumstances and/or the application of some practical or technical knowledge (not theoretical, but the type known to an experienced practitioner of the trade) to an atypical situation. Does *not* extend to very complex problems requiring much originality, theoretical knowledge, or foresight.
5. Problem-solving, involving the necessity of dealing with people or other relatively unpredictable or obstinate things—animals, for example, or fairly complex machines—where a moderate degreee of empathy, insight, or ingenuity is needed to effect small to moderate changes in outcome. Routine selling and auto repairing would fit here.
6. Complex problem-solving, requiring a substantial but not an exceptional degree of insight, originality, or thought. This may involve many variables, but the relationships among the variables will not be extremely complex.
7. The setting up of a complex system of analysis and/or synthesis in which little is fixed beforehand, many variables are involved, their relationships are complex, and outcomes are hard to predict.

C | Longitudinal Measurement Models for Men

Self-conception and Social Orientation

The measurement models of the several facets of self-conception and social orientation are summarized in Table C.1. Those for authoritarian-conservatism, fatalism, morality, trustfulness, idea conformity, and anxiety are single-factor models; self-confidence and self-deprecation are combined into a two-factor model, since they are components of a larger concept, self-esteem. As can be seen in the ratios of chi-squares to degrees of freedom, all of the models fit the data reasonably well.

Parental Values

In developing a measurement model of parental values, we build on the exploratory factor analysis of fathers' values presented in Chapter 1, derived from fathers' partial ranking of thirteen characteristics in terms of their desirability for a child of the age and sex of a pre-selected child of their own. While the utility of this forced-choice method of ranking values has been repeatedly demonstrated (see Kohn and Schoenbach, 1980), the procedure does pose methodological problems.

The basic problem is that there is a built-in linear dependency of each of the values on the set of all the others. That is, if one knows how a parent rates any twelve of the characteristics, then (except in cases with incomplete answers or errors in coding) one can predict with absolute certainty how

Table C.1. MEASUREMENT MODELS OF SELF-CONCEPTION AND SOCIAL ORIENTATION

Concept/Indicators	Standardized Path from Concept to Indicator	
	1964	1974
Authoritarian conservatism ($\chi^2 = 120.98$, d.f. $= 111$, ratio $= 1.09$)		
The most important thing to teach children is absolute obedience to their parents.	.61	.68
Young people should not be allowed to read books that are likely to confuse them.	.50	.46
There are two kinds of people in the world: the weak and the strong.	.57	.62
People who question the old and accepted ways of doing things usually just end up causing trouble.	.51	.47
In this complicated world, the only way to know what to do is to rely on leaders and experts.	.58	.54
No decent man can respect a woman who has had sex relations before marriage.	.43	.51
Prison is too good for sex criminals; they should be publicly whipped or worse	.46	.50
Any good leader should be strict with people under him in order to gain their respect	.41	.54
It's wrong to do things differently from the way our forefathers did	.45	.52
Personally responsible standards of morality ($\chi^2 = 12.92$, d.f. $= 15$, ratio $= 0.86$)		
It's all right to do anything you want as long as you stay out of trouble ...	$-.59$	$-.64$
If something works, it doesn't matter whether it's right or wrong	$-.44$	$-.30$
It's all right to get around the law as long as you don't actually break it...	$-.58$	$-.61$
Do you believe that it's all right to do whatever the law allows, or are there some things that are wrong even if they are legal?	$-.33$	$-.26$
Trustfulness ($\chi^2 = 5.29$, d.f. $= 5$, ratio $= 1.06$)		
Do you think that most people can be trusted?	.51	.53
If you don't watch out, people will take advantage of you	$-.52$	$-.61$
Human nature is really cooperative	.20	.11
Self-esteem 2-factor model ($\chi^2 = 166.77$, d.f. $= 112$, ratio $= 1.49$)		
Self-confidence:		
I take a positive attitude toward myself.	.60	.71
I feel that I'm a person of worth, at least on an equal plane with others .	.47	.45
I am able to do most things as well as other people can	.43	.34
I generally have confidence that when I make plans I will be able to carry them out.	.54	.45
Self-deprecation:		
I wish I could have more respect for myself.	.76	.71
At times I think I am no good at all	.49	.51
I feel useless at times	.43	.40
I wish I could be as happy as others seem to be.	.58	.59
There are very few things about which I'm absolutely certain.	.29	.43
(Correlation: self-confidence/self-deprecation)	$(-.29)$	$(-.28)$
Fatalism ($\chi^2 = 2.15$, d.f. $= 5$, ratio $= 0.43$)		
When things go wrong for you, how often would you say it is your own fault?	$-.65$	$-.57$
To what extent would you say you are to blame for the problems you have—would you say that you are mostly to blame, partly to blame, or hardly at all to blame?	$-.59$	$-.70$

Table C.1.   (*continued*)

Concept/Indicators	Standardized Path from Concept to Indicator	
	1964	1974
Do you feel that most of the things that happen to you are the result of your own decisions or of things over which you have no control?................	−.37	−.38
Anxiety (χ^2=213.94, d.f.=159, ratio=1.35)		
How often do you feel that you are about to go to pieces?	.55	.58
How often do you feel downcast and dejected?	.68	.68
How frequently do you find yourself anxious and worrying about something?	.49	.47
How often do you feel uneasy about something without knowing why?....	.45	.50
How often do you feel so restless that you cannot sit still?..............	.47	.39
How often do you find that you can't get rid of some thought or idea that keeps running through your mind?..	.41	.44
How often do you feel bored with everything?.......................	.58	.57
How often do you feel powerless to get what you want out of life?.......	.54	.52
How often do you feel guilty for having done something wrong?........	.36	.36
How often do you feel that the world just isn't very understandable?......	.48	.44
How often do you feel that there isn't much purpose to being alive?......	.45	.37
Idea-conformity (χ^2=15.43, d.f.=13, ratio=1.19)		
According to your general impression, how often do your ideas and opinions about important matters differ from those of your relatives?	−.69	−.64
How often do your ideas and opinions differ from those of your friends? ..	−.63	−.51
How about from those of other people with your religious background? ...	−.50	−.44
Those of most people in the country?	−.68	−.35

Notes:

1. A high score on the indicator generally implies agreement or frequent occurrence; where alternatives are posed, the first alternative is scored high.
2. In all models, the residual of each 1964 indicator is allowed to correlate with the residual of that same indicator in 1974. In several of the models, some intra-time correlations of residuals are also allowed. (These correlations are not shown in the table.)
3. The overtime correlations (1964-1974) of the concepts are:

Authoritarian conservatism	.78
Standards of morality	.65
Trustfulness	.81
Self-confidence	.52
Self-deprecation..	.55
Fatalism	.61
Anxiety..	.53
Idea-conformity	.39

that parent rates the remaining characteristic. It follows that, if one knows a parent's ratings of fewer than twelve of the characteristics, one can predict his ratings of the others, while not perfectly, certainly better than if one did not have such information. (A corollary of this phenomenon is that the magnitudes of the correlations among value-choices are necessarily constrained.) The issue of linear dependency is particularly serious for a confirmatory factor-analytic model of parental values, because it affects the explication of the error structure of the model. We do not propose to deal with the problem in a fundamental way but to sidestep it. Our method is simply to leave some of the characteristics out of the variance-covariance matrix on which the model is based, thus markedly reducing even if not eliminating linear dependency among the remaining characteristics.[1]

To develop a longitudinal measurement model of parental values, we use the data from the subsample of the fathers, 399 in all, who were reinterviewed ten years after the original study. To minimize the problem of linear dependency, we deliberately exclude one pair of characteristics that are highly correlated with each other—self-control and being a good student—the first indicative of self-direction, the second of conformity to external authority. To further reduce the degree of linear dependency, we exclude other characteristics that prove not to be important indicators of the underlying factors. We retain eight characteristics that are particularly appropriate to younger children as indicators in the 1964 part of the model and seven characteristics that are particularly appropriate to older children as indicators in the 1974 part of the model.

Analyses of the data for 1964, when the children were three to fifteen years old, indicate that there are three principal underlying dimensions of valuation: self-direction versus conformity to external authority, maturity (age), and striving for success. Similar analyses of the data for 1974, by which time the children were thirteen to twenty-five years old, indicate that maturity (age) ceases to be an important dimension. One way to deal with this disparity would be to depict parental values as having three principal dimensions when the children are younger and two principal dimensions when they grow older. A comparable but simpler method, which we use here, is to partial child's age out of the variance-covariance matrix on which the confirmatory factor analysis is based and employ a two-factor schema in both parts of the model (see Figure C.1). Nothing is lost thereby, for the maturity dimension has no substantive interest. There is a small gain, in that the 1964 and 1974 parts of the model are fully equivalent. (It should be noted that partialling child's age out of the matrix affects only variations in values related to the thirteen-year span in children's ages at the time of each interview; it does not distort the reality of the entire sample of children becoming ten years older.)

---

[1] Jackson and Alwin (1980) have proposed an alternative method for analyzing "ipsative" data, i.e., data where scores for all respondents necessarily sum to the same constant. Their method uses the actual ipsative data to estimate an underlying nonipsative model that is assumed to exist. We question the tenability of this assumption for data about values, where choice is of the essence; the very concept, values, implies that measurement be ipsative. In any event, our analyses indicate that the two methods yield nearly identical results when the number of characteristics ranked by parents is more than a very few. Moreover, no one has yet figured out a way to apply the Jackson-Alwin method to a model that posits more than one underlying factor, as our model does.

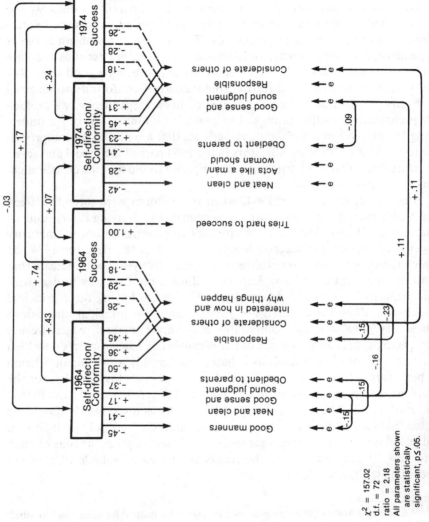

FIG. C.1. MEASUREMENT MODEL FOR PARENTAL VALUES

$\chi^2 = 157.02$
d.f. = 72
ratio = 2.18
All parameters shown
are statistically
significant, $p \le .05$.

For each characteristic included in both the 1964 and 1974 parts of the model, overtime correlations of the residuals of its 1964 and 1974 ratings are tested and retained where statistically significant. In addition, as Figure C.1 shows, there are several statistically significant intratime correlations of residuals. This explication of the error structure results in a good fit of model to data: a chi-square of 157.02, with 72 degrees of freedom, for a ratio of 2.18.

Values-for-Self

The original index of values-for-self, as is evident in Chapter 1, was less than satisfactory, for in modifying the questions about parental values to be appropriate to adults, we had provided the respondents only one characteristic indicative of conformity to external authority. In the follow-up survey, we therefore modified the question about values-for-self to include such characteristics as law-abiding, respectable, and able to keep out of trouble. With the 1964 data as a baseline, however inadequate they may be, and with the new set of characteristics as the basis for a follow-up measure, it proves possible to develop an overtime measurement model of values-for-self (see Figure C.2). This is a one-concept model, the concept being valuation of self-direction versus conformity to external authority. The 1974 portion of the model uses six indicators, two connoting self-direction and four connoting conformity to external authority. The 1964 portion of the model uses the two indicators that connote self-direction and the single indicator of conformity contained in those data. Despite the weakness of the 1964 portion of the model, the overall model appears to be reasonably satisfactory. The fit of model to data is quite good, with a chi-square of 19.10, at 15 degrees of freedom, for a ratio of 1.27. The ten-year overtime correlation of valuing self-direction versus conformity to external authority is .46, which, while not nearly as high as that for valuing self-direction versus conformity for one's children (.74), is at any rate within the range we find for the several facets of self-conception and social orientation (.39 to .81). Clearly, this is not as good a measurement model as it might have been had we asked better questions in 1964, but it is improved by the changes we made in question wording in the follow-up survey.

Alienation

The questions that comprise the 5 component dimensions of alienation are the same as those that comprise some of the dimensions of self-conception and social orientation. Two of the 5 are familiar facets of social orientation, albeit with new names: normlessness is simply another term for what we have called standards of morality, and cultural estrangement is nothing

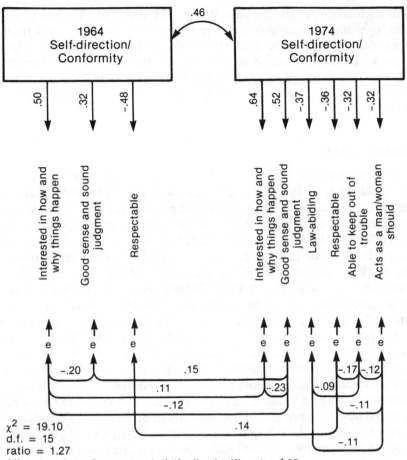

χ^2 = 19.10
d.f. = 15
ratio = 1.27
All parameters shown are statistically significant, p≤.05.

FIG. C.2. MEASUREMENT MODEL FOR VALUES FOR SELF

other than idea-conformity. We have only a single indicator of meaningless-ness, which we have heretofore used as an indicator of anxiety. Powerless-ness and self-estrangement are rather more distinct, but they do overlap with several of the facets of self-conception and social orientation in our other analyses. Thus, to add the 5 facets of alienation to any analysis of the several facets of self-conception and social orientation would be redundant. Yet, the concept, alienation, is of considerable theoretical interest, and can be thought of as another way of conceptualizing orientation, an alternative to the second-order concepts developed in Chapter 6, self-directedness and distress.

A second-order measurement model of alienation (see Figure C.3) has been developed by Bruce Roberts (1982), using our data and building on the

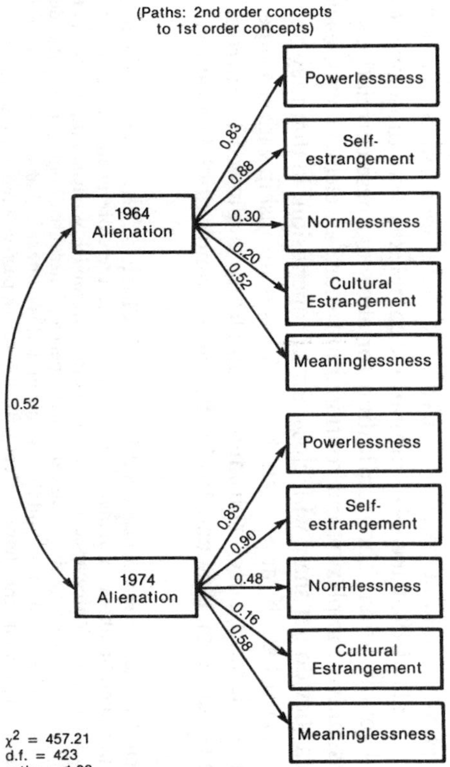

(Paths: 2nd order concepts to 1st order concepts)

(Paths: 1st order concepts to indicators)

Indicator	1964	1974
POWERLESSNESS		
Feel powerless to get what want out of life	.68	.62
Most things that happen result from own decisions	-.23	-.27
When make plans will be able to carry them out	-.26	-.11
SELF-ESTRANGEMENT		
Often feel bored with everything	.50	.56
At times think I'm no good at all	.51	.48
Take life as it comes/no goal	.20	.21
Isn't much purpose to being alive	.53	.46
NORMLESSNESS		
All right to get around law	.58	.59
All right to do whatever law allows	.32	.25
All right to do anything as long as stay out of trouble	.59	.65
If something works, doesn't matter whether right or wrong	.44	.30
CULTURAL ESTRANGEMENT		
Ideas differ from those of people of same religious background	.60	.58
Ideas differ from those of friends	.77	.64
Ideas differ from those of most people in country	.57	.30
Ideas differ from those of relatives	.56	.51
MEANINGLESSNESS		
World isn't understandable	1.00 (fixed)	1.00 (fixed)

1964 Alienation paths to 1st order concepts:
- Powerlessness: 0.83
- Self-estrangement: 0.88
- Normlessness: 0.30
- Cultural Estrangement: 0.20
- Meaninglessness: 0.52

1974 Alienation paths to 1st order concepts:
- Powerlessness: 0.83
- Self-estrangement: 0.90
- Normlessness: 0.48
- Cultural Estrangement: 0.16
- Meaninglessness: 0.58

Correlation between 1964 Alienation and 1974 Alienation: 0.52

$\chi^2 = 457.21$
d.f. = 423
ratio = 1.08
All parameters shown are statistically significant, $p \leq .05$.
For complete question wording, see table 4.1.

FIG. C.3. MEASUREMENT MODEL FOR ALIENATION
(Correlations among residuals not shown.)

analyses of Chapter 4. The model fits the data well, the chi-square being 457.21 with 423 degrees of freedom, for a ratio of 1.08. The overall concept is dominated by the two Marxian dimensions, powerlessness and self-estrangement, but meaninglessness, normlessness, and even cultural estrangement are significantly related to alienation.[2] The model thus provides an empirical tool with which to examine the relationships of social-stratification position and occupational self-direction with the general concept, alienation, not just with its theoretically diverse components.

Occupational Self-direction

The second-order measurement model of occupational self-direction is an extension of the first-order measurement model developed in Chapter 6. We now treat substantive complexity, routinization, and closeness of supervision as "indicators" of the second-order concept, occupational self-direction (see Figure C.4). In this model, we retain the pattern of correlations among the residuals of first-order indicators (for example, the overtime correlations of the residuals of all of the indicators and such intratime correlations as that between complexity of work with things and hours spent working with things). In addition, we include those overtime correlations of the residuals of first-order concepts that prove to be statisically significant, i.e., those for substantive complexity and routinization. Unless we allow other correlations of the residuals of first-order concepts, though, the standardized path from occupational self-direction to substantive complexity would be greater than 1.0. We therefore allow correlations of the residuals of 1964 and 1974 substantive complexity with those of 1964 and 1974 routinization. The justification for allowing these correlations is that substantive complexity and routinization share an element with each other that they do not share with closeness of supervision, in that they both concern the work itself rather than the worker's relationship with his supervisor. In addition, "early" substantive complexity is allowed to correlate with the residuals of 1964 and 1974 substantive complexity.[3] The rationale

---

[2] Meaninglessness was not included in the analyses of Chapter 4, because the data contain only a single question about meaninglessness, and we were therefore unable to construct a Guttman Scale. In developing a second-order measurement model of alienation, it is possible (even if not optimum) to use a single indicator as a "perfect" measure of one of the first-order dimensions. (By a perfect measure, all that we mean in this context is that we have no way of assessing its reliability and thus have to treat it as if it were a perfectly reliable index.)

[3] Alternatively, early substantive complexity could be left out of the second-order measurement model of occupational self-direction, with virtually no change to the rest of the model. Including early substantive complexity as a measurement parameter of combined measurement-causal models, though, strengthens the identification of models depicting the reciprocal relationships of occupational self-direction and values, both values-for-children and values-for-self.

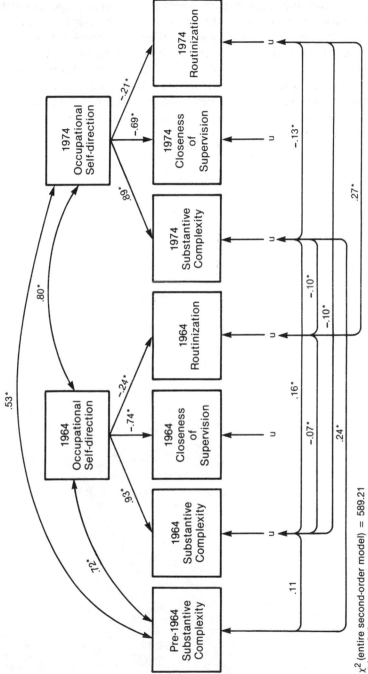

χ^2 (entire second-order model) = 589.21
d.f. = 249
ratio = 2.37
* = Statistically significant, $p \le .05$; other parameters are nonsignificant.

FIG. C.4. SECOND-ORDER MEASUREMENT MODEL FOR OCCUPATIONAL SELF-DIRECTION
(First-order parameters not shown.)

here is that early substantive complexity shares a distinctive component with the substantive complexity of later jobs, above and beyond their all partaking of occupational self-direction. Thus specified, the model fits the data reasonably well, the chi-square being 589.21, with 249 degrees of freedom, for a ratio of 2.37. As we should expect, the substantive complexity of work is the most powerful indicator of occupational self-direction, but closeness of supervision is also strongly reflective of occupational self-direction, and routinization—despite our using only a single indicator—is of more than trivial pertinence.

D | Measurement Models for Women

The measurement models for women are essentially cross-sectional analogues to the 1974 portions of the longitudinal measurement models for men. The models of occupational self-direction and intellectual flexibility are presented in Chapter 8, Figures 8.1 and 8.2, respectively. The models of intellectual demandingness of leisure-time activities, self-conceptions, social orientations, and occupational commitment are summarized in Table D.1. All these models fit the data reasonably well.

Table D.1. MEASUREMENT MODELS OF INTELLECTUAL
DEMANDINGNESS OF LEISURE-TIME ACTIVITIES,
SELF-CONCEPTIONS, SOCIAL ORIENTATIONS,
AND OCCUPATIONAL COMMITMENT, FOR WOMEN

Concept	Standardized Path: Concept to Indicator
Intellectual demandingness of leisure-time activities ($\chi^2 = 9.38$, df=8, ratio=1.17):	
Hours per day watch TV	−.12
Number of times in last six months went to plays, concerts, museums	.43
Number of books read in last six months	.32
Hours per month spent on hobbies	.16
Intellectual level of newspaper reading	.40
Intellectual level of magazine reading	.65
Correlated residual: books/hobbies	.19
Authoritarian conservatism (χ^2=62.76, df=27, ratio=2.32):	
The most important thing to teach children is absolute obedience to their parents	.76
Young people should not be allowed to read books that are likely to confuse them	.45
There are two kinds of people in the world: the weak and the strong	.61
People who question the old and accepted ways of doing things usually just end up causing trouble	.51
In this complicated world, the only way to know what to do is to rely on leaders and experts	.54
No decent man can respect a woman who has had sex relations before marriage	.56
Prison is too good for sex criminals; they should be publicly whipped or worse	.46
Any good leader should be strict with people under him in order to gain their respect	.51
It's wrong to do things differently from the way our forefathers did	.52
Personally responsible standards of morality (χ^2=5.92, df=2, ratio=2.96):	
It's all right to do anything you want as long as you stay out of trouble	−.73
If something works, it doesn't matter whether it's right or wrong	−.40
It's all right to get around the law as long as you don't actually break it	−.58
Do you believe that it's all right to do whatever the law allows, or are there some things that are wrong even if they are legal?	−.21
Receptivity to change (see note):	
Are you generally one of the first people to try out something new or do you wait until you see how it's worked out for other people?	.34
Are you the sort of person who takes life as it comes or are you working toward some definite goal?	−.28
It generally works out best to keep on doing things the way they have been done before	−.63
Self-esteem 2-factor model (χ^2=43.82, df=26, ratio=1.69):	
Self-confidence:	
I take a positive attitude toward myself	.63
I feel that I'm a person of worth, at least on an equal plane with others	.55
I am able to do most things as well as other people can	.44
I generally have confidence that when I make plans I will be able to carry them out	.43

Concept	Standardized Path: Concept to Indicator
Self-deprecation:	
I wish I could have more respect for myself	.67
At times I think I am no good at all..............................	.63
I feel useless at times..	.58
I wish I could be as happy as others seem to be	.54
There are very few things about which I'm absolutely certain	.34
(Correlation: self-confidence/self-deprecation)	(−.66)
Fatalism (see note):	
When things go wrong for you, how often would you say it is your own fault?	−.54
To what extent would you say you are to blame for the problems you have— would you say that you are mostly to blame, partly to blame, or hardly at all to blame?...	−.66
Do you feel that most of the things that happen to you are the result of your own decisions or of things over which you have no control?	−.42
Anxiety (χ^2=123.83, df=44, ratio=2.81):	
How often do you feel that you are about to go to pieces?...............	.63
How often do you feel downcast and dejected?........................	.70
How frequently do you find yourself anxious and worrying about something?	.54
How often do you feel uneasy about something without knowing why?	.45
How often do you feel so restless that you cannot sit still?	.54
How often do you find that you can't get rid of some thought or idea that keeps running through your mind?	.45
How often do you feel bored with everything?	.60
How often do you feel powerless to get what you want out of life?	.56
How often do you feel guilty for having done something wrong?	.31
How often do you feel that the world just isn't very understandable?	.49
How often do you feel that there isn't much purpose to being alive?	.55
Occupational commitment (χ^2=1.16, df=2, ratio=0.58):	
Some people are so attached to their occupation that they cannot imagine wanting to do anything else, while others would be only too glad to change to some other occupation. How about you: would you say that you could not imagine changing, you could imagine it but are not eager to change, you would prefer to change, or would you be only too glad to change?..................	.34
If you were to inherit a million dollars, would you continue doing the work you do now, shift to something else, or retire?...........................	.47
Do you think it is a real accomplishment to be good at your occupation?....	.39
How much good do you think your work does for humanity—a great deal, some, a little, it doesn't help but doesn't hurt, or does it hurt?................	.47

Note: A high score on the indicator generally implies agreement or frequent occurrence; where alternatives are posed, the first alternative is scored high. A χ^2 cannot be computed for a model that has only three indicators; such a model is exactly identified.

E | Classifications of Complexity of Work in Housework

Complexity of Work with Data

Categories	Guidelines for Applying Occupational Codes to Household Work
1. [No significant relationship.]	
2. Comparing:	Reading labels on merchandise
3. Copying/reading instructions:	Writing a note to child's teacher; reading a book on child care; reading cookbooks or recipes in newspaper; reading articles or books on home decorating, gardening, etc.
4. Computing:	Balancing a checkbook/paying bills/writing checks; keeping household accounts.
5. Compiling/reading relevant literature:	Keeping a recipe file; writing a letter complaining about defective merchandise.

6. Analyzing: Preparing income tax returns; planning a major purchase.

7. Coordinating: Planning the week's menus; planning a budget; planning to move the household; scheduling the family's activities.

8. Synthesizing: (probably does not apply to household work; to qualify, the work would have to be something like writing a new cookbook—but that would probably no longer be household work.)

Complexity of Work with Things

	Guidelines for Applying Occupational Codes to
Categories	*Household Work*

1. [No significant relationship.]

2. Handling: Helping in kitchen — cutting up ingredients, making sandwiches; ironing clothes; washing dishes by hand; snow shovelling, leaf raking, cutting grass; straightening-up; setting the table; taking out the trash; carrying groceries; bathing and dressing young children.

3. Feeding-offbearing: Washing dishes by machine; washing and drying clothes by machine; making TV dinners.

4. Tending: (probably not applicable to household work).

5. Manipulating: Vacuum cleaning; gardening; making routine household repairs, fixing the plumbing (unless more than routine), replacing plug on electrical equipment, etc.; sewing (minor repairs, mending, buttons, but not involving extensive use of a sewing machine).

6. Driving-operating: Driving automobiles; using garden tractor (not lawn-mower unless sit-down type).

7. Operating-controlling: Standard cooking: preparing full meals (not just TV dinners), using a variety of techniques (frying, boiling, baking, etc.); operating a sewing machine (but not making entire garments, which would be coded 8).

8. Working on precision devices: Extra-special cooking: baking from scratch, "gourmet" cooking, specialty cooking; making own clothes or clothes for members of the family; substantial maintenance: painting, putting up shelves, repairing damaged furniture, puttying windows.

9. Setting up: Making repairs of equipment, or renovations to house, involving considerable knowledge and skill—e.g., putting in new plumbing, rewiring the house, rebuilding major electrical appliances.

Complexity of Work with People

Categories	Guidelines for Applying Occupational Codes to Household Work
1. [No significant relationship.]	
2. Serving:	Serving meals; handing clothing to spouse.
3. Receiving orders or instructions/helping:	Helping spouse in household work.
4. Speaking-signalling/ exchanging information:	(this is the most common); Speaking with storekeepers; speaking with repairmen; speaking with cleaning women; speaking with spouse about household matters; talking with children's teachers.
5. Persuading:	Convincing a storekeeper to repair or take back defective merchandise.
6. Diverting:	(usually not applicable.)
7. Supervising:	Supervising household help—this means time spent in assigning tasks and over-

seeing the work. In the "typical" situation of having a cleaning lady once or twice a week, supervision is *not* an important part of respondent's household work.

8. Instructing: Teaching household help complicated tasks or procedures.

9. Negotiating: Negotiating on buying a house or property. Negotiating with contractors on making major renovations to house.

10. Mentoring: Unusual in household work other than with children, which is not coded here; probably would apply only in such situations as respondent's counseling an emotionally upset spouse or other adult member of the household.

Complexity of Particular Aspects of Housework

Complexity of Work with Written Materials ("Bookwork") This is a simple count of the number of the following tasks done: (1) helping child(ren) with homework, reading to children; (2) reading cookbooks/ keeping recipe files; (3) reading books and articles on child care; (4) reading books and articles on home decorating, gardening, sewing and other topics pertinent to household work (but not fashions, per se).

Complexity of Cooking

1. Respondent specifically denies cooking./Respondent does not mention cooking.
2. Only helping in kitchen, cutting up ingredients, making sandwiches, etc.
3. Warming things up, making TV dinners.
4. Cooking, unspecified.
5. Standard cooking: preparing full meals (not just TV dinners), using a variety of techniques.
6. Extra-special cooking: baking from scratch, "gourmet cooking"; specialty cooking.

Complexity of Sewing

1. Respondent specifically denies sewing./Respondent does not mention sewing.
2. Minor repairs, mending, buttons, but not involving extensive use of sewing machine.
3. Sewing, unspecified.
4. More than minor repairs, but less than making entire garments, e.g., hemming (with or without a sewing machine), making curtains or tablecloths.
5. Knitting; needlepoint, etc.
6. Making own clothes or clothes for members of·the family.

Complexity of Household Repairs

1. Respondent specifically denies making household repairs./Respondent does not mention making household repairs.
2. Routine upkeep: replacing light bulbs, air conditioner filters, fuses, etc.
3. Making minor repairs: replacing a washer, replacing a plug on an electrical appliance, etc./Unspecified repairs.
4. Substantial maintenance: painting, putting up shelves, repairing damaged furniture, puttying windows.
5. Major and highly skilled maintenance and renovations, involving considerable knowledge and skill: putting in new plumbing, rewiring the house, rebuilding major electrical appliances, putting in tile floor.

Complexity of Gardening

1. Respondent specifically denies gardening./Respondent does not mention gardening.
2. Only most routine activities: lawn-mowing (except with sit-down tractor), leaf raking, weeding, keeping the garden neat.
3. "Ordinary" gardening: transplanting, growing annuals, etc. on a relatively modest scale./Unspecified gardening.
4. More elaborate gardening: extensive flower, vegetable, or fruit gardens and/or growing special varieties, hybridizing or otherwise working at a high level of skill and interest.

References

Adorno, T. W., Else Frenkel-Brunswik, Daniel J. Levinson, and R. Nevitt Sanford
    1950   The Authoritarian Personality. New York: Harper.

Aiken, Michael, and Jerald Hage
    1966   "Organizational alienation: A comparative analysis." American Sociological Review 31(August):497–507.

Aldrich, Howard, and Jane Weiss
    1981   "Differentiation within the United States capitalist class: Workforce size and income differences." American Sociological Review 46(June):279–290.

Allardt, Erik
    1965   Samhallstruktur och Sociala Spanningar. Tammerfors: Soderstrom.

Alwin, Duane F.
    1973   "Making inferences from attitude-behavior correlations." Sociometry 36(June):253–278.
    1976   "Attitude scales as congeneric tests: A re-examination of an attitude-behavior model." Sociometry 39(December):377–383.

Andrisani, Paul J., and Ronald P. Abeles
    1976   "Locus of control and work experience: Cohort and race differences." Paper presented to annual meeting of the American Psychological Association, Washington, D.C., September 3–7.

Andrisani, Paul J., and Gilbert Nestel
    1976   "Internal-external control as contributor to and outcome of work experience." Journal of Applied Psychology 61(April):156–165.

Antonovsky, Aaron

 1979   Health, Stress, and Coping. San Francisco: Jossey-Bass.

Antonovsky, Helen F., and Aaron Antonovsky

 1974   "Commitment in an Israeli kibbutz." Human Relations 27(March): 303–319.

Archibald, Peter, Owen Adams, and John W. Gartrell

 1981   "Propertylessness and alienation: Reopening a 'shut' case." Pp. 149–174 in R. Felix
        Geyer and David Schweitzer (Eds.), Alienation: Problems of Meaning, Theory and
        Method. London: Routledge & Kegan Paul.

Argyris, Chris

 1973   "Personality and organization theory revisited." Administrative Science Quarterly
        18(June):141–167.

Bakke, Edward W.

 1940   The Unemployed Worker: A Study of the Task of Making a Living without a Job.
        New Haven: Yale University Press.

Baltes, Paul B.

 1968   "Longitudinal and cross-sectional sequences in the study of age and generation ef-
        fects." Human Development 11(3):145–171.

 1982   "Life-span developmental psychology: Observations on history and theory revisi-
        ted." In R. M. Lerner (Ed.), Developmental Psychology: Historical and Philosophi-
        cal Perspectives. Hillsdale, NJ: Lawrence Erlbaum Press (in press).

Baltes, Paul B., and K. Warner Schaie

 1976   "On the plasticity of intelligence in adulthood and old age." American Psychologist
        31(October):720–725.

Becker, Howard S., and James W. Carper

 1956   "The development of identification with an occupation." American Journal of So-
        ciology 31(January):289–298.

Bengtson, Vern L.

 1975   "Generation and family effects in value socialization." American Sociological Re-
        view 40(June):358–371.

Bennett, H. S.

 1938   Life in the English Manor—a Study of Peasant Conditions: 1150–1400. Cambridge:
        Cambridge University Press.

Berg, Ivar, Marcia Freedman, and Michael Freeman

 1978   Managers and Work Reform: A Limited Engagement. New York: The Free Press.

Berk, Richard A.

 1980   "The new home economics: An agenda for sociological research." Pp. 113–148 in
        Sarah Fenstermacker Berk (Ed.), Women and Household Labor. Beverly Hills:
        Sage.

Berk, Richard A., and Sarah Fenstermacker Berk

 1979   Labor and Leisure at Home: Content and Organization of the Household Day.
        Beverly Hills: Sage.

Bernard, Jessie

 1981   "Class and the female world." Chapter 7 in Jessie Bernard, The Female World.
        New York: Free Press.

Bernstein, Basil
    1971   Class, Codes and Control. Vol. 1. Theoretical Studies Toward a Sociology of Language. London: Routledge & Kegan Paul.
    1973   Class, Codes and Control. Vol. 2. Applied Studies Toward a Sociology of Language. London: Routledge & Kegan Paul.

Bertram, Hans
    1976a Gesellschaftliche und Familiare Bedingungen Moralischen Urteilens. Doctoral dissertation, Universitat Dusseldorf.
    1976b "Probleme einer sozialstrukturell orientierten Sozialisationsforschung." Zeitschrift fur Soziologie 5(April):103–117.

Bielby, Denise Del Vento
    1978   "Career sex-atypicality and career involvement of college educated women: Baseline evidence from the 1960's." Sociology of Education 51(January):7–28.

Bielby, William T., Robert M. Hauser, and David L. Featherman
    1977   "Response errors of black and nonblack males in models of the intergenerational transmission of socioeconomic status." American Journal of Sociology 82(May):1242–1288.

Blalock, Hubert M., Jr.
    1960   Social Statistics. New York: McGraw-Hill.
    1963   "Correlated independent variables: The problem of multicollinearity." Social Forces 42(December):233–237.
    1964   Causal Inferences in Nonexperimental Research. Chapel Hill: University of North Carolina Press.
    1967   "Path coefficients versus regression coefficients." American Journal of Sociology 72(May):675–676.
    1969   "Multiple indicators and the causal approach to measurement error." American Journal of Sociology 75 (September):264–272.
    1971   "Simultaneous-equation techniques." Pp. 153–157 in H. M. Blalock, Jr. (Ed.), Causal Models in the Social Sciences. Chicago: Aldine-Atherton.

Blau, Peter M.
    1955   The Dynamics of Bureaucracy: A Study of Interpersonal Relations in Two Government Agencies. Chicago: University of Chicago Press.
    1960   "Structural effects." American Sociological Review 25(April): 178–193.
    1970   "A formal theory of differentiation in organizations." American Sociological Review 35(April):201–218.

Blauner, Robert
    1964   Alienation and Freedom: The Factory Worker and His Industry. Chicago: University of Chicago Press.
    1966   "Work satisfaction and industrial trends in modern society." Pp. 473–487 in Reinhard Bendix and Seymour Martin Lipset (Eds.), Class, Status, and Power. 2nd ed. Glencoe, IL: Free Press.

Bloch, Marc Leopold
    1967   Land and Work in Mediaeval Europe. Berkeley: University of California Press.

Blum, Jerome

  1960 The European Peasant from the 15th to the 19th Century. Service Center for Teachers of History Publication no. 33, Washington, D.C.

  1961 Lord and Peasant: Russia from 9th to 19th Century. Princeton, NJ: Princeton University Press.

Bogardus, Emory S.

  1928 Immigration and Race Attitudes. Boston: Heath.

Bohrnstedt, George W.

  1969 "Observations on the measurement of change." Pp. 113–33 in Edgar F. Borgatta (Ed.), Sociological Methodology, 1969. San Francisco: Jossey-Bass.

Bonjean, Charles M., and Michael D. Grimes

  1970 "Bureaucracy and alienation: A dimensional approach." Social Forces 48(March):365–373.

Bonjean, Charles M., Richard J. Hill, and S. Dale McLemore

  1967 Sociological Measurement: An Inventory of Scales and Indices. San Francisco: Chandler.

Bose, Christine E.

  1973 Jobs and Gender: Sex and Occupational Prestige. Baltimore: Johns Hopkins University, Center for Metropolitan Planning and Research.

  1980 "Social status of the homemaker." Pp. 69–87 in Sarah Fenstermacker Berk (Ed.), Women and Household Labor. Beverly Hills: Sage.

Bowles, Samuel, and Herbert Gintis

  1976 Schooling in Capitalist America: Educational Reform and the Contradictions of Economic Life. New York: Basic Books.

Braverman, Harry

  1974 Labor and Monopoly Capital: The Degradation of Work in the Twentieth Century. New York: Monthly Review Press.

Breer, Paul E., and Edwin A. Locke

  1965 Task Experience as a Source of Attitudes. Homewood, IL: The Dorsey Press.

Brousseau, Kenneth R.

  1978 "Personality and job experience." Organizational Behavior and Human Performance 22(October):235–252.

Burt, Ronald S.

  1973 "Confirmatory factor-analytic structures and the theory construction process." Sociological Methods and Research 2 (November):131–190.

  1976 "Interpretational confounding of unobserved variables in structural equation models." Sociological Methods and Research 5(August):3–52.

Bury, J. P. T. (Ed.)

  1964 New Cambridge Modern History. Vol. 10. The Zenith of European Power (1830–1870). Cambridge: Cambridge University Press.

Cain, Pamela S., and Donald J. Treiman

  1981 "The Dictionary of Occupational Titles as a source of occupational data." American Sociological Review 46(June):253–278.

Campbell, John D.

1978 "The child in the sick role: Contributions of age, sex, parental status, and parental values." Journal of Health and Social Behavior 19(March):35–51.

Carchedi, G.

1975a "On the economic identification of the new middle class." Economy and Society 4(February):1–86.

1975b "Reproduction of social classes at the level of production relations." Economy and Society 4(November):361–417.

Caudill, William A.

1973 "The influence of social structure and culture on human behavior in modern Japan." Journal of Nervous and Mental Disease 157(October):240–257.

Chinoy, Ely

1955 Automobile Workers and the American Dream. New York: Random House.

Christie, Richard

1954 "Authoritarianism re-examined." Pp. 123–196 in Richard Christie and Marie Jahoda (Eds.), Studies in the Scope and Method of "The Authoritarian Personality". Glencoe, IL: The Free Press.

Clark, John P.

1959 "Measuring alienation within a social system." American Sociological Review 24(December):849–852.

Clausen, John A.

1974 "Value transmission and personality resemblance in two generations." Paper presented to the annual meeting of the American Sociological Association, Montreal, August 27.

Clyde, Dean J., Elliot M. Cramer, and Richard J. Sherin

1966 Multivariate Statistical Programs. Coral Gables, FL: University of Miami.

Coburn, David, and Virginia L. Edwards

1976 "Job control and child-rearing values." Canadian Review of Sociology and Anthropology 13(3):337–344.

Cohen, Jacob

1965 "Some statistical issues in psychological research." Pp. 95–121 in B. B. Wolman (Ed.), Handbook of Clinical Psychology. New York: McGraw-Hill.

1968 "Multiple regression as a general data-analytic system." Psychological Bulletin 70(December):426–443.

Cole, Robert E.

1979 Work, Mobility, and Participation: A Comparative Study of American and Japanese Industry. Berkeley: University of California Press.

Constantini, Edmond, and Kenneth H. Craik

1972 "Women as politicians: The social background, personality, and political careers of female party leaders." Journal of Social Issues 28(2):217–236.

Cooley, William W., and Paul R. Lohnes

1962 Multivariate Procedures for the Behavioral Sciences. New York: John Wiley.

Coser, Rose Laub

1975 "The complexity of roles as a seedbed of individual autonomy." Pp. 237–263 in Lewis A. Coser (Ed.), The Idea of Social Structure: Papers in Honor of Robert K. Merton. New York: Harcourt Brace Jovanovich.

Coser, Rose Laub, and Gerald Rokoff

1971 "Women in the occupational world: Social disruption and conflict." Social Problems 18(Spring):535–554.

Costner, Herbert L., and Ronald Schoenberg

1973 "Diagnosing indicator ills in multiple indicator models." Pp. 167–199 in Arthur S. Goldberger and Otis Dudley Duncan (Eds.), Structural Equation Models in the Social Sciences. New York: Seminar Press.

Cottrell, W. Fred

1940 The Railroader. Stanford, CA: Stanford University Press.

Crawley, C. W. (Ed.)

1965 New Cambridge Modern History. Vol. 9. War and Peace in an Age of Upheaval (1793-1830). Cambridge: Cambridge University Press.

Cussler, Margaret

1958 The Woman Executive. New York: Harcourt Brace.

Dalgard, Odd Steffen

1981 "Occupational experience and mental health, with special reference to closeness of supervision." Psychiatry and Social Science 1(March):29–42.

Davis, Fred, and Virginia L. Olesen

1963 "Initiation into a woman's profession: Identity problems in the status transition of coed to student nurse." Sociometry 26 (March):89–101.

Davis, Kingsley

1937 "The sociology of prostitution." American Sociological Review 2 (October):744–755.

Dean, Dwight G.

1961 "Alienation: Its meaning and measurement." American Sociological Review 26(October):753–758.

Denitch, Bogdan Denis

1976 The Legitimation of a Revolution: The Yugoslav Case. New Haven: Yale University Press.

Dubin, Robert

1956 "Industrial workers' worlds: A study in the 'central life interests' of industrial workers." Social Problems 3(January):131–142.

Duncan, Otis Dudley

1961 "A socioeconomic index for all occupations," and "Properties and characteristics of the socioeconomic index." Pp. 109–161 in Albert J. Reiss, et al., Occupations and Social Status. New York: Free Press.

1966 "Path analysis: Sociological examples." American Journal of Sociology 72(July):1–16.

1967 "Some linear models for two-wave, two-variable panel analysis." Psychological Bulletin 72(May):177–182.

1968 "Ability and achievement." Eugenics Quarterly 15(March):1–11.

1970 "Partials, partitions, and paths." Pp. 38–47 in Edgar F. Borgatta (Ed.), Sociological Methodology, 1970. San Francisco: Jossey-Bass.

1975 Introduction to Structural Equation Models. New York: Academic Press.

Duncan, Otis Dudley, Archibald O. Haller, and Alejandro Portes

1968 "Peer influences on aspirations: A reinterpretation." American Journal of Sociology 74(September):119–137.

Dworkin, Rosalind J.

1981 "Prestige ranking of the housewife occupation." Sex Roles 7 (January):59–63.

Edwards, Alba M.

1938 A Social-Economic Grouping of the Gainful Workers of the United States. Washington, D. C.: U. S. Government Printing Office.

Edwards, G. Franklin

1959 The Negro Professional Class. Glencoe, IL: Free Press.

Elder, Glen H., Jr.

1974 Children of the Great Depression: Social Change in Life Experience. Chicago: University of Chicago Press.

Elder, Glen H., Jr., and Richard C. Rockwell

1979 "The life-course and human development: An ecological perspective. International Journal of Behavioral Development 2:1–21.

Ellis, Godfrey J., Gary R. Lee, and Larry R. Petersen

1978 "Supervision and conformity: A cross-cultural analysis of parental socialization values." American Journal of Sociology 84(September): 386–403.

Encyclopedia Britannica. 15th ed. S.v. "History of Scandinavia."

Farrar, Donald E., and Robert R. Glauber

1967 "Multicollinearity in regression analysis: The problem revisited." The Review of Economics and Statistics 49(February):92–107.

Featherman, David L., and Robert M. Hauser

1976 "Sexual inequality and socioeconomic achievement in the U.S., 1962–1973." American Sociological Review 41(June):462–483.

Finifter, Ada W.

1970 "Dimensions of political alienation." American Political Science Review 64(June):389–410.

1972 "Introductory notes" and "Concepts of alienation: Introduction." Pp. 1–11 in Ada W. Finifter (Ed.), Alienation and the Social System. New York: Wiley.

Firkowska, Anna, Antonina Ostrowska, Magdalena Sokolowska, Zena Stein, Mervyn Susser, and Ignacy Wald

1978 "Cognitive development and social policy: The contribution of parental occupation and education to mental performance in 11-year olds in Warsaw." Science 200(23 June):1357–1362.

Foote, Nelson N.

1953 "The professionalization of labor in Detroit." American Journal of Sociology 58(January):371–380.

Ford, Robert N.
  1950 "A rapid scoring procedure for scaling attitude questions." Public Opinion Quarterly 14(Fall):507–532.
Fox, John
  1980 "Effect analysis in structural equation models." Sociological Methods and Research 9(August):3–28.
Franklin, Jack L., and Joseph E. Scott
  1970 "Parental values: An inquiry into occupational setting." Journal of Marriage and the Family 32(August):406–409.
Freidson, Eliot
  1970 Profession of Medicine: A Study in the Sociology of Applied Knowledge. New York: Dodd, Mead, and Co.
Furstenberg, Frank F., Jr.
  1971 "The transmission of mobility orientation in the family." Social Forces 49(June):595–603.
Gabennesch, Howard
  1972 "Authoritarianism as world view." American Journal of Sociology 77(March):857–875.
Gagliani, Giorgio
  1981 "How many working classes?" American Journal of Sociology 87 (September):259–285.
Galtung, Johan
  1971 Members of Two Worlds: A Development Study of Three Villages in Western Sicily. New York: Columbia University Press.
Gauger, William H., and Kathryn E. Walker
  1980 The Dollar Value of Household Work. Information Bulletin 60, New York State College of Human Ecology at Cornell University, Ithaca, NY.
Gecas, Viktor
  1976 "The socialization and child care roles." Pp. 33–59 in F. Ivan Nye, et. al., Role Structure and Analysis of the Family. Beverly Hills: Sage.
  1980 "Father's occupation and child socialization: An examination of the linkage hypothesis." Paper presented to the annual meeting of the American Sociological Association, New York City, August 27–31.
Gerth, H. H., and C. Wright Mills (Eds.)
  1946 From Max Weber: Essays in Sociology. New York: Oxford University Press.
Geyer, R. Felix
  1972 Bibliography Alienation. 2nd ed. Amsterdam: Netherlands Universities' Joint Social Research Centre.
Goldberger, Arthur S.
  1964 Econometric Theory. New York: Wiley.
Goldman, Paul, and Donald R. Van Houten
  1980a "Uncertainty, conflict, and labor relations in the modern firm I: Productivity and capitalism's 'human face'." Economic and Industrial Democracy 1:63–98.
  1980b "Uncertainty, conflict, and labor relations in the modern firm II: The war on

labor." Economic and Industrial Democracy 1:263-287.

Goldthorpe, John H., David Lockwood, Frank Bechhofer, and Jennifer Platt

1968   The Affluent Worker: Industrial Attitudes and Behavior. Cambridge: University Press.

1969   The Affluent Worker in the Class Structure. Cambridge: University Press.

Gordon, Frederick M.

1978-1979   "Marx's concept of alienation and empirical sociological research." The Philosophical Forum 10(Winter-Summer):242-264.

Gordon, Robert A.

1968   "Issues   in   multiple   regression."   American   Journal   of   Sociology 73(March):592-616.

Gould, Stephen Jay

1981   The Mismeasure of Man. New York: W. W. Norton & Co.

Grabb, Edward G.

1981a   "Class, conformity and political powerlessness." Canadian Review of Sociology and Anthropology 18(3):362-369.

1981b   "The ranking of self-actualization values: The effects of class, stratification, and occupational experiences." The Sociological Quarterly 22(Summer):373-383.

Gross, Edward

1968   "Plus ca change ...? the sexual structure of occupations over time." Social Problems 16(Fall):198-208.

Gruneisen, Veronika, and Ernst-Hartmut Hoff

1977   Familienerziehung und Lebenssituation: Der Einfluss von Lebensbedingungen und Arbeitserfahrungen auf Erziehungseinstellungen und Erziehungsverhalten von Eltern. Weinheim, W. Germany: Beltz Verlag.

Gusfield, Joseph R., and Michael Schwartz

1963   "The meanings of occupational prestige: Reconsideration of the NORC scale." American Sociological Review 28(April):265-271.

Guttman, Louis

1944   "A   basis   for   scaling   qualitative   data."   American   Sociological   Review 9(April):139-150.

1950   "The basis for scalogram analysis," and "The scalogram board technique for scale analysis." Pp. 60-90 and 91-121 in Samuel A. Stouffer, et al. (Eds.), Measurement and Prediction. Princeton, N. J.: Princeton University Press.

Gwatkin, H. M., and J. P. Whitney (Eds.)

1957   Cambridge Medieval History. Cambridge: Cambridge University Press.

HEW Task Force

1973   Work in America: Report of a Special Task Force to the Secretary of Health, Education, and Welfare. Cambridge, MA: M.I.T. Press.

Habermas, Jurgen

1979   Communication and the Evolution of Society. Boston: Beacon Press.

Hall, Richard H.

1963   "The concept of bureaucracy: An empirical assessment." American Journal of Sociology 69(July):32-40.

Hall, Richard H., and Charles R. Tittle

    1966   "A note on bureaucracy and its 'correlates'."American Journal of Sociology 72(November):267-272.

Handlin, Oscar

    1951   The Uprooted. Boston: Little, Brown.

Hauser, Robert M., and Arthur S. Goldberger

    1971   "The treatment of unobservable variables in path analysis." Pp. 81-117 in Herbert L. Costner (Ed.), Sociological Methology, 1971. San Francisco: Jossey-Bass.

Heckscher, Eli F.

    1954   An Economic History of Sweden. Cambridge, MA: Harvard University Press.

Heise, David R.

    1969   "Separating reliability and stability in test-retest correlation." American Sociological Review 34(February):93-101.

    1970   "Causal inference from panel data." Pp. 3-27 in Edgar F. Borgatta and George M. Bohrnstedt (Eds.), Sociological Methodology, 1970. San Francisco: Jossey-Bass.

    1975   Causal Analysis. New York: Wiley.

Heise, David R., and George W. Bohrnstedt

    1970   "Validity, invalidity, and reliability." Pp. 104-129 in Edgar F. Borgatta and George M. Bohrnstedt (Eds.), Sociological Methodology, 1970. San Francisco: Jossey-Bass.

Hodge, Robert W., Paul M. Siegel, and Peter H. Rossi

    1964   "Occupational presitige in the United States, 1925-63." American Journal of Sociology 70(November):286-302.

Hoff, Ernst-Hartmut, and Veronika Gruneisen

    1978   "Arbeitserfahrungen, Erziehungseinstellungen, und Erziehungsverhalten von Eltern." Pp. 65-89 in H. Lukesch und K. Schneewind (Eds.), Familiare Sozialisation: Probleme, Ergebnisse, Perspektiven. Stuttgart: Klett-Cotta.

Hollingshead, August B., and Fredrick C. Redlich

    1958   Social Class and Mental Illness: A Community Study. New York: John Wiley.

Horn, John L., and Gary Donaldson

    1976   "On the myth of intellectual decline in adulthood." American Psychologist 31(October):701-719.

Horner, Matina S.

    1972   "Toward an understanding of achievement-related conflicts in women." Journal of Social Issues 28(2):157-175.

Horton, John

    1964   "The dehumanization of anomie and alienation: A problem in the ideology of sociology." British Journal of Sociology 15 (December):283-300.

House, James S.

    1980   Occupational Stress and the Physical and Mental Health of Factory Workers. Report on NIMH Grant No. 1R02MH28902. Research Report Series: Institute for Social Research, University of Michigan, Ann Arbor.

    1981   "Social structure and personality." Pp. 525-561 in Morris Rosenberg and Ralph H. Turner (Eds.), Social Psychology: Sociological Perspectives. New York: Basic Books.

Howe, Louise Knapp
  1978   Pink Collar Workers. New York: Avon.
Hudis, Paula M.
  1976   "Commitment to work and to family: Marital-status differences in women's earn-
         ings." Journal of Marriage and the Family 38 (May):267–278.
Hughes, Everett Cherrington
  1958   Men and their Work. Glencoe, IL: Free Press.
Hyman, Herbert H., and Paul B. Sheatsley
  1954   "'The authoritarian personality': A methodological critique." Pp. 50–122 in Ri-
         chard Christie and Marie Jahoda (Eds.), Studies in the Scope and Method of "The
         Authoritarian Personality". Glencoe, IL: Free Press.
Inkeles, Alex
  1960   "Industrial man: The relation of status to experience, perception, and value."
         American Journal of Sociology 66(July):1–31.
Israel, Joachim
  1971   Alienation: From Marx to Modern Sociology. Boston: Allyn and Bacon.
Jackson, David J., and Duane F. Alwin
  1980   "The factor analysis of ipsative measures." Sociological Methods and Research
         9(November):218–238.
Joreskog, Karl G.
  1969   "A general approach to confirmatory maximum likelihood factor analysis." Psy-
         chometrika 34(June):183–202.
  1970   "A general method for analysis of covariance structures." Biometrika 57(Au-
         gust):239–251.
  1973a "Analysis of covariance structures." In Paruchuri R. Krishnaiah (Ed.), Multivari-
         ate Analysis-III. New York: Academic Press.
  1973b "A general method for estimating a linear structural equation system." Pp. 85–112
         in Arthur S. Goldberger and Otis Dudley Duncan (Eds.), Structural Equation
         Models in the Social Sciences. New York: Seminar Press.
  1977   "Structural equation models in the social sciences: Specification, estimation, and
         testing." Pp. 265–286 in Paruchuri. R. Krishnaiah (Ed.), Applications of Statistics.
         Amsterdam: North Holland Publishing Co.
  1978   "Structural analysis of covariance and correlation matrices." Psychometrika 43(De-
         cember):443–477.
Joreskog, Karl G., Gunnar T. Gruvaeus, and Marielle van Thillo
  1970   ACOVS: A General Computer Program for Analysis of Covariance Structures. Re-
         search Bulletin 70–15. Princeton, N. J.: Educational Testing Service.
Joreskog, Karl G., and Dag Sorbom
  1976a "Statistical models and methods for analysis of longitudinal data." Pp. 285–325 in
         D. J. Aigner and A. S. Goldberger (Eds.), Latent Variables in Socioeconomic
         Models. Amsterdam: North-Holland Publishing Co.
  1976b "Statistical models and methods for test-retest situations." Pp. 135–170 in D. N.
         M. deGruijter, L. J. Th. van der Kamp, and H. F. Crombag (Eds.), Advances in
         Psychological and Educational Measurement. New York: Wiley.

Joreskog, Karl G., and Marielle van Thillo
  1972 LISREL: A General Computer Program for Estimating a Linear Structural Equation System Involving Multiple Indicators of Unmeasured Variables. Research Bulletin 72-56. Princeton, N. J.: Educational Testing Service.
Kabanoff, Boris
  1980 "Work and nonwork: A review of models, methods, and findings." Psychological Bulletin 88(July):60–77.
Kahn, Robert L.
  1972 "The meaning of work: Interpretation and proposals for measurement". Pp. 159–203 in Angus Campbell and Philip E. Converse (Eds.), The Human Meaning of Social Change. New York: Russell Sage Foundation.
  1975 "In search of the Hawthorne effect." Pp. 49–63 in Eugene L. Cass and Frederick G. Zimmer (Eds.), Man and Work in Society: A Report on the Symposium Held on the Occasion of the 50th Anniversary of the Original Hawthorne Studies, Oakbrook, IL, November 10-13, 1974. New York: Van Nostrand Reinhold.
Kalleberg, Arne L., and Larry J. Griffin
  1980 "Class, occupation, and inequality in job rewards." American Journal of Sociology 85(January):731–768.
Kanter, Rosabeth Moss
  1976 "The impact of hierarchical structures on the work behavior of women and men." Social Problems 23(April):415–430.
  1977 Men and Women of the Corporation. New York: Basic Books.
Kelman, Herbert C., and Janet Barclay
  1963 "The F Scale as a measure of breadth of perspective." Journal of Abnormal and Social Psychology 67(December):608–615.
Kennedy, John F.
  1964 A Nation of Immigrants. New York: Harper & Row.
Kerckhoff, Alan C.
  1976 "The status attainment process: Socialization or allocation?" Social Forces 55(December):368–381.
Kessler, Ronald C., and Paul D. Cleary
  1980 "Social class and psychological distress." American Sociological Review 45(June):463–478.
Kessler, Ronald C., and David F. Greenberg
  1981 Linear Panel Analysis: Models of Quantitative Change. New York: Academic Press.
Kirscht, John P., and Ronald C. Dillehay
  1967 Dimensions of Authoritarianism: A Review of Research and Theory. Lexington: University of Kentucky Press.
Kohlberg, Lawrence
  1976 "Moral stages and moralisation: The cognitive-developmental approach." Pp. 31–35 in T. Lickona (Ed.), Moral Development and Behavior. New York: Holt, Rinehart, and Winston.

Kohlberg, Lawrence, and Carol Gilligan

1972 "The adolescent as a philosopher: The discovery of the self in a post-conventional world." Pp. 144-179 in Jerome Kagan and Robert Coles (Eds.), Twelve to Sixteen: Early Adolescence. New York: Norton.

Kohn, Melvin L.

1959 "Social class and parental values." American Journal of Sociology 64(January):337-351.

1963 "Social class and parent-child relationships: An interpretation." American Journal of Sociology 68(January):471-480.

1969 Class and Conformity: A Study in Values. Homewood, IL: The Dorsey Press. (Second edition, 1977, published by the University of Chicago Press.)

1971 "Bureaucratic man: A portrait and an interpretation." American Sociological Review 36(June):461-474.

1972 "Class, family, and schizophrenia: A reformulation." Social Forces 50(March):295-304, 310-313.

1973 "Social class and schizophrenia: A critical review and a reformulation." Schizophrenia Bulletin 7(Winter):60-79.

1976a "Occupational structure and alienation." American Journal of Sociology 82(July):111-130.

1976b "Social class and parental values: Another confirmation of the relationship." American Sociological Review 41(June):538-545.

1976c "The interaction of social class and other factors in the etiology of schizophrenia." American Journal of Psychiatry 133 (February):177-180.

1977 "Reassessment, 1977." Pp. xxv-lx in Melvin L. Kohn, Class and Conformity: A Study in Values. Second Edition. Chicago: University of Chicago Press.

1980 "Job complexity and adult personality." Pp. 193-210 in Neil J. Smelser and Erik H. Erikson (Eds.), Themes of Work and Love in Adulthood. Cambridge, MA: Harvard University Press.

1981a "Personlichkeit, Beruf und Soziale Schichtung: Ein Bezugsrahmen." Pp. 203-235 in Melvin L. Kohn, Personlichkeit, Beruf und Soziale Schichtung. Stuttgart: Klett-Cotta.

1981b "Personality, occupation, and social stratification: A frame of reference." Pp. 267-297 in Donald J. Treiman and Robert V. Robinson (Eds.), Research in Social Stratification and Mobility: A Research Annual. Vol. 1. Greenwich, CT: JAI Press.

In press "On the transmission of values in the family: A preliminary formulation." In Alan C. Kerckhoff (Ed.), Research in Sociology of Education and Socialization: An Annual Compilation of Research. Vol. 4. Greenwich, CT: JAI Press.

Kohn, Melvin L., and Carrie Schoenbach

1980 "Social stratification and parental values: A multi-national assessment." Paper presented to the Japan-U.S. Conference on Social Stratification and Mobility, Hawaii, January.

Kohn, Melvin L., and Carmi Schooler

   1969   "Class, occupation and orientation." American Sociological Review 34(October):659–678.

   1973   "Occupational experience and psychological functioning: An assessment of reciprocal effects." American Sociological Review 38(February):97–118.

   1978   "The reciprocal effects of the substantive complexity of work and intellectual flexibility: A longitudinal assessment." American Journal of Sociology 84(July):24–52.

   1981   "Job conditions and intellectual flexibility: A longitudinal assessment of their reciprocal effects." Pp. 281–313 in David J. Jackson and Edgar F. Borgatta (Eds.), Factor Analysis and Measurement in Sociological Research: A Multi-Dimensional Perspective. London: Sage.

   1982   "Job conditions and personality: A longitudinal assessment of their reciprocal effects." American Journal of Sociology 87(May): 1257-1286.

Kon, Igor S.

   1967   "The concept of alienation in modern sociology." Social Research 34(3):507–528.

Kornhauser, Arthur

   1965   Mental Health of the Industrial Worker: A Detroit Study. New York: John Wiley.

Kusatsu, Osamu

   1977   "Ego development and socio-cultural process in Japan." Keizaigaku-Kiyo (The Journal of Economics) 3(1&2):41–109; 74–128.

Labovitz, Sanford

   1967   "Some observations on measurement and statistics." Social Forces 46(December):151–160.

Ladinsky, Jack

   1976   "Notes on the sociological study of careers." Paper presented to an SSRC Conference on Occupational Careers Analysis, Greensboro, NC, March 26–28.

LaRocco, James M., James S. House, and John R. P. French, Jr.

   1980   "Social support, occupational stress, and health." Journal of Health and Social Behavior 21(September):202–218.

Lawley, D. N., and A. E. Maxwell

   1971   Factor Analysis as a Statistical Method. 2nd ed. New York: American Elsevier Publishing Company.

Laws, Judith Long

   1976   "Work aspiration of women: False leads and new starts." Signs: Journal of Women in Culture and Society 1(Spring):33–49.

LeMasters, E. E.

   1975   Blue-Collar Aristocrats: Life-Styles at a Working-Class Tavern. Madison: University of Wisconsin Press.

Lewin, Ellen, and Joseph Damrell

   1978   "Female identity and career pathways: Post-baccalaureate nurses ten years after." Sociology of Work and Occupations 5(February): 31–54.

Lewis, Archibald R.

   1958   Shipping and Commerce in Northern Europe, A.D. 300–1100. Princeton, NJ: Princeton University Press.

Linn, Erwin L.
 1971 "Women dental students: Women in a man's world." Milbank Memorial Fund
    Quarterly 49(July):63–76.
Lipset, Seymour Martin
 1959 "Democracy and working-class authoritarianism." American Sociological Review
    24(August):482–501.
Lipset, Seymour Martin, Martin A. Trow, and James S. Coleman
 1956 Union Democracy: The Internal Politics of the International Typographical Union.
    Glencoe, IL: Free Press.
Locke, Edwin A.
 1976 "The nature and causes of job satisfaction." Pp. 1297–1349 in Marvin D. Dunnette
    (Ed.), Handbook of Industrial and Organizational Psychology. Chicago: Rand
    McNally.
Lofquist, Lloyd H., and Rene V. Dawis
 1969 Adjustment to Work: A Psychological View of Man's Problems in a Work-oriented
    Society. New York: Appleton-Century-Crofts.
Lopata, Helena Znaniecki
 1971 Occupation: Housewife. New York: Oxford University Press.
Lord, F. M., and M. R. Novick
 1968 Statistical Theories of Mental Test Scores. Reading, MA: Addison-Wesley.
Lukes, Steven
 1972 "Alienation and anomie." Pp. 24–32 in Ada W. Finifter (Ed.), Alienation and the
    Social System. New York: Wiley.
McKinley, J. C., S. R. Hathaway, and P. E. Meehl
 1948 "The Minnesota multiphasic personality inventory: VI. The K scale." Journal of
    Consulting Psychology 12(January-February):20–31.
Manning, Sarah H.
 1968 Time Use in Household Tasks by Indiana Families. Research Bulletin 837 (Jan.).
    Lafayette, IN: Purdue University Agricultural Experiment Station.
Marx, Karl
 1964 Early Writings. Edited and translated by T. B. Bottomore. New York: McGraw-
    Hill.
 1971 The Grundrisse. Edited and translated by David McLellan. New York: Harper &
    Row.
Mason, Robert, and Albert N. Halter
 1968 "The application of a system of simultaneous equations to an innovation diffusion
    model." Social Forces 47(December):182–195.
Mason, William M., Robert M. Hauser, Alan C. Kerckhoff, Sharon Sandomirsky Poss, and
Kenneth Manton
 1976 "Models of response error in student reports of parental socioeconomic characteris-
    tics." Pp. 443–494 in William H. Sewell, Robert M. Hauser, and David L. Feather-
    man (Eds.), Schooling and Achievement in American Society. New York: Academic
    Press.

Meissner, Martin, Elizabeth W. Humphreys, Scott M. Meis, and William J. Scheu
1975   "No exit for wives: Sexual division of labour and the cumulation of household demands." Canadian Review of Sociology and Anthropology 12(4) Part I:424–439.

Menzel, Herbert
1950   The Social Psychology of Occupations: A Synthetic Review. Unpublished M.A. Thesis, Indiana University.
1953   "A new coefficient for scalogram analysis." Public Opinion Quarterly 17(Summer):268–280.

Merton, Robert K.
1952   "Bureaucratic structure and personality." Pp. 361–371 in Robert K. Merton et al. (Eds.), Reader in Bureaucracy. Glencoe, IL: The Free Press.

Meyer, John W.
1977   "The effect of education as an institution." American Journal of Sociology 83(July):55–77.

Middleton, Russell
1963   "Alienation, race, and education." American Sociological Review 28(December):973–977.

Miller, Alden Dykstra
1971   "Logic of causal analysis: From experimental to nonexperimental designs." Pp. 273–294 in H. M. Blalock, Jr. (Ed.), Causal Models in the Social Sciences. Chicago: Aldine-Atherton.

Miller, Daniel R., and Guy E. Swanson
1958   The Changing American Parent: A Study in the Detroit Area. New York: Wiley.

Miller, George A.
1967   "Professionals in bureaucracy: Alienation among industrial scientists and engineers." American Sociological Review 32 (October):755–768.

Miller, Joanne
1980   "Individual and occupational determinants of job satisfaction: A focus on gender differences." Sociology of Work and Occupations 7(August): 337–366.

Miller, Joanne, and Howard H. Garrison
1982   "Sex roles: The division of labor at home and in the workplace." Annual Review of Sociology 8:237-262. Palo Alto: Annual Reviews, Inc.

Miller, Joanne, Carmi Schooler, Melvin L. Kohn, and Karen A. Miller
1979   "Women and work: The psychological effects of occupational conditions." American Journal of Sociology 85(July):66–94.

Miller, Joanne, Kazimierz M. Slomczynski, and Melvin L. Kohn
1982   "Job conditions and intellectual flexibility: A life-course analysis of Polish and U.S. data." Paper presented to the convention of the International Sociological Association, Mexico City, August 16–20.

Miller, Jon P.
1970   "Social-psychological implications of Weber's model of bureaucracy: Relations among expertise, control, authority, and legitimacy." Social Forces 49(September):91–102.

Miller, Karen A., Melvin L. Kohn, and Carmi Schooler
1982 "Educational self-direction and psychological functioning." Paper presented to the annual meeting of the American Sociological Association, San Francisco, September 6–10.

Mills, C. Wright
1953 White Collar: The American Middle Classes. New York: Oxford University Press.

Mongeau, Beatrice, Harvey L. Smith, and Ann C. Maney
1961 "The 'granny' midwife: Changing roles and functions of a folk practitioner." American Journal of Sociology 66(March):497–505.

Morgan, William R., Duane F. Alwin, and Larry J. Griffin
1979 "Social origins, parental values, and the transmission of inequality." American Journal of Sociology 85(July):156–166.

Morris, Richard T., and Raymond J. Murphy
1959 "The situs dimension in occupational structure." American Sociological Review 24(April):231–239.

Mortimer, Jeylan T.
1974 "Patterns of intergenerational occupational movements: A smallest-space analysis." American Journal of Sociology 79(March):1278–1299.
1976 "Social class, work, and the family: Some implications of the father's occupation for familial relationships and sons' career decisions." Journal of Marriage and the Family 38(May):241–256.
1979 Changing Attitudes toward Work. Work in America Institute Studies in Productivity. Vol. II. Scarsdale, NY.: Work in America Institute.

Mortimer, Jeylan T., and Jon Lorence
1979a "Work experience and occupational value socialization: A longitudinal study." American Journal of Sociology 84(May): 1361–1385.
1979b "Occupational experience and the self-concept: A longitudinal study." Social Psychology Quarterly 42(December):307–323.

Mortimer, Jeylan T., Jon Lorence, and Donald Kumka
in prep. Work, Family, and Personality.

Muraskin, William
1974 "The moral basis of a backward sociologist: Edward Banfield, the Italians, and the Italian-Americans." American Journal of Sociology 79(May):1484–1496.

Naoi, Atsushi, and Carmi Schooler
1981 "Occupational conditions and psychological functioning in Japan." Paper presented to the annual meeting of the American Sociological Association, Toronto, August 24–28.

Neal, Arthur G., and Melvin Seeman
1964 "Organizations and powerlessness: A test of the mediation hypothesis." American Sociological Review 29(April):216–226.

Nelson, Joel I.
1968. "Anomie: Comparisons between the old and new middle class." American Journal of Sociology 74(September):184–192.

Nettler, Gwynn
    1957 "A measure of alienation." American Sociological Review 22 (December):670–677.

Nie, Norman H., Dale H. Bent, and C. Hadlai Hull
    1968 Statistical Package for the Social Sciences: Provisional Users Manual. Chicago: National Opinion Research Center (mimeo). (Second edition, 1975, published by McGraw-Hill.)

Nilson, Linda Burzotta
    1978 "The social standing of a housewife." Journal of Marriage and the Family 40(August):541–548.

Nowak, Stefan
    1981 "Values and attitudes of the Polish people." Scientific American 245(July):45–53.

Olsen, Marvin E.
    1969 "Two categories of political alienation." Social Forces 47 (March):288–299.

Olsen, Nancy J.
    1974 "Family structure and socialization patterns in Taiwan." American Journal of Sociology 79(May):1395–1417.

Olsen, Stephen Milton
    1971 Family, Occupation, and Values in a Chinese Urban Community. Ph.D. dissertation, Cornell University.

Olson, Joan Toms
    1979 "Role conflict between housework and child care." Sociology of Work and Occupations 6(November):430–456.

Oppenheimer, Valerie Kincade
    1970 The Female Labor Force in the United States: Demographic and Economic Factors Governing its Growth and Changing Composition. Westport, CT: Greenwood Press.

Ossowski, Stanislaw
    1963 Class Structure in the Social Consciousness. London: Routledge & Kegan Paul.

Otto, Luther B., and David L. Featherman
    1975 "Social structural and psychological antecedents of self-estrangement and powerlessness." American Sociological Review 40(December):701–719.

Pearlin, Leonard I.
    1962 "Alienation from work: A study of nursing personnel." American Sociological Review 27(June):314–326.
    1971 Class Context and Family Relations: A Cross-National Study. Boston: Little, Brown.

Pearlin, Leonard I., and Melvin L. Kohn
    1966 "Social class, occupation, and parental values: A cross-national study." American Sociological Review 31(August):466–479.

Perron, Roger
    1971 Modeles D'Enfants, Enfants Modeles. Paris: Presses Universitaires de France.

Peters, Charles C., and Walter R. Van Voorhis
    1940 Statistical Procedures and their Mathematical Bases. New York: McGraw-Hill.

Petersen, Larry R., Gary R. Lee, and Godfrey J. Ellis
    1982   "Social structure, socialization values, and disciplinary techniques: A cross-cultural analysis." Journal of Marriage and the Family. 44(February):131–142.
Piaget, Jean
    N.D.   The Moral Judgment of the Child. Glencoe, IL: Free Press.
Poulantzas, Nicos
    1975   Classes in Contemporary Capitalism. London: New Left Books.
Reid, Margaret G.
    1934   Economics of Household Production. New York: Wiley.
Reiss, Albert J., Otis Dudley Duncan, Paul K. Hatt, and Cecil C. North
    1961   Occupations and Social Status. New York: Free Press of Glencoe.
Rheinstein, Max (Ed.)
    1954   Max Weber on Law in Economy and Society. Cambridge, MA: Harvard University Press.
Riley, Matilda White (Ed.)
    1979   Aging from Birth to Death: Interdisciplinary Perspectives. Washington, D.C.: American Association for the Advancement of Science.
Roberts, Bruce
    1982   "A confirmatory factor-analytic model of alienation." Paper presented to the convention of the International Sociological Association, Mexico City, August 16–20.
Robinson, John P., Robert Athanasiou and Kendra B. Head
    1969   Measures of Occupational Attitudes and Occupational Characteristics. Ann Arbor: Survey Research Center, Institute for Social Research, University of Michigan.
Robinson, John P., and Philip R. Shaver
    1969   Measures of Social Psychological Attitudes. Ann Arbor: Survey Research Center, Institute for Social Research, University of Michigan.
Robinson, Robert V., and Jonathan Kelley
    1979   "Class as conceived by Marx and Dahrendorf: Effects on income inequality and politics in the United States and Great Britain." American Sociological Review 44(February):38–58.
Roof, Wade Clark
    1974   "Religious orthodoxy and minority prejudice: Causal relationship or reflection of localistic world view?" American Journal of Sociology 80(November):643–664.
Rosenbaum, James E.
    1976   Making Inequality: The Hidden Curriculum of High School Tracking. New York: John Wiley and Sons.
Rosenberg, Morris
    1957   Occupations and Values. Glencoe, IL: Free Press.
    1962   "The association between self-esteem and anxiety." Journal of Psychiatric Research 1(September):135–152.
    1979   Conceiving the Self. New York: Basic Books.
Rosenberg, Morris, and Leonard I. Pearlin
    1978   "Social class and self-esteem among children and adults." American Journal of Sociology 84(July):53–77.

Rotter, Julian B.
   1966   "Generalized expectancies for internal versus external control of reinforcement."
          Psychological Monographs, 80(1), Whole No. 609.
Rubin, Lillian Breslow
   1976   Worlds of Pain: Life in the Working-Class Family. New York: Basic Books.
Ryder, Robert G.
   1965   "Scoring orthogonally rotated factors." Psychological Reports 16(June):701-704.
St. Peter, Louis Glenn
   1975   Fate Conceptions: A Look at the Effects of Occupational Tasks on Human Values.
          Ph.D. dissertation, University of Nebraska.
Schoenbach, Carrie
   1982   "Effects of husband's and wife's social status on psychological functioning." Paper
          presented to the annual meeting of the American Sociological Association, San
          Francisco, September 6-10.
Schooler, Carmi
   1968   "A note of extreme caution on the use of Guttman scales." American Journal of
          Sociology 74(November):296-301.
   1972   "Social antecedents of adult psychological functioning." American Journal of Soci-
          ology 78(September):299-322.
   1976   "Serfdom's legacy: An ethnic continuum." American Journal of Sociology
          81(May):1265-1286.
   1980   "Psychological and social perspectives on status attainment." Paper presented to
          the Japan-U.S. Conference on Social Stratification and Mobility, Hawaii, January.
Schooler, Carmi, Karen A. Miller, and Joanne Miller
   1982   "Work for the household: Its nature and consequences for husbands and wives."
          Paper presented to the annual meeting of the American Sociological Association,
          San Francisco, September 6-10.
Schooler, Carmi, and Karen C. Smith
   1978   "...and a Japanese wife. Social structural antecedents of women's role values in
          Japan." Sex Roles 4(February):23-41.
Schweitzer, David
   1981   "Alienation theory and research: Trends, issues and priorities." International So-
          cial Science Journal 33(3):523-556.
Scurrah, Martin J., and Abner Montalvo
   1975   Clase Social y Valores Sociales en Peru. Lima, Peru: Escuela de Administracion de
          Negocios Para Graduados.
Seeman, Melvin
   1959   "On the meaning of alienation." American Sociological Review 24(Decem-
          ber):783-791.
   1967   "On the personal consequences of alienation in work." American Sociological Re-
          view 32(April):273-285.
   1971   "The urban alienations: Some dubious theses from Marx to Marcuse." Journal of
          Personality and Social Psychology 19(August):135-143.

1972a "Alienation and engagement." Pp. 467–527 in Angus Campbell and Philip E. Converse (Eds.), The Human Meaning of Social Change. New York: Russell Sage Foundation.

1972b "The signals of '68: Alienation in pre-crisis France." American Sociological Review 37(August):385–402.

Sennett, Richard, and Jonathan Cobb
1973   The Hidden Injuries of Class. New York: Knopf.

Siegel, Paul M.
1971   Prestige in the American Occupational Structure. Unpublished Ph.D. dissertation, University of Chicago.

Simon, Herbert A.
1957   "Causal ordering and identifiability." Pp. 10–36 in Herbert A. Simon (Ed.), Models of Man: Social and Rational. New York: Wiley.

Simpson, Miles
1972   "Authoritarianism and education: A comparative approach." Sociometry 35 (June):223–234.

Skvoretz, John V., and Ubol Kheoruenromne
1979   "Some evidence concerning the value hypothesis of intergenerational status transmission: A research note." Social Science Research 8:172–183.

Slicher Van Bath, B. H.
1963   The Agrarian History of Western Europe: A.D. 500–1850. London: Arnold.

Slomczynski, Kazimierz M., Joanne Miller, and Melvin L. Kohn
1981   "Stratification, work, and values: A Polish-United States comparison." American Sociological Review 46(December):720–744.

Smith, Donald E. (Ed.)
1922.   New Larned History. Springfield, MA: Nichols.

Smith, Karen C., and Carmi Schooler
1978   "Women as mothers in Japan: The effects of social structure and culture on values and behavior." Journal of Marriage and the Family 40(August):613–620.

Sokolowska, Magdalena, Anna Firkowska-Mankiewicz, Antonina Ostrowska, and Miroslaw P. Czarkowski
1978   Intellectual Performance of Children in the Light of Socio-cultural Factors: Warsaw Study. Warsaw: Polish Academy of Sciences.

Sorbom, Dag
1975   "Detection of correlated errors in longitudinal data." British Journal of Mathematical and Statistical Psychology 28(November):138–151.

Spaeth, Joe L.
1976   "Characteristics of the work setting and the job as determinants of income." Pp. 161–176 in William H. Sewell, Robert M. Hauser, and David L. Featherman (Eds.), Schooling and Achievement in American Society. New York: Academic Press.

1979   "Vertical differentiation among occupations." American Sociological Review 44(October):746–762.

Spector, Paul E.
 1982 "Behavior in organizations as a function of employee's locus of control." Psychological Bulletin 91(May):482–497.
Spenner, Kenneth I.
 1977 From Generation to Generation: The Transmission of Occupation. Unpublished Ph.D. dissertation, University of Wisconsin, Madison.
 1980 "Occupational characteristics and classification systems: New uses of the Dictionary of Occupational Titles in social research." Sociological Methods & Research 9(November):239–264.
Spoerl, D. Tilden
 1951 "Some aspects of prejudice as affected by religion and education." Journal of Social Psychology 33:969–976.
Srole, Leo
 1956 "Social integration and certain corollaries: An exploratory study." American Sociological Review 21(December):709–716.
Stafford, Frank, and Greg J. Duncan
 1980 "The use of time and technology by households in the United States." Pp. 335–375 in Ronald. G. Ehrenberg (Ed.), Research in Labor Economics. Vol. 3. Greenwich, CT: JAI Press.
Staines, Graham L.
 1980 "Spillover versus compensation: A review of the literature on the relationship between work and nonwork." Human Relations 33(February):111–129.
Stern, Robert N., and William F. Whyte (Eds.)
 1981 Economic Democracy: Comparative Views of Current Initiatives. Sociology of Work and Occupations 8(May): Special Issue.
Stouffer, Samuel A.
 1955 Communism, Conformity, and Civil Liberties: A Cross-section of the Nation Speaks its Mind. Garden City, NY: Doubleday.
Sudman, Seymour and Jacob J. Feldman
 1965 "Sample design and field procedures." Pp. 482–485 of Appendix 1 in John W. C. Johnstone and Ramon J. Rivera (Eds.), Volunteers for Learning: A Study of the Educational Pursuits of American Adults. Chicago: Aldine.
Sweet, James A.
 1973 Women in the Labor Force. New York: Seminar Press.
Temme, Lloyd V.
 1975 Occupation: Meanings and Measures. Washington, D.C.: Bureau of Social Science Research, Inc.
Treiman, Donald J.
 1977 Occupational Prestige in Comparative Perspective. New York: Academic Press.
Treiman, Donald J., and Robert M. Hauser
 1977 "Intergenerational transmission of income: An exercise in theory construction." Pp. 271–302 in Robert M. Hauser and David L. Featherman (Eds.), The Process of Stratification: Trends and Analyses. New York: Academic Press.

Treiman, Donald J., and Kermit Terrell

1975 "Sex and the process of status attainment: A comparison of working women and men." American Sociological Review 40(April): 174–200.

Troll, Lillian, and Vern Bengtson

1979 "Generations in the family." Pp. 127–161 in Wesley R. Burr, Reuben Hill, F. Ivan Nye, and Ira L. Reiss (Eds.), Contemporary Theories About the Family. Vol. 1. Research-Based Theories. New York: The Free Press.

Tudor, Bill

1972 "A specification of relationships between job complexity and powerlessness." American Sociological Review 37(October):596–604.

Turner, Arthur N. and Paul R. Lawrence

1965 Industrial Jobs and the Worker: An Investigation of Response to Task Attributes. Boston: Harvard University Graduate School of Business Administration.

United States Department of Labor

1949 Dictionary of Occupational Titles. Washington, D. C.: U. S. Government Printing Office. Second edition.

1965 Dictionary of Occupational Titles. Washington, D. C.: U. S. Government Printing Office. Third edition.

United States Women's Bureau

1976 The Role and Status of Women Workers in the United States and Japan. Washington, D.C.: U. S. Government Printing Office.

Vanneman, Reeve and Fred C. Pampel

1977 "The American perception of class and status." American Sociological Review 42(June):422-437.

Walker, Charles R.

1957 Toward the Automatic Factory: A Case Study of Men and Machines. New Haven: Yale University Press.

Walker, Charles R. and Robert H. Guest

1952 The Man on the Assembly Line. Cambridge, MA: Harvard University Press.

Walker, Kathryn E., and Margaret E. Woods

1976 Time Use: A Measure of Household Production of Family Goods and Services. Washington, D.C.: Center for the Family of the American Home Economics Association.

Wallace, Michael and Arne L. Kalleberg

1982 "Industrial transformation and the decline of craft: The decomposition of skill in the printing industry, 1931–1978." American Sociological Review 47 (June):307–324.

Wallerstein, Immanuel

1974 The Modern World-System: Capitalistic Agriculture and the Origins of the European World-Economy in the Sixteenth Century. New York: Academic Press.

Weber, Max

1947 The Theory of Social and Economic Organization. (Translated by A. M. Henderson and Talcott Parsons.) New York: Oxford University Press.

Werts, Charles E., Karl G. Joreskog and Robert L. Linn

1973 "Identification and estimation in path analysis with unmeasured variables." American Journal of Sociology 78(May):1469–1484.

Werts, Charles E., Robert L. Linn and Karl G. Joreskog

1971 "Estimating the parameters of path models involving unmeasured variables." Pp. 400–409 in Hubert M. Blalock, Jr. (Ed.), Causal Models in the Social Sciences. Chicago: Aldine-Atherton.

Wesolowski, Wlodzimierz

1969 "The notions of strata and class in socialist society." Pp. 122–145 in Andre Beteille (Ed.), Social Inequality: Selected Readings. Harmondsworth, Middlesex, England: Penguin Books, Ltd.

1979 Classes, Strata and Power. London: Routledge & Kegan Paul.

Wheaton, Blair, Bengt Muthen, Duane F. Alwin and Gene F. Summers

1977 "Assessing reliability and stability in panel models." Pp. 84–136 in David R. Heise (Ed.), Sociological Methodology, 1977. San Francisco: Jossey-Bass.

Whyte, William Foote

1948 Human Relations in the Restaurant Industry. New York: McGraw-Hill.

1961 Men at Work. Homewood, IL: The Dorsey Press.

Whyte, William H.

1956 The Organization Man. New York: Simon and Schuster.

Wilensky, Harold L.

1960 "Work, careers, and social integration." International Social Science Journal 12(Fall):543–560.

1961 "Orderly careers and social participation: The impact of work history on social integration in the middle mass." American Sociological Review 26(August):521–539.

Williams, Gregory

1975 "A research note on trends in occupational differentiation by sex." Social Problems 22(April):543–547.

Williams, Robin M., Jr.

1960 American Society: A Sociological Interpretation. 2nd ed. New York: Knopf.

Wilson, John

1980 "Sociology of Leisure." Annual Review of Sociology 6:21–40.

Witkin, H. A., R. B. Dyk, H. F. Faterson, D. R. Goodenough, and S. A. Karp

1962 Psychological Differentiation: Studies of Development. New York: John Wiley.

Wolf, Wendy C.

1977 "Research note: How biased are sex comparisons of occupational attainment when wives of male respondents are utilized as the sample of women?" Working Paper 77–17, Center for Demography and Ecology, University of Wisconsin, Madison.

Wright, Erik Olin

1976 "Class boundaries in advanced capitalist societies." New Left Review 98(July-August):3–41.

1978a   "Varieties of Marxist conceptions of class structure." Institute for Research on Poverty Discussion Papers, University of Wisconsin, Madison, August.

1978b   Class, Crisis and the State. London: New Left Books.

1979   Class Structure and Income Determination. New York: Academic Press.

Wright, Erik Olin and Luca Perrone

1977   "Marxist class categories and income inequality." American Sociological Review 42(February):32–55.

Wright, James D., and Sonia R. Wright

1976   "Social class and parental values for children: A partial replication and extension of the Kohn thesis." American Sociological Review 41(June):527–537.

Zollschan, George K., and Philip Gibeau

1964   "Concerning alienation: A system of categories for the exploration of rational and irrational behavior." Pp. 152–174 in George K. Zollschan and Walter Hirsch (Eds.), Explorations in Social Change. Boston: Houghton Mifflin.

Zurcher, Louis A., Jr., Arnold Meadow, and Susan Lee Zurcher

1965   "Value orientation, role conflict, and alienation from work: A cross-cultural study." American Sociological Review 30 (August):539–548.

Index